SACRIFICIAL SELFISHNESS

SACRIFICIAL SELFISHNESS

and a girl who lives forever

A TRUE STORY OF
EVOLUTION'S PASSION

KEITH FRASER

ISBN: 978-1-6653-0549-5 - Paperback
eISBN: 978-1-6653-0550-1 - eBook

♾This paper meets the requirements of ANSI/NISO Z39.48-1992 (Permanence of Paper)

You can contact the author, who is **looking for a traditional publisher**, at theunfoldingevs@icloud.com or by calling: 770-364-3191.

0 4 2 3 2 4

CONTENTS

PREFACE

At a blues bar one night, a friend of mine, Mark B, told me the best joke I've ever heard:

This high-earning New York stockbroker has had it up to here so he gets on the net and books the first cool trip he sees—a 10-day wildlife tour in Alaska. It's in a remote region run by an Alaskan Indian tribe—perfect. He needs something, anything that's different. As he steps off the plane in Fort Yukon, he hears drums in the distance—they seem to be coming from the mountains. He asks about the drumming sounds but nobody at the airport wants to talk about it. "Odd," the guy thinks. A Native Indian helps him with his luggage and another Indian, a talkative cabdriver, takes him to his hotel near the tundra. As he opens the door to the taxi, he notices the drums are louder with catchy drum rolls and tom-toms, so he says "what are the drums all about?" as he pays the fare. "Drums good, when drums stop, that's bad," the driver says with a worried look on his face, and drives away quickly. "Hmmm," the stockbroker smiles, "this place is weirder than I thought—I like it." The guy gets to his room and walks out onto the back balcony for a smoke. Facing the mountains, the drums are more prevalent now and he can make out cymbal sounds and a cowbell, when he hears a knock. It's the bellboy, who carries in his luggage. The stockbroker says to him "what's with the constant drums?" "Drums good, when drums stop, that's bad," says the frowning bellboy and he exits without his tip.

Perplexed but more tired, the guy hits the sack. He wakes to the same noise, hops another cab toward the mountains, and joins the safari group. As the group heads into the tundra in a huge, open, all-terrain vehicle the drums keep getting louder. The guy says to the native safari guide, "can you explain to me what these constant drums are about?" "Drums good, when drums stop, that's bad," says the guide looking away and as the guide tries to change the subject, the guy interrupts and says, "what is so bad about when the drums stop?" "Oh," says the guide with a deathly expression…"when drums stop……bass guitar solo begins."

I love jokes that obliterate all my assumptions. Our minds scurry toward them. At concerts we tolerate long drum solos but our hearts kind of sink when the bass player, the nondescript member of the band, follows with a long solo and we don't say anything. Having been a bass player myself, I tell several bass player jokes. "Did you hear about the bass player who inherits 20-grand from his uncle? He goes right to the store and orders a new Fender Jazz bass guitar, a Marshall stack with a 5000-watt amp, some digital effects, etc., adding "money is no object." The clerk taking the order says, "that's fine sir but this is a grocery store."

Not every bass guitar player drives a song along like *Another One Bites the Dust* or *Treat Her Like a Lady*. Unseen, they blend the drumbeat with the melody and there's a kind of bass player in every family too. It can be an epiphany to identify that person—it might be you. This overlooked domestic is the one who's always stitching the family quilt back together. More often they are seamstresses but sometimes they are tailors.

Men think the bass player joke is hilarious and women barely chuckle though they like the grocery store joke. Men have more schadenfreude (delight in the perceived misery of others) than women so men will come up with a supposed weak link in anything. That's but one example of the disparate ways the sexes think and these supposed discrepancies did not evolve to conflict with each other. The genders evolved on separate paths to see a different side of life more clearly because it worked for survival.

We think we have problems now but for a million years our ancestors fought daily to survive and those two brains brought us here. Cavemen got brute strength and a simple, focused brain—a vector for survival—to tame the dangerous environment. Cave women got the more dangerous birthing job, plus an empathetic, quite verbal brain to articulate a very different perspective on things, double insuring our species against the unknowns and intangibles that were to come. How the genders evolved to perceive love and how to show it are in different languages too and to understand evolution is to understand us. "It's almost like being in love," Lerner and Lowe wrote in the musical *Brigadoon,* showing us our polarity.

Today we quietly worry what may happen next during what is ostensibly the peak of human existence. We wonder what the next war will be like or how stacked the deck already is, then shrug and try to make more money for our families. We are remiss not to think that something old or new, something borrowed, something green, or some unknown trend is afoot. Like no other animal we can predict the future, however, we in the western world are so rich that we think the future is being taken care of. That's a red-carpet mistake. We also take hidden treasures for granted—the unsung bass players, the Huckleberries who look out for us—and these are the fixers of the future we don't realize we need.

Priceless song lyrics tell us about ourselves too and I credit all musicians and comedians because they've taught me as much as the Nobel Prize winners have. Philosophers and scientists have discovered much about the human condition that we already heard in a song. Music is simple, aesthetic philosophy (no need to look up words) and the singer-songwriters of the 20th century beautifully stitched our 100-year history together for us. Sometimes they created the future.

You'll get a bit more from this book if music played such a part in your life that it changed you as a person. Most of us fit that description whether we know it or not because good music slips incognito into our unconscious minds, where we dream. I will show that the songs you love, the dreams you don't, and your precious memories all live together in the same place. It's a place deep in your subconscious brain just above the back roof of your mouth (Chapter 17).

INTRODUCTION

The book starts with how humans survived a million years of hell, and that hell, plus the fortitude to overcome it, still reside side by side in our DNA. Next, we'll explore how our human nature (genetics) and our human nurture (childhoods) slowly evolved, which completely changed how strangers interacted. These also exists a mysterious complement only humans have beyond nature and nurture which is an intangible I call "free will," and we alone have options beyond instinct and environment. We are profoundly influenced but the future is ours more than any before us. We can change how we follow or lead; we can climb from dependent to independent; we can change the mandates of some of our genes with simple thought and action techniques.

Although the vestiges of our anxiousness still thrive in our DNA, we can free ourselves from the anxieties we inherited from those first million years. For 3 examples, we can learn how to stop grinding our teeth at night, learn how to confront our Stockholm Syndrome, and change how our birth order or the family pecking order still impacts us as adults. Most but not all of these solutions involve interpreting our unconscious dreams.

Between the covers of this unlikely science book is a sundry of fresh and old topics devoid of unnecessary detail. I noticed a little hole in the shelf at the local Barnes and Noble, my favorite store, and that hole was a simple blue-collar book on evolution and philosophy. I had to read many evolutionary and philosophical concepts over and over until I understood them; for you I will put them into short sentences you can easily understand.

Evolutionary scientists may find it amusing how I sell evolution, psychology, and philosophy more emotionally as I go while readers will truly get a feel for them. Those three infinitely linked subjects are made of and born of passion. Our brains are half rational and half emotional, for survival, so if we know something and feel it too it sinks in, and if I can make you laugh, I've accomplished both.

There are short sections of salient history in these pages to help make my major points, and for entertainment, I will include some historical fiction later, and let you know about it when it's not obvious. My audience is any lover of reading and learning who hasn't assumed a fixed stance on philosophy and doesn't mind a little spice and controversy. I will show you some overlooked hues of philosophy and tell you a half dozen soul-warming animal stories, whence our essences originated.

(Instead of spelling out numbers in this book I write the number itself, plus, mya means *million years ago*, and I have abrupt scene changes.)

ABOUT THE BOOK

My wife Jeanne, raised in India on the King's English, is an indispensable editor and most of my thankyous for this book go to her. For her, evolution was a new subject. We met in 1987 when she called me for guitar lessons so as you can guess she usually made more money than I did, which eventually allowed me the freedom to write this book. She likes to be chauffeured around our little village in West Georgia, where we live on a sleepy farm, so I wear that cap. I call it "driving miss lazy" (the copper skin girl likes getting chauffeured by the white guy) but I talk too much about this book so *Sweet Georgia Brown*[1] calls it "driving miss lazy crazy."

In retirement on the sleepy farm, we hear wind and birds but not people or cars. It's a near perfect place to write about nature. We are getting up there in the years so I joke that we don't take time-release capsules anymore—afraid we might be wasting our money. My sneeze is super loud and with 60% of the US having some Teutonic (German) blood, [2] when the wind is dead still, I occasionally hear "Gesundheit" from 3/8ths of a mile away. "This is all the heaven we got, right here right now," [3] as the great songwriter Mark Knopfler reminds us. A musician's musician, Mark's lyrics pop up here and there because he's a poet who tells it like it is.

When there is no word for something I occasionally make up a word or phrase. I call them "obvyisms," and *idiot genius*, for example, is how I describe a man. It fits most of my buddies and me. An *obvyism* (a synonym of neologism) is a new word that is instantly clear and examples are: *funky, gnarly, dork,* Shakespeare's *swagger*, Paris Hilton's *that's hot*, or Dr Seuss's *nerd*. Children have the capacity and the need to learn many more words and obvyisms are funny, childlike, instant brain twisters that help 2 minds meet and is how language began long ago.

We love idiot geniuses when we get to see the whole picture because they are awkward, smart, and funny. Peter Sellers played one in every movie, and Edith—the protagonist *and* the antagonist of her life (aren't we all?)—loved being there and laughing through them.

The Germans call a new word an "unwort," and you will find German words in these pages because many of them replace entire English sentences. Germans are more than just exceptional engineers; the organization and complexity of their language rivals any. Psychologically, the Germans are the most observant too, with huge blind spots like all of us, however, they've made the deepest inroads into the catacombs of the quirky human mind.

Carl Jung, Albert Einstein, and Buddha pop up often because they were good psychologists, scientists, and philosophers. I'm not a scientist. Everything I know about philosophy and evolution came from other authors or looking around, listening, and thinking, so I'm more of a translator and an investigator. I'll bring back Buddha's insight and explain Einstein's theory of relativity in such simple language you'll see the picture you might be missing. My favorite quote, "if you can't explain something to a teenager, you don't understand it yourself," is attributed to many notables but its origin is unknown. It's fun to simplify strange concepts for curious adults which was a skill I honed during 13 years of teaching.

The smartest person who ever thought and wrote, in my humble, was the overlooked Carl Jung (pronounced Yoong). I have the evidence to possibly convince you of that and since you are reading this, the fun part is that Jung, you, and I seem to like the same subjects. Jung took a naked metaphysical dive into the human condition because his ego was just fine as it was, and, in his almost shy way, he brought us the deepest understanding of our nightly dreams, our subconscious minds, society, and war.

Karl Marx too is a surprising hero in many ways and what Americans have been taught about him amounts to a diversion, because historians, rather than trying to understand him, pick sides. Marx's brilliance as well as his mistakes are plainly stated in this book, but he was a free speech advocate and freedom fighter in the rawest sense when colonialism defined his 19th century.

Christopher Hitchens is one of my all-time favorite writers, though I disagree with him half the time, and he captures the true spirit of Karl Marx. Schooling us with those British adjectives (used perfectly of course, after I looked them up) Hitchens makes his invidious points emotionally exact, with the clarity of a vector. And these adjectives *are* British, we must admit. "Hitch" (friends called him until his untimely death) possessed a dry wit, more than most any modern writer, and he brought something of great value to literature: a skeptical, very British, jaded mind. When Hitch was a young teenager his mother would say, "the one unforgivable sin is to be boring,"[4] which helped him avoid the common mistake of glossing over British history. I never understood this world until he explained the gory details of his mother country.

Twice, my wife and I went to India for a month. I easily got to know people, started learning the history, and learned something more fun—their nonwestern psyche (Chapter 24). The people in India, who still welcome westerners, were cautiously polite when the British came into India in 1612. Not knowing what colonialism was, they welcomed aliens as the Native Americans did in North America. The people in the Middle East had the opposite reaction to the west which hasn't changed since the west re-divided that part of the world into new states with new borders after each world war. These are opposite psychological responses indeed and are born of different religious and psychological histories. When we don't learn about these diverse, ancient, encrypted mindsets we can't know why people think the way they do which creates historical blunders of biblical magnitude.

Meditating and reading are both mirror images of supply and demand because they combine consumption and work while leaving us unaware of both. When meditating or reading we forget the time of day; we consume what we want to without knowing we are working because we're not doing what someone else wants us to. I learned psychology and economics, not so much from textbooks but from stories. Reading is the secret to life, and of course always keep a thing of Scotch Tape in the kitchen.

If we all had the same philosophy, it wouldn't be a subject—life would get boring. Philosophy is anybody's game because everyone is their own favorite philosopher and though imagination, heurism, and fantasy are crucial in philosophical thinking we are privy to classical blunders and moved north by timeless truisms that a few rare souls have imagined for us. I will show you a cadre of philosophies—there aren't that many—and tell stories of the missteps and the sidesteps and the fixes.

This book may be both the first emotional row for evolution and the funniest—once I get warmed up. Certainly, it is the first to come out of the red dirt south, having been written by, "some Georgia farm boy."[5] Nature gave us more tools than any other animal, including the risibility to laugh at our contradictions, and we are losing one of our best learning tools—our sense of humor. Help is on the way. Evolution provides us with a sea of untapped humor—irony and personification. Since "the Jester's on the sideline in a cast,"[6] I will fill that void to give evolution back the emotion it gave us. I will talk as if evolution had a sentient mind too, it doesn't, but the *little engine that could* has an excruciatingly slow, unknown way of using information to build complexity and intelligence, which is the most peculiar of things.

Although I write about the government-religion-corporate pyramid, a long storied interlaced triopoly that we do live inside, I try to think outside the triangle. Our elusive free will (Chapter 9) is waiting for us beyond that sheltering, manipulating, hovering digital cloud that herds us toward living similar lives. Still, we are the auspicious ones. We inherited the wind[7] at our backs and our opportunities increase too rapidly. Ironically, at the same time it's so comfy inside the western pyramid that our free will is decelerating. We are leaving an invisible debris field behind; we don't go back and pick up the pieces or even notice them. What have we left behind and what have we replaced that with? Well, I will quickly move from obvious concepts to more complex ones and you won't agree with some of my conclusions, so I will carefully explain them to help you see how I got there. Although there are many aha moments designed into this book as well as new methods for alleviating anxiety, this isn't really a self-help book because I don't know you. Everyone is different and I can merely pass on what I have learned.

About This Unauthorized Biography

The first 1/4^{rth} of the book is about how we evolved—academic, comedic, and tragic—with authentic stories of how we used to live. Then begins the story of Edith's lineage which spans 4 generations of 20th century military families and 4 American wars—we won 2, we tied in Korea, then we lost in Vietnam. This true story reads like a novel and I am privileged to be able to tell you a few never told war stories that Edith's people had to fight. I focus on how the kids grew up, how each generation changed, and how these changes came close to ending war itself. These stories will unfold into the untold variations of the 21st century western psyche.

Although Edith's emotional intelligence puts her ahead of the *roaring crowd,* she never overestimates herself. She can imagine being somebody else—duality of mind—knowing she didn't have a damn thing to do with being born a straight white girl named Edith. She balks at quick, binary questions because she lives in the rarest of places, the colorful middle—the place to be for the duration. "Why are we given only 2 choices on so many things?" she wonders, as so many artists and painters do. Up to this point, there is nothing written about Edith's life and the unbelievable story of how her diaries came into my possession is at the end of Chapter 5.

We will paint a picture for you, and instead of this world, we'll attempt to render a slightly more beautiful one. I will explain the scientific mystery surrounding Edith's immortality—and maybe yours. I didn't discover this; a little birdie, another author, told me about it. Sometimes Edith Virginia (Virginia, middle name) does nothing all day. Theodor Rosyfelt wrote, "people say nothing is impossible but I do nothing every day."[8] The band Genesis wrote, "why do a single thing today, is tomorrow sure as I'm here?"[9] To give you a completion early the 100-year story ends and the final chapters blends psychology, art, dreams, economics, and philosophy into a living package—open at one end.

Author contact, 770-364-3191
email: theunfoldingevs@icloud.com

CHAPTER 1

A Long Walk Off a Short Pier

I will begin with a seldom told children's story for adults. Let's look at how an animal can become a new animal.

400 mya (million years ago) crustaceans like crabs and lobsters crawled out of the sea and evolved into tarantulas and roaches. The roach is unkillable as we know and like the spider has shrugged off every would be extinction. A few of the fishes, not to be outdone, played in the shallows and evolved remedial feet on the ends of their 4 flippers. We named them *tetrapods* and the brave pioneer was the iconic tiktaalik from 380 mya, who crawled from the icy ocean on flippers. Now extinct, they would occasionally grow up to 9′ long and could see 70 times farther when free of the ocean.[1]

What made it possible for a fish to live on land? My guess: no predators, more oxygen, and no competition for food. These mudpuppies were the first slimy animals to dine at the fruited table of Pangea, when the 5 continents were pinched together into one land mass. One small sect of tiny crabs, with no water to hold them down, later took to the air. Many flying and walking insects soon evolved and the fight for food on land began.

The tiktaalik could stay out of water for long intervals. Their gills slowly became funny looking ears and their bladders morphed into lungs. They developed 6-8 digits on each "leg," but evolution whittled it down to 5. The 5-digit animals simply lived longer on average than the 6-digit ones.

A simple glance at your own hand reveals the product of hundreds of millions of years of tiny incremental refinements that have optimized one of nature's most envied tools. Look at the arm and hand of a baby macaque monkey and you will see your child's hand. Just a finger means discovery. A finger can check the temperature, define surfaces, cut and scrape, pet a duck (who can walk, fly and swim), point, effortlessly break open a pistachio, and peel back 1 page in a book. Most animals cannot pluck a bug off their body. The combo of the shoulder, elbow, and wrist, evolved into a 9-axis machine with more degrees of freedom than any manmade machine. With a brain to match, humans can get into position to fix anything, whereas a chimpanzee has the same 9-axis machine but doesn't have the brain to notice something is broken and repair it.

While still living in the water, tetrapods developed toothy reptile-like jaws—biting instead of sucking in food as fish do—and kept evolving better ears. Evolutionist Matt Ridley writes, "the middle-ear bones of a mammal, now used for hearing, are direct descendants of the bones that were once part of the jaw of early fish."[2] That jaw worked so well on land that it culminated in the 6′ long T-Rex jaw and re-formed into the bird beak about 150 mya. The T-Rex came in many sizes, sometimes covered with feathers, and those birds were perplexingly smart, still are, so the dinosaurs must have been smart too.

After the tetra-pods evolved into the first amphibians they improved into reptiles, but still laid eggs, leaving caviar laying around everywhere. About 275 mya, before large dinosaurs, one female reptile enjoyed an incredible genetic mutation caused by an envelope virus which formed the first uterine sack and kept her eggs inside. Her kids got that same mutation. These were the first little mammal-reptile hybrids, and they would be put to the test immediately. The catastrophic Permian extinction 250 mya wiped out 9 out of 10 species with a furtive 9° Celsius increase in heat and somehow many smaller animals survived.

Scientists have traced the origin of all mammals to a little nocturnal rat called the "morganucodon," from 200 mya—the first hairy animal to suckle its young—who could sit on her haunches and do things with her hands.[3] Those rats who didn't become dinosaur dinner accelerated the rise of the mammals 65 mya with foreign aid from a 6-mile-wide comet that landed at a steep angle in the Gulf of Mexico at almost 10 miles per second.[4] A grain of space sand the size of Mount Aconcagua created the largest debris field since life originated here and encompassed the earth with cold dust, choking the land animals. The radiated Chicxulub crater at the north end of the Yucatan Peninsula reveals what spelled the end of the larger dinosaurs while the puny mammals stayed warmer underground. These insectivores, as their lizard cousins were, popped out to find tiny scraps of food and reproduced safely in their burrows as the generations went by, waiting for the nuclear winter to disperse. Intermittent fasting was hard-wired into our DNA from 65 mya and that sounds anti-Darwinian, but mammals were forced to fast so often that their bodies adapted to it.

Hooved animals (ungulates) evolved about 55 mya. We know mammal hooves evolved from mammal paws and have the same basic bone structure. One of the most intriguing variations in the physical evolution of any animal began shortly after hooved animals evolved.

Once upon a time the indohyus (skinny dog) and the pakicetus (skinny deer) roamed what is now the coasts of India and Pakistan. Paleontologists have their skeletons but we don't know exactly how they looked on the outside—a tapir comes to mind, not far from an aardvark—and they waded into the ocean on hooves or paws or both to find a new source of food. Due to predators, or too much competition for food on land, these mammals decided to go fishing—forever. They swam awkwardly and developed webbed feet for more speed but they lost their sense of smell and their underwater vision was terrible. Out of necessity, they evolved the ability to secrete liquids from their harderian gland to protect their eyes from salt water, [5] their corneas thickened to mechanically push back against water pressure, and they retained the ability to move each eye independently.[6]

They lived off fish for millions of years. Their tails thickened, lengthened, and became powerful flippers. Evolution put the locomotive in the back to propel them through water—it wasn't a fluke of nature—and the dogs swam faster than they used to run. I bet it was fun. This prehensile mechanism was already in place with the dogs and deer wagging their tails—a motor-skill primates would acquire millions of years later, and humans would lose millions of years after that. As millions more dog years passed, the back legs on this new ocean predator shortened to reduce drag, then disappeared altogether. Now the thigh bones are vestigial structures composed of tiny useless stubs of bone, buried under blubber. The pelvis all but vanished. The tiny pelvis floats there, surrounded by muscle, and helps with making new whales.

"Use it or lose it," they say, and the stubs for the back legs are still there in case they need to go for a painful walk. *Use it or lose it* isn't what changes an animal though because rare is the living thing who genetically changes after birth. About 70-100 random mutations occur after conception and some of the luckier mutations are serendipitous mistakes. For the ancient aquatic dog, if a few of these mistakes happened to make her a better swimmer, she lived longer and had more babies, passing these improvements along.

A few million years later these former 4-footed animals became whales(!), after something very strange happened. The nose vanished and reappeared on the top of its head.

The miracle of the whale ends with the blowhole. The last thing we want is a hole in the head, but evolution will try everything once. With one lucky litter of dolphins, the nose reappeared at the top of the head where the soft spot on a baby's head is (fontanel), and became a breathing snorkel for hunting. Simultaneously, a hole had presented itself at the roof of the mouth, creating a passage exactly where the young dolphins needed it. While still in the womb the dolphin brain folded over and created this air passage.[7] This mind-blowing breathing transformation occurred from a mutation that changed the shape of the brain in the fetal stages and completed the breathing tube. This perfect deformity probably occurred inside one mother, who couldn't believe her eyes when she saw her babies, and had no idea that she'd put the finishing touch on a new species. The blowhole was so successful that it spawned 90 different whale species, and as scientists would say, "the blowhole went to genetic fixation."

There were no mammals living in the ocean 50 mya and 25 million years later there was a diverse family of cetaceans: dolphins, porpoises, killer whales, dugongs, manatees, blue whales, and narwhals—thanks to a hopeful hairy 4-footed land mammal who took a risk.

Paleontologists call this bizarre transition, deer to whale, the "Rosetta Stone" [8] of evolution because they have so many complete bone fossils from different stages that tell similar stories of this subtle but arduous transformation. The sea lions and otters (pinnipeds) happily stopped in the middle and have fingers and toes with heavy webbing between them for swimming or land movement. Those same finger bones and wrist bones are inside the dolphin's fins, reshaped. These animals also have dog whiskers that they use to feel the human face, as they did with my family swam when we swam with the dolphins in Acapulco. I tried to explain to the workers at the aquarium where dolphins came from. They just smiled and nodded.

Nobody knows, but it's possible that predators didn't chase them into the salty water in the first place. Maybe one deer got a bit of free will and decided to take a long walk off a short pier. She decided to try fish, kept eating them, and became *Free Willy*. This bizarre change could very well have been from choice instead of necessity and may have become the most copied meme up to that point in evolutionary history. Throughout endless time, animals have found it advantageous to leave the ocean or return and there are packs of sea wolves in Western Canada today who swim into the Pacific Ocean and live off fish. The fish haven't done so badly since the invasion and still hold the overwhelming biomass in the ocean.

The deer radically changed their weather, so to speak, which is a testament to Charles Darwin's theory of adaption, meaning that no matter what happens, life in some form will move up. When we say, "the weather is perfect," what we mean is we have perfectly evolved to suit the weather earth happens to have. The cloven deer did the same but in a more forbidding environment telling us humans we've barely scratched the surface of our physical evolution.

Indeed, the people who live in and around the high elevations of Nepal have evolved tinier blood vessels to carry oxygen further, and the Bejau Laut people—deep free divers who've worked underwater for centuries in the Western Pacific—have experienced radical changes in several internal organs that help them stay under longer. The spine tingler is that the children of these 2 groups are born with these same adaptations, meaning, lifestyle alters a population's DNA.[9]

Maybe dolphins have an advantage with a floating, colder brain (air-cooled too by the breathing tube) and that's why they are smarter than dogs or chimps? Maybe using hands and making tools is only one way to look at intelligence and with a 50-million-year head start on brain evolution dolphins may communicate better than we do. Dolphins invented music long before we did. Whistling and singing to each other sounds emotional so we have no idea where one dolphin word ends and another begins. They make clicking sounds too, to convey mathematical information or lie. They are much like us but our cognitive speech set us on a very different path than the dolphin's emotional communication, which may be a universal language. Dolphins have near vertical foreheads, bigger brains than we do, and their IQs and communication are, to us, encrypted. When I talk later about intelligence (so far undefinable) I'll offer telling examples of how dolphins are beginning to unencrypt how we think, faster than we're unencrypting how they think.

Primates, dogs, cats, elephants, and dolphins, etc., have highly evolved limbic systems. That's that little area deep under the outer brain that I mentioned in the preface, where our emotions, dreams, precious memories, and the songs we love, live. Our highly developed subconscious minds draw us toward these animals in a profound sense because like us they are more aware of love, loss, and self, than other animals. And interestingly, most of them like living with us. They get free food and shelter but dolphins may have the most emotional limbic system because they don't like the captivity of aquariums. Like humans, they get Stockholm Syndrome?

Traveling halfway across the world to find a mate, one day a free and wild female dolphin will shoot through the water at 33 mph, break the surface, and stretch herself horizontally 10 feet above the water. She'll look around and think, "there is a world and it is flat." She'll be the first dolphin genius—if it hasn't already happened—because she got the wrong answer like we did, but she perceived there was a *world*. The vast majority of animals are all ego and move through the world without ever knowing it's there.

The transformation from 4-footed animals to dolphins (both in the ungulate order) makes it much easier for us to wrap our minds around how a few smart chimpanzees started the human race. It would be difficult to find many scientists or dolphin trainers who do not agree that this is how whales and humans got here. In the next couple chapters, we'll explore how our physical evolution was dwarfed by something else—our meteoric emotional evolution.

From that fateful day when stinking bits of slime first crawled from the sea and shouted to the cold stars, "I am man," our greatest dread has always been the knowledge of our own mortality.

Gene Wilder, in *Young Frankenstein*

CHAPTER 2

Sacrificial Selfishness

This chapter contains an introduction to every topic in the book.

Raised As Animals

The primate story started in a galaxy far away because the Milky Way was far from where it is now. About 55 mya ungulates evolved and a few of them took to the ocean while their cousins—4-pawed, long-faced lemurs—thrived on land. Today lemurs are going extinct unlike smaller mongooses and meerkats who were built 45 mya for moving in treetops, but lemurs can stand up, move upright, and grab things. The paws of early primates possessed an unmatched dexterity and the more primates fought and fed themselves with their hands the flatter their faces got. This was a brilliant improvement because attacking with the mouth put all 5 senses in danger. The primate tongue shortened and the teeth kept shrinking—a trend that hasn't stopped.

40 mya, at the start of an earlier ice age, monkeys branched up from lemurs and about 20 mya, monkeys evolved into apes, some apes getting fortuitous mutations others didn't. These advanced creatures were named "hominids."

The best apes as it turned out were the chimpanzees who could easily walk upright when needed, as if they couldn't decide, and as their bones, skulls, and brains changed from there a few of them evolved into the crudest pre-humans—Sahelanthropus and Australopithecus. These were still "hominids" but were the first cave people from 5-6 mya,[1] though to you and I they would look more like chimps. Scientists had to look at their bones and teeth closely to find hints of evolution because the vast majority of changes from one species to another are microscopic.

I'm moving fast with our physical evolution because I can't wait to get into our psychological evolution—even more fun. Most of our evolution was in brain growth and the details of how one chimpanzee family kicked off the evolution of humans, about 6 mya, is in Chapter 25.

5 mya life was uncomfortable to say the least but with nothing to compare it to the cave people couldn't have known that. They were so much tougher than we are today it seems improbably that we could go back and do it again—we would though, for our children. We owe everything from the terrible art on the refrigerator to the concepts our kids come up with that we can't comprehend to those ancient fathers and the mothers who somehow held babies for years, in a forbidding world. The chattel didn't get to do anything they wanted to do, the men had to follow wounded animals for days, and the clan slept with their wooden spears and babies with one eye open, as dolphins literally do. It's mind-blowing to contemplate what they endured to intentionally bring us to this wonderful place we have today no matter where we live or how much money we make.

An educated guess would be that a generation for cave people was 15-20 years, though monkey and ape generations were longer. It took early man some time to catch up to the established primates who were not at war while the cavemen often were. We had one tool—a long, sharp stick. Our first cognitive innovation, long before speaking in complex sentences, was for killing at a safe distance and Johnny Cash reminds us that *winner take all* is still in our DNA: "I shot a man in Reno, just to watch him die."[2]

Subconscious animal instinct, not so much reason, drove the cave people and this necessary survival device evolved to match the dangerous environment. You had to have a quick nervous system to survive in the wild so if you'd been there, you would have watched what you said and did. As we say in the south, "you don't want to get your ignorant ass knocked into next week."

Their dreams were probably much like their waking lives, making it easier to switch between the two for survival. I've noticed that lower animals seem to pop in and out of sleep much faster than we do because as we grew into our bigger, more cognitive, outer brains and summarily conquered the wild, we developed two distinct minds: conscious and subconscious. Today, so safe and secure, we almost think of them as two different people. One of the best feelings is lying in bed on Sunday morning, unconcerned, as we drift between dreaming and thinking, seamlessly, letting our 2 minds blend together as the cave people could.

The strongest man, the spear leader, ferociously protected his harem but probably had to share with some of his best warriors because most of them had copied his sharp stick. Another clever man figured out how to attach a sharp broken bone to the end and became a new ladies' man until the others had copied that too. All those spears fed the whole clan but they didn't often try to kill the chief because they hero-worshipped him.

We still have these emotional instincts. We revere a president and ignore his sexual indiscretions while chastising the guy on the other side for doing the same. The mega corporations borrow heavily, advertise, then cash in of our tribal emotions. Tens of thousands went out and bought a Cadillac because they saw Matthew McConaughy driving it in a commercial and these obsessions are genetic from cave people because food, sex, tools, and power, still equal status.

About 2 mya (paleolithic era) the hind legbone of any medium-sized mammal made a great club (we were smaller) and in battle we held that sharp stick in the other hand. One caveman learned to sharpen a rock on one side, hold the round part in the palm of his hand, and chop pieces off an animal he'd killed. He applied the same knapping method to make a spear tip but it often broke off the stick and that's why he needed other guys with spears. From those humble beginnings we began evolving into wandering hunter-gatherers because these weapons made hunting, fighting, and travelling, safe. About 1 mya, a branch of pre-humans (hominids) improved into Denisovans (recently discovered) and these advanced *hominins*[3] (people like us) were roughly the start of our hunter-gatherer story. Hominin fighting was worse than hominid fighting because hominins could make much better weapons.

There was so much unused land in Africa it baffles me the various versions of humans killed each other but a million years later the colonists were killing the Native Americans too. However, and this is very important, 1 mya land was not the issue at all. Sex with another tribe tempted much of the prehistoric violence, often cheered on by the lower echelon males who weren't getting any. Peering through the matted vines at the females of another tribe is how the herd of average males first learned about the fruits of conquest.

Today the sight of an early hominin would make a train take a dirt road. It wasn't Raquel Welch and Charleton Heston fighting dinosaurs in loin cloths. "Macht nichts" (mox nix) as they say in Germany, we were genetically wired to spread our genes as far and wide as possible. The best synonyms for evolution were *lust* and *fury*, now they are *passion* and *longing*.

The ancient mothers and fathers who succeeded in getting their kids to puberty—age 7 or 8—are the story of us. Since the average lifespan was about 25 years, 40,000 human generations ago equals about 1 million years. It's easier to imagine the 40,000 generations who made you than to wrap your mind around 1 million years going by (an epoch). To see your 40,000 generations, you'd have to be in an amphitheater the size of a small town but those quite short people are the unsung heroes of you. If you look closely, you'll find a smattering of pre-humans of this sort or that, dozens of homos erectus (late cave people), many Denisovans and many more Cro-Magnons, and 400-600 cute Neanderthals, not to mention all the hybrids we are still discovering, there in your personal amphitheater.

If any one of those people had been in the wrong place at the wrong time you wouldn't exist. You came through a dangerous, twisting worm hole to get here so statistically you shouldn't be here. You and I essentially won the genetic lottery, so to speak, many times in a row. Somebody had to. My numbers are illustrative only but there's a 99.999% probability, considering all the sperm and egg who never met, were discarded, died in vain, or didn't make it to puberty, plus a super volcano, that we shouldn't be here. We each had a snowball's chance in hell to exist, but the caveat is, it wasn't all luck. Many of the human lotteries were genetically rigged from the git go—slightly better genes spelled success—so we are about as lucky as the quadrillions of people, who never got to exist, are, unlucky. We could say all those non-people are dead and we were all dead too before we were born but we don't lament *those* lost years.

If a hunter-gatherer made it through childhood, he or she had a decent chance to reach 50. This sought after longevity was maybe 40% luck (happenstance) and 60% a good survival kit (will, learning, improving instincts). We've gradually diminished the luck in the human equation ever since and gotten to where we can plot a course to age 85 with maybe 2 or 3% luck—a quantum leap. In this time of blame, we have little to point to. Nobody knows nature's ways but we get 51% or more of the good genes in every mix, [4] so during the last million years and those 40,000 generations, we had 3 angels watching over us: moms, dads, and nature. With those compounded dividends, we modern folk are genetically superhuman. History might one day record that a taller, skinnier human species evolved with free will and a higher performing brain, late in the hunter-gatherer era, or maybe farming era. This next species after Cro-Magnon we could call "Exactus." The "caveman" era lasted about 4 million years and the hunter-gatherer era about 2 million and we were farmers for only 10,000 years—now comes the era of Computus Exactus? The eras are getting exponentially shorter.

Who Were Hunter-Gatherers?

After we noticed the sharp teeth, pointed beaks, horns, and treacherous claws animals had, we refashioned them all. One man finally fastened that sharp rock firmly to a long, notched stick with some strong grass, ½ mya. This alpha male spear maker was the first inventor, the first teacher, and spent all day getting others to sit on a log and knap away at a flintstone, yelling "chook, chook……chook." "Cut," was the only word they heard. As the eloquent Brian Greene puts it, "we can pass on hard-earned knowledge, substituting the ease of instruction for the difficulty of discovery."[5] Pretty soon everybody had the modern weapon. It's a good thing the alpha male couldn't patent the new spear because multiple spears often meant dinner for everybody.

The spears would rule for ½ million years, and some primatologists say those spears started monogamy in humans.[6] Lots of spears did keep the strongest males away from a man's sisters because getting injured was usually all she wrote back then but assuming that hunter-gatherers were monogamous is a stretch for me. It seems they have a desire to reach that conclusion. The great apes, our direct ancestors, established monopolies on breeding and today we are still flirting with monogamy.

Primatologists and sociologists have a propensity to call hunter-gatherer societies "egalitarian," meaning *equality of outcome*. Brute force doesn't lend itself in that direction. The inner-tribal competition was fierce which helped them stay strong against other tribes and this fashioned a steep hierarchy within a tribe. This *inequality* meant that the most valuable and strongest members got more of everything. The hierarchy kept evolving into more civilized forms of governing and human value eventually showed hints of the future: individual smarts and innovation that went beyond weapon making.

For instance, if a woman could bear children and had a midwife, and a man could make huts and another with weak knees could strike a fire (Chapter 23), they could each trade that for food and protection. A little economy based on value and coincident interest inched its way along, unseen by most, and, I will try to prove that this ushered in not egalitarianism but a more reasonably refined *inequality* that we are still refining today. Most were unaware of the widening division of labor and the tribe slowly evolving toward individuality. The tribe seemed to run by itself. If we could transport ourselves back there and explain to them that the unconventionalities individuals came up with were pulling everybody up slowly, they might not be able to grasp what we were talking about. "Self?" they might say, "what is self?" Like animals, they all knew subconsciously they were individuals, but few knew it cognitively because most of them were barely involved in tribal decision making.

Considering many hunter-gatherer studies, we're pretty sure everybody in the tribe got food—some hunters being more equal than others (*feed the studs,* they say in sports)—but tribes were hardly egalitarian. There was an unequal distribution of benefits among the stronger and the weaker males.[7] The women, who worked twice as hard and ate half as much, and still do, always carried the babies and most heavy loads. The hunter-gatherers travelled constantly and Jared Diamond, researching their bone yards, showed the kids were spaced 4 years apart. The women carried the 1-year-olds, the 5-year-olds had to walk, and the middle ones were left behind. Occasionally if a kid looked or acted strangely, they would get rid of it, driven by an ancient, utilitarian concern for the welfare of the tribe as a whole.

If we could interview those dead children or their mothers, they might not define their tribes as "egalitarian." I doubt if they were egalitarian *or* monogamous, as author Johnathan Haight intimates: "the love/sex infatuation lasts about 2-3 months, which is how many ovulating cycles it takes for most women to get pregnant." [8] The hunter-gatherer woman thought "my job is starting" and the man thought "my job is done" but now I have to make a bigger hut and hunt more. Given that brute strength sustained life, sexism would have been a given in hunter-gatherer society, which further annulled egalitarianism.

The *forager* men (a better name for hunter-gatherer) often didn't know or sometimes care whose children were whose. Sex was simply an inevitable thing—a *relationship* was hardly what we think of one today—and the forager women were better at guessing which kid belonged to which man. Women observed secluded propensities in children—even with little monogamy and worse—and were naturally better at noticing uncommon attributes, both outward and inward. I think the males governed the tribe, a conclusion any space alien would have come to had he been spying on them, and these speculations are based on the assumption that the differing mindsets of males and females have remained fairly static until recently.

Having evolved from foragers—monkeys were hunter-gatherers before us—the ways of the first foragers are our ways. With groups of 100-200 people (Robin Dunbar's number) we foragers had maybe 7-10 nightly campfires. More than men, the women probably moved between campfires, got involved in wider social circles and busied themselves with match-making, if given the chance. Advice was more appropriate in our hunter-gatherer days because it was often all the information we got. To this day we see the arranged marriages galore, people giving advice from Malta to Gibraltar (but going the long way) and researchers say our social networks still consist of about 100-200 people.

Each of us could name 150 acquaintances if we had to—a few are chiefs, most are followers, and a few are unclassifiable. Modern social media allows us to stay put while we move between campfires and learn more about others, give advice, compare, confirm status, and feel superior or jealous. The pyramid is in our DNA and we still cling to a social power structure because we retain an age-old fear of individualism, bucking the norm, going rogue, whistle blowing, and breaking precious molds. Ironically, these are the rocket boosters that lift all societies and take us north—nothing upgrades a static population like strange new idea. And it is these family created free radicals who go on to recreate themselves into good shamans and rock the world out of its holding pattern, or worse.

And yes, we do have about 150 acquaintances but our worries, our communications, our thoughts, our joys, and our foodstuffs are hoarded among 15-30 people—spouses, kids, their spouses, the dreaded in-laws, and the grandkids. If we practice egalitarianism, it's for them.

"Wanderlust" the Germans Say

"Our nature is to explore." Stephen Hawking said that. 70 thousand years ago, unbathed humans who looked like us, left Africa and started repopulating Eurasia. [9] Small groups had begun exploring in mass again after a massive volcanic cloud subsided, leaving only the healthiest and smartest. Some foragers paddled to Spain, some walked the long way to Greece; the new clans crossed seas and mountains because they were there. And they wanted to create more space, hopefully downwind from a bigger tribe who lusted after their women, and settle in a far-off valley near a stream where the grass was always greener. Long ago they knew what "location, location, location," meant. The biggest forager guy with the biggest spear hit the butt into the ground 3 times and all understood, that for now, this was home. They all got butterflies in their stomachs. The tribe was their world and born was the comfortable feeling of nationalism. The personal nuclear family wasn't their whole world *yet* because they couldn't survive on their own.

Walking made us endurance kings, enhanced our nightly dreams, and invigorated our brains. Dr Yuval Harari (author of *Sapiens*) and other researchers write of the rapid growth of the human brain between 70 and 30 thousand years ago, after the remigration. (This book will offer you a stark alternative to Harari's view of what the human condition is evolving into. More with each chapter, I'm going to be challenging some popular sociological presumptions.)

The evidence shows that cooking meat enhanced our internal

combustion engine, the stomach, so it could get smaller and we could get taller. Processing protein more efficiently grew our brains, and evolving more molars with teeth in a horseshoe pattern instead of rectangular, [10] enabled us to chew meat into smaller pieces, and create more surface area. Our canine teeth had all but disappeared because we killed with spears and cut the animals up with Acheulean axes. The reason our jaw got smaller and smaller was because it was a big tool we no longer needed and evolution saw fit to reroute that extra energy to the brain. A big jaw, like fangs or a useless tail, was baggage that shortened a forager's life slightly, thinning out his or her lineage. And running faster as legs got longer, making better weapons, winning battles and spreading genes, kept raising our IQs.

The foragers, both Neanderthal and Cro-Magnon, enjoyed ever different landscapes that constantly put new pictures, sounds, and smells into their minds. Imagine you are a child raised in a big, safe room because you have no immune system (*The Boy in the Plastic Bubble* movie 1976) so you don't get enough exercise and, as important, your scenery never changes. The neurons in other children's brains who get to play outside will fire more, make more connections, and brighten their dreams. The good news for the boy in the bubble is he can read books and see the world that way.

The wilderness humbled and inspired the foragers. Learning only made them want to learn more. They developed "amazing powers of observation"—as Pink Floyd puts it—and this brain growth, over millenniums, made us super learners and teachers. Nature (genetic changes) is slow without nurture (good habits) and a little free will to get the cart up the hill. With this new 3-cylinder engine evolution finally achieved the thus far, unbeatable, state-of-the-art human brain. After 3 billion years evolution had accidentally on purpose solved the Rubik's Cube.

As a radical baby boomer, I got cabin fever working in large organizations. They felt like pleasant, air-conditioned, white-collar jails. The show *The Office* is so funny because none of the workers want to be there. We foragers were super fit or dead so sitting and staring at a computer screen is an abrupt change. A forager didn't exercise for 20 minutes, stare at a computer for 8 hours wishing he were elsewhere, then go get an unhealthy dinner on credit. Equally bad, we live indoors in front of screens and the onslaught of electromagnetic waves creates a strange new weather for us. We suffer from an invisible neurosis—blasé shock from the screen and the clock—always trying to get ahead of the future the pyramid is creating, while deep in the brain the hypothalamus is trying to correct these chaotic rhythms (Chapter 17). That dichotomy and the stagnant air are the newest environmental adjustments our psyche and immune systems are adapting to, or not.

Still, I believe we're more influenced by nurture than nature because as our outer, cognitive brain grew it became more programmable than our old, inner subconscious. Our outer cognition gets incessant input from our environment, parents, and acquaintances, constantly changing it, while our inner, subconscious, emotional, primordial brain lives a firewall away from that programming. That's why our dreams seem so crazy: a firewall evolved between the inner and outer mind, separating them, and nature's firewall is as good as any 6-layered encrypted computer firewall at keeping hackers, even ourselves, out. Besides having fleeting memories of our dreams when we wake up, our 2 minds don't talk to each other that much.

Another polar contradiction we have is that we consider the brain and body separate systems while nature doesn't distinguish between them. Evolution sensed our blunder so instilled within us a cure-all: wanderlust. When I hike, exercise, or fly to a new place, my brain improves that day, as if somebody hit the master switch. In idyllic Banff Canada, a dry wintry wonderland, you can snow ski a mile high between the Rocky's peaks or golf in the valley at the Freemont Resort while getting chased by massive bull elk. You can stroll around Lake Louise which looks like one of Edith's oil-paintings—both have mystifying color and contrast. You could walk the skyscraper deep Athabasca glacier in the Columbian ice fields or visit the Yamnuska wolf/dog sanctuary to pet hybrids.

The Canadian nightlife was fun, full of young people, and on the big screen we watched, again, the 2010 video of K D Lang singing *Halleluiah* at the Winter Olympics in Vancouver. It's nice to know that old Leonard Cohen was still alive to hear it. Lang took the song to a new place. She may as well have been arrested because she killed the song and wellnigh assumed ownership of it, which was such a compliment to Cohen.

There are too many places I'd still like to go see but I can't decide whether Banff Canada, Tuscany Italy, or the Cayman Islands are the loveliest places on earth. In Tuscany we rented a villa for a week, hiked endlessly through the rolling vineyards—no fences to speak of—and spoke in broken Italian to farmers who had watched WWII planes fly over them as toddlers. My wife and I found more amore in the little quaint Tuscany towns than the medium size cities.

In Cayman, the only trash we saw were the steel ship wrecks sitting on the ocean bottom. As I popped through the top hatch of one ship's hull, I watched a cruise ship going over me, 50 feet up. With an escort of 6-foot barracudas and 1/8th of a mile visibility, we dove 100 feet down the 5-mile-deep sheer cliff of the Cayman Trench. In the shallower water, about 25 feet deep, we petted and fed hundreds of stingrays. These boneless, sharklike scavengers who evolved 150 mya seem to have no mouth because that organ is underneath their sonar-equipped noses so they can skate along the bottom and scoop up mollusks. They would encircle us like a spinning blanket and take turns gobbling bits of fish from our extended palms. My scuba buddy had the bag of fish food and got accosted by 15 of these little puppies but their stingers were relaxed—they only wanted lunch, fast. Like a scorpion, they sport a prehensile tail and if you corner them and stare at them as Steve

Irwin did, they will get apprehensive. They can sting a diver a dozen times in the heart, inside a heartbeat, like a jackhammer.

In Banff, my wife's nephew Josh and I, plus 2 buddies, golfed at the Freemont Resort and saw bull elk lying in the grass with oozing holes in their sides, some fading fast. The *only* advantage the younger bulls had is the choice of when to attack. The winning bull elks were slowly roaming the course, saving energy for the next fight, and bellowing deep haunting sounds (*the rut)* from the chamber of the valley which echoed off both sides of the Rocky Mountains. Hundreds of cows lazily ate the golf course and would only gaze at us to chew while a rather small number of studs watched us carefully and seldom ate. It was the peak of mating season for sure and it seemed that 5 or 6 bulls were happy to share about 250 cows, but somewhat annoyed about the useless golfers sharing their property.

Antlers evolved far behind the head so the bull elks could eat but they had no qualms about putting their mouths down, their eyeballs up, and charging. Scientists speculate that cows (female elk) can count up to 10 and will try to avoid a male with 9 antler points if another male has 10. Even wasps can count so female elk can probably count or at least estimate which bull will help their sons win a future fight.

We golfers weren't yet aware of how special elk were until a bull, proudly standing alone on a high green, watched us as our little white balls bounced around him. As we approached, he lowered his head and came at us so we sprinted back to the golf carts, skipped that hole, and left the four balls there. At about 900 pounds he had the biggest rack on the course, about 5′ across, and the deer family kills the most people, beside bacteria. Elk antlers can grow 1 inch per day and we started wondering if we were trying to golf or get ourselves into the next installment of the Darwin Awards.

The staff at the Freemont told us they didn't attack golf carts but we had fast ones thank God because the staff was wrong. The 2nd time we were attacked an 800-pound bull elk ran at us so we floored the accelerators again and drove 30 mph through bumpy hills and dales, not knowing at the time that elk are one of the fastest land mammals per pound at 45 mph. Not tipping the cart over was priority one, so I risked a quick glance back and he was still on our tail. This monster ran after us at high speed for a full minute. We drove many holes away, finally safe, and started playing golf again from whatever hole that was.

The next day, Josh and I fed the wolves by hand at the Yamnuska Sanctuary. We weren't supposed to pet too them but we did anyway. These wolves were 1/8th dog and they greedily stared at my palm while devouring the handful of treats. One grey wolf, twice the size of a large dog, wouldn't take his eyes off mine while eating out of my hand. With those super close eyes, he gave me the creeps. It was one of the coldest days I can recall and the wolves were not only at ease but grateful. Because of travel, I warmly remember these moments as if they happened yesterday.

Good Genes Have Permanence

When I write about the work/love gene, the war gene, or the depression gene, I am simplifying a more complex phenomenon of our DNA. These genes make up a more complex molecule called the "chromosome," which was gradually assembled by nature over a few eons (billions of years) with no particular end in mind. The story of existing species is the story of stronger genes and those who still carry them.

Dinosaurs still walk the earth, in Florida for example, and the crocodile still thrives with the strongest bite on earth. They can kill water buffalo. Although the croc is adaptable, it was nature's best dinosaur and didn't need to change much. Besides some crocodiles flying away and becoming birds with 4-chambered hearts too, and the rest of them going from 2 legs back down to 4 and shrinking to half their prehistoric size, crocodiles have survived almost unchanged for 200 million years. Like humans, only one species of croc made it and the same croc genes have stayed alive inside croc lineages for 200 million years (Richard Dawkins 1976). This gene longevity shocked the world as well as the discovery that human genes occupy management offices inside our subconscious minds and tell us what to do.

Evolutionary thinkers have come to a daunting conclusion: animals are chiefly on autopilot. Even a human is both the proverbial elephant (the ruling genes) and the idiot riding atop the elephant so the hapless passenger is pretty much along for the ride (Johathan Haidt 2012). Our genes knowingly shove us around by creating many bad and good sensations. One sensation, the best 7 seconds of the week, we can't refuse and a baby doesn't cross our minds during evolution's sneaky attempt at fruition. In a sense, Buddha knew we were slaves to our genes and tried to conquer all his pangs 2500 years ago but he wasn't, in a word, proactive.

As our free will tepidly pecks its way out of its primordial shell, we can experiment more with overruling some instincts and genes and perusing new options. This is scary, virgin territory. We can think so well that we can decide to not think at all, or, we might decide to grab the reigns and *pilot* the elephant more. We are just starting so it's important to know what we're up to, as opposed to simply experiencing a change, because we can make the elephant turn right or left but we want it to be for a reason. The human race is waking from a million years of too many emergencies so with all this free time and countless options, nobody could possibly know what will happen next.

When I write that "the same genes" have been living inside a species for millions of years they usually aren't the exact same genes because genes evolve too. Plus, identical twins have slightly different mutations and evolve genetically further apart by living different lives. When you hear "humans are genetically 99% the same as chimps," that's a true oversimplification. Our brains are 3 times bigger and perform at a much higher level—we choose from countless more options—so our intelligence genes have evolved into a larger sphere of consciousness.

While most species have not evolved enough free will to rewrite their determined futures, what human brains have done is confront the status quo of their instinctual condition, argue with their stubborn genes, and do the unexpected. Adam and Eve, the only people without belly buttons, would be shocked to see our technology and shocked again to see the 8 billion spirits on earth and our unsurpassed longevity. Yesterday we were swinging from trees; today we are preparing to land female astronauts on Mars.

A Wealth of Attitudes

After much travel, something clicked and everywhere I went I saw hints of human evolution. I saw differences in features and vaster differences in attitudes worldwide. There are short people in one country, tall people in the country next door, and men with very deep-set eyes, or not. There were protruding bottom lips in Australia but not in the UK and boundless different ear lobe shapes. Cameras don't seem to bring these features out. I noticed the ubiquitous lazy left eye, the vast majority of hair parts on the left, and so many Scotch-Irish people with a mole under the left eyebrow. The hound dog who started that mole must have caught a rabbit or 2.

Many groups are caught in the technological divide and seem too far behind to catch up but their kids will catch up fast. People get smarter continuously, according to study after study, because the incredible brain both leads and adapts to technology and psychology. In some countries we get lots of advice, in others we get none, and some countries value individuals while others still value groups. Even Europeans and Americans have different attitudes about so many things. Europeans subtly people watch while Americans do overtly, like toddlers. Americans are more outgoing and gregarious while Europeans work together better because of the proximity of nations, while keeping their cards close to the vest. Americans have a singular, independent spirit which can be wildly creative, obnoxious, or misinterpreted.

Europeans, who yawn at sex scandals, were amused when Janet Jackson accidentally showed her breast for a half a second at the Superbowl and perplexed when millions were lost after the long lawsuits. Strangely though, Europeans are the ones who don't mind lots of rules while Americans hate them. Humans are chockfull of contradictions. Asians are calmer and historically less warlike than we were taught (Chapter 24).

When we furtively people watch we can't help it because we get to see the best and most recent chapter of human evolution. Whether we feel superior or a little jealous when we look around, no matter, evolution doesn't care about individuals, only the species as a continuance. You could copy Bill Murray in the movie *What About Bob*—think of people as telephones—and if one of them doesn't like you, just say, "this one's out of order!" We covet our ultra-precious individuality but it's superfluous to mother evolution who maintains a Freddie Mercury attitude toward a single death—"another one bites the dust."[11] You can think of evolution as a lesser god who doesn't personally love you but is really taken with your species.

The lower animals can't grasp either of these concepts, they accept events as they transpire, but sentient individuals arrived which began an eternal conflict: Is evolution still running the show or are we taking over? Humans will invent anything to live as long as possible while evolution has countless clever ways to rid the world of old people who no longer reproduce—it doesn't give a rat's ass. We are winning and it's a great time to be in the club.

Sacrificial Selfishness

"Every life is an unfinished life." *Alexander Solzhenitsyn*

Sacrificial selfishness describes our core value, our core contradiction, and who we are. This polar duality is far and away our forte. For now, consider the meaning of each emotional word—*sacrifice* and *selfishness*—which seem so far apart they cannot be linked. The two words blend like a Möbius strip and they will force me to contradict myself here and there in this book. Though we are logical, robotic creatures too, sacrificial and selfish are both emotional words—drivers of our free will—and are the pilots of our lives.

With backing from other evolutionists, I've estimated we are 90% selfish but we become roughly half selfish when we raise a family, which 90% of us do. Those 25 years are by far the most demanding—and literally derailing—yet the happiest as we are one with nature with our cup half full. Nature wasn't asleep when it made living for yourself almost impossible. We can't be selfish all the time—without polarity life would have no contrast—and Albert Einstein said "we start living when we learn to live outside of ourselves."

After copying our genes our psyche lives half outside of ourselves and we become exposed, real people. With a family we have as much to lose as we have to gain and can't declare victory—life is a tie and the kids aren't what we expected anyway. We rarely get back what we give them; we teach the kids how to love the next generation. After the kids leave, we relinquish control, trust society, and this compels us to make sane laws for everybody. Sacrificial selfishness is felt by everyone, biologically or consciously, I just gave it a name.

Marriage, with the un-coerced consent of both spouses, gained traction in the 1700s but the majority of the western female population didn't demand it until about 1900. That was the inflection point when roughly half of the women were able to choose a husband out of free association and mutual attraction. I learned this from author Stephanie Coontz and the poignant research in her book, *Marriage, a History*, exposed the hidden timeline. Mutual attraction in relationships triumphed in Europe and America at the same time (not many other places) and since 1900 most westerners have worked toward that elusive, antievolutionary, monogamous marriage.

"I feel as though, you ought to know, that I've been good, *as good as I can be*." [12]I guessed John Lennon wrote that song with a splash of sarcasm but Paul McCartney said he remembers writing it alone.

There is no precedence for any mutuality or monogamy or any combination of the two in our history, in fact, it's a bizarre development according to Coontz. The predictable friction that followed this curious development is from laboriously rewriting our programming after a million years of genes that dictated the use of force. The tsunami of male brute momentum took so long to overcome, and reverse, I'm surprised the female powered, *expert gene detector* (Chapter 5) survived a million years of dormancy. It turns out too that women are slightly better at picking stocks, food, clothes, and winners and losers in general.

Each relationship is different and *mutual attraction* can mean absolutely anything so it's a quasi-scientific concept. It's risky to try to put a number on it—let's just say "free association is rapidly increasing." We can see that women now have 51% of the *psychological* power—a modest understatement—so the stragglers, a dwindling minority of powerless women and overly controlling men, must marry each other. They "don't believe in modern love."[13]

The slave/master relationship is the most inefficient engine because it psychologically sickens both sexes, or both groups, as Thomas Jefferson was painfully aware of.[14] When we win all the time, we don't realize we're slowly boring ourselves to death and when we're oppressed, our first victory excites us with life energy. That's why we cheer for the underdog. Most landowners in Jefferson's day had black slaves, simply from having been born rich and white, which generationally passed on a psychological sickness through black families, and in turn, made the slaveowners feel omnipotent and Godlike. Unlike Jefferson, most slaveowners had no clue they were getting psychologically sicker and sicker until those relentless, undecipherable nightmares haunted them later in life.

Marriage was a glorified form of slavery for longer. When women finally cast off their masters, they finally grabbed the reigns of Darwin's brilliant, if now obvious, observation of *sexual trait selection* and changed the very nature of children. Think about it: for a million years far less than half the population, only the strongest men, could practice sexual trait selection and they were the least discerning group.

By picking men more for their psychology, women civilized their love lives and changed the gene pool. They hooked up with guys whom evolution had previously considered geeky, unfit men—you know, those guys with pocket protectors—and women changed everything. "Someday love will find you," [15] and nowadays we even hear the off story of a woman giving birth to a Love Child 9 months after a Star Wars convention. "He definitely doesn't drink or do drugs—I can see that from here—and I don't really care if he goes to church or not," the female Trekkie's thought. Enter the era of the nice guy—a guy who wouldn't know what to do with a slave if he had one—and the girls liked that too.

Long before that strange thing happened, evolution had thrown a curveball to the latter-day primates and from monkeys to apes to us it kept taking longer to raise a baby. And because of the dangers of childbirth men lived longer than women until doctors reversed that sometime in the 1800s. Even with a shorter life, women had the highest workload and have evolved the strongest work/love gene of any living thing, not to mention baby's heads never stopped kept getting bigger. [16] A minority of women cultivated the nice guy for hundreds of years and the daughters watched and learned, until most granddaughters finally got to pick their kid's genes. Simultaneously, they got a near full return on their investment and some professional help with delivery.

The chimpanzees have a similar dose of the work/love gene we do but they have less work—their babies grow up faster—and they have simpler souls. We feel the moral and ethical dilemmas of life and always want more while chimps simply feel an undying emotion that something bad happened, and they can rarely negotiate justice. Humans make huge sacrifices to correct small injustices. There is a quantum difference between chimps and us, in fact, we see them as pathetic creatures.

Still, any animal will fight any bigger animal just to give their offspring an extra 30 seconds to escape, and will feed only their own offspring in good times and bad. Any species that wasn't viciously altruistic *and* selfishly violent to protect their offspring would have ended up in that "great gig in the sky."[17] If any mother felt too much pity for other families and occasionally neglected her own children, her genes would go extinct. This ancient selfishness was in the first fish too, who have similar emotions and feelings that are akin to mammals.[18]

With the wasps on our little farm, occasionally we must poison their nests but they refuse to abandon their young. Gasping through those tiny spiracles in their armor, they try everything less they miss the outside chance to save their offspring, then, after the last flap of their wings, the poison shuts down their nervous systems and they sadly drop to the ground with little popping sounds. And the smart fat birds make nests under our roofed decks too, right where we hang out. "You look at them and they look at you,"[19] as two conscious minds meet but they won't fly directly to their nests until we look away. Much smarter than the wasps, they still don't know that we know where their nests are. Most every Georgia animal has walked up to our farmhouse, except the alligator.

Lastly, evolutionary scientists write much about our core *fight or flight* gene which tells us, when in danger, whether to engage or flee and sacrificial selfishness is so powerful it turns half that gene off! When our offspring are in danger, we automatically fight any battle when there's but a 5% chance to save our derivative genes. Or, we make *Sophie's Choice* and sacrifice 1 and save the rest, knowing we can make more souls later.

Any species, including humans, can also find themselves free of predators for many generations, gradually turn down the flight gene, and get eaten. Psychologically we are experiencing this now and getting slowly consumed.........but that's for much later.

Advice Anyone?

We slowly learn that advice can be good or bad—habitually bad psychologists say—with the exception of some generic advice and of course children need advice (not too much). Adults who copy or live inside a psychological construct of their own making might invite other adults inside their little pyramid. It gets lonely inside so residents freely advise us it's a swell place. Advisors are selling us their pyramid, mainly to reassure themselves, by increasing the population inside their own construct. The late Sheldon Kopp wrote an excellent book alluding to this—*If You Meet the Buddha on the Road, Kill Him*. The older we get the clearer we see Kopp's allegorical message and ironically the more advice we get from people who still live their lives inside their little triangle.

Poor innocent Buddha though! Couldn't Kopp pick on Friedrich Hegel, King Herod, or Confucius instead? Kopp was really making fun of Buddha's own schtick though—Buddha himself would warn us not to take his advice.

Buddha didn't tell us how to live, he suggested we shut our eyes and dwell on our troubles. The feeling of revenge goes away, something better appears, and the self-styled Buddhist John Lennon called it "waves of sorry, pools of joy."[20] The real Buddha, the first denial-anger-acceptance guy, didn't say what might appear next because every person is different and he knew that too. Buddha's brilliance was telling us that he didn't know everything and I don't think he ever said that per se, however, it was hiding inside everything he said. Legend has it that he was born in Nepal, bringing up the question once again: do colder brains work better?

Buddha knew he didn't know it all......what other philosopher taught us that? As the philosophe Carl Jung said, "I found no answer, or too many.[21] Carl Jung—psychiatrist/evolutionist—is the only other I know of who admitted he didn't know everything and his self-acknowledged lack of omnipotence was often the beginning of a patient's trust. After trust, the real struggle can begin. The west laughs about the rabbits with antlers that these idiot geniuses (Jung and Buddha) pulled out of their hats because westerners always want closure. Closure is an infinite process. There are no real gurus out there. Looking for them is our foolish folly and the gurus know it and love it.

The motivation for kibitzing (unsolicited advice) is not altruism though that's how it's packaged, sold, and bought. The advisor assumes that he or she is trying to help but they're using others to reconfirm themselves—**advice is a gift from the advisor back to the advisor**.

When John Lennon got remarried and Yoko had their son he wrote: people would "give me all kinds of advice, designed to enlighten me." They envied his iconic accomplishments and when he relaxed, the self-appointed advisors told him he wasn't "on the ball." Lennon did whatever he wanted to do in life, his advisors hadn't risked that, so they masked their jealousy with advice. I found yet another guru, Linji lu, who basically told us to watch out for gurus.

Master Chán, a great drinker, was a Chinese Zen Master 1500 years ago and one of his students, Linji lu, echoed this interesting take on advice. "The treasury of my True Dharma Eye will be destroyed by the blind donkey," Linji said, and added, "do not except other people's delusions."[22] If someone had told him they had the answer to everything he might have said, "you need counseling." We might want to run from anyone who tells us how to live our lives because they couldn't possibly know the answer. Those who tell you how to live have lost their personal infinity and want the creepy pleasure of watching yours disappear too. They are on autopilot and need the comfort of greater numbers along their trodden path—they pretend they have FOOMO: the fear of *others* missing out.

When parents realize a new child is an infinitely complex individual, they may also realize they have little or no idea who that child will become. There are no kid categories really so we give them countless options because we don't know where they will excel or what they might think they missed out on. Edith's unhurried parents had lots of free time and knew this ancient, smalltown wisdom. That's where she learned it and would later tell her kids, "remember......you're unique, just like everyone else," and laugh, "it's your superpower......the only one you get." The faintest line hides between teaching and preaching.

Herbert Spencer's richly understood *survival of the fittest* means that our biological and psychological infections won't be our grandchildren's infections, however, they will have new ones. Charles Darwin, an unassuming, humble, and polite naturalist, called it *natural selection* after he amazingly saw the transformation of animal life in 1 short lifetime. As weak genes fizzle out, stronger traits are simply *selected* by nature to live longer and be fruitful and multiply, like flatter feet or a better brain or a whale's blowhole. So brilliant, so simple, were the one-liners *natural selection* and *survival of the fittest,* that people will leap through a construct of imaginary hula-hoops to not understand them.

Innocently, the affable chap Charles Darwin (adored at dinner parties as gentleman are) never set out to upset anyone but ended up putting a history of literary work into question. He found a nicer way to burn books, "creative destruction" intellectuals call it, and the tens of thousands of scientists who continue his work no longer consider his theory, a theory. More amazing is that he invented a new branch of science that since 1859 no one has been able to dislodge. [23] The Galapagos Islands, where Darwin somehow read the writing on a speeding bullet (the #1 observation of all time) are metaphysically the most important islands on earth. Galapagos hosts a raft of tropical penguins at the equator, almost 10,000 klicks north of their icy habitat.

After sailing the world, Charles Darwin married late at age 30 and had 11 children. They were a churchgoing, upper crust, educated, British family and publishing *Origin of the Species* presented the couple with a risk, even in Europe. If Darwin had released this gem in a Muslim stronghold "his shoulders would be lonesome for his head."[24] According to the movie *Creation* (2009), Charles' wife Emma read the book, he gave her the option to burn it while he was gone, and upon his return she said "publish it."

The author Robert Wright (*The Moral Animal*, 1994) made an educated guess the strait-laced Charles may have been a 30-year-old virgin when he married his first cousin Emma.[25] It was frowned on for elite Brits to engage in "wenching" in the redlight districts but kissin' cousins were common. 3 out of their 10 kids did die before age 11, maybe from those recessive genes, but both parents were aware of the risks.

Britain, with so many firsts, started the evolution revolution and American writers followed. The American authors let their hair down a bit and talked more about themselves and their families, which made their books more real for me, so I did more of that. I'll never forget the late Robert M. Pirsig and his book *Zen and the Art of Motorcycle Maintenance* which catapulted my absurd teenage mind to the next tier. Pirsig's son asked, "what should I be when I grow up" and Pirsig said, "honest"—non-specific, generic advice. His main message was that we each experience the world differently. We are taught that we're watching the same movie everybody else is watching and nothing could be further from the truth. Once we get that, duality of mind follows which is enriched by reading good books, finding our heroes, and having deepening relationships.

Brian Greene, another name that invariably pops out, is a striking thinker and writer. After a few of his paragraphs a question usually pops into my mind and he answers it in the next paragraph as if he can read my mind. I found almost 2 full pages in one of his books where he didn't use the word *and*, once. That's hard to do. There are so many good writers. We can roll the evolutionary authors into a big ball and ask, "where is the ball rolling?"

The answer is uphill, away from *gravity* and *entropy*. Those are the 2 horseman of the apocalypse who bring the inevitable end to nearly all things. Entropy says, "out with the old" and life says "in with the new." Entropy's mayhem is nearly an axiomatic law in the universe—ashes to ashes, dust to dust, methane to methane—and this vigilante decays atoms, breaks everything, burns out stars, collapses galaxies, and eventually might collapse the universe. On a smaller scale you can have a couple of boys and over the next few years watch them destroy thousands of dollars-worth of stuff—that's entropy too. They'll probably play hockey inside the house. You might name them *Wear* and *Tear* but after a decade or 2 of mayhem, they build in an uphill fashion—that's *work*—which brings us to positive entropy: *positive* entropy disperses their goods and services throughout an economy.

We start as mostly empirical learners so we define the world by watching how things work (experience combined with reason). We learn about gravity first because toys hit the floor when we let them go—they break, we get to see what's inside—and we get to learn how they were made. We learn that balls never roll up hill but we can make them do that. Living things are the unquantifiable *lifeforce* that fights uphill against the downhill racers of entropy and gravity. It takes purpose to travel up an inclined plane and Isaac Newton said it takes *work*. By using muscle or mind we can only create wealth by engaging in *intelligent work*—it doesn't answer to any other name. I call working for the sake of working, "nervous working" because we need that time to contemplate future priorities. That's intelligent work too. Work should be *our* slave and when we don't put philosophy and contemplation before action, we work like nervous robots.

Something else does work which is why salmon swim upstream to spawn. Evolution itself performs work accidentally on purpose. It can't match our speed but in a poorly understood way it builds complexity as deliberately as we do. Evolution, in a sense, is alive. Whatever tiny motors are inspiring that draftsman who never sleeps (philosophe Robert Pirsig calls it "Dynamic Quality"[26]) we have the same motors; we are the same thing evolution *is*, we simply have the best biological and emotional engines, synchronized to do inconceivable things.

After Charles Darwin upset the applecart, many realized that the great pyramids of Egypt were built for no reason and the Pharoah's people were enslaved for nothing. The government-religion-money pyramid of modern western society also builds the biggest baddest[27] monoliths often for bragging rights. Some of these valueless monuments—the digital surveillance clouds and the off-the-books spending—go unseen and are not for bragging rights. I will clearly define these later—those deepfakes that we put up with while continuously fine-tuning individual work—but you probably know what I'm talking about. The reason we've put up with them is because they've always been there—the hierarchy of tribal nationalism lingers in our DNA.

One reason we shrug at philosophy is that most of the old philosophers were beholden to a king, pope, caliphate or mogul, and wrote to please them. Those philosophes got longwinded, obsessed with big words, and bored us into disliking the most interesting subject, maybe for a reason. With the exception of Aristotle and a few others, little changed until about 400 years ago. In order of their deaths, from René Descartes 1650, Locke 1704, Hume 1776, Smith 1790, Kant 1804, Marx 1883, Spencer 1903, to Rand 1982, each philosopher tried to break some of our societal chains. They saw the material and psychological zeitgeist of any society as an absolute reality and knew that individuals could correctly perceive these concepts too. The loner Nietzsche (1900) begged to differ. He stayed an entertaining character and fantastical dreamer while most philosophes knew that people grasped abstractions.

When we create a new environment together—an awareness of sexism, racism, or the expansion of free speech, a welfare state, or a buildup to war—we can accurately perceive these in reality, unless the pyramid goes to great lengths to hide them. We think in pictures and although reasonable people have different opinions about a state of affairs, the genius of the masses is usually right.

Strange environments however, like nano worlds or our dream worlds, which we don't understand, are just out of reach. Quantum physicists have long been mining into the atom but we don't see the picture—we conceive but don't perceive—because *they* don't have the picture yet, which summons speculation. Like humans, atoms are 99.99% empty space and we don't know what goes on inside that expanse either. When we believe we understand more than we can see we begin seeing much more of it.

Sigmond Freud, Frederick Pearls, and Carl Jung saw our emotional subconscious (our main driver) and tried to show that world to us. The irreverent Buddhist Henry David Thoreau lived on cloud 9 and balanced a short industrious life with nature's infinite richness. The Buddhists too have been suggesting we take a peek inside and tackle the riddle from there.

Apophenia

"An unexamined life is not worth living." —*Socrates*

Every good citizen once believed the earth was the center of the universe—the Ptolemaic system—and many who disagreed were burned at the stake. Science slunk along under a red threat level and humanity stayed in the wrong orbit for centuries. This fear of science, brought to us by the old pyramid, led us to misdiagnose all orbits. We used a bad reference point—our planet—and when we measure others instead of ourselves we are often wrong because we are using a bad reference point—ourselves. This egocentricity also bestows us to see unfairness as pointed at ourselves while unfairness is stitched into the fabric of the universe.

One little drawback to the safe modern world is that we aren't required to get reality right, as opposed to cave people who had to, to survive. To ensure we get some wrong answers we tend to believe information that makes us feel better and doubt things that make us feel worse—mostly when we're not at work. This simplicity of mind is as good as randomly filling in answers on a true-false test. We see this phenomenon everywhere except in the mirror and if we think someone else's delusion is obvious we can use that to ignore our own for another day or talk about that other person's delusion until we end up in La La land.

Benjamin Franklin wrote it better: "I imagine a man must have a good deal of vanity who believes that all the doctrines he holds are true and all he rejects are false." This egocentrism goes beyond heurism in that it is the refusal to venture off autopilot, and, when we bid adieu to our free will. For a haunting example, imagine if all scientists and engineers had believed whatever made them feel better and didn't believe whatever made them feel worse. We would have no machines and might still be living in the wood.

Apophene, the original spelling of the word, was coined in 1958 by a German, Klaus Conrad. Apophenia (the way the English say it) is the tendency for people to make connections between unrelated things, like seeing patterns few others see, or, making connections in their heads that have no counterpart in reality. A crazy idea can turn into a brilliant idea, hinting at our free will, or, on the downside, many of our personal thoughts can be completely delusional. Like everything else, apophenia has polarity. We hide our true desires from our conscious minds and Sigmond Freud knew we were oblivious to our deepest motivations.[28] These apophenic misconceptions are precious and personal—the psychological candy is unique to the 7-year-old inside us all—and we protect our delusions like we would a newborn baby. Nobody can point it out, take it away, or even joke about it.

Before World War II, apophenia made the Arian race think they were far superior and the damage stunned the world. Mass apophenia can turn hordes of people into psychopaths and author Hrishikesh Joshi says, "when too many like-minded individuals gather, they become fanatics quickly."[29] The psychiatrist Klaus

Conrad thought of apophenia as a mental disorder (not really a delusion) but it certainly can be when unnoticed for decades. How could we be so delusional after so much mental improvement?

Deception is firmly-seated in our DNA (creatures great and small are experts) and it has a positive side. For humans, it *was* a selected, psychological overreaction from long ago, to cope, defend, hide, or to stand out from the crowd. After learning the art of deception, self-deception followed. This was the jagged sidestep we had to take in our long circuitous journey toward becoming individuals. We needed the all-powerful tribe for protection but most of us were being abused by the steep hierarchy too. Each person tried any tactic, often unconsciously, to gain some freedom or find a loophole in the tribal laws. We certainly didn't want the tribe to see what we were up to and we accidentally began fooling ourselves.

Half the information we need hides inside our subconscious leaving us all half free to revise our own histories so we don't have to single out anyone. A psychology degree is great if we can also uncover our cloaked motivations (our *confirmation biases*) but college is a far cry from therapy. We can't learn to play soccer by studying it. Many of our statements are designed to distract others, which is fine, and consciously knowing when we are doing it will tell us whether it's an obsolete reflex from yesteryear or a necessary distraction to keep fools and neurotic investigators at bay.

When we do cursory, personal studies of the human condition we are sure we are removing ourselves from the equation, which is impossible unless we've learned to think like a scientist. Nature has honed our heurism to be oh so accurate but it has polarity; heurism can unknowingly prioritize our worst biases and produce self-congratulatory gobbledygook. The first chapter in the hypothetical book of life is the study of self. Not only is that the longest chapter by far but therein lie the tools we'll need for the rest of the short chapters, if there are any. Diagnosing others before self is rearranging knickknacks in your display case when there's a stranger in your house. Skipping self-diagnosis also makes us terrible counselors because we are simply making damn sure our assessments of others don't interfere with or confirm our own delusions. After we intrude on our negative thoughts they lose their deceptive power—that void is filled with awareness—and we can start sleeping like a baby again.

Humans are the most refined measuring devices known and even the crudest of measuring devices need periodic recalibrating. Recalibrating the superlative measuring device is learned: meditation, dream awareness, laughing, music, and therapy are the only cerebral scrubs I've found. I'm a book taught, amateur meditator but simply stopping your mind from taking in constant information or worry, or trying to, makes a soothing difference, especially when repeated. Will Rogers said "worrying is paying on a debt that may never come due." Those little bio-gears in our heads get gummed up during childhood innocence when nature and nurture shove us around and cleaning that foreign debris off without removing the grease gets tedious. Half of us skip that step and don't realize the staircase ended there, so we happily pretend we're still climbing.

For most of our evolution we knew few words so lived more inside our heads. Now we are constantly bombarded with words. "Noise" is what the scientist Dr Daniel Kahneman calls it and when we turn off the noise, the brain cleaning starts. " So I rose above the noise and confusion, just to get a glimpse beyond this illusion."[30] The first 2 easy noise reducers are the hardest: turn the TV off then take a brave breath and shut down your cellphone. You'll get a feeling of fear because you are in a strange new peace.

We cannot help but be heuristic. It is in our DNA and Kahneman politely calls it our "availability heuristic." What he means is, we pick the low hanging fruit—the easy answers and the quick answers—and ignore the rest of the tree. We "jump over synapses" and redact lots of data. When we pick those lazy genes, we begin judging the veracity of information based on how it makes us feel—like children see the world. The most controversial example is those who get all their information from TV and convince themselves there is a pointed difference between the republican and democrat party. This claim makes me vulnerable early in the book but I'll provide excellent examples—when topics come up—of how both parties smugly pretend they're at odds with each other but have eerily similar cores.

A cool trick for seeing through any difficult concept is to reverse everything. I imagined: "what if the loser in every presidential race had won the election," and concluded that the bad wars and bad bailouts would have happened anyway yet more couples per capita are getting divorced because of opposite party affiliation. A haunting analogy is when we divorce then marry a refreshingly dissimilar spouse and realize years later that we married the same person. That's double learning though.

The perfection complex is the illusion that stops struggle and growth so often becomes a permanent plateau. With no blowback from ourselves or others our perfection becomes "I'm rubber, you're glue, everything you say bounces off me and sticks to you." Perfect people don't think they make mistakes either and mistakes present us with the #1 opportunity to learn. Flawless people become legends in their own minds—the straighter the arrow the bigger the kink—and we happily pick them to lead us. We misdiagnose ourselves, then them, because we think we need them—these *ringers* need us more (a ringer is a person who has a different goal than the one he's selling). Identifying one of them might entail, I don't know, maybe they're selling us smiles and their sentences are perfect but there's no spontaneity. We are drawn to their false pretenses and distracting charisma because believing lies is long seated in our DNA (Chapter 22). There are thousands of creepy hunches we get from our guts—hard to put into words—and that My Pillow guy gives me the same feeling.

Perfection (a distant synonym of greed) is a fatal conceit[31] that emboldens the ego to protect itself at any cost by never investigating its own irrational biases. The perfect feign concern for the imperfections of the masses so listeners will buy their empathy and perfection as a package. With personal growth stymied for years the perfect offer up counterfeit emergencies which foster corruption, invasion of privacy, divorce, violence, then war.

Perfect apophenia can be likened to Gollum (from *The Hobbit* by Tolkien) and his obsession with the powers of the magic ring. When we point out someone's acute apophenia we get the same repulsion as we would trying to take the magic ring away from Gollum. "My precious," Gollum would say, coveting his apophenia and not seeing that he was the vampire in the mirror. Evanescence sings, "save me from this thing that I've become," telling us we don't love our delusions, we are *in love* with them, and direct hits glance off our deflector shields because we have no awareness of our dream world. Don McLean sang, "you know I've heard about people like me......but I never made......the connection." [32] P.T. Barnum made a fortune with this simple observation: "the public appears disposed to be amused even when they are conscious of being deceived."

At a weekend party you may hear someone say, with an impish grin: "they're saying now that Bruce Willis is gay." They never say who *they* are and talking about and Richard Gere or Jamie Lee Curtis is so 90s that they need to freshen up the distraction. Not only do they not care if Bruce is gay or not and will probably never know but what they're saying is, "we're not even rich but we're well adjusted!" They certainly got the first part right. Hunting for strawmen is our favorite distraction from ourselves.

When we start telling someone else's story it's "1 step up and 2 steps back," as Bruce Springsteen puts it. That adds up to 1 step back every time we tell someone else's story instead of our own and some are 10,000 steps behind. We don't realize it because it's so crowded back there in psychological self-protection land. It feels like a party but it's an incarceration because our children learn to tell other people's stories—fake stories take on an extended shelf life—and our whole psychological lineage feels prevalent as if fades to fiction. Entire governments do this too until the "system" begins running itself, for itself.

I haven't been to therapy in decades but the best thing I did in my 20s was spend 5 years in group therapy and learn the techniques as a lifelong maintenance program. It started after I read an easy book on dream interpretation.[33] Interpreting your dreams is an emotional leap over a bottomless pit and hopefully clawing your way up the other side (isn't that encouraging?) but anybody can learn it. Once you interpret a dream right and learn something about yourself you never dreamed you would, you'll periodically interpret your dreams and keep getting better. When my mindset bogs down, I start interpreting my dreams again, which, if done right, is no fun—dreams show us what we don't want to know about ourselves. Our brains want us to do something difficult because they are greyhounds itching for a challenge and built to get better at self-discovery. For an example from about 2005, I realized I casually overrated myself and casually underrated others. Stuck in the Us vs Them paradox, I used those 2 wrong watermarks to understand the human condition which is like using a broken tape measure as a search engine. Strangely, after that realization, I gradually stopped watching football and the democrat vs republican show started boring me too.

Here's a 2nd example: I didn't mind picking up debris in our big yard—though my back is not great—but I did mind picking things up off the floor of the house. I had a glaring inconsistency: I thought the yard was my job and the house was my wife's job. Now that I've made the connection—negating my absurd apophenic connection—my back hurts less with both clean-up jobs. My psychology changed my biology.

For a final example, many people I met seemed lost in space as if they were looking in all the wrong places. Then, I had a dream that I was lost in space. My spaceship was superfast but every solar system I went to in the endless scary universe didn't have an earth. It was surreal. I feared I'd never get back home. The next morning, I diagnosed the dream: I had been working at improving my underground utility business so intently that I was neglecting my family. Since I wasn't telling my own story my dreamer did it for me. With dream interpretation there is a catch—we have to pay the price of admission.

Men will overrate themselves with abandon while women will rate the value of ideas and gifts based on their opinion of the person from whom they originated, leaving others one step away from deciphering their bias. A recent twist in this Us vs Them evolution is both sexes overvaluing their group which degrades into maternal genes battling paternal genes. After a million years of men trivializing maternal bonds (women were pedestalled 2nd class citizens) the biggest trend in the west now is maximizing them so we are in the trenches of the biggest and most accelerated psychological switcheroo humans have ever gone through. The gender war, which isn't in full bloom yet, will eventually change the world more than crossing the oceans did.

Most people still pick the revisionist history of their same sex parent and end up in sibling conflicts without a clue as to why. We even divide up liars and nonliars by sex and how related we are to people and don't know we're doing that. Humor is judged, not by wit, but by the status of the deliverer within the dominant group. When we pick one parent over the other instead of scrutinizing this hornet's nest, we toss out 50% of the learning.

Some people bank heavily on luck and lies. Like water running downhill, they buy state lottery tickets every day. Others tell lies reflexively or dig into whatever is none of their business and have no sensation they are taking the least resistant path. They want to know what gossip you know and who told you and when, so they can figure out their next chess move. Only to protect ego, their lives are about controlling the narrative so they can know when to exaggerate, lie, or say nothing. When they meet another dumpster-diver they don't particularly like them.

The best way to bungle a future is to inaccurately assess yourself, then others, and a situation, which is a rough definition of the Dunning-Kruger effect. For a bad example, some believed the story about how "the Apollo 11 astronauts found a Timex watch on the moon, still ticking," which was something I repeatedly told people right after the first moon landing. Hey, I was 13.

Unchecked apophenia is so powerful a person can be sexually abused when they are young and much later—unaware that they are psychologically transferring and projecting—manipulate those same fears into their own children though nothing like that happened to them. Pink Floyd sings, "mamma's gonna put all of her fears into you." This apophenia sprouted wings when neurologist Sigmond Freud contended that all repression was from sexual abuse in childhood. This isn't true.

Freud was visiting Carl Jung's office one day and Freud happened to tell Jung his recurring dream. Jung interpreted it. Freud didn't understand what had happened, but Jung realized that Freud had been sexually abused as a child, and, knew that Freud had based his entire psychological theory for all of us, from his own repressed memory. [34] It was a classic case of transfer and projection. The tactful renaissance man Jung wrote about this historic epiphany so subtly but the reader knew what had happened.[35] Sexual abuse is of great import, but violence, neglect, parent to child disgust, and psychological brutishness were and are more prevalent. It gets stranger because Freud was worshipped in Europe because of his 5-syllable-words and those esoteric books of his that they didn't understand—it's that hero worship again—while he was helping make people unduly paranoid and even delusional.

Psychotherapists are quite prone to coax and induce false memories of sexual molestations into their patients. [36] The old abuser who now lives inside us can create events that never happened, if not psychologically confronted. It can build up like creosote in a chimney and start another fire inside another person. Deception not only marginalizes real victims of abuse but regifts psychological truancy person to person like a virus. Better to create a strawman or say you're possessed by a demon than to go back and figure out what really happened, or didn't.

The point of mining your head isn't a small one. The organ of happiness and health, the brain, is the only organ we can rebuild and repair simply by getting to know its oddities. We can take the good brain programming with the bad and leave it as is or reprogram it daily into an engine of happiness. I said earlier that every generation is smarter; I meant *cognitively*, not *emotionally*. This has a good side and a bad side. The rate at which we progress emotionally and subconsciously *is* the rate at which humanity progresses. Archetypes change at a snail's pace and that is the good side. Our cognitive minds are racing ahead, stretching the rubber band, and a current course and speed one day it's going to snap. That's the bad side.

We relentlessly race toward money around the beltway—bumper to bumper at 2 mph—and away from our psychology. We do more maintenance on our cars, condos, corporations, computers, and cats than we do on our cortexes. We're enjoying rich, half-lives and our kids feel the missing piece. We're already rich and they want the other half of life. This is why the human condition is discomforted and a good start is to turn Sunday afternoon into a free-for-all family therapy session—attendance optional, no advising.

We are exercising, dreaming, travelling, egocentric, empathetic, contradictory creatures by nature—gifts from evolution—yet we chase the almighty dollar as if it were the only value and laugh at our dreams. The evidence of this dichotomy is in the pandemic of our broken sleep. Insomnia is THE disease of the western world—the gateway to the other diseases—and our emotional night brain is trying to reinforce our psychological immunities and repair our bodies.

When I "sleep real good," as we say in the south, and dream real good, my hair looks better and I can sometimes write a decent paragraph on the first try. When we're sleep deprived, we can't think well and don't feel like exercising or eating well either so we spiral down. The cure is to get more sleep. Do an 8-hour reboot—clean the garbage from your hard drive—and in the morning look at what your sleeper was trying to take to the dump (Chapter 17). We have to finish the cleaning while awake because if we skip that, the debris field will hover like a halo and blind us to our repeated mistakes. Since examples are such a good way to learn about new intangibles, like dreams, you will get to know several characters rather well in this nonfiction book and I will tell you their dreams, and interpret them best I can.

Value is Personal

A burden on society is what the old fraud Robert Malthus considered a newborn, because he miscalculated where value came from and who was responsible for maintaining that value, as many 19th century philosophes did. The evidence was right in front of them, scurrying through the house and knocking over vases on their way to the great outdoors. Unlike Malthus, those kids were going somewhere. Malthus thought a *society* had values and in a blurry way they do but one aristocrat thinking he can define them is a wild guess, plus, he saw a society as an ant colony, humbly waiting for his next brilliant theory. Socioeconomic policymakers look down on humanity while "economies and living things evolve from the ground up."[37]

Nature has already made us experts at taking care of kids—a million years of acquired knowledge will do that—and each parent does it differently because each kid is different. We know this but are taught that our problems and values are national or universal, and not personal or subjective, which has created innumerable high paying jobs for the Neo-Malthusians.

The turbid ideas Robert Malthus employed in Britain led to eugenic horror stories, similar to Vladimir Putin's singular idea of national value, while value, in the abstract, is as diverse and varied as anyone's assessment of it is. The underpinning reason why the west became so rich is that the state, for so long, left value choices to each.

Metaphysically, all lives have the same value. However, sacrificial selfishness improves life by forcing parents to make the *correct mistake* of way overvaluing their own children. It's 2 personal desires dove-tailed for future out of body rewards. 1 + 1 = a coterie of 3—*Hello World*[38]—and this is the most productive duality of mind. Each kid is half of each parent, plus intangibles, so is higher in value than either parent—maybe higher than both combined—making each kid not only greater than the sum of its parts but giving the family a loftier reason to survive and thrive. This is where value starts, manifested later in happier kids with brilliant new ideas, and how each generation improves. We see increasing value everywhere—intelligence, laughter, music, health, security, frivolity, science—and it starts so early inside families.

Copying your genes is pure *vanity*—as well as out of our control for most of history—so we can remove that word from the list of deadly sins. Vanity is a delicious, *lively* sin and hard to avoid. We sacrifice a score of our lives after selfishly copying our genes so the high price we pay verifies our vanity. But nature has ensured that parents cannot make copies of themselves so we settle for hybrids that no other couple can create and our vanity gamble becomes our future.

Risk too, is such an individual assessment that the study of economics gets muddy, vague, and fewer should attempt the profession. Risk and value are subjective, meaning you and I know nothing of a stranger's needs or wants while an economist, sabotaged by epistemological oversight, doesn't know he doesn't know that. Living economies evolve from the ground up and economists don't pay that pesky truism any mind either. They overlook the basic building block that initialized modern economics—the nuclear family. Economics, like philosophy, is rather simple. In addition, economists meddle with the infinite division of labor instead of letting it take shape by itself. Elected officials don't make the economy, they inherit *our* economy, because an economy is only as good as its tap-roots.

To put an exclamation mark on how personal value and risk are I posed a hypothetical to our love thy neighbor friends. Let's say you get home from work on Friday, flip on the TV, crash in your recliner, and your phone rings. It is a cop informing you your daughter has been in a rollover wreck on the freeway and she's now in an ambulance headed for the hospital. He is not allowed to tell you much more. As you rush to get your stuff together, hands shaking, out of the corner of your ear you hear a news flash that a nuclear bomb has gone off in San Diego at the Mexican border. You race to the hospital praying for your daughter, get to her room, and find her alert and talking to you. She's banged up but the doctor says no internal injuries and you thank the doctor like he is a god. A weight has left your soul and only then does your mind return to your 2nd worry—San Diego and Tijuana—with probably millions dead and dying. Your mind scans through a list of friends and relatives in the area, you give a quick thought to your stock, then you look back at your daughter and smile. It's the happiest day of your life—your genes are intact. Collection plates are already circulating in the waiting room and you drop in $100.

Nobody took issue with my hypothetical. We are selfish. We are selfish down to the bone marrow and up to the last rung in the double helix. If we weren't, we wouldn't exist. But then......you are informed by the cop that they found crack cocaine in her car. I'm kidding.

There have been many little studies comparing longevity between childless adults and adults with children. Having children gives us a slight edge on a longer life because of the oxytocin boost—the cuddle chemical—we get from our children for decades, if not longer.[39] If you never had kids, you missed out on a big one but I do envy you got to travel the world when young because that's more fun than limping around Europe after the kids have flown, looking for a bathroom.

There's gotta be a public restroom in Place de la Concorde, Paris—I never found it. I finally had to walk through this big restaurant to the very back and pee in this tiny bathroom the size of a phonebooth and get this: when Superman came out a French waiter followed me out to the street and tried to chew me out because I wasn't a "patron." He was way too empowered for what had transpired, and what he meant was: "fat Americans who aren't *patrons* cannot use our microscopic bathroom." I guess *that* little piece of claustrophobic nanotechnology was designated for the 150 paying *patrons*. After I'd spent 45 minutes looking for relief, I smiled and said, "time to go back to work."

Brain Genes

Claus Wedekind, a Swiss Zoologist, suspected that human females could smell the pheromones in a man's sweat, because scientists knew female mice could. If you haven't heard about his 1995 discovery, 44 men slept 2 nights in their dirty T-shirts and put them in plastic bags in the morning. Then 49 women sniffed the T-shirts and rated them by smell. Women rated their brother's T-shirts as the worst smell and the T-shirts that smelled the best were worn by the men with the opposite immune systems. This instant and crucial knowledge was confirmed by DNA tests. Nature equipped females with this individual primordial knowledge long ago but most women throughout history—no matter their place in society—simply got "picked" by some man.

The pheromones that women smell in a man's sweat somehow tell them how many recessive genes the two of them might be sharing in the future and the communication isn't verbal or mathematical. It's a smell to brain language that scientists have traced down into the hypothalamus[40] and the amygdala,[41] where this information is electrochemically processed, turned into emotion, and action or no action is decided. Think about it, it's a quadratic equation with too many variables and countless unknowns that women solve in fractions of a second which haunts us to learn that the subconscious brain can process that much information that fast. It shames the best Artificial Intelligence algorithm.

When a woman explains why she picked one man over another, be skeptical. She'll tell you the other man smoked or had an irritating fascination with cosmology but down in the nanoworld, she picked the one whose immune system could kill 7 of her kid's diseases and not the one who had the genes to kill only 5. If the genes had been a tie, she'd pick the smarter one.

The *Flynn Effect* (research from New Zealand) shows that we have gained an average of 30 IQ points in 100 years—paralleling the rise of women. Every new generation could be called the "greatest generation," sorry Tom Brokaw, because the next one is a smidgen less neurotic, more aware, and lives longer.

Intelligence genes are highly heritable compared to other genes.[42] Imagine the 2nd Friday of each month is *pick a husband day* at the mall and the women get to interview the men. Let's assume in this hypothetical that all immune systems are identical. A woman will pick a man with vigor, height, and smarts—ugly ones or limping ones—and leave the slightly slower brains on the shelf. The carnage at the mall restarts on some other Black Friday, 25 years later, when the daughters pick husbands, and the best brain genes again disappear from the shelves. Bear in mind that intelligence has never been defined, never will be defined, and each of us sees intelligence from a different angle.

A University of Utah study found a gene that makes Jewish people a little smarter than the average bear.[43] Typically, this intelligence gift is attached to a disease gene commonly found in Ashkenazi Jews in Europe.[44] Einstein was one of them. Higher intelligence and Gaucher's disease come in a paired allele (short for allelomorph, pronounced uhleel) which is a different version of a *similar matching* gene we get from each parent. Either can be good, bad, or indifferent. Alleles are the same 2 genes from 2 parents that butt up against each other on the double helix, however, no 2 things are the same. Alleles are a bit like the difference between a possum and an opossum (their tails are different) which is something we struggle with in the south.

If you have 2 Jewish parents with bad versions of this allele you have a chance of getting higher intelligence, plus the disease. If you have one Jewish parent with a good version nature somehow tries to give you that one and you won't get Gaucher's disease and your IQ could be 5-10 points higher than average. In any family too, if each parent has a different philosophy, the kids get to see 2 *more* life choices and can choose between the 2 when it counts, according to their needs and preferences throughout life. Nature made opposites attract for this benefit, however, life choices and genes are almost synonyms in the sense that they are difficult to employ because both require the elusive butterfly of free will.

Over 20% of the Nobel Prizes since 1900 have gone to Jewish people which is pretty good for 0.2% of the world population,[45] hitting 2 classes above their weight. Jewish contributions in science and literature represent 2 orders of magnitude higher than the rest of earth's population. In the US (2.5% Jewish) we think of the Jewish population as higher, probably because of higher IQs, and if not for World War II their population would be higher.

After the world wars, arranged Jewish marriages began going out of style late in the game and some began marrying outside of their culture (moms didn't pinch *all* their son's cheeks at the weddings) spreading more smart genes throughout the population. Today about 3% of westerners have an IQ of 125 or above so there are many powerful brain genes and if merit continues to be rewarded these genes will push toward genetic fixation. All these crafty brain genes walking around allow more of us to marry up because we want those genes for our kids as well as more immunity variations so nature can pick health over sickness 51% of the time.[46]

Loving your work is the kindling for blazing a trail to innovation and as David Rubenstein says, "nobody ever won a Nobel Prize hating what they were doing." This high mindedness might be a better explanation of how the phrase "God's chosen people" evolved. Voluntary Jewish marriages spawned scientists, business people, theatre professionals, songwriters, comedians, brilliant Dershowitz's, etc., but maybe weren't the best genes for combat, sports, and grasping spacial relationships.

I think the "ingenuity gene" (a good name because it sounds like *engine*) created the capacity for us to expand the If-Then-Next-Else statements. Most of us know the If-Then statements from computer programming and it started an eon ago with crude animals sagely assessing risk, and winning more because of that.

Bruce Springsteen says, "you can't start a fire, worryin' about your little world fallin' apart."[47] The ingenuity gene enabled sellers to ponder how large groups of buyers might be thinking in the future, and how to pre-respond. It's a thrill to predict the future and be right. For so long we worried about distant armies that got too neighborly and as our *better angels* deselected violence[48] the ingenuity gene had time to evolve statistics, psychiatry, medicine, and policymakers/bankers who would fundamentally change the nature of economics. When I'm looking for a doctor, I often look for Jewish names, helping me realize that ingenuity genes create value for creators and consumers alike.

Combining this advanced thinking with *economies of scale* catapulted a few families to a new prosperity. Good for them but the reason it's fantastic is because making more widgets faster made everything cheaper, and families noticed the double benefit. Small businesses popped up everywhere. Wealth exploded the population, or vice versa, creating many more buyers and sellers, and competition shrunk the profits, benefitting everyone again.

Karl Marx foresaw this shrinking profit and believed that as profits got smaller, capitalism would collapse into revolution. It didn't, but it's odd that Karl Marx and Thomas Jefferson knew the tree of liberty needed to be fertilized with blood every so often—both getting there from opposite philosophies. Marx's mistake was in thinking value is held by *classes* of people instead of individuals, which cloaked, at least to him, the gradual obliteration of class structure in the west.

Today what somebody's father does for a living is superfluous information. The son doesn't always become a made man, creating more freedom for talented outsiders to climb the ladder. An individual in any group now, has a unique sense of value, sees different opportunities of scale, and finds a niche. In at least one exceptional way, you are the smartest person in the world.

Value is personal so whenever we can buy something cheaper or buy something we can't find anywhere else we have benefited from the transaction more than the seller did, except the seller has many buyers and makes miniscule profits from each, so it adds up nicely. As this phenomenon of opensource, free-thinking widened, shoppers paid less for the same goods and had money left over to buy other things. This created an unexpected leap of wealth from the Middle East to Europe which paralleled, not coincidentally, the weakening of throne and alter.

In Asia, economies of scale happened late. Full-scale free trade didn't click in the Asian head maybe because of mistrust of the west, or arranged marriages, or the Ming Dynasty, or Confucius and Buddha promoting suffering to end suffering, or mistrusting profit in general. "How can we allow strangers to ethically profit from strangers?" they thought. The concept of profit is a sophisticated way of thinking—logic that's difficult to grasp—but competitive capitalism, when not subsidized into monopolies, will keep shrinking profits.

The top-down command and control economies of China and Russia do not let their best minds freely flourish because many citizens outside the tight circle of controllers would gain wealth, however, that's not their real worry. Eventually, the private sectors in Russia and China would create the dreaded free market of ethical ideas too, prompting citizens to want justice across the board. Shortly after that *enlightenment*—250 years behind the west—they will hang Putin and Jinping so both must systematically squash their people, their words, their thoughts, and the entire economy.

Today the world is going bananas with ingenuity genes. The mental acumen of brilliant manufacturers and CEOs who create new services, make their customers, on the whole, richer than they are. Each customer knows this because value is personal but getting a nation to understand how capitalism turns water into wine is an uphill battle. When a new entrepreneur gets rich, it's because he outsmarted other entrepreneurs by making his customers a little richer and without the profit motive he wouldn't have tried it. If a country's policy is anti-profit, complacency sets in and a general shrinkage occurs.

Discovering during childhood how to predict the future accurately, then as an adult, and expanding that clairvoyant macroeconomic thinking horizontally across landscapes, markets, and national borders, creates wealth for all families during peacetime. Customers know a good bang for their buck and become sellers themselves by finding untapped markets. It's the only possible explanation for the rise of the west: free trade + free association + smarts – war = wealth.

Genes Are Memes

After reading Susan Blackmore's book *The Meme Machine*, and seeing her on TV, I can tell you she's a fun person. This new word, meme,[49] she says is any interesting idea that is copied or improved upon. Intelligent mate selection accelerates meme production because 2 people are trying their best to create an advanced, new meme machine. The new kids and their new ideas will ripple through society and live forever or die like a bad gene. Think of an economy as an open input universal operating system that the new kids on the block constantly improve with fresh ideas. The system appears to arise from groupthink but the operating system itself cannot think, and is simply the natural summation of the best individual ideas.

Susan Blackmore told a lovely story about a lady dolphin trainer she knew who taught dolphins tricks, fed them little tasty fish, and had a neat way of scolding them when they wouldn't do the trick correct. When they screwed up or didn't copy her meme, she would walk far from the pool for a whole minute, then come back. One day a dolphin performed a trick well but the lady accidentally gave that dolphin a spiney hard-to-eat fish. The dolphin dropped it, swam away to the far side of the pool, and stayed there for *1-minute* before coming back! This may be the most revealing observation of how smart dolphins are. The dolphin was flattering the trainer, mocking her, and abstracting a passive aggression. If we could decipher their sophisticated language, we could grasp a new sphere of consciousness.

Funny Women and Lightly Battered Men

Women, instinctively, still want a fierce protector with high testosterone because they over fear crime. Our overactive emotions and anxieties were built when cave people lived in a much more dangerous environment (Tooby and Cosmides, 1992). I heard a female comedian talking about her macho but not so smart husband and she joked, "I told him to just have sex with me and guard the perimeter." She apparently ran the family and wanted a Minute Man in both the guardian and reproductive sense. She was quite smart and funny and married people tend to have similar IQs so chances are he was smart too, in spite of her joking about her *tempura man* (a lightly battered Johnny Depp-type husband). She didn't let go of her ancient emotional fear of violence and would sick her husband on would be perpetrators as the first and best sacrifice.

Less than a century after that mutual consent marriage year, 1900, female free speech blossomed too and the new shamans became Ella Fitzgerald, Madonna, Lady Gaga, Taylor Swift, and Beyoncé. Using different lyrical devices than men—poetry woven with rancor—they tell their stories without preaching and teach by example.

As if we needed more testimony of the female upsurge, Phyllis Diller, Joan Rivers, Carole Burnett, and Rosanne Barr suddenly slipped ahead of the best male comedians. Now, in the intangible, undefinable art of standup, we have Sheryl Underwood, Jennifer Coolidge, Bonnie McFarlane, Amy Sedaris, and of course Maria Bamford from the great port of Duluth Minnesota. These standups almost killed me a few times. Bamford talks about depression but says she's more "paralyzed by hope," and says "even babies are starting to see their sippy cup as half full." That's when my analogy of the half full cup vs the full cup started germinating. "Some people love life," she says "I've always been on the fence about the whole thing." Maria was talking about her new tempura boyfriend and how she "can't wait to get married because we can go grocery shopping together." Her new boyfriend walks around the apartment saying "I don't have a job, I'm broke, and nobody likes me." Maria, who rarely takes a shot at anybody or any country, answered "Hello Europe!" That's the first mother Europe joke I've heard in a minute. I joke Europeans don't need a ticket to get on a commuter train, they just need a grocery sack with a long piece of bread sticking out of it. When Maria was single and lonely, she met a very happy couple—something she didn't want to see—and she asked the new wife, frowning, "don't you guys have any problems?" and the wife said, "well.........he doesn't like onions." Maria says her mother is so positive she can squeeze some joy out of an AT&T call. Women got funnier than men, and we can't leave out Flo from the insurance commercials.

Tempura husbands like Jamie from the same commercials replaced the old, blowhard archetype of manhood. Jamies can't yell out their wife's name from the other end of the house anymore. A husband knows he can't ask his wife a string of questions and can't ask his wife to do something when she's already doing something. The wife can do these things, these are the new unwritten rules, and ignorance of the law is no excuse. The wives can answer a question with a question, taking a cheeky move out of their dad's playbook, but the husband can't do it without getting the stare, and I won't get into who superintends the vacations.

If a man tells his wife that she's acting neurotic like her mother he'll get a fierce glance and when she tells him he's acting like his crazy father it's okay. To this day, neurosis has sexist connotations and even inquiring into what motivated a woman to say or do something will get a man on thin ice. "You told me that story yesterday," wasn't spoken by the greatest generation mothers, who learned forbearance by having to listen to their husband's stories, over and over. They knew their place. It was a small place and some of those mothers, who had to smile when slicing potatoes, were named "Dot."

The lady revolt has never been so vividly portrayed than by Quinten Tarantino in his *Kill Bill* movies. "If mamma ain't happy ain't nobody happy," southern bumper stickers read and our families were the opposite in 1960. Remember when we said "if dad wasn't mad, everybody was glad?" I don't, I made it up but all the baby boomers thought it.

Western society is now about who wears the skirt because of 5 events: abuse from the fathers of history, the feminist revolution, no arranged marriages, birth control, and the realization that the insufferable sexist, evolution, gave women fewer options and the hardest jobs—without a vote. Cavemen didn't decide to start lifting weights until their shoulders were huge, then start running everything. Evolution did that. It only took a million years to revolt against nature's taxation without representation and now women can say, "you told me that story yesterday....and a few weeks ago....and on our first date."

Paul McCartney

1969 was the bewitching year when the "weaker sex," as we said back then, entered the workforce in mass. Women decided to make their own money and had to since the dollar had lost most of its buying power since 1913. Raising a family had tripled in cost and the buying power of the husband's blue-collar paycheck stopped growing in 1969 too (the Great Decoupling). True to form, the pyramid's media parroted that the economy was "fantastic." Strangely, sperm counts had dropped by half from the 1950s to the 1970s,[50] and more adults then ever moved back in with their parents.

When women no longer needed man money Paul McCartney artfully expressed this dilemma in his 1969 song, *Oh Darlin.'* I've always been a sucker for a great pop song and the teenage Paul McCartney (a pre-baby boomer born in *The Summer of 42*[51]) learned to write lyrics listening to African American music, called "devil music." In *Oh Darlin,'* McCartney screamed, "when you told me, you didn't need me anymore, well you know I nearly broke down and cried" and he screamed it out like he was in a black church. He had learned how to make it sound like Jesus was in the building and I didn't make that connection until the mid-

90s when my family attended a service at Ebenezer Baptist Church. It then hit me that Paul learned how to emote from the black churches across the pond and from the gospel to blues to rock revolution in general. He became a triple threat: the brilliant young southpaw bass guitar player could sing from his soul and write songs, and in 1957 John Lennon didn't see this genius coming. They both had that irresistible vulnerability but Paul infuriatingly edged out John on that contest too.

Paul learned to sing one melody while playing a different melody, erased many Ringo drum tracks and redid them himself. Paul was growing shyly while John was trying to save the world—something that will usually get you killed. John, the atheist who said "God is a concept" told the world to "come together…over me," whereas Paul, who wrote an insane baseline for John's song, "woke up, got outa bed, dragged a comb across [his] head."[52]

The universal language of emotional music flies past our cognition and straight into our subconscious minds. We don't like to go in there enough so music opens the back door silently and we can't say *no*. The best way to get a 5-month-old baby to smile is to sing them a song like you mean it and we have no idea how that precious information lights up a baby's hypothalamus but they will hear the same song years later and smile inside. Even nonverbally, they know a good song when they hear one and isn't it strange that we detect foreign accents readily yet when people sing in another language we can't tell? Radio waves don't stop at checkpoints either because they move at lightspeed, and broadcasting the emotion of freedom worldwide brightened up Carl Sagan's pale blue dot as music splattered like a goblet across the world.

McCartney loved those old American records, from gospel to the blues to 1950s rock and roll, and went back to music school as did most of the songwriters in the British super bands. They learned the new bluesy style along with how to write edgy, stark lyrics, which took McCartney from *I Wanna Hold Your Hand* (1964) to *Why*

Don't We Do It in The Road (1968).

Later I will talk about this mega transformation that appeared out of nowhere—the blues to swing to jazz to soul to rock and roll—because it was America's renaissance. Once African American musicians get full credit for pulling rock and roll out of a hat they'll get full credit for America's only art renaissance too. The western musical ear devoured the biggest and fastest cultural disturbance in classical music's 3000-year history and it started in about 1900 (there's that number again) in a tiny poor region of one small state—Mississippi—where the best rags to riches story began (Chapter 27).

McCartney rode the waves of the renaissance with works like *Got to Get You into My Life* in 1966, *Silly Love Songs* in 1976, and in the pivotal year 1969 he wrote *Golden Slumbers*. "Once there was a way……to get back homeward……once there was a way………to get back home, sleep pretty darlin' do not cry, and I will sing a lullaby," and for some reason we all knew what he meant.

After my wife and I moved across town to a bigger place, our daughter used to say, "I wanna go home," and we all want to go back to the cradle, back to that comfy first little house where we didn't know people had problems. We want to be "back in daddy's arms,"[53] as Peter Gabriel says, and there are so many songs with this message. My favorite is *Neptune City*[54] and these songs remind us that we can't really go back home to Kansas, as Dorothy did, because the zeitgeist is gone. Paul lamented too and in *Let It Be* he introduced us to his late mother Mary, another bass guitar player who held the family together and died at age 47. She imparted to him that the parted still had a chance to see, so unlike John, Paul left the religion door ajar.

At this point I will broaden these concepts and explain the unseen factors and rote habits that may be changing humans faster than ever.

Men's singing voices have been migrating from deep to high from the greatest generation to the millennials. Lennon was an edgy baritone we don't hear much anymore and McCartney is a tenor. With the timbre of male voices rising and women's dropping we hear dark brown voices and can't identify the gender. Sperm counts are still dropping like a rock in the west and we don't know why (diet?). We can deduce that men feel the loss of power—that psychology moves through their biology—and men are becoming more androgynous because women are. What changed is women started liking those geeks more, so did the economy, and we are living through a sexual-economic divergence.

Since everybody is pairing off now, including those men who were excluded from the gene pool for so long, and most of those premature babies are surviving too, we will be seeing an increase in hybrid children. With the alpha male waning and the alpha female waxing, perhaps we'll keep using the basic abc genes and def genes, and will be toying with some tuv and xyz genes. Whether one sees the world falling apart or falling together, these newish genes will be the catalysts for the eventual reconstruction of the archetype of society (the sum of a civilization's thoughts and beliefs).

We may need a longer alphabet or we could stop using labels altogether because our genomes are bifurcating like feral cats. We have preteen hackers, reasonable kids, forest fires, those still questioning, neo-geniuses, uncategorizable kids, and some who have baffling emotional heart attacks. We unleashed the entire male gene pool, new sets of parents, and rarely do they have 3 kids now. These small families raise super kids who get more nurturing, a new biology, more androgyny, too much instant communication, and we should fully expect the unexpected. The social network is a quest to understand what changed in the world and "how do I now fit in?" Kids can't know that, because Venus crashed into Mars before they were born and trillions of pieces are still going in every direction and there's nothing anybody can do about it.

Speaking of alphabet kids, the L could stand for *Love Child*—a match made in heaven? Leonardo da Vinci was the Love Child of possibly another Love Child (his young mother Caterina, probably a slave) and long before Henry David Thoreau he went on to transform esthetics and science as if they were one. Leonardo's painting of *Virgin on the Rocks* is a world-class example of his abstract fusion of utility and art.[55]

To make a Love Child is easy, or, evolution knows how valuable one is and *makes us* do it at dark 30, knowing that forbidden love is irresistible. Genetic mining doesn't start with a date, it starts with a date-date, intercourse leads to intercourse—*Steppin' Out* as Joe Jackson tells it—and dynamic economies are looking forward to hiring your biologically upgraded Love Child. A Love Child "who's got his own"[56] will be smart, cheap labor, for a few years anyway, then they'll figure out how to make their own economy.

I can't shake the notion that a bigger male orgasm, where maybe Love Children come from, gives the female more options for choosing the 1 best sperm cell. Researchers contend that a low stress environment makes for a bigger female orgasm which brings more interesting eggs out of hiding too. The strong links between ovulation and female orgasm are surfacing, including the discover that during orgasm the cervix "tents" and sucks in more sperm.[57]

Then the cat fight starts. Out of about 15 female eggs only the healthiest egg makes it into the pole position for the hopeful conception. With sperm counts falling the chance of conception dwindles but it gets more complicated. The fastest sperm doesn't win the race you see, conversely, the female egg seizes the day by giving off a gradient, analogous to a smell, and that gradient attracts the healthiest sperm cells for that particular egg.[58] Our chromosomes in our gametes (egg and sperm cells) are already split down the middle for the hopeful rejoining, exposing their innards and maybe more smell. The alpha female egg can somehow scrutinize this small circle of would-be winners who made it into her inner sanctum, fight some off, and pick the lucky one.

Whereas a female orgasm increases the chances of conception 10-15%,[59] a tiny male orgasm decreases it because the female egg doesn't have as much genetic material to choose from. Whether it is big or little, she can reject all the sperm, and herself, through a phenomenon called "apoptosis" (cell suicide) knowing something we don't.[60] The younger a woman is the better her tiny bits are at recognizing and aborting troublesome genetic combinations. 60 couples donated sperm and egg for a study at St Mary Hospital in England and the eggs did not particularly prefer the sperm of a spouse over a stranger. Scientists will forever be researching natures conception variables and why a woman may like a man but her egg does not like his sperm, or vice versa. After conception though, an embryo can change.

Recently, we have discovered the C Child. Chimera Children come from 2 eggs or more, and 2 sperm cells or more, to form 1 zygote. The zygote will usually become a healthy multi-DNA individual and possibly up to 10% of people walking around are assimilations of what could have been 2 or 3 people. A male zygote and a female zygote (twins) can join in the womb—it happens—and make a gender hybrid or even a child who is unrelated to the biological father.

One couple had a child who was not the father's child and 23andMe reported it was the father's nonidentical twin brother's child. But he never had a twin brother. When they were more than microscopic, his zygote had subsumed his twin brother in the womb and later the father had a son who was roughly 50% his mother's genes and more of his non-existent twin brother's genes than his own. With interminable gene mixing, by now all people are getting a little chimera DNA which is making men more sensitive and women less.

If evolution didn't super experiment with every species constantly it would eventually risk saying goodbye to all of them. It has already had to say goodbye to 99.99% of all species so it's probably trying every possible microscopic miracle to save every species (highly likely). Or, with humans, it thinks there are too many of us and it's diminishing reproductive potential (highly unlikely). It probably doesn't think earth is a planet in crisis, in that ageless unknown way it thinks, but in a primordial way it divines 3 things: asteroids, ice ages, and super eruptions are overdue and unknown viruses are patiently waiting.

Some will live through these near extinctions and I believe that evolution has always created hybrid children to maintain a super adaptive population for when things change dramatically. Or, evolution is helpless and we're changing our nature ourselves on purpose or through innate survival knowledge (medium likely). It's even possible, with all the population apocalypse books and disaster books out there, that people feel guilty having more than 1 child.

What changes a species the fastest is a new diet or isolation from the main group and humans are so integrated that it must be diet that is responsible for some of our seemingly inconsistent shape and behavior. Each pre-historical Armageddon created a scarcity of food which produced more female births as if evolution knew the population should drop if the food supply was going to. The Trivers-Willard Hypothesis (1973) also found that more male children cultivate more successful hunting and thus more sex in general. Another way to say it is that a female can make about 1 new person a year and a male can make about 10, so we've actually inherited a tendency to give birth to more boys when we feel optimistic. Non-nutritious food fosters more female births, as in Eastern Europe, and fewer kids in the long run, so we could say their optimism is low.

We can go further and venture that processed food and worse is driving a change toward a more effeminate population. Earth still hosts 1-2% more boys but since the mid-1800s we've been putting too much poison into every meal and a change in diet alters a species fast. Bread and sugar are great for us but we only need a little—a little more than a little is a little poison, yet we live off of it. Cave people had to pig out every chance they got or risk death and we got those genes in droves but the tables have been turned. It's effortless for us to eat right and is the hardest thing to do because our over-evolved taste buds saved us almost as often as our eyes did.

How Much Freedom Do We Want?

There's a word that describes the fear of losing freedom or the fear of gaining freedom—*Eleutheromania.* It may be born of reason or be an irrational disorder, unless we are caught in no man's land which is an in between place the people of every region find themselves in from time to time. People who already have freedom come to love it, fear losing it, and oppressed people fear gaining freedom because they've never had it and don't know what happens next. The imaginative author Anas Abdulhak illustrates this condition beautifully in his book, *Eleutheromania.* The enchained boldly break out of their chains and find themselves wandering around, not knowing what to do. Minus the long familiarity of the comforting chains, they feel naked, and put them back on. We fear abrupt change and feel a certain honor toward our captors.

Some people get Urbach Wiethe disease—a rare recessive gene that attacks the amygdala and leaves one without fear of anything. This disease is selected in the southern US noted by the occasional bumper sticker which reads: "Ain't Skeered." I was going to make a bumper sticker that said "Honk if You Love Cheezits," but refrained 'cause some a those guys ain't skeered a nothin'—they stand in front of the mirror like Dinero and say "you talkin' to me!?"

Last but not least, *passive eleutheromania* is experienced by people who have never lived under an oppressive government—Americans and many Europeans—and the freedoms they think are permanent, slowly slip away, unmeasured.

Since we've come this far, any individual may put his chains back on but isn't qualified to tell anyone else to. The self-enchained get a hollow feeling at the sight of free spirits waking around and they reflexively want to stifle that. My wife says "you're a dog in the manger, if you don't want something [freedom] but don't want anybody else to have it either."

That above information will help you understand my new twist on why America and France evolved differently. One group risked revolution and won, and the other group risked it and lost. It's unlikely to transition from monarchy or imperialism to freedom in 4 generations, or even 8—skipping so many steps in between—but it happened in America. The impetus for freedom was long in America's European blood and gaining political freedom plus personal freedom led directly to prosperity. Many in the west still don't grasp that this opulence was a psychological achievement that took 1000 years to evolve in Europe. The author Joseph Heinrich explains this incredibly well in *The WEIRDest People in the World*. His book is an historical marker and here's my quick take on his work.

> The old wealth from 1000 years ago was about kinship and extended family institutions which were not only the oldest institutions but everyone's first cognizance of the world. As some Europeans intuitively risked jumping up a tier and going beyond family into the economy at large, some pre-catholic factions cultured them further along. In the 13th century the church taught people to stop marrying close cousins and in the high Middle Ages people learned to not marry *any* cousins at all, or in-laws, unless they must. It wasn't total individual freedom; it was freedom pecking its way into the unknown again, as will always happen, or we don't discover anything new. The genetic and economic rewards snowballed in Europe, creating a tectonic shift in fair trade preferences away from kinship and toward strangers. It was the beginning of the end of nepotism and old money, as people began preferring outside money, without strings. A rather small group of Europeans evolved the involuntary socialist family into the extended, voluntary capitalist family, void of the emotional and incestual DNA attachments. Free trade blossomed and Europe became a zeitgeist where good ideas led to better ideas, spurred along by

> the 18th century French *Enlightenment*, [61] which gradually opened up more minds, one at a time. As monarchies teetered, profits spread out which precipitated an explosion of wealth in the latter half of the 2nd millennium.

Besides the snow monkeys of Japan, we are the only primate who adapted to snow. The Europeans were colder than the rest, which forced them to invent heating machines, accelerating all manner of machinery. Living in cold areas has other strange charms: it spawned the industrial revolution, people lived longer, were nicer, and seemed to be smarter, and better yet, they lived more as individuals.

Revolutionary France, ahead of the sexism in colonial America, was full of forward, flirtatious, Chantilly laced women called "the great ladies" of glittering Paris. Equally open-minded, Benjamin Franklin was adored in France as a quirky, homespun, rustic American who could talk philosophy, party, or play chess with the best of them. Little did the French know that Franklin was the quintessential bass guitar player of diplomacy and with the fewest words possible he would save the American revolution by patiently stitching France and America together.

As for the "great gentlemen" of Europe, the Catholic church was caught flatfooted with the natural philosophical thinking of Spinoza, Lafayette, Diderot, and Voltaire, and their ideas made it across the 3500-mile pond to the American colonies. Baruch D. Spinoza, an early free speech radical from Amsterdam, kicked off enlightened thought in Europe saying, "fear cannot be without hope nor hope without fear," highlighting the human contradiction.

In 1754, Benjamin Franklin revolutionized the colonists early with an either/or: Join or Die. As the thought of war heated up, Thomas Paine wrote *Common Sense* in 1776 and the atheist rabble-rouser radically ignited the Americans to fight the revolution against Britain—his mother country. Philadelphia had many printing presses—more newspapers than London—and *Common*

Sense was #1 on the charts,[62] with a bullet. At the time, the 13 colonies were not much different than separate, competing countries, and they were staunchly protestant, however, it was mass printing that rippled through the pond and educated so many minds quickly toward freedom. Paine, America's first shock jock, got a little too thick too early with atheism, and faded from glory.

Back in England, King George III wanted his vassal state, America, to be a commonwealth but he attacked the colony that had been enjoying a higher birth rate than any country in Europe,[63] with the possible exception of Britain's nemesis, France. While the American Tories—hearts loyal to the crown—stayed quiet or got their property confiscated, in 1778 24-year-old Louis the 16th and the 72-year-old Benjamin Franklin signed the treaty of alliance in 1778.[64] Spain allied with France, though 50 years earlier Spain had chased them out of Tejas, and the colonies got some real foreign aid in 1780 as the largest French fleet ever set sail for the New World. 1779 had ended with the worst colonial winter in 40 years, stalling the British invasion,[65] and the colonial forces had time to lick their wounds and regroup.

In late 1781 seasoned French forces and American forces defeated General Cornwallis at Yorktown and 7000 British soldiers surrendered, temporarily ending British designs on America. The French had twice as many militiamen defending America as America itself had and only 5000-7000 Americans died in land battles during the Revolutionary War.[66] America couldn't pay France back until the 2 world wars. The British King finally signed the treaty in 1783, getting virtually no concessions from the stubborn American negotiators. America was a triumphant, poor, fledgling country and secured a $2-million 5% interest loan from 3 Dutch banks and a bigger loan from France.[67] After America's unlikely miracle, a new kind of government popped out of this improbable place with *peaceful* transitions of power from one president to the next,[68] and much more—individual rights.

Back in 1768 Voltaire had said, "if we didn't have a God, we'd have to invent one." He was referring to Kings/Gods, I think, making fun of his fellow Frenchmen (the whole world really) who still had dyslexia about which was which and who was who. Though old and wrinkled the wizened Voltaire was angling for a total separation of church and state in a catholic stronghold. Diderot wrote thousands of pages on natural philosophy and was chosen to write the French encyclopedia too. He knew it would take years for the monarchs to read all the volumes. Diderot dutifully penned the religion chapter, outlining the history of Christianity and how the French monarchs were conduits of God, and he ended it with this: "we don't know exactly how the soul attaches to the human body." His footnote read, "inquire with monarchy."[69]

France had the best modern philosophers. Maybe the best comedic duo in history, Voltaire and Diderot were sandwiched in time between René Descartes (17th century philosopher) and John-Paul Sartre (20th century existentialist), who weren't particularly funny. Voltaire and Diderot usually had to cloak their beliefs in humor on the outside chance a disgruntled member of the monarchy would drop the guillotine on them. Getting a little too bold, Diderot said "man will never be free until the last king is strangled by the entrails of the last priest." Even the religious Isaac Newton said, "the world will end in 2060," came around to natural philosophy near the end of his devout, enlightened, yet womanless life.

100 years after John Locke wrote "life, liberty, and property," the Marquis de Lafayette (Thomas Jefferson's buddy) wrote the first *Rights of Man*. Borrowing ideas back and forth, Lafayette's words "life, liberty, property, and *pursuit of happiness*" would ostensibly kick off the French Revolution in 1789. King Louis the 16th signed off on the *Rights of Man* with reluctance as American revolutionaries were adopting the phrases of Voltaire and Diderot. Septuplet brothers from different mothers were the philosophes Locke, Voltaire, Diderot, Franklin, Paine, Jefferson, and Lafayette (in order of their deaths from first to last). These were the first

teachers without borders and they didn't talk much about money, just liberty.

The redhaired, statuesque 6′ 2″ Thomas Jefferson, the 5′ 7″ Alexander Hamilton, and the 5′ 4″ James Madison, had authored a constitutional republic based on Norman natural philosophy and Lafayette's individual rights.[70] The American colonies had drawn a line in the sand between power and the people while France teetered on the fence between freedom and the old order. Ironically, the culmination of the French Enlightenment was the 1789 *American* constitution—finally securing the right to own property for opaque males.

It appeared as if France might make the move to individual rights too when the French Camelot slipped into a bloody revolution. It would be á propos to say that the natural philosophes started a grassroots rebellion in 1789 that went too far too fast—they tried to exterminate the Catholics—earning them the new name *vandals* and Napoleon dropped the guillotine on the French revolutionaries.

"The more the cause of revolution advanced in Paris, the more America's old comrades seemed to lose their eminence, or their liberty, or even their heads."[71] The old French monarchy spared the lives of Diderot, Lafayette and most of the heroes but reintroduced the French mind to theocratic-military rule. The new military dictator of France, Napoleon Bonaparte the 1st, declared an end to the bloody revolution in 1799 though the civil war dragged on till he became emperor in 1804.

After the French got an ungodly amount of money from America from the Louisiana Purchase, what might happen next? Napoleon Bonaparte invaded half of Europe and the overextended French army was crushed from multiple angles, with a vengeance. The country that practically wrote the Bill of Rights for America, royally screwed up. Good ideas cannot be killed and the great French intellectual breakthrough resonated in Scotland, Holland, Scandinavia, and later Britain and Turkey. In a quantum leap of thought, people the world over grew the

French gift of natural philosophy into science.

How could a country that started world enlightenment destroy their own blossoming republic? It was eleutheromania combined with denial of spirit. Their revolt into natural philosophy rejected the concept of deities but neglected to fill that void with anything. We have the spirit of our 40,000 generations and everything they believed inside of us. When we can't demarcate between the power of the state, the church, and the power of spirit, we throw the baby out with the bath water. Most of Europe itself would turn fascist or communist (synonyms) and destroy the religious symbols of society, replacing the crosses with swastikas, hammers, and sickles. We can't instantly destroy countless centuries of belief, real or imagined, without destroying the whole of society. Diderot and Voltaire sold unbelief to the French without offering to what new heights it would take them. Carl Jung wrote: "no psychic value can disappear without being replaced by another of equivalent intensity."[72]

America didn't make that mistake. They postponed the religious debate, or, simply let it take its course. They held to their common spirit and formed a government that didn't involve itself with theology. It took will and grace to overcome the inertia of Parliament's Stockholm Syndrome, brave the unknown future with independent hope, and having a brand-new continent helped. I will talk about the colonial genocides in Chapter 24 and the beauty and flaws of the US Constitution in Chapter 10.

I'll finish this chapter with a curious look at how we got so smart in so many different ways, rendering intelligence, IQ, and standardized tests almost worthless.

No Claws No Fangs No Venom

Evolution gave us the weakest bodies in the animal kingdom and the strongest brains, rolling the dice once more before the casino closed. It worked. In the midst of a million-year war between the latter-day primates in Africa evolution saw an infinitesimal advantage—intellect. The slightly smarter human won the fight 51% of the time. We are all descendants of the quick, not the dead, and that slight tip of the scale eventually tripled the size of our brains.

We know that evolving wisdom is how we survived and elevates all lives yet we walk on potato chips when talking about how this catalyst varies from person-to-person or from group to group. The subject makes academia squirm; however, the Buddhists have always reminded us of the polarity of all things. This is an interesting discussion because intellect is what has produced the vast wealth and the easy life we all enjoy today. Of course, comparing groups of people is hurtful and usually ludicrous anyway, and we're getting rid of that old, very powerful gene slowly, at least in the west.

Mental comparisons between individuals though are something we do every day. This should not make us fidgety because we all won the mental lottery. Stuck in the *comparison paradox*, it's as absurd as me fretting that my Ferrari is "challenged" or isn't as "snazzy" as your Lamborghini. Those stuck in the comparison paradox always compare themselves to others, or their group to another—half the time their egos win, half the time their egos lose—and they never consider how unique they are.

Recent books attribute prosperity to geography, weather, or disease eradication but we can look around the world and see so many countries, right next to each other, where one is poor and the other prosperous.[73] Environmental factors are somewhat still in play but those explanations belong to yesteryear because as intelligence spreads exponentially, each generation adds up to more than the sum of its parts. The agency of voluntary marriage, which most of the world lacks, makes for better gene combinations, and societies evolving towards equal rights under the law provide us with a safe playground to work or live in. These countries are sought-after destinations but we still see strange, gaping demarcations between countries inches apart.

In the 1990s, the average North Korean was 6" shorter than the average South Korean and nightly satellite photographs showed a lit up south and a dark north.[74] The Dominican Republic has a happy, upbeat feel to it and the other half of the island, Haiti, doesn't. Haiti rightfully rebelled but didn't upgrade their government after French imperialism—only the dictator's name changed—and they found themselves back at square 1. As in the Russian Revolution, the absence of ideas other than "get revenge then copy the last tyranny" replaced one mess with another.

The United States is rich and Mexico is poor so a family's hope for the future—what drives us—remains starkly different depending on which side of the Rio Grande you are on. Most of us know the good nearby countries from the bad with a quick glance at where people and businesses are migrating to and from. We often avoid that country and never wonder *why*. We can surely trust the innate principles from our upbringing—if our dinner table was a free speech zone—to filter out the distractions and get to the main ingredient.

Mexico, a country where journalists have the shortest lifespan, has free speech but if you read through the many stipulations to this law, you'll realize that they don't have free speech and know why Mexico is poor, and violent. Every transaction, psychological or material, begins with a conversation, and when you can't talk to the good guys or the bad guys because you can't tell them apart, or could be murdered by either one, you don't talk to strangers. The absence of free speech haunts Mexico down to Chile and screws up everything which is why the world is screwed up.

The Irish people are funny and the Scots, 12 miles away, are serious. We get some of the best philosophy from taxi drivers because they meet so many different people. One taxi driver I met talked about how the Irish were going to out-populate the imperialists occupying the top 1/7th of their island. The British still can't seem to leave well enough alone. Beautiful Irish girls would give their all to seduce young men into the IRA. A great singer-songwriter wrote, "and I will lie like a rose upon you pillow, and I will twine the laurel in your hair."[75] With that tenacity of spirit, the family Irish never gave up on the other sovereign isle.

Australia is relatively advanced compared to the countries dotting the Pacific Rim and is the preferred destination for troubled islanders. The Pacific Asians are telling us about their governments with their feet, saving us from a detailed study. The Chinese government controls marriage, reproduction, education, and import-export, leaving their people a few generations behind. It's odd that smart but poor Russia sits next to the enviably rich, neutral, Scandinavian countries and affluent Western Europe. After finally escaping communist rule, Eastern Europe is still trying to sort through their eleutheromania and blend into the western free markets—also generations behind. Like so many places, the eastern bloc parents did the best they could under a stultifying occupation but when the kids left home there was no opportunity because Russia had clamped down on those economies for 5 decades, as they had always clamped down on their own economy. The eastern bloc teenagers thought, "I've got a strong urge to fly but I've got nowhere to fly to, fly to, fly to," as Pink Floyd put it.[76] Good countries have 3 attributes: contrarily evolving brains, flexible economies, and a government that evolves along with both at the same speed.

It is odd that evolutionary scientists know evolution hones every organ in the body to work better, in vastly different ways, yet hesitate to write about intellectual advantages or disadvantages. Every so often I search the internet for *smart genes* or *intellectual genetic advantages*, read 40 articles and conclude—not much. Each study disagrees with the previous one, every gene does good, bad, and unknown things, and yes, we get our smarts, likes-dislikes, and physicality from our parents.

When we meet someone, we asses them in a few seconds and evolution did ensure that our appraisal is usually accurate. However, after a million years of gene mixing evolution doesn't know what's happening anymore, so, we have to slow down and constantly reupdate our paradigms. I'm forced to talk out of both sides of my mouth and conclude these 2 phenomena:

1. We are reticent to compare intellects out loud and that came from political correctness but it really didn't. That's simply the safe response of "don't be rude," which accidentally gets the right answer not unlike all the broken clocks that often display about the right time of day. We have to back up, start over, and know that in some cases it's necessary to compare smarts between people—marriage, hiring, risk, talent, productivity. And in some cases, it's fruitless—art, culture, friendship, lifestyle, happiness.

2. In the grand scheme of things, IQ is undefinable, individual, and attraction to another IQ is a matter of taste. Matching up IQs for reproduction is similar to shopping for art all day only to come home with something most other people wouldn't buy. We admire it for a bit too long; others nervously glance at it. When individual taste can roam free it creates more options which improve families, brains, and the world. Intermingling, more free trade, and more genetic mixing works, because each individual can inch closer to finding that unique key or lock that maximizes their genetic potential.

It's laughable that I'm attempting a general explanation of why some general explanations are right and some are suspect. Intuitively, we know which is which; we feel the answers in our gut. The body and mind align to formulate pretty good answers so we don't need artificial intelligence when we have the real McCoy. For instance, would we like for a crack team of genetic researchers to decide who our best friend for life is? A best friend is something we just *know*, and only one other soul feels it. We all fall in love too but we each experience it differently—same with grieving—and nature wasn't asleep when it did that.

Aside from the necessary and fairly accurate heuristic assessments we make, another great way we can learn is from the macroeconomic/macro-psychological evidence—what the world looked like then, what it looks like now, and what changed. Genetic brain advancement can flourish (maybe 51%) or it can fester (maybe 51%) and every tomorrow will show us more. Since we humans evolved together with ever-advancing brains which matured way beyond our physical capabilities we are impelled to look at our modern evolution as a psychological-economic one, and economy won. Nevertheless, 2% of our body (3 pounds) has been doing most of the evolving and Robert Trivers, a giant in the field, writes "our neurons express half of our genome."[77]

CHAPTER 3

Stockholm Syndrome Detected, Violence Rejected, Learning Selected

We have a lazy left eye. We are 90% righthanders so we usually protect with our left side until we attack with our right. When we were cave people, we developed a slight squint to protect the left eye from club blows, debris, and blood splatter, while never taking our eyes off the attacker. When we fought with sword and shield, we would stand at a 45°angle to our foe and defend until we saw an opening in our opponent's defense. Our left arm held the shield to face our attacker, and the right arm, led by the ambitious wider, right eye, stayed back to take advantage of a full swing for the coup de grâce.

The *oculus sinister* medicine aptly named our left eye and it is really a droopy left eyelid. This and the left hair part evolved to keep that eye protected and unobstructed after a million-year struggle with clubs and axes. The lazy *right* eye is now rare but Rafael Nadal, Bruce Willis, and Ken Jennings have one. I guessed they were all lefthanded and they were. Lefthanders are mirror images of righthanders and often have a lazy *right* eye and the hair part on the right to leave the right eye unobstructed. David Frayer found we are the *only* 90% righthanded animal and it started ½ mya. The evidence for our righthanded nature is in our tools, in the marks on our teeth, in our lefthanded brains, and in our language.[1] Sophisticated language was well on its way ½ mya.

We've all heard tales of how lefthanders are smarter but don't live as long as righthanders. Neither are true because most statistics are analyzed too quickly. As Stephen Pinker says, "mistaking a non-random pattern for a non-random process is one the thickest chapters in the annals of human folly, and knowing the difference between them is the greatest gift of rationality."[2]

There was so much fighting in our history it reshaped the bone structure of the male face. This masculine face still holds to this day—more in some places—and that face is sexy to women. The bridge of the nose is bigger and the forehead extends further over the eyes. Darwin himself had a pronounced brow sticking 1.5 inches past his eyes (twice that of mine) and we may be happy that those features vanished from females but females still want a man who at least looks a little violent. Ancient boys were simply born with nature's eye protection, including gradually thicker skulls, and these boys had more "relations" (as Eddy Murphy calls it) and passed on those same skull genes.

The Valiancy of Height Selection

"They called him Little Joe 'cause he scraped the ceiling."[3]

—Richard Thompson

Being the only *being* stuck in the comparison paradox, one thing we never stopped comparing with other families is the height of our children, if only in our minds. Increasing height is an evolution women create—they want their children to be looked up to—and this preference is redesigning our furniture and houses. Too tall is happening right in front of our eyes—much easier to spot than the tiny differences in finch beak's that Charles Darwin noticed. We assume tall people are smart too so a women might ignore smart, short men and marry a tall man but accidentally on purpose get a man of average intelligence. A 2014 study at the University of Edinburgh did find a small correlation between tall and smart and this trend will propagate because tall kids get more college scholarships. Tall people have more mates to choose from too so the reasons to make our kids taller keep piling up while we ignore the cons.

What about our knees, backs, and circulation as we get taller? Women don't look at those so closely. Although short people have fewer diseases and live longer than tall people, human evolution holds many secrets and one of them is *fortune favors the bold*. Using our free will to push the envelope is hardly a determined, random process, and women are gambling with sacrificial selfishness. Without risk there's no reward and women have decided quality of life wins over longevity because we are done reproducing when disease hits us.

Mammals got bigger after most of the dinosaurs died so increased size must also be a naturally selected, net evolutionary improvement. Consider the ancient eohippus. The early horse and the camel—America's gifts to the world from 50 mya—were the size of today's dogs, because of severe heat. 60 mya the elephant was the size of a rabbit, and the blue whale came from a mouse. With modern humans, the 4rth US president, James Madison, never weighed more than 100 pounds,[4] and the Revolutionary War uniforms would fit our elementary school kids. Height was so important back then that the height of some of the other founding fathers, well over 6′, are the most exaggerated numbers in history. After the Civil War, American women who tote almost half of the *tall genes*--boys often get their mother's father's height and hair—had to start over with short guys after so many tall ones had been killed. A study showed that they could do enough choosing even then to make the very next generation of men taller. The height of the average American woman now is about what the height of an American man was when the US went into Vietnam. To illustrate how fast we've been growing, if we keep gaining 4″ every 65 years, in 1000 years we'll be 11 feet tall(!) and the heights of the sexes may converge after those 40 generations. "Go ask Alice.........when she's 10 feet tall."[5]

Female preference and *diet* drive up our stature faster than anything, and diet is how the Dutch passed the US in height in 1979. Tall couples, however, can never be sure that their children will be taller than they are. The tall gene combinations can look ordinary or seem like a "freakish conspiracy" as Stephen Pinker says.[6] Tall, smart parents can occasionally have short, average intelligent kids but when the kids are taller, we notice it more. That's what women want. Although marriage is willfully designed to produce taller children, as well as higher IQs, the statistical results say that anticipation is greater than event. Nature's idea of a healthy child is not nearly as narrow as ours.

To make statistical analysis easier, when you guess there is an 80% chance of something bad happening, cut it in half to 40% and you'll be close to the right answer. On the other side of the coin, we think of ourselves as empathetic, charitable people—maybe 55% empathetic and 45% selfish. That's a pat on the back because most of us are 90% selfish toward ourselves and our family—*twice* what our guess was. Our egocentric observations are off by a factor of 2.

Flashback to the First Genocide

> In the south we say "everything should go pretty well if the neighbors don't start shootin' and the crick (creek) don't rise." With no police or infrastructure, the cave people were constantly on guard. The risk of nature's fury or surprise attack was ever-present and naturally, we all acquired a psychological condition called "Stockholm Syndrome." I'll return to modern times in 4 pages after I again tie the violent past to the present.

After Australopithecus and Africanus, came Homo habilis, then Homo erectus (fire starter with a brain half the size of ours[7]) then Denisovans, Neanderthals, and Cro-Magnons came last. As brain size increased a little with each evolutionary jump, the latter three used stone tools, wore crude clothes, and made campfires. Besides brain growth, flatter feet for walking, and changes in the throat, countless intermating tribes put us through a sea of other microscopic evolutionary changes.

The smarter tribes could organize bigger groups and could eventually string words together so well everyone in the tribe knew what would happen next. Well, most of them could; there were some who didn't get it but knew enough to copy the others which is how I survived school. Our violent tendency didn't wane with higher intelligence—we simply made better weapons—and the fighting amongst the groups drug on with bloody efficiency.

Whales eat whales but only for sustenance, not to wipe out an entire subspecies. Our closest *cousins*, or *breeds*—because they could usually intermate—were Hobbits, Boskops, Neanderthals, still some Denisovans, and possibly some Mungos, to name a few. We Cro-Magnons do have 400-600 Neanderthal genes still inside us, by injection, and I'll talk about those artistic, intelligent, extinct people in a minute.

We are a cult of one, Cro-Magnon, and our human and pre-human cousins, many of whom looked hauntingly like us, are gone. Evolution tried for eons to make the apex predator yet was probably surprised when we wiped out the top 1/3rd of the primate tree of life, leaving a vast void between chimpanzees and us. Some scientists say "wait a sec, life was rough all over and we don't know why the other hominins went extinct" but this gap (ape to man) has no parallel. Most animal classifications show fairer competition, many hybrids, a steady procession of larger and more complex cousins, and survivors from each epoch. With humans, this isn't so. Either God intervened or we did and wiped out every race between apes and us. In the family of primates, many have gone extinct but *all* species who competed directly with us are gone. The circumstantial evidence is overwhelming.

There are still a hundred different lemurs, hundreds of species of monkeys, and a couple dozen apes. Most primates have used sticks to ferret food from little holes but only Cro-Magnons thought to make long sharp sticks to hunt and fight. Lower male primates murdering the occasional neighbor did and does happen but we alone have the genocide gene.

In the tree of life, Cro-Magnons branched off from Neanderthals 600,000 years ago[8] but that date is disputed. Prehistory shows that's it's better to branch off from another animal than to have an animal branch off from you, be smarter, and kill you. The upright walking Neanderthals left Africa 75,000 years ago, *occupied* Eurasia, and happily flourished in the cooler air. The Cro-Magnons followed in their footsteps. The real first world war—not organized or planned—was the biggest genocide in history per capita. Imagine a 20th century where the German Army killed everybody in Eurasia, leaving only the Aryans. 30,000 years ago, World War I ended after about 45,000 years, only to start never ending wars in a fight for Eurasia amongst us Cro-Magnons.

Both Neanderthals and Cro-Magnons verbally communicated, routinely struck pyrite rocks together to spark fires, and took care of the sick and injured. With a slightly sloped forehead Neanderthals had less space for the all-important prefrontal cortex (the CEO of a person) but how underdeveloped the Neanderthal pre-frontal cortex was, is also disputed. Cro-Magnons could organize groups of fighters a little better and the Neanderthals might not have been the sharpest knives in nature's war chest, along with other weaknesses. Cro-Magnons were taller, the clubs came down harder, and the world war greedily selected tall genes for longevity. Some real evidence is in the bashed in skulls. We can guess the Cro-Magnons made better weapons and consider too that some common or extinct disease may have wreaked havoc on Neanderthal immune systems, while maybe 1 gene protected us. Neanderthals lived to about age 40 while Cro-Magnons sometimes pushed 60,[9] partially because of the war.

Scientists who studied Neanderthal throats agree they could talk which is how they came much closer to populating earth than any human before us. Speech genes are highly varied but the Neanderthal FOXP2 gene is identical to ours[10] and if you got a phone call from one today you wouldn't be able to tell her from a Cro-Magnon.

Creating art, as Neanderthals did, tells us that that lifeform is scary smart. Maybe Neanderthals were more artistic and emotional than Cro-Magnons, evidenced by the 65,000-year-old Neanderthal fingerpainting art found in Ardell's cave on Spain's Iberian Peninsula. Neanderthal art, 20,000 years older than any known Cro-Magnon art, led the discoverers of the paintings to speculate there is nothing older, in an aesthetic sense made by humans.[11] Neanderthal art is evidence of their carefree frivolity and maybe their free will too because creating art was not in their gene pool, they came up with it.[12] Neanderthals were possibly better lovers than fighters—didn't come up with a projectile weapon—and maybe evolved a free artistic flair a bit too early, having had their run of Eurasia for so long.

When everything is going well smart humans get a feeling something bad might happen and it did: Cro-Magnons, only 14 miles away, saw Spain from Africa, rowed north and started wiping them out. Scientists estimate there were only 100,000 Neanderthals in Eurasia,[13] spread thin in noncommunicating, small groups, and they had no idea they were getting methodically eliminated. The high smoke from those damn campfires pinpointed the tribes for us Cro-Magnon super travelers—good as a GPS—and after the raid there were indulgences to be had, not to mention a fire was already roaring.

We Cro-Magnons suffered much during the long, costly win over the Neanderthals which first proved Frederic Bastiat's broken window theory: destroying things *doesn't* increase wealth. War *does* shake up, smarten up, and unleash the tenacious gene pool across oceans. War is selfish with an unintended sacrificial component in that it smartens up both the invader and often the invaded by transferring precious bodily fluids across vast distances, creating more dynamic change than with static populations.

Starting with our proclivities for sex and genocide, we later evolved cooperation, organization, playfulness, and much later, a sprinkle of altruism. A great way to grasp the entire process of our evolution—chaos to order—is to understand my favorite childhood joke: **we went to a fight and a hockey game broke out**.

The last Neanderthal fossil (found in Portugal) was only 25,000 years old—no more were made after that. If the war had tipped to the Neanderthals, we would likely still have computers, satellites, better art, and may have been spared the music of the 70s. The DJs call it "the shevendiesh." Maybe it's a guy thing but if you were born in the late 70s you didn't miss much. It wasn't all bad—there was Motown, Pink Floyd, and that song...*Seasons in the Sun.* Unlucky Chapter 13 is about America's tipping point, 1969—the last season in the sun.

Stockholm Syndrome

The late Robin Williams said "there are no funny people in Germany, they killed them all." For thousands of years Jewish people have been persecuted for heresy or inciting heretical behavior and blamed for foreign invasions, ice ages, recessions, and diseases. But they were simply better capitalists than most, good at raising children too, and the *ressentiments*—the jealous who thought economics was a zero-sum game—didn't notice that Jewish families lifted up economies. The fortunate Jews who did escape the 1940's Holocaust acquired Stockholm Syndrome (SS for this chapter) and learned that the use of force is the fault in the human condition.

Oppressed groups were put through such stress tests that Jewish people and African American slaves were forced to learn things most of us could overlook. Even with us fully knowing that several large groups in Africa were wiped out during our lifetimes, we don't really grasp SS. Think about how countless children have inherited a generationally induced fear that everything they have and love could vanish in an hour. Most of us never knew the eerie feeling that our mother needed to go to the store but was afraid to go, or, God forbid, knew families who had to kill people to live. We can relate though because the universal disease of SS is still there in our DNA. We went through a million years of distress, and despite 3-5 generations of freedom from fear in the west, we sense the presence of those old chains we can't slough off.

Heavy SS is a psychological phenomenon experienced by kidnap victims or severely abused people who, believe it or not, fall in love with their captors. This irrationally rational bizarre response for survival is the key to understanding how violence or worse distorts the human brain. Worst case scenario: Under threat of being put feet first into a tree shredder, citizens routinely began worshipping Saddam Hussein, Colonel Kaddafi, and the Ayatollah Khomeini. In our lifetimes, people threw themselves at the feet of these fascists and begged to do their bidding. The victims themselves would murder innocents on command, or do it voluntarily, because heavy SS removes the essence of what it is to be human. Humans don't even realize SS has changed their brains or that they now love their abusers. Once these consummate initiations have fully infected the brain, victims regift it without knowing it, and create psychological slaves of their own.

We can readily see heavy SS in cowering dogs and we rescue them. Women, thus far having absorbed the brunt of SS, will often devote themselves to an abused dog not knowing they are transferring and projecting to the little dog the rescue they wished they'd gotten in their own innocent childhood.

Even the best parents give their kids some light SS and before each of us can recall that and reexperience that, we can remember smaller more recent SS events. Twice I've sat handcuffed in the back of a police car on my way to jail and twice the cop turned around and took me back to my car. The infractions I committed were small (2 crimes north of ripping off a mattress tag) which were shooting fireworks in the city limits and driving with a 2-year-old tag. I was young, belligerent, and talked back to the cops both times but knowing I was going to jail turned me from arguer into negotiator. I've always dreaded but never known what a night in the slammer was like and the thought gave me SS so I suddenly became nicer and the cops liked having that effect.

Forrest Whitaker tells a story to one of his Irish Republican Army captors in the great movie *The Crying Game*, as both are becoming aware the captor probably has to kill Forrest because he can identify the Irishmen. Forrest, angling for his one slight chance of freedom, starts charming his captor: "did you hear the story of the scorpion who finally convinces the frog to carry him on his back over the water to safety, but halfway across the water the scorpion stings the frog anyway?" The captor stares at Forrest, gun in hand, not responding, so Forrest continues: "why did you do that?" the frog cried as they both started sinking and drowning, and the scorpion replied, "I can't help it, it's in me nature." To no avail, Forrest got the message to his captor...and Forrest looked sadly down at the floor. His thoughts change to his girlfriend, whom he was worried about and talked his captor into taking care of her after the dreaded inevitability of his death.

A Preexisting Condition

How can SS, an activity people choose to partake in or get entrapped in, get into our DNA? The world was always a dangerous place and we were raised in seemingly dysfunctional, violent families for so long that the children who adapted to SS fit in better. They became more plentiful and thrived because they had to be raised as the next line of defense against rival tribes in Africa. Most couples trained their kids as they were trained and everyone eventually took SS for granted. If you were lucky to get to age 8 you knew how to kill or you might not make it to 9, when you start making your new SS family. Raising a family to be ready for violence wasn't considered by nature to be dysfunctional at all. This necessity came with a psychological loss though, as violence always does. SS made most males mean, many females depressed, and those live and let live dreamers who didn't fit the ancient social norms were often weeded out of the gene pool, along with their innovative ideas.

Some cave kids with less violent parents had trouble fitting in because they didn't play rough enough but some of those oddball genes did stay in the gene pool. This is probably because these freer thinkers were entertaining, had an occasional great idea, or maybe nature slyly keeps all brain types in play. After a childhood of abuse, most wore it proudly you see, like a badge, and they wondered why some kids hadn't gotten the badge.

Genetically passed on SS is a peculiar concept to grasp so think of the cavemen who were adept at fighting with clubs. Those guys lived longer and had more kids who were more likely to have those same talents. As bad as SS is for the brain—no matter—we had to learn anger and hate before we could kill efficiently. Pretty soon most cavemen were *natural born killers* (Oliver Stone 1994) and cave women needed them for food. The tribe was everything and they had to instill SS into all to survive and reproduce within their own clan. SS went to genetic fixation. Think of SS as the first psychological caveman vaccine to achieve herd immunity against the violence everybody knew was coming.

Leaping forward 2 million years, it was only 1945 when *genocide*—a word coined by Raphael Lemkin in 1943—seemed to get its first pause and baby boomers the world over felt liberated. An enlightenment occurred in many families and for the first time we consciously whittled away at our SS, however, SS is too engrained to rid ourselves of it in 1 generation. The baby boomers remain in conflict: our conscious minds love our greatest generation abusers, our subconscious minds hate them, and we usually retain that dichotomy for life.

In this new world we are usually protected from violence—foreign armies and domestic strangers—but many kids are still stuck with abusive parents. A tiny bit of violence only damages young brains a tiny bit and a childhood of it creates so much repression that kids may block out whole chunks of their lives. When a toddler is getting beaten (2-5 is the common age) the child thinks one of his two favorite people is trying to kill him and that psychological trauma compromises the brain, then the immune system. Stress robs us of long-term health in exchange for immediate defense. In her book, *No Visible Bruises*, Rachel Snyder says the brain scans of domestic abuse victims are similar to the brain scans of prisoners of war.

> *The adorable psychopath Karl, who in the movie Sling Blade had just gotten released from a 25-year stint in the nervous house, was sitting on a dock one afternoon with his young friend Billy, talking about life, when Carl gazed out over the lake and said, "I don't think nothin' bad should ever happen to children, I think they should save up all that bad stuff for them folks that done got older, that's what I think......ummh huh."*

Religion was a unique search for the human spirit in each ancient tribe until continuous war organized religion into nation states. After this U-turn, bad interpretations by charlatans turned religion into a tool to subjugate people by inventing the crime of "heresy," which means *choice* in Greek. [14] Scary. Shaming sexuality was their favorite sword, they used Eve and her apple as the excuse, and began prosecuting sins never committed. As we devolved into the manmade folly of original sin, the 2nd step was to cut the genitals of babies—after spanking them first. Carl Jung said that sex was both God and the Devil,[15] and the old men in robes might have been courting the devil early, on day 1.

Half of the Middle East remains religiously dogmatic and choiceless, akin to the pre-reformation in the west, and many grow up unintroduced to and unable to grasp the concept of SS, sexual freedom, or not having a king or a religious icon. Incredible as this is to us in the west, billions of people feel insecure or at least uneasy without a trillion-dollar potentate ruling over their country. In stifling cultures people subconsciously learn the worst lesson—nothing is going to change—and this inertia must be maintained with the threat of force. The threat of force makes citizens 1-dimensional by stopping many neural connections and in turn, stopping innovative, conceptual thinking.

Using genetic inheritance and family nurturing, western parents have grasped many complicated concepts—like free choice—and fought to the death to establish decent governments. Hopefully our idyllic Camelot isn't brief so the scant few nations who demanded an end to controlling societies can spread world-wide. In the west, the first step is to understand our subliminal tendencies toward original sin and Stockholm Syndrome and consciously avoid teaching them to our very young kids. The research that the quality of life we will lead is wired into our psyche by age 5 is clear, and a comprehensive, ongoing Arizona State University Study on early childhood development states:

1. 90% of brain growth occurs by age 5, whether a child is nurtured or neglected.
2. At times during childhood we form at least 1 million neural connections per second.
3. Success in school is hampered by early neglect or violence, or, in those 5 years, the seeds of a successful, happy life is planted.

Except for the million connections per second, don't we all, deep down, know those 3 bullets above? It's a reminder—people forget. We have really bad days and come home angry. "Every second, the eye transmits 10 million pulses through the retina to the brain at a speed of 270 mph,"[16] so every disturbing incident tells a thousand words as does every positive glance, sound, smell, and touch.

Learning Selection and Teaching Selection

"It's a Family Affair" —*Sly Stone*

We all try to marry up to selfishly copy our genes with a complementary set and raise the kids a skosh better than our parents raised us. We nurture them with the best within us and this improves emotions, attitudes, intelligence, and happiness. Do I mean that the institutions and the social planning are not the prime movers of our brains? Yes.

Since we all do good and bad things, and it's usually a strange blend of the two, it's maddening to separate good intentions from bad. With our first family though, we get to observe 2 decades of how our parents and siblings act. This is the crucial learning experience of our lives—the struggle that makes us—which nature has statistically vetted over and over. Next, we have another family and with hopefully well-wired brains we teach beyond our parents and continue learning "through the good and lean years and the in between years." [17] Evolution doesn't let the struggle ever stop because it knows that when the struggle stops, we stop. Always jagged around the edges, the 2 families still stand as the quintessential educational experiences of our lives and where we indeed learn the concepts of love, hate, loyalty, betrayal, revenge, sovereignty, motive, independence, manipulation, evasion, force, sustainability, and victimhood. We each learn unique versions and sad it would be if we all learned the same ones.

Life is therapy and we build on everything we learn by listening to other people's stories because we never can get enough story. Stories make us feel more normal yet woefully uninformed until we've read a thousand of them and listened to how hundreds of other people were raised and how they lived. Only then do we get an inkling of what the hell is going on. This is why uniform *family values, metadata,* and *community standards* are leaky bromides.

Beware of these advisors because every crazy human depicts the world in a newfangled way and these self-appointed seers are advising everybody into a corner. We don't want to miss the real show with the real people and we'll create our own metadata thank you. Many try to emphasize the state, the church, the school, or big tech as our formative experience. It's not nice to fool mother nature with her million years of familial experience. She was a little wordy but Jackie Kennedy said something like this: "when you don't raise your kids right, nothing else matters."

Learning Selection and Teaching Selection are volitional decisions made by parent and child alike. The main job for the parent is to spark curiosity and the main job for the kid is to not believe everything they are taught. We parents might keep reminding ourselves of that until we remember it ourselves. Learning selection is more powerful than Teaching selection because we can lead our children to water but we can't make them drink. The rebel children (growing in percentage) are unique free-thinking radicals, learn different lessons, and can end up charting new horizons for us, or become drug addicts, or do both.

Learn shouldn't be the passive voice of *teach* either because learn is an active verb too, as it is in German, and we could teach the young that learning is an act of will. Cave people had to learn how to survive before they could teach it. We are inadvertently teaching the young that they must be taught to learn and Ira Gershwin wrote, "it ain't necessarily so." America's most formidable Revolutionary War mother, Abigail Adams, in a letter to her young sons jumping from school to school in France, wrote "learning is not attained by chance but must be sought for with ardor."[18]

Getting back to the Arizona study, we are all born with a unique capacity for brilliance and our first 5 years add or detract from that potential more than all else combined. Do I mean that the programs, institutions, and social planning aren't the prime movers of our brains? Yes. It's those first 5 years that more influence how well we'll do in whatever school we go to and beyond. The giant step in education is brought to us by our parents and teachers must work with what they've got.

After they teach kids how to "add, subtract, multiply and divide…by 2," [19] teachers are instructed to get the kids to memorize as much as possible. Better it might be to coax them into understanding dilemmas people were in and the thought processes they went through to solve those problems. Economics, for instance, is super easy to learn. Ask a class of 7-year-olds to each think of a toy they'd like to trade for a toy another kid has. Let them think for a minute. Boom! You've practically taught them economics. Notice money wasn't mentioned and after school a rare little economy might start. Most kids are reticent to play the barter economy because they think their parents own the toys—not so—and teaching them this will educate them on the concepts of ownership and value.

As they get better at math in a fun way, we can also give kids a simple picture of the big 4 subjects—evolution, economics, psychology, and philosophy—and ask them, "what is the common thread connecting the big 4?" A 9-year-old might say the common thread is me! That's the right answer! 9-year-olds think egocentrically of course (don't we all?) and next a teacher might nudge them toward thinking outside of themselves and looking for deeper threads. Kids will next learn coincident interest and see their own face in the face of every other child. From that vantage point they can begin making more connections among those 4 subjects. Notice the kids haven't memorized anything yet.

Long after I took 3 advanced calculus courses and passed by memorizing the processes, I took the bird's eye view of calculus and finally understood it. They didn't teach me that view, they taught me the process to get the grade. Simple math doesn't involve the concepts of time and infinity, but calculus does, and Isaac Newton created this incredible tool to calculate simultaneous but different rates of change along a constant—time. We don't know what drives infinite time or even what father time is, but Newton was a conceptual pioneer who blended forever with math.

Math and science concepts should be taught using word problems before teaching with numbers until all the kids get it. The faster learners can draw pictures at their desk (learn on their own) while the concept dawns on the others which is how I became a pretty decent artist in school. It wasn't that *I* caught on fast, I wasn't paying attention at all (I have the typical male ADHD and dyslexia). It was later when I started thinking conceptually that I started understanding calculus, philosophy, and the global problem of Stockholm Syndrome.

Modern Stockholm Syndrome

"Don't know a soul who's not been battered, don't have a friend who feels at ease, don't know a dream that's not been shattered, or driven to its knees." —*Paul Simon*

On the outside of the body, the visible evidence of internalized trauma, obesity, is everywhere we look in America the beautiful. Young people eat to form a protective cushion around an implausible childhood and they are in no uncertain terms setting a perimeter around themselves. Obesity began with the baby boomers and hasn't stopped, telling us of a major change: instead of projecting violence some Americans internalized it. Having lived through this, in the next paragraph I will venture an incautious guess as to what the baby boomer dilemma was.

Boomers were born into a world of sudden positivity with the highest of expectations and the greatest generation parents overshot it. This generational transition would be a slow one as usual but hope changed too fast and despite winning WWII the same old unruly world was still sitting there in front of everybody. With the mixed messages of individual freedom and harsh group discipline, vegetables and fast food, Vietnam or no Vietnam, and with male children still favored, anticipation for the boomers was keener than event. Darkly, they noticed that they inconvenienced their parents as the other generations had which surprised them—life wasn't supposed to be like that anymore. The boomers thought they were special. Their young minds went off-center—in good, medium, and bad ways—and some got fat, some stayed skinny, and some harbored hate for the boomers who weren't beaten. The silver lining was that people were expanding into individuals after making the general observation, maybe mistakenly, that the greatest generation was all the same person. Nearly the entire greatest generation was beaten too but accepted the violence—"maybe I deserved it"—stayed strong, and stayed at their married weight for life. And, they weren't told they could be anything they wanted to be and then stopped from being anything they wanted to be, as the boomers were.

One greatest generation girl who got these mixed messages is my personal choice for the greatest singer who ever died: the sweet but resilient, 220-pound Ella Fitzgerald. She ran away from the boarding house she was sent to after her mother died because she was getting beaten by the teachers with sticks. Ella told those maids they couldn't tame her and they wrote that down in the school ledger because they were starting to agree with her.[20] She was probably a Love Child—she had the voice even then—but they did tame that super skinny teenager in a way. Ella gained weight from stress she didn't deserve. She *had her own* though and conquered the world with her voice. I saw colors when she was singing and the first smells of fall sometimes take me back to her *September Song*. Music is therapy when it takes us back decades to a place we forgot we used to be.

The greatest singer was also the first iconic female singer-songwriter! I've always thought that adversity and pressure create the most unexpected rarities, like when you squeeze a piece of ice between your fingers until it shoots over the crowd. Along with Billie Holiday, Ella broke the old mold of the male singer-songwriter and with the deck stacked against her created an intimidating volume of material over 5 decades. She wrote the words and the music—something that can't be taught—and as nature sees the mind-body as one thing, so Ella saw the words and music of song. She, as all African Americans do, knew Stockholm Syndrome in every form from overt to benign and like that piece of ice that shoots across the room they started a music revolution America didn't see coming (Chapter 27). Elle lived right through the eye of the storm. She was the eye of the storm.

The Baby Bloomers

"Everybody's gotta fight to be free." —*Tom Petty*

The effect the baby boomers *did* have was the rejection of

violence except for defense. Although I am a bias, non-violent member of this generation, I watched this happen and the evidence for a rapid decline in physical discipline, starting with Generation X, is a search from your fingertips. I don't know any Xers who beat their kids and I don't know no any boomers who weren't beaten. Beating a toddler is now unfathomable for most everybody—we changed our brains—and I think the decline of physical abuse during these generations precipitated the steep crime drop in the west more than birth control did.

The boomers were also the first to be half economically *and* psychologically spoiled—born into the wonderfully confusing Goldilocks Zone of history—and that little window of freedom let in a little light. As 40,000 generations of parents had thought, the boomers also believed they could raise better families than their parents had, even in the clumsy 60s, and they went further. It was radical to confront the old long-standing institutions and attack racism, sexism, violence, and war in synchrony. Boomers selected abstract learning in mass and innocently stole the whole show, it would turn out, because the silent majority hasn't yet had a comeback.

The boomers, lucky enough to not have a world war dropped into their laps, were in the first sweet spot with their cup half full. They stopped the war in progress, not caring who won, and I'm not disparaging the dedicated people in our military—I'm angry at their political bosses. Mark Knopfler sings of warriors as "deep and strong, brave and true," but the people they worked under weren't. Vietnam simply wasn't our business.

This wasn't just advice from the boomers, it was a polar shift; they didn't tell people what to do, they told them what *not* to do. The generations prior always told their kids what to do every minute, leaving them no time to ponder, and the boomers were left half free to ponder and hope. The changes didn't happen in every baby boomer family but enough to make generation X the psychologically healthiest because the boomers started a generational super trend with many intended and unintended consequences. Today, daughters have a good chance to be valued more than sons. In one generation college graduates went from about 60/40 boys, to 60/40 girls. And we even make friends with our kids and I think that has more pros than cons but I'm culpable there so won't be getting into it—it's not what the book is about anyway.

Boys want love too. From early primates to latter day primates, fathers have remained in competition with their sons for life. This is in male DNA from when a man's sons were the most likely culprits to steal from his harem. The father wanted to do the gene mixing but the better hunters his sons were the more the tribe ate, making them more attractive to women and more of a threat to dad. Thus, fathers still make friends with their daughters a little easier than with their sons. A successful friend of mine was complaining that his 80-year-old father always denigrated his accomplishments. I said, "all fathers do it, so it's not personal." He stared at me. Competition is in male blood; a million years of competition courses through those veins.

As fathers recognize this stale throwback from evolution, they can modernize the instinct and make a home into a safehouse. Boys encounter competitive stress everywhere they go and need 1 demilitarized zone where competition is for fun and free-spirited idiot geniuses are loved.

Scorpions don't change but we do and we're getting there from those post-war marriages of *Beauties and Beasts* (a great cartoon that says it all). After nature's software our parents are the 2nd tier of programmers—we will feel the gaze of both parents for life, they are that powerful—and understanding what they thought they had to do is half the battle.

CHAPTER 4

Epistemology

We know human characteristics go back 7 million years, perhaps 10. Archeologists found a pre-human skull in Africa from 7.2 mya and human footprints almost that old, along with more bones from 7 mya that prove we were getting around without hands. [1] Evolving alongside beavers, who still build damns like they did back then, pre-humans began improving on everything they built. After millions of years of off-the-charts brain growth with much more to come, the first modernish humans left Africa travelling in tiny groups as early as 500,000 years ago. 450,000 years later they had covered the globe like a can of paint. The microscopic evidence is continuously telling us the prehistorical knowledge we seek and one day we will have the chronological DNA of the many scattered tribes who eventuated in the smartest hybrid: us.

When we live with someone long enough, we say we start looking alike, but this does happen in small populations—countries too—when a group is isolated long enough. I have a photo of our cab driver in Glasgow Scottland where Mark Knopfler is from and they look exactly alike. When a subgroup gets separated from the whole it isn't often from geographic chaos—flood, volcano, fire—it is caused by a radical shaman who has new ideas, good or bad, and 5 or 10 people steal away with him at 3am. A new leader thinks he knows things others don't or yearns to find out something he doesn't know. Even on a hunch, he's convincing and they follow, which changes their diet and eventually their mutations. These mixtures of nurtures and natures and wills change people much faster than that sloth evolution would on its own.

What often starts a little new branch is two rebels from two tribes, say John Smith and Pocahontas, who cop some of evolution's passion, eyeball to eyeball, and steal away without benefit of clergy. They had only one Lovechild but Pocahontas taught John epistemology by showing him things "he never knew he never knew."[2] The study of knowledge, epistemology, hinges on knowing what we know, knowing what we don't know, and being aware of both. Untold troubles begin when we think we understand something that we don't, and our dreams are epistemological puzzles too because we know what they mean but don't know we know that.

How do we *know* we are conscious? Pienso luego existo, Spanish for *I think therefore I am,* came to us via René Descartes in 17th century Holland when philosophy was brilliantly simple and conjecture wasn't running amuck. Today we've dumbed Descartes down to "I think therefore I make money." Many are addicted to the dollar, some are preoccupied with renaming streets, and some want to know the flavor of the week—who Brad Pitt is dating. As we stumble confidently sideways, we often come across the remains of the same campfire we had a few nights before and it dawns on us we've been walking in circles—while some just get déjà vu.

The first humans were confused too because the philosophy of individualism, which some eerily felt, didn't make sense yet. The tribe seemed to have a momentum and they couldn't make out any collective conscious running it. The engine was usually a strong spear leader, a cult of one, from which individualism sprang and worked its way down to the others. On some level each tribal member had their own inkling of *I think therefore I am* and pondered the 3 subsets of philosophy: epistemology, ontology, and metaphysics. They couldn't corroborate these thoughts with others because their vocabulary was for immediate problem solving. These concepts were within their grasp though and could have been confirmed had there been many more words and one other person to deliberate with. And they couldn't discuss the subject that had long towered atop philosophy and its 3 subsets—evolution.

Scant few of them saw evolution although a parade of eerily similar animals—with all the organs in the exact same place, neatly increasing in complexity—was front and center to nudge them in that direction. Early humans couldn't make out this mysterious mechanism that kept pushing the nervous system toward a more individual existence.

Their cognizance of ontology, the study of *being,* was also in a nascent state but early man knew ontology 101: I own my own body. Property rights started roughly a million years ago and when a man made his first rocky-topped spear, he knew he owned that too because he built it with his own work. He alone maintained it because only the owner will. A few of them put 2 and 2 together and realized that every other man knew he owned his own body too. This was our giant leap toward coincident interest and this rare common good came from individuals. Ownership became self-evident to almost every man and it would be a long time before women knew they owned their own bodies. It would be 1973—Jane Roe vs Henry Wade.

The conceptual realization of ownership and value lives in the abstract, in and beyond humans. The proof of this is that the lower animals make no mistake of knowing they own their own bodies too. The difference is that they cannot bridge that with coincident interest and form contracts beyond gene relatedness.

Unlike the religious Descartes the early humans knew their days were numbered but couldn't communicate that to each other because they didn't have the words. "A penny for your thoughts or a million dollars"—it wouldn't have mattered—but they could see it in each other's eyes. This was our first metaphysical dilemma (we're still working on it) and "you reap what you sew" was known long before religion evolved.

Epistemology too, as Pocahontas taught John Smith, was on their minds. They knew what they knew and knew what they didn't know—inventured to know both better—and it was another bond they felt but couldn't describe to each other. At night the old devil moon[3] was in the west, in the morning it was in the east, and they thought they were being spied on by twin gods. The gods would just hang there, motionless, staring at them.

It never crossed their minds they were the top of the bio-chain and in natural fact it is usually naïve to assume that. Conjuring up a God gave half of them hope and half of them fear—eleutheromania—and they started worshipping objects in the sky, or the biggest guy with a spear when necessary. If aliens ever land here Richard Dawkins said the first thing they'll want to know is "have they discovered evolution yet?"[4] We had to wait until 1859 for Charles Darwin to spill the collection plate on how we got here and wait for the 1860s to know about dinosaurs. Early humans had simple metaphysics on their minds too—their original *relationship with the universe* was to kill, eat, avoid death, and reproduce. They became efficient enough to find precious time to contemplate much more than that and an idle mind is not the Devil's workshop. Philosophy finally broke out of the stanchion because this was the dawn of the prefrontal cortex—the peripheral vision of their awareness widened—and the pre-ancients would gradually come to know everything they didn't know.

Bob Seeger sang, "I wish I didn't know now what I didn't know then"[5]—sometimes knowledge is the burden of modern life—but the foragers wanted to know what they didn't know. The ancient, great unwashed had no choice but to keep thinking; they had to discover reality or live the lawless, static existence of animals, corralled forever inside their instincts.

Armageddon?

Besides Chevy Chase getting a late-night talk show, the most destructive event in human history occurred 75,000 years ago[6] and this force majeure, or act of God, killed most humans. A super volcano erupted in Indonesia covering mother earth with ash for months—some say years[7]—and the story would make a good Stephen King novel. Most of Toba Mountain in Sumatra, an island in Indonesia, shot 50 klicks into the troposphere and some of the debris went into rarified air or reached escape velocity. The rest of the diamond dust got trapped inside our ultrathin troposphere and reflected light back into space, making the sky white and the earth cold. Many small packs of wandering humans were in Asia by then and they longed for the bountiful Africa they had adapted to as they starved and froze in the dark.

The mountain of volcanic dust obeyed entropy and circumvented earth, robbing plants of life-sustaining sunlight, as the underground seeds patiently waited there for a pinhole of sunlight. The sky, a never-ending cloud, choked or starved most land-dwelling animals and almost wiped out the fledgling human race. The nuclear winter began far away in Indonesia, as they usually do, where our DNA brethren were enjoying paradise in East Africa. To fathom how destructive the ancient Mount Toba explosion was, it was roughly 50 times bigger than the Mount Tambora eruption in 1815 which created a year without a summer, and 100 times bigger than the 1883 Krakatoa eruption, which gave the sky a dark, greenish glow, all the way to Switzerland.[8]

1/2 mya earth's human population was about 30,000 and climbing fast but after the Toba eruption, DNA tests confirmed that the low number of mutations found in those 74,000-year-old bones in Africa, told scientists the entire population had dropped to between 40-1000 humans. In large populations, each birth has about 100 new mutations which arise from "1 mistake in every 100 million nucleotides of DNA per generation,"[9] and when 90% of the population died, 90% of new mutations died too. This haunting event in earth's most populous place slowed down the genetic clock, leaving a skeleton crew of 40. I'm being a little dramatic here because some studies show there were 1000-10,000 people left on earth and yet others found scant evidence of survivors on other continents, however, the disaster does help explain our genetic similarities planetwide.

Even with little rainfall and rivers drying up, East Africa was the place to be—location, location, location. The unfortunate humans who had gotten to the Middle East, Asia, and Europe didn't have what the people in East Africa had—thick, lush vegetation. The 40 survivors were *lucky* enough to live in what is now the country of Malawi—home of the still-trickling Shire River—and with little meat they had no choice but to eat their vegetables. Like herbivores, they had to munch all day, exhausting their jaws but creating the energy for sex and healthy breast feeding. Living in dirty, cold air, the strong lungs survived—those are the strong lungs we have today—and the smarter, more industrious brains were heavily selected too. The philosophe Nietzsche said, "what doesn't kill you makes you stronger," and in a dark, forbidding, mathematical way this is where the slower humans and the smarter humans parted paths.

"A Man is Just a Dick with Ears"

My late friend Kevin, a natural born wordsmith, used to say "a man is just a dick with ears." "Pecker heads," is how Richard Pryor put it. These guys were philosophers.

There is scattered historical evidence that during plagues, hyper weather events, and wars, or whenever we feel threatened, sex, prostitution, and wouldn't you know it, pregnancies increase. We steal away and make strong, all important, Love Children.

With snow at the equator after the eruption, we shivered, ate, and huddled together in that little spot, and earth almost lost its favorite son save for the crude programming of the *any port in a storm* male. Eminem said, "I'm tryin' to get my head straight so I can figure out which spice girl to impregnate." With most every endeavor the reward comes after you finish a task but evolution made the male orgasm such a reward that with Armageddon staring us in the face and 40 humans left, we screwed our way back. If a praying mantis or black widow could talk, they could tell us how important sex is to a male. Evolution made sure we created many children and was confident many would survive because of the parent-child bond it instilled into us. Not much has changed in 75,000 years for the predictable male, as the songwriter Mark Knopfler says, "the ghost of dirty dick is still in search of little Nell, that's what it is." Mark's gettin' old now. After 50 years of great songwriting, he wrote: "Chasin' after Little Red Ridin' Hood......I don't......do it no more but I......used to could."

We've had no E.L.E.s (extinction level events) since. The youngest super eruption, Mount Toba, was earth's 5th known ELE and precious few species survived all 5. If all species had died though, worry not, 1-celled creatures would have lived through the long cold night, or appeared again, morphing into multi-celled creatures as they did eons ago and similar animals would have flourished, if not identical ones. With the perpetual motion machine of life, there is no Murphy's Law. It's virtually a mathematical certainty that if something can go right it will.

Jim Bowler found a new species of humans, Mungos, in Australia and the bones were 50-60,000 years old![10] These 6′ tall human remains were buried adorned with intricate jewelry when nobody was supposed to be Down Under. Mungo skulls were too big to be a Cro-Magnon, and these 200-lb men weren't Neanderthal or Homo erectus either, and had bigger teeth than any human. This separate reality threatens our belief that all humans came out of Africa because there is no trace of Mungo Man anywhere else—so far. Studies from the John Curtin School of Medical Research found that Mungo's mitochondrial DNA was different from any other human who ever existed.

3.5 mya, "Lucy," hung out in what is now Ethiopia. Lucy was a great find, though still in Africa, because they found her whole skeleton. Don Johansson et al found Lucy's bones in 1974, measured her at 3.5 feet tall and she was not a monkey, ape, or chimpanzee. She was an Australopithecus and became the oldest pre-human celebrity. She had shorter arms than a chimp, flatter foot bones, and her pelvic bone more resembled a pre-human. Her knee bones were shaped for bi-pedal motion so she walked upright and had a smaller brain than an ape—1/3rd smaller—as pre-humans did back then. With long fingers, toes, and tail, she could hang out in trees if necessary and had teeth for eating both plants or animals—pre-humans were already scavenging for meat.

5.6 mya, pre-humans were walking upright and their all too human footprints were preserved in the mud which had hardened into rock. 5.5 mya ago Gibraltar was mashed against Africa and the Mediterranean Sea temporarily dried up, so all kinds of primates walked from Africa to Europe. There are Barbary Macaques native to Southern France (monkeys) and lemurs and apes got to Europe about when humans did too.

Paleontologists recently uncovered a 7.2-million-year-old pre-human jawbone in Greece. Apes and monkeys have 2 or 3 nerves going to each front tooth but this jawbone had 1 nerve going to each front tooth, like we do. This and the later discovery of flatter footbones—flatter than apes had—were the first 2 little changes toward becoming human. Scientists studying these fossils think our split from chimps may have happened much earlier because the first pre-humans got to Europe over 7 mya! That's a very long walk, plus raft rides and the jury is still out on these pre-humans, named *Graecopithecus*.

The 3 terms, anatomically modern *humans, sapiens,* and *Cro-Magnons,* are loosely interchangeable and that sparked my dyslexia and maybe yours. The origin of us is heavily debated because most of these skulls only date back 40,000 years but there is evidence that they lived in Africa 130,000 years ago as a small population.[11] In the book, *Why Nothing Can Travel Faster Than the Speed of Light,* they place Cro-Magnon origin at 300,000 years ago.[12] The book *Work* agrees with that[13] but Chris Stringer's lifelong DNA study concludes that Cro-Magnons split from Neanderthals between 500,000 and 650,000 years ago. This DNA evidence sounds so wishy-washy but remember there were so few of us in the beginning, much sleeping around, and our DNA changed a trifle every generation. How and when did the first German appear on earth? It would take a book to formulate an educated guess.

Let's make another academic guess that smart humans of different species decided to explore the pale blue dot 1 mya. The spear and the boat were the beginning of globalization.

Boats

The first ocean boaters followed prominent coast lines exposed by the ice age and although there is almost no evidence of these boats, humans were almost everywhere they shouldn't have been. Homo erectus, Neanderthal, and Cro-Magnon, crossed the seas and probably passed down the knowledge of navigation by the stars because the stars were the only things in the sky that were in the same place every night. Let's start with boating in biblical times then make our way down to 1 mya.

Archaeologists found 3,300-year-old South American coffee in Africa, inside King Tutt's 19-year-old stomach. We think coffee is expensive now so imagine how much gold the poor deformed Egyptian had to pay for *that* coffee, and probably tobacco, plus shipping. Unless people could walk on water back then, we were boating across the major oceans over 3000 years ago and returning home with money or goods. Heyerdahl, the Norwegian who wrote *Kon Tiki*, built a small raft in 1947 and went halfway across the Pacific Ocean to prove it could be done.

There is similar human DNA throughout Polynesia, to Chile, and all the way up to Columbia South America(!) proving that people were crossing the Pacific 1,200 years ago, and that genetic mixing spans 7000 miles of open ocean.[14] Which direction they were sailing is another question altogether. Some scientists say that people were on the west coast of South America some 15,000 years ago which would be improbable since the first Americans from Siberia got to Alaska 14,000 years ago and hadn't had time to walk all the way down to South America. There is a 13,000-year-old skeleton of a Chinese-looking teenage girl found on the Yucatan Peninsula of Mexico and earlier evidence of campfires in Brazil. The Siberians and Chinese, who didn't need boats to become Native Americans, may not have been the first American settlers because the Polynesian people might have gotten to South America first. However, there is some evidence that the first Siberians began coming into Alaska 28,000 years ago and footprints in New Mexico from 22,000 years ago[15] which starts the debate as to which group discovered America.

People were living in Papua New Guinea 60,000 years ago and boated east across the Pacific for tens of thousands of years. What slowed them down so, is they had to cross the deepest part of the Pacific (few islands). Did they get to South America first in such small numbers that they were wiped out by the larger land-loving tribes heading south from Mexico? Whover got their first, or if it was a tie, all these ancients were from the area we now call China.

Recent mind-blowing research by Jason Lau shows evidence of modern Cro-Magnons reaching Australia 50,000 years ago, Neanderthals getting to the island of Crete 130,000 years ago, and Homo erectus regularly crossing the Mediterranean .5 mya[16] and even 1 mya.[17] With some continental landings, more drownings, more starvations, and many untold Gilligan's Island stories in between, the brave star followers created pockets of civilizations.

In premodern times, Egypt had some of the first sailing vessels that we know of and those usually clung to the Nile River. Like the Middle East, Australia, and most tropical islands, there were no pine trees for building large sailing vessels or the humid hemp fields for making miles of rope to hold up the conifer masts. Whether trimming the sail with or against the free wind, or wasting away in the expensive doldrums, it was hard work for Britain, Scotland, France, Italy, and Spain to ply the seas and ropes into safe 2-way tickets. Northwestern Europe was the ideal setting to perfect large transport ships for intracontinental trade and the European Kings saw a world technologically behind, and theirs for the taking. Who wouldn't have?

From wooded Ireland to the Clyde shipping company in green Scotland the great wooden ship builders on the Isles always called their ships she-names and they guided their ships with a sextant. The sailors, with short life expectancies, knew they would find some strange on every continent and those long maiden voyages in the sea of love may be how our dreams about vast bodies of water evolved to be about sex. Mare means *sea* in Latin—we still name our daughters after Columbus's ships—and Jimmy Buffet sang "mother mother ocean, I have heard you call, wanted to sail upon your waters since I was 3 feet tall."[18] Not to belabor the point, but Mark Knopfler sang, "let's go down to the waterline," and Al Green sang, "take me to the river." By the early-1800s the UK had come up with steam powered steel hulled ships and ice cutters, retiring the wooden ship to inside a wine bottle.

If the Middle Eastern people had perfected ship building before Western Europe did, what would the world look like now? About the same, and their most distant colonies would be singing *Losing My Religion*[19] too. The Middle East got their sea legs late or we might be speaking Arabic and praying 5 times a day. That thought will pucker up the average westerner a bit, as it puckers up an Arab when an American or British aircraft carrier passes 400 meters from one of their major ports. Imagine going fishing early one morning on the Hudson River, and a light-duty Iranian, nuclear powered, nuclear armed, aircraft carrier silently floats by.

You could easily make a case I'm too hard on imperialist Britain considering 2 small countries joined at the waist, Britain and

Scotland (120 miles by 420 miles!) are wellnigh why the world looks and sounds like it does today. Even with their bad teeth and driving on the wrong side, that tiny island started globalism and world trade. Looked at by itself with no strings, this was a penetrating positive, however, there was a catch—paper money.

The Chinese call 1850-1950 the "century of humiliation" as Britain, Japan, and Russia grabbed Asian territory while Britain ruled ocean trade with cannon, paper money, and illegal opium. The Chinese people had already figured out how to crudely refine opium and had long been coerced into getting paid with paper money too, by their own rulers.

The British bought tea from China and opium from India, both on credit, and resold the shiploads to the other country in exchange for silver or gold coins. Historians tell us that the crown-sponsored drug dealers used *bills of exchange* from London banks to prefinance the operations, and their twin, the US bank, began issuing those bills having seen how they were used to pay American farmers for crops. What historians don't tell us is how this piece of paper worked its magic.

These bills were how farmer Thomas Jefferson got paid for his tobacco, and he, maybe one of the few to notice, realized there was a catch to the British method. Though the bills of exchange were not real money, as coins were, all Britain's colonies were pressured into accepting them as such, and rare was the chap who could figure out that the IOU would eventually create twice as much money as existed prior. A bill of exchange represented a couple grand of value in North America and sometimes it paid for a farmer's entire crop. When sold back in Britain, the British shipper received a couple grand of existing, circulating money. This payment was sometimes silver or gold, and sometimes paper money, which they were told represented some precious metals saved in some vault somewhere.

A British merchant usually sold a shipload in a colony for gold or silver too, then bought a shipload for the return trip using a banknote and a smile. The smile was the *distraction* and if that piece of paper was accepted for payment, that constituted the *prestige* of the trick. I say *trick* because the bill of exchange wasn't money that had been earned, the British banks simply printed it up in the backroom, and if the ship later went down with all the goods, the bank lost no money. They would just print another one for the next outgoing ship and keep going. If the shipment. picked up in some colony, made it back to Britain, the captain got paid in real money for the shipment, though he didn't use real money to buy it. This trickery created twice the original amount of money which caused a slight inflation in prices, far from England.

The only way the trick would work was if that piece of paper, usually left in some colony, would also buy domestic goods. It usually would in the many British colonies and beyond as the *weightless* British pound rapidly became the world currency. It's just as if you bought a guitar from a friend with a fancy piece of paper imprinted with the seal of the Royal Bank of England and he had to go find somebody else who would accept the paper for another payment. You got a free guitar, minus the small bank fee and the king's tax, and the new money would then go into circulation forever, with all the rest of the circulating money. The bank may ask you for a little favor later, but hey, you're in the club!

With cargo ships, roughly a couple thousand new dollars were created with each pickup and delivery, after the bill of trade went into circulation in China, India, Africa, or the American colonies. Everybody knew what they knew about money but didn't know what they didn't know about it.

This extra money, whether it was used for buying, selling, or imperialism, began a tiny inflation on several continents and few noticed. People everywhere were partial to using coins made from precious metals but paper money seemed to work OK too—it was a monkey see monkey do type thing. Populations were also increasing rapidly which masked the inflation and this paper trick is how the British could afford the massive expense of centuries of imperialism. There is no way the crown could have afforded half the world by taxing its own people, most of them poor.

In comparison, and minus Mao's genocides, China was and has been a total pacifist, internationally. Taking the frontiers, Tibet and Mongolia, was like the US taking the west. Imperialism begats communism and the Chinese communists began taking over China in 1949.[20]

Japan had ostensibly taken Formosa (Taiwan) from China in the late 19th century, then China lost it again to rival Chiang Kai-shek in the 19th century, and now China wants it back. The world wars, WWI and WWII, never really started or stopped, invasions blended together, and Taiwan and many more of these previously war-torn countries are now independent sovereign countries. Should every border on earth get moved back to where it was according to some date in history? Which date?

The UK fought in most of the *early* world wars and has the best win/loss war record in history. What an island. Every army since Adam had house cats took whatever their technology could grab so the guilt of the west is having made the best boats, guns, global trade routes, and funny money. Everyone has sins to atone for and bigger boats with bigger shipments bought with disguised credit simply made for bigger sins.

After all this delectable deleterious history, we're not supposed to say that every single nation is creating banknotes or that English is the world language. The Brits took bits and pieces of most other major languages through wars, shipping, trade, computers, and music, and after all that imperialism, funny money, and positive interference, the English language has evolved into the dialect of freedom. And how refined the pronunciation and phrasing of it tells a million more words.

If some other country had overpowered Britain, my guess is that they would have acted similarly and the world would be using another language and different money. As we are versed in the cruelty of light-skinned men during the long age of imperialism we don't hear so much about the global history of all males stealing land and enslaving groups worldwide.

CHAPTER 5

Clever Instincts

A mother and a baby experience an emotional and chemical bonding that is truly the stuff of science fiction. For instance, a baby likes the people its mother likes which proves that the brain and body are one inextricably connected mechanism. Science has but scratched the surface of this evolutionary miracle which is more intense with female children and the mirroring is for life, deepening with each child. I often observe this metaphysical strand that lives through my wife, daughter, and granddaughter, and cannot put it into words.

Women automatically kiss their babies to ingest their pathogens, build up resistances to these pathogens, and pass the immunities into the baby through breast milk. Mothers get living fetal cells through the common blood stream that morph into chimera repair cells to heal weaknesses in the mother's organs. This foreign DNA, almost half from the father, acts as an evolutionary, micro-mechanical repair team that helps women stay healthy and live longer so they can have more babies.

Minus the dangers, pregnancy is a beneficial relationship and now men are getting in on the mystery, nervously picking at their fingernails and scrunching up their faces. The husband helps with the Lamaze classes, the birthing, then blindly dips his toe into the cuddle chemicals. Only then does he first see, after a million years, the hardest job in the world. After having a baby, actress Christina Ricci said she and her hubby were "sleep deprived, exhausted, starting to see things and talking to God."[1]

Besides the odd human we have but 1 stalker left: micro-organisms. Medical science has made incredible but expensive remedies for the bacteria and viruses that stalk us but women are solving this problem on the house. They've always been subconsciously suspicious of tiny things that make us sick and are now shopping for genes that kill them. They aren't really looking for a soulmate; they are looking for a unique set of genes that will help their kids live longer, smarter, and happier. *Subconsciously suspicious* sounds contradictory but I will try to prove otherwise.

The only built-in defense we have against bacteria, viruses, and cancer, is our immune system which consists of a dozen or so genes out of about 20,000 from each parent, doing most of their work from the stomach. Since women were nominated to improve our immune systems long ago but never had the chance to flash that around until recently, we are getting healthier faster.

Women can get a schematic of a male's genes by smelling his pheromones in his armpits or pubic hair and researchers say that this phenomenon occurs in 100th of a second from up to 10 feet away. To match up her immune system and the rest of her genes with a man she not only smells his genes but must also biologically *know* about her own genes too, in order to dovetail this baffling liaison. This priceless info is in an unknown language encoded deep inside the female brain where she dreams and absorbs romance novels. Our sense of smell has long been devolving while our sight has long been evolving, hurting and helping how women detect healthy men. A picture tells a thousand words and she is developing the ability to *see* inside a man, always with the goal of producing Mother's Finest.[2]

What women see and smell is a man's MHC (Major Histocompatibility Complex) along with the man's face/body symmetry—indicating generally healthy genes—and much more. One stray researcher found that groupie girls in Minor League

Baseball can more accurately pre-pick the guys who are headed for the Major Leagues than talent scouts can.[3] My wife offered "those groupies are hot and that helps the minor league players get to the big show." My nephew, a PhD in microbiology, told me about the MHC, which is specifically called the "HLA" in humans. The *human* leukocyte antigen system consists of 100-200 variable, adaptable genes only 2-3 people out of 100,000 have very close matches with. This makes reproduction not quite the gamble I'm insinuating and makes transplants difficult beyond the immediate family (identical twins are ideal for transplant).

Researchers at Abertay University in the UK found that women can "see" the immune system and the testosterone in a man's face. Sexy male faces had the most compatible immune systems, the most testosterone, and both were confirmed by DNA testing. A sexy face and a healthy inner male are the same thing—by design. Keats wrote, "beauty is truth, truth is beauty." Long thick hair is another clue that the reproductive levels and immune system are strong—published in Psychological Science Magazine. Long eyelashes are beautiful because they keep debris out of our eyes and both sexes study the face because a *face is a map of the world.*[4] All that detail in a small area contains a banquet of genetic information that we process in an instant and the same thing happens when we scroll down to the derriere walking away, where our eyes go next. That's the mechanical room—the heart of the plumbing—and the joke there is that sometimes what you see is "a cross between a donkey and an onion—an ass that brings tears to your eyes." Women take a snapshot of the derriere in a fraction of a second and don't get caught while men stare, dumfounded. Humans, of course, didn't invent any of this. Evolution perfected the plumbing and software for *Love Potion #9* long ago; tiny, multi-celled organisms were chasing each other around like teenagers before they decided to leave the ocean.

Canadian researchers found that just seeing a sick person boosts the observer's immune system and published these findings in Psychological Science Magazine too. Conversely, our immune system suffers when somebody we love expresses contempt for us,[5] and words or looks—little drops of poison—change our glandular secretions. Mark Schaller of the University of British Columbia showed that both disease and pathogens can be psychologically detected in humans by smell or sight. A woman can probably see other women being proactive and psychologically generate a little more testosterone, or its equivalent, for herself. How our senses and thoughts machinate inside of us is a scientific mystery, however, the anecdotal evidence that the body-mind oneness exists, crashes the scales, and we now know we can turn emotion into a physical event.

Dr Trisha Stratford says love at first sight is real and it's all in the gaze. If the gaze is returned you get a tiny shot of nature's heroin from a good drug dealer—evolution. Evolution is cheering for you to round 3rd base and head for home but finding a soulmate is your problem. The high divorce rate tells us that Mr *slow to learn* evolution only wants lots of *physically* healthy kids.

The evidence is trickling in that men also have a crude 6th sense and they tip dancing women quite a bit more when they are ovulating[6] and find the *silhouettes* of ovulating, dancing women on film significantly more attractive.[7] None of the thousands of men in these studies knew the women were fruitfully peaking and couldn't smell them so men aren't detecting genes, only fertile woman. The *any port in a storm* male is programmed for macro-reproduction and the female for micro reproduction.

I've always wondered why it makes us squirm to imagine our parents having sex. Maybe we revere them as godlike (why wouldn't we?) and picturing them acting like animals, muddies that up. Our dads were probably thinking about baseball and our moms were probably thinking, "I hope he's not thinking about baseball." The main reason most of us squirm is probably that during puberty we each develop a sexual attachment to one or both of our parents.

Before 1969, "girls were girls and men were men[8]," and since then, we've been choosing to acquire more traits from our opposite sex parent because parental roles have blurred so. Better it may be to avoid parental binarism altogether and pick the best qualities from each, but picking the opposite sex parent shouldn't create confusion about our sexuality. Androgyny (having acquired traits of both sexes) and homosexuality, with androgyny growing faster, are very different. Now we're seeing countless freewill spinoffs of androgyny and Martin Short isn't a bad example. His impersonation of Katherine Hepburn is, if you're old enough, sidesplitting. Cast off binary thinking, from personal to politics. The world is too colorful for either/or, but who am I to give advice?

Until recently women couldn't use the power of clever instincts as men usually picked the mates, and longevity had to wait. It reminds me of an old joke: did you hear about the 90-year-old couple who got divorced? They wanted to wait until all the kids had died. I'll bet you a Ruth's Chris Steak House dinner that humans can see and smell longevity genes too. It had to be one of the first things nature thought of and as we learned to seek those genes more, we found ourselves in virgin territory: we live 85 years and are married for 60. The new psychological experience of 60-year marriages is our conundrum because we have no imbedded experience with that in our DNA.

Getting back to trait selection, if both parents have similar immune systems their children will have much less disease protection and this is why evolution—in its ordeal to rise above trial and error—made an opposite immune system smell hot. If a woman was forced to marry her cousin, their son would be unequipped for longevity—a mother's nightmare—and she would be sending him into battle, so to speak, with 3 swords, instead of a sword, a helmet, and a Kevlar jacket. The son of a ladies' choice couple stands a much better chance of having all 3 tools and is better armed for longevity—she robs Peter (husband) to pay Paul (son). When she gets to pick a guy with an opposite immune system, many of her weak genes are overridden by the partner's stronger ones. Since women are now picking the phenotypes (sum of all genetic information), they *are* the new evolution.

William J. Behe, in his incredible book *The Edge of Evolution*, explained mutations, the automatic micro-processing that goes on inside our cells, and a little philosophy too. He wrote "in the real-world Darwinian evolution has no gaze to focus; it is blind……there can be no intentional building on a single trait."[9] He's more than hinting at heavenly intelligent design but hold on a sec. Women are part and parcel to evolution so if I'm right about our volitional sacrificial selfishness—evolution attached to a super computer with free will—then women are speeding up evolution's gaze. With intent, women are cultivating unseen positive traits. When the *vast* majority of western women finally got to pick their man by 1969, women **took over** human evolution. I had no intention of coming to this conclusion—this is where the research led me—and we must also conclude something bigger: women are *teleological.* [10] They are accidentally on purpose creating better humans much faster, with intent, because now they know they can do it.

The phrase, clever instincts, is not an oxymoron. Smelling pheromones is an instinct from the ages but now men know about it too. With awareness of this ancient automation, we can promote that knowledge from unconscious mind to conscious mind by crossing the firewall between dreams and cognition. When we cross this wall, an instinct gets cleverer because we can consciously decide whether to follow it or do something else. A woman who might not want children can now weigh her natural attraction to a man's immune system against another man who is nicer, richer, has no facial hair, or is a more interesting conversationalist, and let her genes bid the world adieu.

Sometimes When We Aren't Looking

After our daughter graduated college, she bought a cute house and moved out in 2015, so Jeanne and I went on a little trip through the heartlands, which turned out to hold a hidden surprise. From our little farm in West Georgia, we headed north in my packed to the gills dented Tundra to escape the summer heat. After I sped through Tennessee with Jeanne telling me to slow down, she took over in Kentucky, hardly speeding, and got a speeding ticket in Paducah. She damn near joked her way out of it. We laughed later because the only other time she'd been pulled over, her joke worked. She had gone through a reddish light (she told the cop it was yellow which didn't help) but then she looked at him with those 2 big brownies and said "it was actually orange." He looked at her, and let 'er go. She disarmed him with a joke. Cops love jokes.

This time though, the Kentucky cop handed her the ticket and softly said "get outa here" as I smiled because I had stuffed my *one for the road* Coors Light down into the pocket of the passenger door. Hey, it was almost 3pm. Anyway, she turned left at the next highway taking us just above the bootleg of Missouri and headed straight west along I-60. We'd never seen the endless Ozarks.

Something told me if she hadn't gotten pulled over, she might have kept going north. She doesn't take kindly to reprimand or getting pulled over for having out-of-state plates or brown skin and thought, "to hell with Kentucky." She headed straight west. She wasn't going to drop a dime in Kentucky. "Done and done," as she put it but it doesn't matter where you go in the south, there's always a shade tree mechanic or a *malfunction junction* close by—they fix you right up.

The hills of southern Missouri were gorgeous, or maybe the weather in our minds was beautiful, as we drove into a small town. The early autumn in Alton, population 200 forever, was splendid and she was tired of driving but not that tired. She doesn't seem to get tired. Evolution made sure women would be like that.

We wanted dinner in a bad way—you know that car appetite—so we decided to see about lodging. Before seeing any motels we drove past a little house for rent sitting on a secluded lot surrounded by ancient black oak trees—$75 a night—and the little town seemed perfect for a few days. A real-estate lady showed up in minutes and it was one of those quick small-town transactions. In Alton "you don't need no credit card,"[11] and there were no confirmation numbers, passwords, or 1-way streets. The rental house smelled clean as we left our bags in the hall and went right for food. We walked back in time to the little town square where the Five and Dime and Ben Franklin store used to sit and went for some sweet corn at the Corn-Fed Rascal. The next day we hit a couple estate sales and Jeanne the collector found some table-top antique statues she'd never seen before—cash only.

I had already come up with fresh angles to prove evolution to a doubting public and these ideas were about people but not about specific people. I worked on the book in that little rental house and it crossed my mind to just make up a story, when something possessed me to go up into the attic. As I pushed back those cobwebs, I stumbled upon an old trunk full of letters, diaries, and ancient pictures. I started reading this antique cursive writing and for me anyway the trip to Missouri turned into a Huckleberry. An old man named Jesse, probably long dead, had kept ungodly amounts of information about his daughter Edith Virginia who wrote to her parents about her life and her children's lives. At the bottom were older letters written by the grandparents of Edith and her husband. There were old documents, photos, snapshots of her paintings, medical documents, military records from her husband's family, and hundreds of letters—starting from the 1880s—speckled with little brown spots.

After reading how different each generation was, I started piecing together a psychological evolution of 20th century Americana. I left out the last names in the story, that's immaterial—nobody in her family was famous anyway. When I had finished reading all of this material, I knew Edith, and soon you will too because she didn't leave much out.

The real estate lady stopped by the next day making a smalltown visit and I asked her about the stuff in the attic. Though she was surprised I went up there, she apologized and said the guy who was supposed to take it to the dump hadn't shown up yet. I didn't say anything. It took an hour, but I got the whole trunk out of the attic and into the bed of my dented truck. Knowing nobody would miss it or knew it was there, I still felt dirty like a thief, stealing a rare, innocently written, perspective on America.

Edith's letters were so precious to her mother Helen, it helped her live longer and she read them over and over—especially the crazy conversations that defined Edith's family. After her mother passed in 1962, Edith pretended she was still alive and kept writing to her, hoping her dad wouldn't read them for reasons you will see. Edith also wrote about her dad Jesse and a buddy who had found some old treasure maps and started digging for gold in Ozark caves. She knew he was losing his marbles but couldn't help still love him because for a turn of the century, antebellum head of the household, he was never violent or knowingly mean to her.

Having no hateful bones must feel pretty good but Edith doesn't have the foggiest idea she is the stuff books are made of, or that she changes the world. Her story will tug at you in your sleep because she talks to herself, revealing some of your unspoken sentences. Edith held on to her innocence longer than most but she had a flaw or a defect you see...imbedded into her long ago and inadvertently coaxed along by her parents. We all have one. It's our pensive sadness......our undertow......our propensity to never be satisfied and where our empathy and selfishness collide. We're all born with a hole in our hearts that never quite closes.

Edith was trying to figure all this out in her mid-30s after her mother's death, but she had no idea she was writing the story of the decline of America. She never noticed that what happened to *her* happened to *it* too, though she had a front-row seat to both.

CHAPTER 6

And the Story Begins

"A story is about significant events and memorable moments, not about time passing."
—Daniel Kahneman in *Thinking Fast and Slow*

In the spring of 1947, 19-year-old EDITH VIRGINIA was nervously packing for a 3-week solo trip to the east coast by rail. She had forgotten to do a load of clothes, forgot a few other things, and decided last minute she couldn't part with her kitten, Spotty Ann Feisty. Her parents couldn't talk her out of it so her dad Jesse had to buy cat food on the way to the station and Edith fed Spotty there in the backseat of their new Chevy Coupe. He had bought her a train ticket because when he talked of airplanes he'd say, "too many of 'em hittin' the dirt," in that classic Missouri accent.

Edith's mom Helen cried like a baby at the loading dock and Jesse seemed impatient. "The parting was awkward," Edith thought as she dragged her big bag with one hand, held her cat and purse with the other, and grabbed the closest window seat to wave goodbye to them. Her anxious parents smiled and waved back to their only child. As Edith grinned at them the conductor yelled, "all aboard!" and she nearly jumped out of her skin. She got a lump in her throat as the train slowly left the station so she took a brave glance back and her parents were no longer there.

She lit up her first cigarette in 2 hours and watched St. Louis go by the window.

Edith, from the tiny town of Alton Missouri, the colorful middle of America, was going to get to see New York! She couldn't decide if she was excited or nervous or was making her second mistake of that spring. Her first possible mistake might have been breaking up with Miles, her high school boyfriend, however they did stay friends and he took a job in New York as an electrician—and got married. Edith had butterflies in her stomach about the visit but wanted to see the big city. She was tossing these things back and forth in her head when the train made an unscheduled repair stop in "Warshington DC" as the Missourians pronounce it, and she decided to get off and do some errands in the allotted 3 hours. She mailed the letter she'd written to her parents about the long train ride and bought a big wall clock for Miles and his new wife.

Edith headed for DC town center lugging her stuff and the cat. In 30 minutes, she was in the middle of it all, looking around and smiling breathlessly. Passersby were saying "hello" like the people in her small town did. She then saw a sign in a store window that read, "Clothes Washed Here" so she ran in and put her laundry on the counter. Nobody seemed to be around, but all the lights were on. After checking her little pile of silver quarters, she wrote a quick note for them to wash and fold the clothes and she'd be back to pick them up in an hour. She finished some other errands, was running late—no surprise there—and rushed back to the store. Her clothes were still sitting on the counter where she'd left them. A man was looking at her. "Why didn't you wash my clothes?" Edith asked, puzzled. The man said, "this is a sign shop ma'am, we make signs here." They both stared at each other, and she hurried out to find another place.

After finally getting her clothes washed and chasing Spotty around the capitol Edith Virginia got hit with what the German's call "fernweh"—a sudden panicky feeling that you should be somewhere else. That would be the train station, and she guessed that the train might be pulling out about now. She liked DC and the friendly people there with the possible exception of that guy at the sign shop. Maybe the springtime smell of cherry blossoms grabbed her, and, almost subconsciously, the thought crossed her mind to stay there. Edith walked back to the Post Office and mailed the clock to her high school x-boyfriend with a "sorry, change of plans" note scribbled on the box. She nervously made a phone call to her parents in Alton Missouri, asking them if she could stay in DC, and they reluctantly agreed. That's when Helen reminded her that her Aunt Mary lived there in Foggy Bottom with her daughter Betty—both secretaries in DC.

Edith and Spotty Ann Feisty moved in with them. Edith taught them why animals should have 3 names, "because they are people too," and they taught Edith the art of drinking—Mary and Betty never missed happy hour. With candy apple red lipstick, pre-curled brown hair, and cigs dangling, the 3 flappers had no idea that they were the European stereotype of American women.

After Jesse wired Edith some out-of-state tuition money, she entered college at George Washington University, majored in art and history, and oil-painting became her forte. Less than a year later, Betty, who was dating a Navy pilot and was perplexed about Edith's lack of dates, set her up on a blind date.

It happened so fast. Edith found herself on a date with a handsome G.I. (government-issue 2nd Lieutenant)) and they were both so nervous they couldn't stop smiling. It helped they were both coincidentally from Missouri (both pronounced it *Missoura*) so the conversations weren't monkied up with pauses. It took him a second to size up her figure, though it was hard to tell how skinny she was with all those curves. One glance at her uptown belt pulled tight around that fetching waist, told the age-old story. "She can't weigh 115 pounds dripping wet," thought the officer and gentlemen, forgetting to look away from her tall, more than Greek figure as their eyes met again. No matter, this wasn't Edith's first rodeo and despite her parent's advice she knew to test drive the car before she bought it.

Prodigious Prospects

America had ended World War II with a knockout punch, winning simultaneously on 2 hemispheres and everything seemed to be looking up for the yet unnamed greatest generation. They daftly assumed it was the last war. Violence was Europe's to bear but after 1945 the US assumed ownership and power turned to pride, as it will. Many from the greatest generation didn't peer into themselves after that great victory—it's what winners forget to do—and 1947 would seed new troubles. Not having the wisdom to skip Vietnam would be the final blunder, but still, they raised their expectations, their grand old flags, and their kids, with pride.

The romantic war (1941-1945) didn't appear to have a religious slant to Edith as that undercurrent lay hid by those who do that sort of thing. America was King with or without a God and trust in Uncle Sam filled that precarious void. Presumptions ran amuck in the backrooms of Washington DC and momentum gathered to recreate the world in its own image—a seemingly flawless idea. The US had given the tattered world a big dose of hope and the Yankee God redrew boundaries and created new countries out of whole cloth. There were more winners than losers and we could say the US did an *awful* lot of good, exporting opportunity worldwide, even to our previous enemies. The word *awful* used to mean *awe full*, the opposite of what it means today—I'm using it both ways. We'll never know what the world would look like if the US had remained an isolationist country. Imagine removing US foreign policy from post-WWII history and let your imagination soar.

They got married young on May 15th, 1948 and would have 4 military brats. Edith's fever for the future was high and laughing came easy for her in America the beautiful but she had no idea she'd be moving household 30 times, or that the army would send them packing all over the world. Edith learned other languages and even started dreaming in other languages which was a new one on me. She *felt* immortal the way young people do but had no earthly idea she would live forever. All she knew is she loved life and had the big family that she had missed growing up. Everything was hunky dory with the promise of a wonderful life and the new couple slow danced to "from now on our troubles will be miles away,"[1] smiling 1950s style, into each other's eyes.

The 3rd Floor

Hoping doesn't always work. A year after the wedding Spotty Ann Feisty died early—never having had a litter—and although it was her 3rd cat it hit her hard. Even with all the worry and trouble that cat was, Spotty had made Edith miss the train, learn how to drink, and find a husband. Edith found a spot in her little vegetable garden between the cucumbers and tomatoes, surrounded by flowers and buried Spotty there.

She started wondering if her precocious cat had free will. "Could something that brought me so much joy be simply one of nature's curious robots? Maybe my life is determined by outside forces too," Edith said to herself. She happened to look out the kitchen window and saw the burst of color that was now Spotty's tomb. "It might be easier to untie Gordian's Knot, than to find my own free will," she said out loud, not knowing in 15 years she would be standing in front of Gordian's Knot. "I should call my mother and tell her about Spotty," Edith said in the empty house, "or maybe that would just make her sad for me." Most people talk to themselves, however, Edith the only child did it more than most. She came by it honestly. She sat down and penned another letter to her mother, burying the bad news somewhere in the middle.

Having grown up driving Fords since he was 11, Edith's husband decided to try his first Chevrolet—a Fleetmaster—after hearing Edith rave about her parent's Chevy Coupe. He'd gotten orders to head for postwar Germany, and though he knew the car would be a bit big for the streets, the couple wasn't using any birth control and the car might fill up fast.

From 1948-1952, the Army dispatched Edith and her now 1st

Lieutenant husband to 3 brand new US military bases: Frankfurt, Stuttgart, and *Nurnberg* (as the German's say it) where they had 1 daughter in each city, 3 years in a row. Edith had post-partum depression after each birth, thought it was just her, and strangely it reminded her of a feeling she had long ago.

The Nuremburg trials (as we say it) for the Nazi war criminals were wrapping up as Edith arrived in her first of many foreign countries. Bombed out Berlin was still inhabited by 2.5 million women and children and the Berlin Airlift was in full swing bringing planeloads of food from the west. After losing 360,000 Russian soldiers taking the last city, Berlin,[2] Stalin was happy to let the Berliners starve out of a well-earned revenge. The Germans had prayed to God for General Patton to get there before Stalin—both men often referred to God[3]—and those prayers fell on deaf ears.

Of course, the family always lived on the 3rd floor with no elevators and the 3 baby girls made sure Edith had little sleep. She could forget about oil-painting and writing letters for a while. Like most moms, she couldn't wait for each kid to enter kindergarten, as she carried groceries and a baby daily up the 36 stairs to her tiny apartment, leaving one baby there and one at the bottom, then going back down to get her with the oldest tagging along the whole way. Back then you could leave a baby or two alone for a minute and nobody said anything. They moved to 9 different apartments in Germany in those 3 years, always flying in those loud Army propeller planes while the Army trucked their furniture to the new address. Whenever Edith got to a new apartment, her simple furniture was in place, even the infamous red and white checkered breakfast table with that shiny silver aluminum band around the edge.

Rachel, Electra, and Mary, Edith's precocious toddlers, would steal candy at stores, break milk bottles for fun, eat sand and aspirin, pour contractor's paint on themselves, and tell people: "if you swallow an apple seed, an apple tree will grow in your stomach." Once, while Edith was painting, they smeared feces all over the master bed. Diapers didn't bother Edith but for the first time Edith thought the bedsheets stank to "high heavens," and concluded it was the smearing that tipped the scale. She spanked them, if we could call it that, and later overheard the oldest girl Rachel say to the other 2 crying sisters, "don't worry, we'll do it again sometime." After Rachel had reassured the other 2 girls, Electra, who for some reason didn't really mind getting spanked, got a bit jealous. Rachel was doing the reassuring, which always made Edith laugh, and Electra took the cue and assumed the top position in the sister triad.

Rachel did not say a word during her year in kindergarten and Edith's husband spanked her good for that. The couple finally had their first real fight that day because it didn't take much for him to spank a toddler. Each parent had 1 vote on everything but he was the tie breaker. "They're just children," she said wide-eyed to her husband, loud enough for the neighbors to hear.

Edith, the bass guitar player of the family who blended the drumbeat with the melody, finally coaxed Rachel into saying 1 word. On her way out to kindergarten playtime, when the other kids were running ahead of her, she yelled out "stop!" It's a big bad wonderful world out there, and Rachel finally found her public voice at age 5. She also had an overdose of curiosity, had a 10-year-old's view of the world, and for years Edith treated everybody with Rachel's inquisitive sentence structure, "what man doing mommy, where man going mommy?" Rachel said it again, watching from a window, as an excited German man drove away in their new looking Chevy Fleetmaster. Their 3-year stay in German was over. The car was a lemon, the doors didn't shut right, and when they got back to the states, Edith's husband bought another Ford—a 1952 Victoria.

Unaware that she was living her dream with all that work, the 3 girls got Edith into army shape and by the time they moved to Champagne Illinois, then Alexandria Virginia, then Fort Belvoir Virginia, Edith was as tough as Rosie the Riveter. Fort Belvoir is where she had her last child, and named him Miles after her high school boy friend but her husband didn't need to know that. Edith's husband thought, "Miles? That's like naming a German boy,

Kilometers." A year before Miles was born Edith's husband had watched a nuclear bomb go off in New Mexico, from 8 miles away—though he was told not to watch—and walked through the area a couple hours later. He joked he didn't think he could have another child after that. Edith's 4^{rth} child, from sperm just a skosh radiated, was a surprise since they were using the rhythm method, and was Edith's most difficult birth—Miles came out backwards. "A breach birth," they called it. A hen's egg turns around right before it comes out and that same gene from reptiles flips the baby 180° in the 3rd trimester. Maybe that gene got zapped?

The doctor spanked the bloody baby who screamed a primal scream and peed all over him. After the army nurse cleaned it up Edith held him for the first time and looked weakly into his eyes and at the indentations the prying forceps had made around his head. Then something made her look back into his eyes—1 was blue and 1 was green. "Somebody musta messed around with a cousin sometime back," she thought, "probly on my husband's side." As most women in the 1950s, Edith happily smoked and drank through all 4 pregnancies, so who knows.

Instead of sending Edith's husband to the Korean War, they sent him to West Point New York where he got the *cushy* (word from India) job of teaching physics at the military college. Even after taking physics courses at 3 different colleges, he had to study every night while Edith was in heaven with Rachel, Electra, Mary, and Miles asleep. The girls had started school and she could spend her days painting nature's bounty along the Hudson River. With gas on military bases at 27¢ a gallon in 1959, sometimes she would drop Miles off at the daycare on the base and go into the Big Apple to shop. At stop lights she would people watch and one day she thought she saw her old boyfriend Miles eating lunch at an outside café, by himself, and her heart started racing. She kept driving. She skipped the shopping and went straight back home to get busy cleaning—married women just didn't do that.

It was now 1960 and very near the end of the 3 years at West Point. Everything was on base and the parents strolled a few blocks to cast their votes for JFK while the 4 kids walked to a movie about Sinbad and the 1-eyed Cyclops. The theatre was not a mile from their apartment but they had to walk through a huge cemetery to get there faster, which always spooked them. They started running. Boom, they were at the theatre—spent almost 50¢ on tickets and popcorn—and sat in the middle of the front row filled with anticipation. As the movie progressed without showing the cyclops for a good while, Sinbad heard "boom, boom......boom" and the theatre shook. The booms were so far apart they could imagine how massive the monster was but it was even scarier because they hadn't seen the cyclops yet—the tension mounted. The booming sound of each step gave them brontophobia; the same feeling they got when their father stomped down the hall toward the bedrooms but they didn't make the connection. Finally, the cyclops appeared and it was that 1 eye that scared them the most because they knew the primeval monster lacked intelligence.

Stalk-Home Syndrome

Rachel had a new dream one night where she changed a rough spanking from her father into a dark scene from the Middle Ages. In the middle of the night, she saw a Knight in black armor wielding an axe, slowly approaching her in the dimly lit hallway. The Knight drifted right up to Rachael. Feeling sure she was about to die she punched the Knight in the stomach as hard as she could and to her surprise the black armor was only thin plastic. Her little fist went through the plastic like paper, the Knight was hollow inside, and he collapsed. Rachael woke up the next morning, relieved. But she was more than relieved, she felt triumphant, and some of her father fear vanished.

Your subconscious mind is the dream director. It's a wild concept when you think about it: you are watching a movie you make while you are making it. A dream is a form of literary historical fiction too: it's telling you your real history in a made-up, present tense, fictional way. Everything in your dream is a part of yourself, in the broadest sense, so if you dream a plane is crashing into your house you are scared or angry. Pretend you're the plane and yell about how you want to smash the house until you accidentally say something that reveals who you are flaming mad at. Or, pretend you are the house and talk about how you feel as this plane is about to destroy you. Notice there's never anybody helping you in a dream so you can learn to consciously take control of a dream—make a dream lucid as Rachel did—by planning on it when awake. Your dream director will keep showing you a similar movie until you consciously take control of it.

We dream about the worst feelings. Too often it's about the final test day in class and we haven't been to class all semester. That's the universal *fear-depression* dream with an overdose of the dread feeling strangely brought to us by academia. These dreams came from long ago. Some lazy cavemen had subconsciously put off gathering firewood for a month than had a nightmare about it and woke up freezing. When they looked around, the forest was covered in an icy dread.

In modern dreams we are powerless to say, "to hell with that paper or that test, I lost the battle but not the war." It might mean we fell short of parental expectations long ago and saw the disgust in their faces, and were devastated. The dream is telling us to go back in time and relive what happened.

At 3am, we find ourselves alone in a strange daylit room. We don't yet know what will happen next but we know it won't be good. The room looks unfamiliar but feels eerily familiar at the same time because our dreamer knows us well, yet wildly exaggerates our surroundings. We know we've been there before but when? The room might represent an all-encompassing loneliness we felt while our parents' played cards in the kitchen—clowns laughing and joking—while we suffered. As adults we have to do exactly what we don't want to do and go back into that damn room many times while awake. If we lived a childhood of violence, returning to the room seems impossible. We haven't stopped running since but find ourselves back inside that room, with our next family, because we never interpreted the dream.

David Gilmore said, "kicking around on a piece of ground in your hometown[4].........runnin' over the same old ground, what have we found, the same old fears, wish you were here."[5]

Coast to Coast, Around the World

Leavenworth Kansas was their next home. They lived in a tiny 3-bedroom apartment with a master bedroom, Rachel and Electra sharing another bedroom, and Mary and Miles the other. It was called the "Beehive" which was a 5-story complex almost a quarter mile long. Army housing was free of charge—no debt but no equity—and doctors and dentists were free too. A military family had to have 4 kids to get an apartment at the Beehive and of course they lived on the 3rd floor again with no elevators. As their parents were, the kids were fit as fiddles from riding their bicycles all over the base, and on Sundays they reluctantly trudged their way to Bible School. With her husband always at work and Miles in school now, 34-year-old Edith finally had the days to herself so the year in Leavenworth raced by.

I will formally introduce you to Edith's husband in the next chapter. The kids called him "daddy" and called Edith "mommy" and they said "good riddance" to Leavenworth and "hello" to 3 weeks off. It was 1961 and their next base was Monterey California. While Russian and American tanks faced-off across intersections in Berlin, and Khrushchev said he had "30 nukes earmarked for France and 50 each for West Germany and Britain," [6] Edith's family went on vacation. Edith's husband turned into a great daddy at vacation time and he was excited as they headed to Missoura to visit the 4 grandparents in Alton and Bolckow. The grandparents lived 400 miles apart (opposite corners of Missoura) so the family usually killed 2 birds with 1 stone.

First stop, they arrived in the 2-doctor town of Alton in July to visit Edith's parents, Jesse and Helen, when the kids were 8, 12, 13, and 14. The 2 docs were Doc and Vera and they were married to each other. As soon as daddy delivered the family to Edith's parent's house he made a bee-line to Doc's house and finally got his cheap vasectomy. To save money the pure Scot would have gone to a veterinarian. If you have 4 kids and are in the military you have to be frugal, and he put saving money over the family jewels, for, in effect, experimental surgery at the time. Doc made up outlandish stories and performed too many surgeries with his lips firmly attached to a whiskey bottle, but the vasectomy worked and Jim the old rooster still got his standing ovation. "No more kids," daddy thought, as he added up that saved money plus the no-charge from Doc. He would say, "we don't have a refrigerator because I don't believe the light goes out after I close the door."

Doc's favorite story was of a rare lawn mower accident in Alton when the mower blade hit a rock, broke off, flew across the road and cut the neighbor lady's head off. But that's not how it went according to Edith and her father Jesse, as they had taken the lady to Doc himself for a bunch of stitches.

Next, they drove from Alton to Bolckow (population 160 forever) and visited the other grandparents, Walter and Laurinda at their little house in the middle of the street. The grandparents were getting up there and the army doesn't tell military families exactly when they'll be going overseas or when they'll be coming back. It would be the last time they saw Walter.

Dad let the oldest 2 girls drive the car around in that sleepy little town when they were 13 and 14. He enjoyed teaching them, with his right elbow on the open passenger window of his newish 1957 Ford Fairlane and his hairy ape-like middle finger clinging to the roof, *so the other 10 could rest.*[7] The "missing link," the girls called him but he didn't care, the old rooster still had that rocket in his pocket. He always wore the same watch, wound the spring up every few days, and always wore his Cool Hand Luke sunglasses, being too careful to lose anything. Occasionally he'd yell out, "watch out for that little kid!" and Rachel would slam on the brakes (or sometimes the accelerator) throwing everybody around in the car with no seatbelts. Dad would laugh and say, "just kidding."

A few days later it was time to "hit the road," as dad would always say. They took a few lastminute pictures and said their goodbyes, followed by some hugging—mostly between the adults. Dad's family wasn't that much of a hugging family, well, neither was Edith's, though the adults stood way too close when talking too loud to each other. The men also didn't wait studiously in the car for the women back then—everybody piled in on command.

Before joining Route 66—California or bust!—with Bolckow in the rearview mirror, they went back over the "big bridge" as dad called it. The kids knew from previous trips about the 1-lane bridge just outside of Bolckow which was a pile of rust and rivets over a deep creek and it shook. Maybe the only reason it still stood was because it got an hour of rest between vehicles. Everybody laughed at his sarcastic joke, making fun of his hometown—he was funny on vacations and usually refrained from spanking the kids. The kids rewarded him by laughing every time he said, "big bridge," and laughed more when he yelled, "I ran over a skunk!" when he passed gas in the car. Edith wasn't laughing along though, this time.

When they got to Amherst, dad yelled "fill'er up," and ordered everybody to the latrine. The old black man putting the gas in the Ford Fairlane was thin, gaunt, and looked like he had been working there for 100 years. Dad was happily looking around at the place—it was the Midway, the place he had worked as a soda jerk and 18-wheeler parker 25 years prior.

Miles, who was trying to pee the old brown spots off the inside of the toilet, to no avail, was the first one back to the car. The daughters peed together and piled in the car next, and Edith was last. Something was wrong. With dad still reminiscing around his old haunt, Edith couldn't keep quiet anymore and told the kids about the hug she got from Walter when they were leaving Bolckow. As Walter released the hug, he raked his right hand across her left breast. "It wasn't a mistake," Edith said, "he almost grabbed it." Edith was obviously shaken and none of the kids could believe it but knew it was true. They were creeped out, like when thinking about their parents having sex but worse. Dad jumped back into the car talking about his glory days working at the Midway, not noticing the silent tension. "They paid me 50¢ a day," he smiled as the whole family stared straight out the front windshield and dad hit the road again. Edith immediately lit a cig.

The kids voted to go to the Grand Canyon but they were already in Colorado and the Royal Gorge was closer so to there they blazed a trail with Camel smoke streaming out of both front windows. The kids stared in silence as Edith crawled on her belly across a flat rock and stuck her head over the edge to look at the thread of blue 100 stories below. There were no ropes, no rules, and no one else dared to peer at death so certainly.

Their next station was Fort Ord in Monterey California from fiscal 1962 to 1963. They finally coasted up to this vacant officer's house—with *no steps*—on Salerno Drive. All Edith's furniture was in place, plus an army issue TV and a refrigerator with some food in it. Everybody ate something then took the bedsheets from the boxes to make up the beds, and in the morning, they watched Captain Kangaroo over Wheaties and whole milk. They then remembered that the smell of the beach had dominated their dreams. The Pacific smelled different than the Atlantic, and they couldn't wait to frolic in the warm waves so everybody piled into the Ford. It wasn't a dream come true. The ocean was cold in the summer—the odd, austere beach was almost deserted—and the people who *were* there had matching towels.[8] (joke) The 17-mile drive along the beautiful coast was more to their liking—looking at animals they didn't know existed. They played *kick the can* at night because this was the first place they'd lived where the temperature was the same, day or night.

Occasionally Edith didn't have to heat up those Swanson TV Dinners and sometimes even on a school night they'd pile into the car and go for some fried chicken or something. Dad, unenthralled about spending money, silently took the wheel. Electra slammed the car door on her brother's fingers as he held the centerpiece to climb in the back, this was the 2nd time it had happened, and nobody suspected these were anything but accidents.

Foggy Monterey was crawling with snails and long, steep, slippery ice-plant hills to slide down, ruining the kid's clothes with permanent green stains. Between buying clothes (Edith dressed them well) and spending a day at Disney Land the family damn near went broke. One rare sunny afternoon, dressed to the nines, they went to visit Dad's cousin Herb Miller. The rich, smiling musician had a fancy house and meeting their first celebrity was a pure, subdued excitement, as a good military family would have it. Edith had a ball though—she always seemed to have more fun than anybody else. Even when she hosted, she tossed out the rules, and had her own party. With everybody sitting attentively in the spacious living room, Herb proceeded to tell the family a *story* about World War II when a commoner was arrested in England for calling Winston Churchill an "idiot." The parliament pleaded with Churchill to release the commoner on free speech grounds and Winston said: "I understand but his crime was giving away state secrets during a time of war." This quote is probably apocryphal but the parent's laughter informed everybody it was a joke, and, that she and her hubby were the only ones who got it. Herb and his brother Glenn were part Scottish and dad's 3rd cousins (1/128th related) but could have been mistaken for his brothers. They all had that *no nonsense,* unphased Harry Truman look.

Though both Millers were famous jazz musicians the more famous Glenn had disappeared during a European concert tour in World War II, flying around playing for the troops and leading his new band. He had left his civilian orchestra back in New York, abandoned his Army band, and started the first all-star 50-piece Army-Air Force band. They were heading to newly liberated Paris and everybody was "in the mood."[9] The day they turned up missing a US bomber pilot was dumping his bombs into the

English Channel—after a cloudy mission to Germany—and his belly gunner saw one of the bombs clip a wing from a civilian plane below them, heading the other way. It was December 15, 1944 and Glenn Miller, the 40-year-old patriot, ended up in Davy Jones' Locker.

On average, siblings have ½ similar genes, halfsiblings ¼, 1st cousins 1/8th, 2nd cousins 1/32nd, and so on. Biologically speaking, like animals we will sacrifice 20 increments of our own happiness if it helps a sibling by 41 increments of happiness. It must be greater than half for us to selfishly rationalize an efficient sacrifice. We will sacrifice 10 increments of our happiness to help a halfsibling by 41 increments, 5 increments to help a first cousin by 41 increments, and so on—all other things being equal.[10] Our children and siblings each have half of our genes so why are the children more important than siblings? Children are nature's top tier because we get to choose both sets of genes and they haven't lived their lives yet.

Edith had all Glenn's records—none of Herb's—and when hubby wasn't home, she put the needle on and turned up the heat. With the exception of dad this wasn't a problem because Edith's kids had been baptized in music since leaving the maternity ward, and how. Those melodies, plus the Duke Ellington and Count Basie albums that shook the walls of the house, were the only instrumentals the kids had ever heard. "Why don't they have words in them?" they would ask Edith, having already learned all the Chairman of the Board's lyrics by heart. "I don't know," Edith said. The kids—ages 9, 13,14, and 15 now—found out adults didn't know everything. Dad had never let on to that juicy piece of information.

Edith's family had made it all the way across the country in a seat beltless Ford (NY to CA) and the military brats were becoming quite aware of the world outside of themselves. They had all gone to look for America[11] and the last thing on their minds was they were about to go on a trip around the world, because the parents hadn't told them yet, which reminds me of something I forgot. When they were driving across America the beautiful at 80mph a creepy thing happened. Screaming down Eisenhower's toll-free turnpikes, Electra was sitting in the middle of the back seat for a change, leaning forward and stroking her dad's hairy right arm. Her eyes turned to the rearview mirror and she noticed dad's eyes were closed. "Are you asleep?!" she yelled. He jerked and opened his eyes with the car still heading straight between the little white lines. Everybody nearly had a stroke thinking what could have been so Edith took over the driving after Electra saved the day. It was if all the life had been sucked out of the car but they knew they'd dodged 1 bullet. As Edith drove, she couldn't stop having daymares of horrible car wrecks. Her mind could go anywhere. She would vividly imagine one of her kids getting ejected from the car and landing in the churning blades of an international harvester wheat separating machine.

Dad—the civil-electrical, soon to be nuclear engineer—asked the kids a question right after the scary incident, mainly to lighten things up: "How long do you think those white lines are running down the middle of the freeway?" They seemed so short, ripping by at 70 mph now. The older girls guessed 3 feet, or 5 feet. Everybody guessed but Edith, Mary, and Miles—they didn't care how long the white lines were. "More d'nat," Jim finally said (*more than that* in Missoura talk) "they are 10 feet long." "Oh my gosh," Rachel gushed, "are they really daddy?" She was still trying to bump Electra back a notch in the daddy admiration department. "Oh, you betcha," he replied, pursing his lips. The girls were astounded by the optical illusion and couldn't believe how smart he was. He was back in control. Later, away from the parents, Electra told her siblings to stop calling them "mommy and daddy." She changed it to "dad" and "mother" and most of her siblings obeyed.

Dad, the obvious boss, was so careful about showing favorites because all the kids worshipped him so the very smart Electra decided to crack that code and become his favorite by emulating him. She would repeat over and over, "I wish I was a boy, I wish I was a boy, I wish…"and decided she would try to become a perfect copy of dad.

With dad always at work Edith's daytime world worked pretty well and she hated to spank them—if you could call it that—but when the kids fought, exhausted Edith would tell her hubby at 1730. He would spank them immediately and usually spank all 4 of them just to make sure. Electra kind of admired the purity of that method, so the other 3 kids didn't realize that Electra gradually assumed dad's position until 1730 when he came home. Things changed a bit. Rachel and Mary capitulated and began obeying her backroom commands, and Electra added some enforcement too. Electra was afraid of nothing, not even slimy things and would chase her sisters with worms or snails or anything gooey she found moving on the ground. She would mash them into their hair—it wasn't exactly *the sisterhood of the travelling pants*—and Rachel ended up with a lifetime fear of worms. Electra never would open her own can, having learned from the best. Electra became the daddy's girl, Miles became the mama's boy, and Mary had long been the grandparent's favorite. Helen and Jesse called her "Little Mary Ellen." Electra was dad's favorite but Miles was looking like Edith's favorite and Electra wanted both. Frustrated, she never could establish herself vice president of the family.

The 3 girls had learned to water ski before Miles was born but dad had sold that ski boat before moving to West Point. Dad wasn't all discipline, he had a good side, and when he got promoted to California Captain he of course bought another ski boat. In the summer they went water skiing on the weekends and the kids learned to ignore the cold California water. They didn't camp at the dock with everybody else, they would load everything up into the boat and go find a remote place on the lake to set up shop. Edith set up her painting easel on a large, flat rock near the shore, and the 4 kids skied endlessly. In 2 ways now, Dad was quite the happy "Capm," as they say in Missoura.

Back at home Edith got the bad news and had to make a few trips back to Missoura where her mother was fighting cancer in a St. Louis hospital. The cancer won when Helen was only 57. When

Edith returned to Monterey, she was a person the kids didn't know. "She's the only person who ever loved me," Edith sobbed, sitting in the kitchen with black mascara running down her face. Her sentence and her scary face put everybody, even hubby, on edge. They saw the weight of a mother's unconditional love and its loss—forever. Edith's helpless vulnerability was a fragility that made them squirm and a breakability they never wanted to feel. Each of the kids had the same haunting thought: what if nobody ever loves me like my mother does? It's a worry, or a blessing if you're lucky with a mother as they were but they couldn't grasp why she didn't stay strong and hide her emotions as you were supposed to.

True for antebellum mothers as it was for the lost generation, nobody gave Helen credit for her life but Edith—Helen reproduced, died and was forgot. Helen was cherished by a cult of one.

Edith retired to her bedroom and her mind went back to that morning she gave birth to Miles. She remembered thinking, "I finally have a boy," as their oxytocin levels shot up and they bonded into each other's eyes. The ordeal was over but she remembered getting quite upset when the army nurse whisked young Miles off to some other room, and Edith, exhausted, stared at the other nurse. "Your boy is fine," the nurse snapped—1950's style. Edith barely smiled and the morphine took her further back to that wonderful senior year she had with her boyfriend Miles in high school. "I wonder if he's still in New York? I wonder how his marriage is going?" she whispered, "I wonder how many kids he has?" "How many kids does *who* have?" nurse Ratched[12] barked. "Miles," said Edith. "None," the nurse snapped, "he's only 5 minutes old." Edith laughed at the memory and consoled herself knowing that her mother had gotten to spend so much time with her kids and started feeling a little better.

Edith and hubby finally told the kids where they were going next, Ankara Turkey. The kids had no idea what to think. The parents had learned to speak fluent Turkish at the Foreign Language Institute in Fort Ord as preparation to be good ambassadors and despite Edith missing so many classes because of Helen's sickness, she could speak better Turkish than hubby. Halloween night was especially a scream as the parents would speak only Turkish to the trick-or-treaters: "Hoşgeldiniz," Edith would say in Turkish, meaning *welcome*. "The least you can do is stay for dinner," dad would say in Turkish and pull off a rare crack-up of the whole family.

They sold the 2nd ski boat and headed to Ankara, the capital, for a 3-year stint—and no TV. That summer of 1963, the 4 kids thought the world was ending but it turned out they didn't even miss the "idiot box" as dad called it. On the way to Turkey the army splurged a bit and the family got a shotgun tour of London, Rome, and Vienna. They walked through the bloody Tower of London and went to a live performance of *Oliver Twist*. In macho Rome, the 3 daughters got generous one-sentence offers for sex, in English, from skinny Italian boys standing and smoking by the Coliseum. In beautiful Vienna they walked around during a layover only to re-board another army propeller plane headed for Turkey. The planes were rough, loud, and the kids had filled up several brown paper air-sickness bags by the time they landed in Ankara at dusk.

Edith's family was held up for hours on the main highway from the Ankara airport because of a massive wreck. A speeding car had hit the back of a large cart full of firewood, pulled along by 2 oxen. The cart had no taillights and there wasn't much left of either vehicle. They finally drove slowly past the wreck way past dinnertime. The oxen were crumpled, bloody and dead as well as the cart driver and the passenger sitting in the suicide seat of the car. Edith said she saw a half of a man's head with an ear intact laying in the road but she was very upset. Nobody else saw it. She was probably thinking, "oh, God, I'm taking my 4 children to a 3rd-world country and we're all gonna get murdered!" And it was she who wanted to go to Turkey the most. At least that old daymare she used to have of one of her kids getting ejected from a vehicle and landing in a wheat separating machine wasn't possible in this backwards country. At midnight they finally reached the Merhaba Hotel, meaning "Hello" Hotel, where civil servants and military families stayed for a short while until finding an apartment. The kids were woken at 630 to the Muslim call to prayer and were treated again that afternoon to first *Yankee Go Home* protests in Turkey. It was 1963.

The family checked into the 3rd floor of the Hello Hotel and hubby immediately took a bus to the motor pool to pick up their freshly delivered 1957 green and white Ford Fairlane. Days later they found a large apartment in Ankara (on the 3rd floor) in a Turkish neighborhood, 1 block from the Russian embassy. The kids were well schooled on the evils of the Russian empire and the embassy looked daunting—or maybe it was in their minds—with 25-foot-high vertical slats making up the mile-long perimeter fence. From the photos Edith took it looked similar to the partial wall between Mexico and the US today. At least they were out of downtown where the alarm clock went off at 630 from way up in those minarets that dotted Ankara like slender skyscrapers. "Those people who don't drink sure get up early," thought Edith.

Exotic as Turkey was, they lived in little America, with several department stores on base, American schools, an Olympic size swimming pool with a 3-meter diving board, and groceries at the PX (Post Exchange). A *Nancy Drew* or *Hardy Boy* book was a dollar and a Turkish *One Day the Hodja* book—the teacher with a Yogi Bera sense of humor—book was even less. In downtown Ankara the American theatre had the first *Pink Panther* movie and Edith enjoyed the idiot genius's deadpan humor more than the rest of the audience combined. Having never seen the classics, they also watched *Ben Hur* and *The 10 Commandments* in the geographic center of Islamic Turkey.

There were plenty of American families in the area, Air Force and Army, averaging 3-5 kids each so there were countless kids to frolic and rumble with. The parents were fearless of this exotic world so the kids were too and ran around Turkish neighborhoods night and day unsupervised. Back then parents didn't worry much—America was king, and evil seemed to be taking a wait and see attitude. One night though, Edith's 4 kids were walking down a main boulevard and an older Turkish man, walking the other way, grabbed the youngest of the 3 girls, Mary. He French kissed her, then just kept walking on by, and the 4 kids kept walking too, in shock, as it slowly dawned on them this was their first encounter with sexual abuse. Maria got over it quickly. The kids had been brazened with a hard shell and had also adopted the macabre side of life from Edith, which they turned into a form of entertainment.

9-year-old Miles came home with a new Turkish friend one night when the parents were out at the Officer's Club, and strangely, there were no lights on in the apartment but a flashlight was propped up in a plant shining into the master bedroom. The 2 boys crept down the hall and looked into the room. 1 sister was laying in the floor with her feet sticking half under the bed. The other 2 girls were sprawled in motionless, broken figures across the floor and had ketchup smeared around their necks! The boys screamed and sprinted back to the front door but only the Turkish boy made it outside. Miles hit a Turkish rug at the front door and slid on the magic carpet into the living room, crashed into a coffee table, and broke Edith's new Turkish lamp. The 3 girls came running out laughing, turned the lights back on, and Miles started laughing nervously too but the laughing abruptly stopped. All knew what was coming next because there was no way to hide that broken lamp. Everybody got spanked—corporal punishment style again—and they never saw the Turkish boy again. Imagine if that was his only experience with Americans.

Imagine no TV, no cellphones, no nothing, and finding the world as it is and what it could be. On weekends, when the parents slept in, instead of going to separate rooms the 4 kids would congregate on the biggest bed and pretend it was a raft floating in the middle of the ocean. Oddly, dad hadn't spanked Miles through the tender years but he was getting a *whoopin'* regularly now so finally everybody was in the same boat. They fantasized that they were lost at sea and their parents were dead, like in so many Disney Movies. In reality, they had to be super quiet because the weekends were the only time the parents could sleep in, adding to the tension. It was scary fun, so much so that every second counted as they conjured up the most drastic scenarios possible and tried to figure out how to survive. The fun was intense—knowing you're stranded but not alone—and the bonds between them were never greater than inside those moments. Time had stopped and they were all going to live forever. They never saw a ship, they never got rescued and didn't want to be; all they wanted was to see water in every direction, for the scary game to never end, and for the parents to not wake up.

There were always lots of stray cats in Turkey. Kemal Atatürk, the father of modern Turkey, was secular but he got a little wishy-washy on his death bed in 1938 and told his people he would be reincarnated into a cat. Since Atatürk's disclosure, cats have had the run of the country because no one would cull the herd, thinking it might be him, so dozens of cats collected in the alleys between the buildings every night. The kids would go so sleep to the bloodcurdling sounds of catfights, as if they needed more color and richness to their nightmares. Edith, unconcerned about all that, decided it might be high time to replace—not replace, you know, but move on from—Spotty Ann Feisty.

A few days later Edith had to run out and buy cat food because Allah had heard her wish. A Turkish cat adopted her. The other people in the apartment building said the cat had been hanging around for about 2½ years so she gave the cat a Turkish name: Icki Buçuk (icky boo-chook, translation: 2½ in English). Calico Icki, with kind of a middle and last name, would sit calmly on the narrow 3rd floor railing of Edith's balcony waiting for that tiny cup of milk every day. She finally coaxed Icki into the warm house with the cat food and Icki became a fixture inside, as cats do. With the weekdays to herself Edith enjoyed talking to Icki, unaware that she was talking to herself. She would ask Icki's opinion about a painting or ask the cat if she thought somebody was rude and look at the cat for a second, but the cat, who never purred or even meowed, would just lay there staring at Edith. Icki thought Edith was a likeable nut but Icki had not seen anything yet. In the final year in Turkey, Icki would develop a maniacal fear of Edith and for very good reason (Chapter 16).

The kids came in from playing in 4 feet of snow and were introduced to their first pet ever—Icki! The kids thought cats were icky anyway and would have killed to have a dog but now they had a cat named Icki. Dad didn't like the cat right off the bat and frowned right through Icky, as his jaundiced eye returned to finish scanning the grocery receipt to see what the cat food had cost. She had purchased olives for her martinis, 2 bottles of ketchup, and the cat food. "Ick might be Atatürk," he said, and with that sarcastic statement the kids threw reincarnation off the list of possibilities but you know who didn't. "You never know, you know," she'd say.

At the end of the first year in Turkey, 1963, the kids were moaning about having to go to bed when Edith got the call from the US that President Kennedy had been assassinated. It wasn't a good Friday night bedtime story. The next night Dad told the family about the ready nuclear missiles the US had in Turkey.

The US stationed military families in Turkey to improve international relations with the Turks. Uncle Sam had 15 Jupiter missiles in western Turkey (near Izmir, managed by the Army) and 50 small nukes in southern Turkey at Incirlik Air Force base.[13] The smaller ones could be dropped by little F-104 fighter jets on Russian cities in minutes. The F-104 looks like a dolphin, with those tiny fins on the sides, and at a party one US Air Force pilot bragged about flying his little fighter-bomber 1 mile into Russian territory, then hightailing it out. 100 US airmen or so were shot down and killed during the cold war—some in China but most in Russia,[14]—and by the time Barbie came alive in 1959, the US could fastpitch Russia with nukes, Turkey being right on the border.

Since the US government was always broke, this massive military buildup was floated on credit and Russia financed theirs likewise, impoverishing that serfdom in the east more than it did the aspiring classless society in the west.

In 1962, Russia installed dozens of nuclear warheads in Cuba and after all the secrecy, lies, and ruminations, the missiles are still there in Cuba and Turkey. Other than needing routine maintenance, or occasional upgrading, a nuke has a very long shelf life and any Cuban American will tell you that the missiles are still there—the genius of the masses is usually right.

Recently RFK Jr said that his "uncle [JFK] had made a secret deal with the Russian ambassador to the US, a man surnamed Dobrynin, to remove the missiles in Turkey and Cuba."[15] Nothing of the sort was done. The deep state that JFK inherited was so unafraid of war with Russia, having a hefty temporary nuclear advantage, and so afraid of a future Russia, they considered it hypothetically prudent to sacrifice some US cities. An old Russian General who was stationed in Cuba during the crisis, said on PBS in about 2016 that if the US attacked Cuba again, he was under orders to pepper the eastern seaboard with 80 nukes—probably far above their capacity at the time. Since the Russian government lies for a living, we can guess we would have lost about 10-20 cities and the cold war would have been over.

After Eisenhower's imperialism light in Southeast Asia, and the botched invasion of Cuba, JFK poured cold water on the CIA's eagerness to reinvade Cuba. Worse for the deep state, JFK was contemplating either keeping only the small team of advisors on the ground in Vietnam or pulling out completely and this alarmed the American warlords. According to historian Ken Hughes, who listened to the white house tapes, JFK was planning an unpopular full pullout, including financial support, right after his reelection in 1964. In 1963 JFK and defense secretary Robert McNamara began a documented process to pull all US personnel out by the end of the year or so. Oddly, this known information has been ignored along with corroborating statements JFK made to friends about his wishes.[16] He was still hemming and hawing about helping South Vietnam and saving America's face after almost 3 difficult years in office, however, he was the first president I can think of who wanted self-determination for any country in that region. He wished for the sovereignty and autonomy of all countries, saying, "here in this hemisphere and we hope around the world." Was he saying let civil wars stay civil wars? The industrial military complex, the hegemonic politicians, and their bankers couldn't take that risk. There were loans, the biggest to date, already sitting neatly stacked on huge mahogany tables, and war profits to be made.

There was so much deficit spending and lending on the chopping block that the deep state responded with the inhouse assassination of JFK. After the CIA had deemed JFK a threat to national security and later altered the Zapruder film to show no 2nd shooter, they happened to fall in love with LBJ, [17] who capitulated or at least agreed with them to ramp up the Vietnam War. After the CIA's multiple failed attempts to kill Fidel Castro but succeeding with many regime changes by the same method, and later claiming Salvador Allende of Chile had committed suicide by shooting himself in the back, the ensuing coverup of the 1st US president assassinated in 62 years proved too elaborate. The CIA had long been allowed secrecy without oversight and became pros, like the Russian liars, and the shooting star was gone before most knew he was one.

Lee Harvey Oswald, who knew people at the FBI and had paid a visit to their office, [18] as well as having visited the Russian Embassy in Mexico City, took the rap. I think the federal police knew when he would try to shoot Kennedy and let him. There we so many power players who wanted JFK gone. He had already enraged bankers by ordering silver certificates—a currency that would have competed with their Federal Reserve Note—and with Cuba, the US military, and the Mafia involved too, it was essentially the *Murder on the Orient Express* where everyone on the train was a bit in on it. Jackie Kennedy sensed that the worst had happened and moved her whole family out of America the beautiful to Greece.

In 1964, China tested their first nuke. That raised the number to 5 countries with nukes, after the US, Britain, France, and Russia. Then sadly, the pressure of the 1970s cold war prompted Russia to give India nukes. Next, an Indian Muslim, Dr Abdul Khan who worked with classified material in Europe, stole nuclear secrets from the west and smuggled them into Pakistan. China and Libya helped Pakistan from there to make nukes, and Khan later sold those same secrets to Iran. The smart money now is on China having a couple hundred nukes, Iran/N. Korea having a few each and Indian/Pakistan having a few hundred. The US has a couple thousand and Russia has a few more than that.[19] Israel made their own 100 nukes *they say*. On a lighter note, let's take a peek at the quixotic Republic of Turkey and the unfathomed recovery it made after the collapse of the Ottoman Empire.

Mustafa Kemal Atatürk

Atatürk the army officer had joined the Young Turk rebellion in 1908, forcing the Sultan Vahdettin to partially reinstate constitutional government. This event began a chain reaction and the beset Vahdettin would be the last ruler of Turkey and the Ottoman Empire. In Ottoman Africa, Atatürk held the Italians off at Tobruk (now Benghazi) until finally losing it in 1912, and in 1914, the hard-drinking officer was promoted to Lieutenant Colonel. Vahdettin allied with Nazi Germany at the start of WWI and though western armies were pushing the Turks out of the Baltics and North Africa, Atatürk, to no avail, vocally opposed Turkey's alliance with Kaiser Wilhelm II.

By 1915 Atatürk was a General and revered for fighting off the British, Australians, and New Zealanders at Gallipoli (meaning *beautiful city*) stopping the allies from annexing the only entrance to the Sea of Marmara from which the British navy could flank the Germans and of course Russia if necessary. Surely, Nicholas II and Vladimir Lenin quietly thanked the Turks though Russia was allied with Britain. Atatürk, practicing homeland security, lost ¼ of a million soldiers in the Dardanelle victory and almost that many commonwealth soldiers died in the failed assault. Atatürk was protecting his nearby capital, Izmir, and his Bosporus too (the gateway to the brackish Black Sea) which is just 300 klicks northeast of where the British invasion point was. The young Winston Churchill was responsible for the debacle at Gallipoli and in 1921 Atatürk was promoted to commander of the Turkish armed forces.

After the Turkish parliament finally ousted Sultan Vahdettin, Mustafa Kemal Atatürk became Turkey's president in 1923. Winning generals were all the rage back then but he was far more—he was the JFK of the Middle East. Atatürk moved the capital inland from Istanbul to Ankara—his west coast having been an historical hot bed for sea invasions—and instituted compulsory education throughout the country. Historians tell us that he read the US constitution (fewer than 12 pages back then) and astonishingly introduced "separation of church and state" to Turkey, then gave women all individual rights—voting and divorcing too—when the "countries" to his east didn't have elections. He sensed, knowing how rich the US had gotten, that these non-monetary principles would play out unseen in making Turkey the wealthiest country in the area by freeing up families and businesses. He had already surprised everybody with his military victories, surprised us again by starting a democracy, and he did something much more difficult than expanding an empire: he *decompressed* the defunct Ottoman Empire to within the borders of Turkey. To this day Africa is still religiously split in half at the equator. Because of the Ottoman invasion, the top half (the *maghrib*) has about ½ billion Muslims and the bottom half has about ½ billion Christians.

Under Kemal Atatürk's watch, Turkey—perfectly sculpted with the best beachfront in the Middle East—went from an ageless international trade center to a modern one. After free speech, free trade grew exponentially, especially off the west coast of Turkey and Atatürk earned his legacy as the father of Turkey for reasons many didn't connect. He could be quirky too and with Turkey's long history of fighting Greece and Russia he outlawed the fez hat.

He didn't absorb everything in the US constitution.

From the cradle of human organization, the Tigris and Euphrates rivers send their ancient messages southeast from Antalya (now Türkiye—Turkey) flowing through Iraq and finishing into the Persian Gulf at the Iran Iraq border. From this Islamic throttlehold the modern "Kemal" (now that we're on a first name basis) decided to shock everybody and create a republic. He announced a secular Turkey and told his surprised fans that he was ending jihad (crusade, war struggle) and caliphate. A Caliph is an Arab leader, next in line for power, and a modern caliphate is a revenge killing, or killing one or more infidels (non-believers in Islam). Kemal dispensed with all that, at least in practice.[20] His announcements stirred uneasy murmurs among the fast-evolving Turks but their hero-worship reassured them, probably because 1 person had philosophically modernized the whole country. Kemal had a dark side too and was mysteriously vague about 3 massacres by his own people: the Kurdish in the southeast of Turkey, the Greeks in the west, and the Stalin-style extermination of the Christian Armenians in the east. Rumors still swirl that Kemal's mother was Jewish and maybe the cover rumor is Kemal and mom later converted to Islam.

I was reading a great book online (too cheap to buy it) about Kemal's Jewish roots when it suddenly vanished from the internet. The current Turkish president, *Sultan* Tayyip Erdoğan is destroying everything Kemal did. Erdoğan has personally banned thousands of books, safeguarded the banning of the phrase *Armenian Genocide*, and vanquished freedom of speech in Turkey. Suffice to say Erdoğan stole the #1 slot from China with the most journalists in prison—over 200—and you might prefer a Mexican prison to a Turkish one. Tayyip created hyperinflation for his people, banned Wikipedia for 3 years, outlawed the buying of crypto currency, and jailed many for insult/thought crimes.[21] (I love Wikipedia and for certain quick checks of verifiable events, or science, it is accurate.)

A Pilgrimage into the Middle East

In 1964 the indistinct democrats, Edith and her rock-ribbed hubby, decided to switchover and vote for the anti-inflation, states' rights guy Barry Goldwater. After a couple predinner martinis at the Officer's Club, Edith would tell the military wives, "remember ladies, republicans vote on Tuesday and democrats vote on Wednesday." Missoura Edith liked Barry saying "the left coast and the right coast are draining the middle," and probably didn't know he was a warmonger, but the incumbent LBJ smashed Goldwater anyway. Barry was going to stop deficit spending as so many conservatives had tried, and shortly after Barry, the prototype of the fiscal conservative almost went extinct. The kids too went from democrat to republican as the entire south did, taking every Dixiecrat with them. Eisenhower winning half the south in 1952 was the spark that would become a political transformation of almost biblical proportions.

As a warm up to their pilgrimage through the Middle East, Edith's family camped at Göreme—a strange but natural area in Turkey with a multitude of high pyramid shaped sandstone towers connected by catacombs of tunnels carved underneath. The Christians had laboriously built the tunnels to hide out from the Romans 2000 years ago, hid there from the Ottoman Empire in the next millennium, and again during the Armenian genocide in 1915. The historical site was deserted and the family had their run of the enchanted, haunted Göreme.

In Istanbul they visited the Topkapi Palace and the Blue Mosque, where the kids got a talking to because they were running around the place like it was a playground. With those thick Persian rugs Edith was collecting, they felt like they were at home. From the Mosque on the hill the kids could see a US aircraft carrier silently moving up the Bosporus.

In Greece the family walked up the rocky hill to the Acropolis to watch the light show at the Parthenon. Beautiful loud music echoed from the outcropping as a narrator told the story of the sacred Pheidippides, who had run 300 miles to inform his people of a Persian attack. 500 years before Christ he saved the empire then dropped dead and the girls learned that if you absolutely had to, you might be able to run 300 miles. Miles just figured the telephone system in Greece was broken at the time.

They vacationed in the port of Izmir in the west and Adana on the southern coast of Turkey, where dad, who never needed to go to the doctor, fell ill. His food poisoning kept him in the hospital for a week and the kids hung out at the Olympic size pool on the military base there, not worrying enough because only Edith knew he almost died. He came out of the hospital skinnier than ever, they dodged another bullet, and the family headed back to Ankara. The Ford Fairlane cut out just outside of Adana and everyone silently panicked as dad watered down the thirsty radiator, screwed a hot spark plug back in, and limped to a nearby repair shop. A Turkish mechanic threw the stuck thermostat on the floor without replacing it, replaced 7 of the sparkplugs but couldn't unscrew the one dad, fresh out of the hospital, had torqued in.

On the next trip they visited the sight of Gordian's Knot—put there by Gordius, father of King Midas—and nobody could untie that mess to win the emperorship of Asia (Asia's *Sword in the Stone*). Supposedly Alexander the Great slashed the knot in half with 1 whack of his sword and from there the most winning quarterback did savagely inherit the better part of Eurasia. This Macedonian took over Persia, even part of India and Asia, then took Jerusalem back from the Muslims around 330 BC. He died very young, in 323 BC in fact, because the years were going backwards at the time.

On the way back to Ankara Edith stopped at the little villages to take pictures of huts and falling apart barns. While the Turkish men relaxed and drank tea in the afternoon there were usually *8 maids a milking* in the fields, some of them pregnant. Upper body strength still made the decisions about who did what and the Turkish men all wore sweatpants that sagged down to the knees in the middle so the family jewels wouldn't get too warm. For their reputation as "the best fighters in the world" they were strikingly non-violent and the Muslims rarely drank alcohol but they would do anything for an American cigarette. Turkish men would touch their mouth with their first 2 fingers so Edith would crank down the window slightly and stick a cigarette through the crack. The cig was destroyed in a second as they all grabbed for it. Turkish women never smoked or drank however they had an arm signal not unlike the Italian one, only better.

The 3rd year in Turkey Edith and hubby were down to their bottom dollar. Still filled with wanderlust, they carefully planned a month-long vacation through the Middle East and sold everything they could, even toys, to afford the trip. The kids learned how to create a quick emergency fund but it wasn't enough. Edith was afraid to ask her dad Jesse for a loan so her husband borrowed $400 from his farmer parents and the family of 6 climbed into their 1957 Ford Fairlane to see the Holy Lands for themselves.

In 1965 there was one traffic light in the capital city, Ankara, and the locals would carefully demolition derby their way through it from all directions. As the family got south of town, they found themselves going back in time. The villages looked more biblical, with small mud huts, sheep, oxen, skinny cats, and goats hanging by their back legs from a lone tree, draining from the neck into a bucket. Toilet paper was unheard of and the typical village toilet was a 4-inch circular hole in the ground with 2 elevated foot-shaped places to stand on and squat down.

After staring at the free nativity scenes dotting southern Turkey and taking more photos of bleak village life they arrived at the border of Syria. They took their place in line with a thousand cars and trucks. The delay was caused by soldiers inside the checkpoint beating the hell out of a Syrian border agent who had let somebody through they didn't like. Dad and Miles were now standing in line clutching the 6 passports and watching as they dragged the agent into another room to beat him some more. The one American family finally made it through and arrived late at their hotel in historic Aleppo. They looked at so many ancient, crumbling, absurdly expensive marble palaces (ruins) the next day that everybody was sick of ruins except Edith and she already had to buy more film which surprisingly was on sale everywhere.

They raced deeper into Syria on fairly good roads but the kids got motion sickness again, and the vomit had to go out the window. There were few "latrine stops"—as dad called them—so whenever Edith asked, "does anybody need to tinkle?" nobody said a word. Nobody wanted to be the wimpy soldier who made dad stop. On the road to Damascus, the capital, they gassed up for 28¢ a gallon and Edith talked the kids out of going into the bathroom. They started stopping on the right shoulder, opening up both right passenger doors for cover, and squatting between them. Strangers whipping by could see the bottom curve of their little white butts just under the door. The Turks were white too and on the long drive south the skin began turning olive, then a little darker, as it dawned on them that they were in Semite country.

Entering Damascus in 1965, they learned that they had just missed the 2 bodies hanging from the town square. If caught stealing they would cut off your hands and if convicted of things worse they would hang you. Edith's entourage crashed in a hotel, woke up refreshed, and breakfasted continental style with eggs and fantastic bread rolls. Miles didn't like the eggs, they had a different smell, and Edith said, "if you don't like eggs, you're neurotic." Oh, God, the boy thought," "if it isn't one thing it's your mother." And Edith took that opportunity to remind the kids yet again: "your tonsils will need to be removed one day, but you'll get to eat ice cream!" which never happened. After those appetizing conversations they followed her down a crowded street with dad taking up the rear. The family kept close together because the parents had been warned about "white slavery" and Edith was forced to explain forced prostitution of both kinds to the kids. The smells were even stranger as they made their way to the famous covered bazaar in downtown Damascus, called "suq" by Arabs.

Everything seems bigger when we're young and Edith wrote about the endless bazaar "covered with a massive, taught, canvas canopy 500 feet over their heads." They marveled at the thousands of tables covered with strange, inexpensive items, while the locals, especially the Syrian women, couldn't rip their eyes off the 6 aliens. Some merchants enticed them to their display with a wide smile, advertising their gold teeth with tiny crescents and stars engraved in them. They were proud of that wealth symbol because the largess of the Treasury was in King Hussein's bedroom. Edith was in her element, bargaining with the merchants fearlessly and coming away with some 1-of-a-kind conversation pieces—for almost nothing. She would offer them half what they were asking and walk away. After noticing that Edith was using American dollars, or smelling them, one merchant knew he was already ahead and said, "OK, take it and go!" A couple times she so underbid an artifact the Syrian merchant would take a deep breath, bite the back of his hand, and stare at the item as if it was about to start moving, while his wife was boring a hole through the item with her eyes as if to say, "put it back."

The bizarre was a show to remember and the one Edith wanted to see. From that little town in Missoura (as everybody in the family now pronounced it) and with her college major in history, this gypsy never dreamed she'd get to see anything like it. With hand-carved cooking tools, not seen in the US in hundreds of years, she took home some of Syria's best art, history, and utility. Her husband paid for everything, grimacing as he looked at the funnily shaped items.

They were "in a country where they turn back time,"[22] and time kept moving backwards as they drove further south. Although there were no signs of the US military anywhere south of Turkey, everybody but Edith was relieved as they crossed the Syrian border into Lebanon. She was too excited to have the fears that dogged her and never wanted the vacation to end. Called the "Paris" of the Middle East, Lebanon was a definite upgrade—Beirut residents could snow ski down the mountain or waterski in the Mediterranean. They got a spiffy hotel in the capital, Beirut, and met up with a Lebanese friend of a friend who had a ski boat. All the kids got to waterski in the Eastern Mediterranean which was choppy and warm—unlike the cold smooth California lakes. Exhausted, they went to dinner at the gracious Lebanese man's house. As the kids gobbled up the tasty fresh bread, they wondered why bread was always so much better in foreign countries than in the US. "Or does everything taste better on vacation?" they thought, "almost as good as camping!" Two days later in that summer of '65 they pushed further south into Jordan and to the kids, safe and cozy Turkey seemed a distant base. Ankara seemed to be slipping out of reach and the kids feared they may never see it again. They would have felt the same anxiety about TV but they had forgotten they had forgotten all about it.

After the collapse of the Ottoman Empire Jordan became yet another British protectorate called "Transjordan" until getting its independence in 1946. Edith described it as *magical* and she found an Arabic English-speaking guide who took them through all the biblical sites. They walked through Jericho (a small pile of rocks) and little Bethlehem, then walked the 12 stations marked out for Jesus's last day, with heavy cross and thorny headband, to Calvary. Those annoying Sunday mornings at Leavenworth Bible School finally paid off as the kids connected the history they'd learned with firsthand knowledge. They floated in the Dead Sea, created by the southern flow of the Jordan River, and had to sprint to the water through very hot sand, though there were buckets of water along the way. Most of Jerusalem was in Jordan then.

Though Israel was just over the Wailing Wall, they couldn't get in or point a camera in that direction because the Jordanian guide told them that there were many camouflaged guns facing the holy city. The family had no idea there were intermittent military skirmishes, or that authorities were rounding up Jews, or that a new Middle East war—when Egypt, Jordan, and Syria would sandwich attack Israel again—was less than 2 years away.

Jordan's King Hussein was trying to work things out with Israel when he bowed to pressure from Egypt and allowed Iraqi soldiers to amass in Jordan. What physically started the 1967 war was Israel wiping out the Egyptian Air Force, sparking the triple invasion, which Israel repelled then reoccupied Jerusalem after about a 635-year hiatus. June 5th, 1967 was the start of the war and exactly 1 year later, plus 1 day, Bobby Kennedy was murdered in the City of Angels by Syria's Sirhan Sirhan Jr.

On the way back to Turkey in 1965, they were gassing up again in Syria for 29¢ a gallon (American commodity inflation) when the kids saw it: a bright red Coke machine with a 5¢ slot. Edith and her husband rarely let the kids drink Coke but the kids got lucky that day, on top of all Edith's purchases. The first 3 kids dropped their nickels in and out came their 12-ounce Cokes. The second oldest, Electra, put her nickel in last and out popped a tiny 6-ounce Coke. The kids had never seen one before. The 6.5-ounce coke was introduced in 1916 but as Americans were doubling in size coke followed suit. Electra might have gotten the last 6-ouncer! What crap luck. She was livid, felt juked and just stared at it.

Back in the car she threw a fit as if she'd been cut out of the inheritance and dad made her pour the tiny Coke out onto the pavement. She continued complaining so bitterly that dad made his favorite child get out of the car and walk along the shoulder somewhere in the middle of Syria. He drove about 2 hundred yards past her and stopped. A minute later she caught up, got back in the car and didn't say another word. The other 3 kids chatted and laughed up a storm with their schadenfreude—aided by their sugar buzz—until the relentless rhythm of the wheels sang them to sleep. If they woke up grumpy, they fought in the back seat and had to dodge dad's righthand slapping blindly at anything he could hit while driving.

Follow the Money

Back in Ankara, good to be home, Edith found a magnificent handwoven Turkish rug that filled the spacious living room. With intricate black borders and her favorite reds mathematically woven through it, the rug was the envy of her friends and likely her favorite possession in life. These rugs are so resilient that Turkish rug makers lay them in the street so cars would break them in. They sold them as *Persian* rugs, to Americans anyway, but they were made in Turkey from an old family algorithm. Hubby called it "the $611 rug," so that was the title of Edith's next long letter to her parents. She wrote about the trip through the holy lands like she was reliving it and her writing was improving as was her oil-painting. And though her mother Helen had passed young, Edith kept writing to her about every single thing that happened. Till now, no one has read them but me.

Dad needed a bump in pay to accommodate her spending when he serendipitously became head of US construction in Turkey—the Captain of Industry—including work on those nuclear missile sites he rarely spoke of. Everybody knew he was building roads, airports, and bridges. He had his own plane with a pilot, co-pilot, and a mechanic but never took his family on it because he wouldn't waste a drop the government's gas. Where did those people go? He knew the hum of his own plane engine too and when his plane was flying over the now busy skies of Ankara without him, he knew it. Once in thick fog, he and crew prepared for a trip to Izmir in zero visibility. The pilot couldn't see anything in front of him so hubby squinted at the left edge of the runway, the co-pilot squinted at the right edge, and they guided the blind pilot down the runway and into the air. Using instruments, the pilot never lost the horizon and landed in Izmir 90 minutes later.

After 3 years of site construction the captain offered to give the Turkish government all his road making machinery so they could continue paving paradise. The Army would give them a fortune in machines and train them because shipping the equipment back home was more expensive than the machinery was worth. The Turks said they would take all the equipment but must levy a large tax on the Army for the transaction. Jim refused the offer, and dumped all of the machinery into the Mediterranean Sea. "Close enough for government work," he liked to say. He was promoted to Major in the Army Corps of Engineers—maybe they liked his style—and that Saturday night he threw a party, got stumbling drunk, and quit smoking cold turkey the next day at age 41—the same age his father Walter was when he started smoking.

With no nicotine he lost what little patience he had. The kids kept committing small misdemeanors anyway, and at 1730, when everybody including Edith appeared quite busy, the new Major arrived home and doled out the punishment for the day's "flimflam." He always used a belt for the "whippings" but there was a new twist: dad had a relapse or something and made the kids pull their underwear down to their ankles first and bend over the bed—even the teenage daughters. Edith thought it was too weird, started getting worried, and stopped telling him what the kids did wrong during the day as their 3rd year in Turkey came to a dramatic close. Better it may have been to tie them to the Whipping Post[23] than to mix violence with nudity on a bed.

Edith walked up 3 more floors from her 3rd floor flat and handed the landlord the last month's rent. He grinned and took the money without a word. Edith didn't like him. He stared at her boobs among other things with that unrepentant eye. He would grab kids, even hers, and hold them over the balustrade of the 35-foot-high entrance to the middle of the 6-story building, laughing his head off. He always said "how are you," twice when they happened to cross paths and Edith started answering, "asymptomatic," which shut him up. His name was Ahmet and she named her red pin cushion after him.

Years later she would reminisce about Turkey and Ahmet, every time she heard Guy Clark sing: "pack up all the dishes, make note of all good wishes, and say g'bye to the landlord for me, the sons-a-bitches always bored me." His song *LA Freeway* would loop without permission in her mind and kept reminding her that she'd left a piece of herself in Turkey. She couldn't figure out which piece but thought it had something to do with a dream she had. Her voodoo doll—her red pin cushion plaything—lived in the painting studio with the sewing stuff and she hadn't gone into that chamber for weeks. She had fallen asleep on the couch in there one odd morning and had the most bizarre dream (Chapter

15). After paying the rent she crept bravely back into her painting studio and started packing.

Edith gave poor Icki Buçuk to the childless couple 1 floor below—2 grownups who spent their evenings sitting silently in the living room. Dad sold the Ford Fairlane to a very excited, well-dressed Turkish man and the family flew back "stateside," as they say in the forces. The kids were caught between missing Turkey and kissing the tarmac as soon as they set foot onto terra firma in America the beautiful. Back then they rolled a staircase up to the door of the plane and you were walking on concrete in minutes.

The family stayed at Edith's childhood home in Missoura that spring. The kids had always loved the grandparents' house in Alton because Jesse, Edith's dad, still had that energetic little dog named Snapsy! (I forgot to mention Snapsy from their previous visit to Alton.) Not following Edith's tradition, her parents had only given Snapsy one name because they'd forgotten what Edith had taught them—"animals are people." The kids, who had been dogless since birth and were pissed about that, would have to wait 2 more years to get their own dog.

Before the traditional Easter Egg hunt Edith made the kids dressed up for formal photos as usual but there was sure something missing—Alton was a different place without Helen—and it would be the kid's last visit there. 18 years after Edith had left the safe and cozy little town of Alton it had remained impervious to the rapid change of the 1960s except for, of all things, a car. Edith's first cousin's daughter Linda drove up one afternoon in a spanking new 1964 and a half Ford Mustang—a $25,000 convertible—and all the kids got to ride in it.

Jesse, who had 3 businesses and never seemed to work much, would take the kids to his pharmacy/ice cream shop. On the first visit, after they had their just desserts, they piled back into his car and Jesse let the car idle for a minute. He advised them, "always let a cold car idle for a minute before driving it." Everybody sat there for 60 seconds in silence, and the kids told Edith that he never let the car idle again after that. Jesse also gave Miles a Ryder

BB gun and when Miles got back home 6 hours later, out of BBs, Edith would look at him and say, "hey stinker."

Cutting his spring vacation in half Edith's husband left Missoura and flew stand-by on a free military flight to buy a car in Florida where his sister Jean, an army nurse, lived with her car salesmen hubby "Smitty," and their 7 kids. Jean and Smitty were one of the pioneer working couples in the mid-60s and probably had to be with 7 kids. After selling cars in Bethesda Maryland, Smitty managed a Renault dealership called "Diamond Motors" in Miami and he talked the famous Larry Csonka of the Dolphins football team into being the dealership's spokesperson. Smitty was able to get his hands on one of the last of the discounted 1965 Chrysler Newports, with air-conditioning! It was one of the best cars ever made and crisscrossed the US for 2 decades, with seatbelts—but only in the front.

Edith's hubby drove his spanking white Newport from Florida straight to Missoura to pick up his domestics and they promptly headed southwest to El Paso Texas. Their new station was Biggs Field, formerly Biggs Air Force Base, and all their furniture was sitting there waiting. It was a 1-story ranch and their 2nd house with no steps! Little El Paso was buzzing in 1966 because Don Haskins, the new basketball coach at Texas Western, had shocked the nation—he won the national championship by starting 5 black players. The backroom rule then was you could only start 2. Haskins ignored that rule, squeaked by powerhouses Kansas and Kentucky who had nearly all white players, and changed college basketball forever.

On the way to El Paso, they happened through Stonewall Texas where LBJ had a Texas White House and ranch, when suddenly a white Lincoln Continental pulled out onto the highway right in front of the family. Everybody could see that Lyndon Baines Johnson was driving it. He was putting along, way below the speed limit, and sitting screwy in the seat for some reason, with one butt cheek higher than the other. They followed the president for a spell down Highway 290 with Edith and the kids shouting "pass him, pass him, so we can get a better look!" Dad wouldn't do it; he wouldn't pass his commander-in-chief. LBJ eventually turned off the highway while the carful chatted nonstop at the same time about seeing their 2nd celebrity.

I searched this and LBJ did have a white Lincoln Continental from 1964 until his death in 1973 and it was his favorite car. 3 years after JFK was shot in his black Lincoln Continental LBJ liked to go places by himself in his white one. Long after LBJ was sworn in aboard Airforce 1, I heard him say on TV, "I want a report of the number of people assigned to Kennedy and if mine [body guards] are not less [than Kennedy had] then I want less right quick." James Baker said "yessir." The secret service was pretty relieved after having to follow JFK to every girlfriend's apartment. LBJ had been plucked for vice president so JFK could win Texas in a paper-thin win against Nixon—as close as US elections are now.

LBJ ended up in the hotseat of history after a slow start. He skipped college after high school and went to California to sew his wildest oats. He went back home, graduated college, and started teaching, which I believe was to hone is oratory skills for the big things that were to come. This fast-talking Texan won a seat in congress at age 40 and inherited the white house at age 55. Long after his death his white Lincoln Continental was auctioned off in California and LBJ *did* have an operation in 1966 to repair an abdominal hernia. That's why he was sitting sideways as he drove. Edith's story is nonfiction.

CHAPTER 7

Saving Jim's Privates

Allow me to introduce you to Edith's husband, the indefatigable James Franklin (Franklin, middle name) 4 years her senior. The formal name of *James* is only for paperwork and signing things—his handle was Jim from the git go. You know him a bit, he is deep and strong, brave and true, and loyal to the end. As a stallion of his peer group and that fire down below, he put the family through a basic training of his own, raising the eyebrows of Edith, some of his greatest generation buddies too, and making others jealous. With *Guns and Roses* dispositions, Jim and Edith were the *Iron Butterfly* or the *Led Zeppelin* of the stereotypical 20th century American couple. The Great Depression, farming, the world wars, and being born a Scot had jaded Jim so his cynicism told him the wars would continue into the 21st century. He is right so far. He worked his butt off in case things went south so the family would never go hungry. This chapter is about Jim's rough growing up on his father Walter's farm and after we get past the pivotal year, 1969, you will know him like you know Edith.

Walter Joins the Army

The old letters say that Walter, Jim's Scottish father, was born in 1895 with some aristocratic blood coursing through his veins from his father Alex. Walter joined the army 20 years later. I couldn't how he was educated, you know, to become an officer, but he probably took a test, and he then volunteered to fly those 2-winged fighter planes for America in 1917. He trained with Squadron 1 at Love Field in Dallas Texas, trained with Squadron 30 at the University of Texas (where 4 of his grandchildren would go) and as a flying cadet he was promoted from 2nd to 1st Lieutenant in 1918. Walter was then dispatched to France with the 138th Aero Squadron of the 5th Pursuit Group. He trained on the Sopwith Camel, the French Caudron, the Dutch Fokker—wooden planes reinforced with 2 x 4s—and had too many photos of his buddies' planes after botched takeoffs.

When taking off, Walter had to learn to deal with the torque effect (Coriolis effect) where a quickly revving, clockwise spinning propeller (from the pilot's view) would make the plane yaw down and to the left. To avoid a Baptism of fire on their first try, from this strange magnetic field, pilots had to manipulate the plane up and to the right. Eventually engineers learned to trim the tail rudder 5° to the right on takeoff to counteract the Coriolis effect.

At the start of the world war most pilots shot at each other with pistols but Walter trained on a French 2-winged war plane (the *Nieuport*, Americans called it the "Newport") equipped with a single forward-facing machine gun synchronized to shoot harmlessly through the propeller. The Newports were so effective against the German's they copied a Newport they had shot down,[1] and the Germans re-perfected that synchronizing gun, that they had originally come up with, at the Fokker airplane factory.

In the 1800s the Germans (Prussians until 1871) won wars against Denmark, Austria, and France, saw those victories as productive, and thought WWI would be productive too. In the spring of 1914, the military officers from Britain, Whales, and Scotland thought otherwise and knew they would be back home "before the leaves fell." But from 1914-1918 naked aggression cost 20 million lives only to see the world ravaged by the Spanish Flu, taking 50 million more.

For most of WWI the US supplied war machines to Britain and

France which transferred most of their gold over to the US Treasury.[2] America then bought the Danish West Indies for $25 million in gold while their national debt rose almost 10-fold to $25 billion. The US began sending volunteer help to Europe in 1916 during the million casualties at the 16-month battle for Verdun in German occupied Belgium. In 1917 the US declared war on Germany. By 1918 the trench warfare had turned into a grueling stalemate, and exhausted, the walking wounded simply limped back home without victory or surrender. Russia and China were shunned at the treaty of Versailles, and Germany was only fined for war reparations. They printed paper money to pay the bill which destroyed their economy and cheated those they supposedly paid back. It was a shallow allied victory but for Germany it wasn't a *Farewell to Arms*—it was halftime—and no nation enforced the agreement that Germany not rebuild its army.

Walter was released from duty in 1919, luckily having never seen action, and sent home with a briefcase full of glowing letters from his superior officers. He might not have fared well against the best fighter plane of the war, and the stars of this chapter, Jim and his brother Craig, would never have made it into this book. The pilots who did see action had to dogfight the highly maneuverable D VII German Fokker—nicknamed the *Flying Dutchman*—designed by the Netherland's Anthony Fokker who had to change citizenship to build planes for the Germans. The allies had some Fokker fighter planes of their own since they were originally built in Holland and Germany equipped the Flying Dutchman with double machine guns, prompting the Entente (allies) to double up their guns. To help you remember the Dutchman's Fokker, one ace who flew the plane was the Red Baron (Baron Manfred von Richthofen) who shot down 80 allied planes during WWI. The last but not least of his kills was America's favorite dog/pilot Snoopy from the 1966 fictional song *Snoopy vs the Red Baron.* [3] The allied top ace was Eddie Rickenbacker, a racecar driver, with 26 kills—22 fighters and 4 dirigibles.

Life on the Farm

Walter's immediate Scottish roots were Illinois farmers, some of whom continued further west to Missoura with western expansion and cheaper land. Walter being one of them, married a beautiful petite women named Laurinda just after the *great war*. Both Laurinda's parents were Scottish too, and hailed from farms in Kentucky. The marriage of Walter and Laurinda was probably based on mutual attraction as that freedom had just blossomed in America the beautiful as well as the freedom for Laurinda to vote by 1920. Both of their mothers had neither. Walter may have voted for Cox in 1920 but from what I've learned about him, he thought about voting for Harding.

Walter and Laurinda, democrats as all good poor farmers were, could somehow afford to have 4 "young 'uns" as they called 'em. Craig, Marge, Jean and Jim, spaced 1 year apart, were born right there in that little Missoura farmhouse 8 miles from Bolckow and Dr Wood made house calls in a Model-A Ford. With no real birth control, Laurinda would have no more kids.

Laurinda was exhausted after the marathon, ended up with pneumonia twice that 4th winter of 1923, and Walter had to take her to Colorado for a long recovery. The 4 little kids were split up and taken in by farmer neighbors, who had toddlers of their own, and the oldest 2 were put to work. Walter stayed with Laurinda for 6 months as she slowly recovered in the clear mountain air. It almost sounds like tuberculosis to me.

Their closest neighbors were 2 other farm families—one ¼ mile away, the other ½ mile away—and since the kids had lived with those generous families for half a year they would sneak away to play with the kids whenever Walter turned his back. Walter would reel them in by voice command—he had a booming windpipe—and in the stillness of middle America, his bark went miles. His overworked kids could hear him yelling "git home," and he would pop them with a tree switch 1 by 1 as they ran back inside the house to resume their chores. Walter's kids pleaded, "we were helping out the neighbor." "No, you weren't," Walter said, "I could hear you laughing." This is about when the Scottish kids graduated from "young'uns" to "little shits," author Arthur Herman reminded me.

Complaining, lying, or bragging was illegal and if Jean said she could do something and Jim said "so can I!" Walter would say, "which eye do you want me to soak?" The kids learned about eggcorn reinterpretation and sarcasm all in 1 sentence plus the despondency that that he didn't consider them individuals yet. Walter couldn't let them open that can of worms on a humorless farm and Jim took that as gospel and buried his ego best he could. The kids absorbed mountains of information too from this tiny strange box in the kitchen called a radio.

I doubt if Grant Woods ever knew Walter and Laurinda but they looked like the farm couple on the Wheaties box. Walter's clenching line to the kids was, "I'd rather you kill somebody than lie to me," as Laurinda taught them grace under pressure.

It was the roaring 1920s but nobody in the region or in rural America could tell. Their farm lacked a telephone, running water, electricity, and heat but the house was built over a well and they had a pitcher pump in the house to manually fill large pots by hand and heat them with firewood to take the cherished bath. "Pop," as they called him, rigged up a self-styled gas generator making his farmhouse the first in the area with occasional electricity. When the lights got dim Pop would go out and gas up the engine again and nobody minded the loud noise because they could read again without squinting by candlelight, as Walter kept reminding them, "believe half of what you read and nothing that you hear." Walter's log splitter was an ax. When nature called, there was a modicum of privacy in the outhouse 50 feet behind the little house where they had a few minutes to freeze alone in the dark with their thoughts and a dry corncob to wipe with if they hadn't burned them all to keep warm.

Rumor had it that Craig and Jim made sling-shots out of cat gut and were known as "little Missoura snipers," at least when they weren't tipping over neighbor's outhouses or accidently on purpose burning down Laurinda's canning shed. Though both boys were idiot geniuses it was the wee lad Jim's idea to pile up all the debris in the backyard right next to the jelly shed and light it. Boys can't wait to start a fire. Most of mom's Mason Jars packed with preserves were ruined and Walter didn't spank Jim, he beat him. It was a way of life that all 4 kids knew and had accepted and since nobody really got injured, they kept their spirits surprisingly high. Every so often the boys planned nighttime watermelon raids on the not-so-nearby farms—Marge and Jean always joined in—and the fun was stealing off with a ripe one right before the salt in the farmer's shotgun stung their hightailing butts.

Walter the 1 man show started a farm because "it beats workin' for somebody else." He grew soybeans and feed grain, had pigs, horses, cows, and those chickens who occasionally did run around minus their head for a bit. They maybe only had 2 cows and most of that was for cream. The smart pigs were pretty scared of anybody approaching, not knowing if it was suppertime for them or the farm family, and would run smack into the chicken wire at full speed hoping to bust out.

Farmer Walter was proud, relieved actually, to have 2 sons. Craig, the oldest boy, manipulated the horses to do the heavy hauling and worked like a dog until his 10th birthday when Walter bought his first tractor in 1930. Henry Ford called it the "automobile plow" and the whole family felt a burden leave their shoulders. Little Jim, the youngest, was coming up fast and learned that labor was as good or better than money. What they couldn't afford, they made or did themselves. The iceman would drop off milk and ice on the front porch and collect the money later, if they had it.

The roaring 20s was great for the few. The orgy of bank loans was such that "the average income of the fortunate families at the peak was 630 times the average income of the families at the base."[4] The tried-and-true farms were holding steady as a wave of Americans had left for the cities, following the new money.

Before the 1929 crash only 5% of Americans were farming[5] while *most* Americans had worked on farms 15 years earlier.[6]

Newly fashioned stocks, some embroidered, and the new paper to buy them were renamed "securities," and "liquidity" and became "a honeycomb of loans that could bare just so much strain and no more."[7] By the very early 30s banks were busting 1 by 1—no banks in Canada went under—and the collapse of the honeycomb heard worldwide, but made little sound in the heartlands. Wouldn't that be nice?[8] Anyway, the farms always had potatoes, eggs, *all* kinds of fruit, unpasteurized milk, corn……anybody who didn't have food could rely on the Missoura network. Times were harder and everybody took care of everybody like a close-knit group of hunter-gatherers. Back east, no bailout came for the speculators because the fledgling US central bank was dumfounded after creating the roar and the crash. The cash-credit boom collapsed into thin air and bottomed out into the Great Depression of the 30s.

One July there was no cash on the farm so they couldn't buy milk or ice because they still owed for the previous 2 weeks. The milkman dropped it off on the hot front porch anyway. He knew they'd grab it and use it immediately—everybody helped and everybody got paid, eventually. Wheat and oat threshing season was an example. The nearby farms would get together, combine machinery, and finish the first farm, then go to the next. All souls knew to foster a silent economy—money was hardly the only medium of exchange—and even when a big harvest made crop prices drop, everybody ate.

"Dog soup" was a glass of water if they ran out of unpasteurized milk. If you wanted better, Walter would say, "whadaya want, egg in your beer, or all the tea in China?" They knew what he meant and he pegged some geography and history into their brains too. They were raised lean, mean, and grew the tough skin and the worldview Edith never got. If the farm kids were looking long in the tooth, they had to choke down a spoonful of cod liver oil or castor oil, which scoured them clean. As the depression drug on, Walter picked up smoking for the first time at age 41—filter-less menthol Cools—and all the kids followed suit on the sly.

Both Walter and Laurinda had studied German, Latin, and a little Greek. Rumor had it that Walter knew the derivation of every word so the kids would get out the dictionary and try to stump him while Laurinda baked the fruit pie. They could never stump Mr Blueblood. They had dessert more often than you'd think but it took Laurinda so long to make it from scratch the kids had to be woken up to eat it. Jim would complain the next morning that nobody had woken him up—he didn't remember. He had blind spots. And breakfast wasn't slim pickens either as you might think on this allegedly impoverished farm. Everybody had oatmeal, ham and eggs, fresh biscuits with homemade apple butter and then it was off to the one room school.

Jim and his older sister Jean got to school on a Shetland pony named Winkus who was the daughter of Mabel—the mare they rode as toddlers. The younger 2 siblings were in the same grade and the older 2, Marjorie and Craig, were in the same grade too, although Margorie was 15 months older. Those two rode a horse named Molly to the little building, which was more crowded in the winter when the boys could be spared from the farm. The horses hated bridges, having never evolved with those strange contraptions, and refused to cross. The kids would go get a nearby farmer and as soon as the horses saw him coming, they rushed over the bridge. Eventually, Walter made a board with nails in it and they hit the horses on the butt to get them across. Sometimes the kids were so frozen by the time they got to the old wooden schoolhouse the teacher had to thaw them out by the fire, which was quite painful when she did it too fast. On the worst days the ponies would sink into the snow to their bellies and the kids would trudge to the nearest farmhouse again, borrow a farmer's shovel to dig 'em out, bring the shovel back, and start school freezing and covered with mud. Getting a terrible education, by today's standards, didn't seem to handicap them. Though Winkus was aggressive and naughty he was the favorite horse of all the children and years later, after they moved, Walter let them keep him.

When Jean and Jim were in 6th grade, a bully named Oscar was picking on Jim so Walter told Jean to "take care of it." The next day on the playground the 6th grader Oscar started picking on Jim and Jean beat the crap out of him while the class cheered her on. Oscar and Jim were best friends after that. Doing whatever was necessary to survive, daily, was soon engrained in the whole Scottish, *failure is not an option,* family, and any shrinking violets got toughened up.

Without child labor the dangerous farm work wouldn't get done so labor laws didn't apply to farming. After the Winkus taxi got the youngest 2 kids home from school, they had to gather eggs, milk the cows, clean out the barn, and slop the pigs. "Sui! Sui!" Jean and Jim would shout and the pigs came running. Jim hated pigs and milking cows and Jean hated gathering eggs because the hens would peck at her. Jean wouldn't slap the chickens back like her parents did. When the sunlight faded and stopped all farmwork, they could start on their homework, if they had finished their fried eggs, corn, and potatoes.

Jean and Jim were in the dimly lit kitchen cutting up some construction paper for a school project with the only pair of scissors in the house when the parents told Jim to take out the garbage. They had put the garbage can in the middle of the kitchen and Jim looked around and said he couldn't find it. He had almost knocked it over while looking and Jean started laughing at him. She still had the scissors in her hand when he started chasing her, she tripped, and the sharp end went right into her nostril and out the top of her nose near her left eye. Laurinda patched it up on the spot while Walter spanked Jim which suddenly restored his sight and he took the trash out.

Walter's Presbyterian family often attended church in nearby Maryville (pronounced Maryvul) 19 miles from Bolckow. It was a Baptist church and nobody cared but to cater to everybody it morphed into an ecumenical church. As Walter's kids were entering high school there was a lynching of a black man in Maryville,

January 12, 1931. His name was Raymond Gunn and the mob removed him from a police car, tied him to the roof of the Garret Schoolhouse where a teacher had been murdered and set it on fire. Nobody was charged with a crime after 4000 people marched him through town, beat him and burned him alive.[9] There was some circumstantial evidence Gunn *did kill* the teacher named Velma Coulter but he never saw a jury. William *Lynch*, a Scot who ran his Virginia county with an iron fist back in the 1700s, gave us the name for what they did to Raymond Gunn.[10]

Time has erased our memory of the lynching of an underestimated 10,000 black people in American history. Some historians say there were closer to 2 million murders, counting the *Strange Fruit*, [11] plus the sick slaves they pulled out of steerage and threw into the ocean, writhing in pain from scurvy, along the *shark route* or the *middle passage*. Many more were killed before they got on a ship because when the American privateers and their African collaborators raided a village, those who were too young or too old to be useful, were murdered.[12]

From the way Edith wrote about the pugnacious Walter, he was the kind of guy who, if offered poached salmon might snap back, "who'd you steal it from?" Every so often Walter would put all the cats from the farm into a burlap sack with some rocks and drop it off a bridge. He didn't get along famously with his headstrong female relatives, having had an invective mother, whom he copied. She came to live with them in the last few years of her long life and Walter would always tell her to "stop humming hymnals at the dinner table." She would snap back, "you've never even been baptized." Walter didn't know whether to feel bad about that or not so didn't risk replying. It was a hard life with too much work, so perpetual seriousness was imprinted upon everybody. Edith's childhood, 4 years behind Jim and only 400 miles away, consisted of growing up in a brick ranch house, with a beautiful yard, and no chores—and no siblings.

Walter pulled a hilarious prank on his 2 young sons. When they were both teenagers, he took Craig and Jim with him into town to get supplies. The weather was so bad they left the Model-A Ford sitting there and took a rickety horse drawn cart through a daunting Missoura snow into town to the not-so-local general store. They bought animal feed, fertilizer, nails, and hotdogs (staples). On the way home, the boys needed to pee so Walter stopped the cart but snuck one of the frozen hotdogs out of the burlap sack and broke it in half. He held the 2 pieces together lengthwise and stuck them under his pants and out his zipper, hiding his arm with his coat. As the boys were peeing, he moved closer to them and pretended he was peeing. When they were done, he turned toward them and acted like he was shaking it off. He then let the front half of the hotdog fall into the snow—right in front of his sons' popping eyes. For a minute, they thought his dick had broken off.

After the hotdog thing, Jim's parents, Walter and Laurinda, still in the throes of the Great Depression, noticed an apple in the kitchen with 1 bite eaten out of it. They made all 4 kids take a bite out of the apple and the parents compared the teeth marks. They determined that the dentition was of their youngest, Jim, and ignored his protests. This wasn't a suburb spanking folks, this one was rural. Injustice was a part of life and Jim would use the axiom "nothing is fair" to govern his storied life.

Jean was the naughtiest and most outgoing of the 4 kids, so she got spanked by Walter the most—"it didn't bother her," she wrote—and she probably felt almost justified in seamlessly avoiding that apple spanking. Pragmatism (when what works justifies outcome) is a useful tool because inequity is baked into the cake of life. Dog-faced pragmatism made the greatest generation who they were and the comprehension that "little in life is fair" stopped there. It wouldn't make it into future generations. Years later Jean confessed that she had taken the bite out of that apple and they had a big laugh together.

In 1936 Walter scored well on a test to win the job of Bolckow Postmaster. Farming was over and they sold some of the equipment, rented the big farm, and moved into a tiny farmhouse on the edge town. Their new little house had a cow, chickens, a small barn, and of course Winkus, who got into some grasshopper poison and died. When the older 2 siblings headed off to college, Jim had to do all the work on that 2nd little farm and on weekends he would work at other farms bringing water to the pickers in the fields for 2 silver quarters a day. Long after that fun job—2 buckets on a stick over his shoulders—whenever one of his own kids expected somebody to do something for them, he'd say, "who carries *your* water?" That weekend torture ended for Jim when they got a house in town, 1 block from the post office, and Walter could walk to work. He never wasted a penny. In 1938 a set of 5 new tires for a Model-T Ford was a whopping $40, a pound of coffee was 27¢, and a US senator made $10,000 a year.[13]

The little brick schoolhouse burned down the first time in 1921, 2 years before Jim was born, the 2nd schoolhouse burned down in 1931 with Raymond Gunn tied to the top, and for years they used churches and people's houses for classrooms until FDR's WPA (Work Projects Administration) built them a 3rd brick schoolhouse, where the last 2 children ended up for their final years. Just after Jim and Jean graduated, school bus services began in 1941.

Jean wanted to have parties in the house with music and dancing and her parents said "no." She knew that was the end of it. She was packing for nursing school anyway, Jim was jealous, and told her he would never work anywhere near a farm again. He had no idea that growing up in a farm family, as most Americans did back then, was a free economics degree. The kids learned the art of efficiency by necessity or by example and it stuck because they learned every lesson many times over. Farms were America's educators of the young until megafarms slowly effaced the landscape and brought in hourly migrant workers. Those lucky to grow up on a farm had a charming shyness we don't see much of anymore. Take your kids to work with you and show them everything.

You might remember from the previous chapter that Jim supported himself his senior year in high school by working at the infamous Midway on Hwy 71. Craig had worked there too and

Jim took the same job 3 years later. In 1941, after high school and that job at the Midway, Jim and a friend signed up at the Missoura School of Mines, which was an engineering school in Amherst where his elder brother Craig was a senior and close to graduating in Electrical Engineering. Jim and Craig shared a trailer 3 times the size of a chicken-coop but Jim rarely saw him because he had a date most every night and seniors didn't consort with lowly freshman anyhow. Craig loved flying as a college student and flew his sister Jean around in his own little plane. Nobody could figure out how he could afford it. At 6′ 3″—5″ taller than Jim—Craig almost wasn't accepted as a military pilot but squeezed into the cockpit of the trainer planes and fittingly ended up flying in the roomy cockpit of the P-47. Being the heaviest fighter-bomber of WWII, they nicknamed it *the Jug*. Craig was a fearless pirate in the air and named his personal P-47 the *Jolly Roger*, after Peter Pan's Ship. He probably trained in Texas, as Walter had, and in the rush to training pilots, 15,000 American boys died learning to fly a plane for the first time.[14]

Black pilots were banned from the Army Air Corps at the outset of WWII because some black officers would then outrank white enlisted men and white soldiers would have to salute them. They got around this in 1943 by forming all black squadrons in the newly created Air Force who finally saw action in April of that year. They unleashed their patriotic hell on Italian targets and Field Marshal Rommel's divisions in North Africa. Churchill also didn't allow his white soldiers in India to oblige the darker, ranking Indian officers with a salute.[15]

Put a Helmet on that Soldier

Craig was commissioned as a 2nd Lieutenant in the Corps of Engineers, then went to the signal corps, then the Army Air Corps, where he was promoted to 1st Lieutenant on Christmas Day, 1943. After training he volunteered to go to Britain and help prosecute the war. In 1944 the army assigned Craig to the 366th fighter group containing his 390th Fighter Squadron. He was stationed in Membury England and relocated to a launching base in Thruxton from where Craig's 21 plane squadron could reach Paris in 30 minutes. With a range of only 800 miles, the P-47 had about an hour to find targets, bomb, strafe and dogfight, if necessary, and head home. The Brits said our soldiers were, "overpaid, oversexed, and over here," and Craig probably had that Scottish mole on his left eyebrow but they were so bushy in the photos I couldn't see it. The dog-faced infantry didn't get the girls, the daring young fly boys did. Barbie doesn't really come with the Ken doll, sometimes with the G.I. Joe doll, but more often she comes with the fly boy doll. "The Brits were a bit embarrassed they needed us but they loved us," Craig thought, "especially the girls."

In high school Craig was a football-basketball star and the girls threw themselves at him. His main girlfriend from college, Kathleen, unfortunately didn't get pregnant as far as I know so other than his reputation as a ladies' man Craig immortalized his legacy with the 8-millimeter video tapes he secretly mailed home to his parents after the army had documented them. I've watched them and you wouldn't have wanted to be in a Nazi vehicle when his P-47 was diving at you. He turned trains and trucks into Swiss cheese—all on film—divebombed German troops, and shot down at least 1 German Messerschmitt 109—a faster fighter plane than his P-47.

They all knew they had a 50-50 chance going in and Craig grew up ten years during his year of combat. Some reports of fighter missions to France reported losses of 23%. After 25 missions with the 390th Fighter Squadron, Craig's army service was done so he signed up for another term and flew 25 more missions with the 9th Air Force. Craig had 2 opportunities to go home and declined both, probably guessing that the longest day was coming soon, and he volunteered for a 3rd term.

Before we come back to Craig, here's the strange story of what created Adolf Hitler (misspelled from this father's name Hiedler) and earth's biggest disaster. Hitler was born in 1889 and whipped as a kid along with his siblings, halfsiblings, and mother. He disliked and feared his father Alois Hiedler (original last name "Schicklgrüber," what Churchill call Hitler) for being treated like an animal.[16] Alois died when Adolf was 13. When Hitler was 18 his mother Klara, who was Alois's niece and also treated like an animal, died of breast cancer and Hitler became a hypochondriac, obsessed with cancer. He was sure he was going to get cancer himself and Sam Apple says in his book *Ravenous* that it drove Hitler to hurry the war and attack Russia. Adolf probably hated his father, loved his mother, and was torn between military service and being an artist.[17] He gave up on art and joined the military (picked dad over mom) which cemented Adolf's psychopathy.

I believe Hitler had a vengeful hatred toward his father which he didn't analyze so unconsciously acted it out. If Hitler had spent some time on psychiatrist Dr Carl Jung's nearby couch instead, it might have changed history. Jung had already helped many delusional patients, lost a few to suicide, and these people weren't freaks of nature. They had heavy Stockholm Syndrome upbringings, each reacted differently, and Hitler's remedy was to kill 50 million people to avoid confronting his childhood. I've read similar stories of the childhoods of Japan's emperor Hirohito, Stalin, and Putin. Not only does the economy come from the family but so does war.

Back in 1913 Carl Jung had visions of a Europe "bathed in blood" and world war broke out less than a year later.[18] In 1933 Jung again saw a Europe married to technology, divorced from psychology, and all but predicted the 2nd world war.[19] Luckily, Hitler was a terrible military general but unluckily for him it was the *Flowers for Algernon*[20] story again, as the genius went fully insane and elected to burn in a ditch.

Hitler's insanity was not helped by the incomprehensible 19th century German philosopher Friedrich Hegel whose ideas were so consuming yet so confusing that the Germans had to pretend to understand them. Hegel the racist saw human rights as abstract and fluid—his Germany could do no wrong—and his heavily worded explanations left philosophers lost in his fog. Hegel's philosophy that the "actual is moral" may have been to protect himself from the authorities but he drew no line between the public and private sector. 100 years later Hitler professed to hate Hegel but may have come to fancy himself as the long awaited "Machiavellian genius," Hegel had written about, needed to save Germany. Hitler drew no lines at all and quickly expanded Germany's lebensraum (territory).

At the 1930 Hague Conference they had outlawed hollow point bullets because medics reported that fragmenting bullets turned soldiers into hamburger meat. Near the end of the conference the *Bank for International Settlements* was chartered in landlocked Switzerland and the super innovative Swiss, who couldn't ship much for export, later began exporting paper money. After the crash of 1929, the US had stopped loaning to Germany which helped the fairly well-run Weimar Republic's economy to crash and precipitated Hitler's rise to power. Attempting to gauge their risk and reward, the mysterious *Tower of Basel* funded the Nazi war machine with freshly printed Swiss Francs and continued doing so after Hitler had spent all his gold. Ironically the western financial appeasement recontinued in the mid-1930s with bankers in the US and the UK lending Hitler money while America was busting and Germany was producing war machines like hotcakes. If it wasn't for the banks, Hitler wouldn't have gotten the biggest bang for his buck—ask Daddy Warbucks. What followed this disruption of economic balance was the first peacetime conscription law in the US, passed by congress and signed by Roosevelt in 1940, a week after Jim's 17th birthday. About 10 million were drafted—every 6th man.[21]

Germany had about a dozen countries in their pocket at the start, many neutral ones including rebellious Ireland, and about 6 other countries whose first language was German. To this day the people in countries bordering Germany understand or speak German, including Italy and uranium rich former Czechoslovakia which Hitler took first in 1938. There, videotapes exist of 100s of

Czech protesters getting machinegunned down in Prague but in reality, Eastern Europe was one big fascist block, including Poland who had militarily expanded their own territory by 1938.

With backing from 2-timing Russia, WWII officially began on paper with Hitler invading Poland in September 1st 1939. The end of Poland was a foregone conclusion you see because Hitler and Stalin had a secret pact to split it so right after Hitler took southern Poland, he knew Russia would take the top half.[22] The western allies, still thinking Russia an ally and still thinking Russia was invading Poland and a few other countries for defensive purposes, didn't learn about the secret pact until 1945.[23]

Bloody Stalin and Hitler were secret fair-weather allies and really none of the axis powers were strategically aligned. Each fascist leader was self-absorbed. The fiasco Mussolini and the neurotic Hirohito, who never got a childhood, barely pretended to be loyal to Germany so the lack of planning, learning together, and communicating reduced their chances of winning down to zero. When WWII first started, there was a joke in Germany about Hitler getting a report from a communications officer that Italy had joined the war, and Hitler said, "send 2 divisions." The officer said, "no, their joining the war on our side," and Hitler said, "oh, send 10 divisions."[24] In 1940, Hitler occupied Norway.

Remember the old joke about the only Norwegian fighter pilot during WW II? The joke is so old I'll say his name was Ragnar Schmangee, and he shot down a few German war planes. Years later his daughter Dagny was an anchor woman on the evening news in Oslo, interviewing her aging father, and asked him to recount his most harrowing dogfight. He responded, "I saw 2 fokkers coming down on me fast, and 3 other fokkers approaching on the right, and"………she quickly interrupted her dad and said, "by Fokker, I think you mean the German Fokker fighter plane right dad?" He said, "yaaa, kind of, but zees fokkers vere Messerschmitts."

Russia invaded Finland again, a disaster as usual but kept part of it, as Hitler took Paris a few months later in the summer of 1940. For FDR and Churchill, their best worse choice was to remain Stalin's ally—the communist who was urging collectivism over family. FDR and Churchill were too, in preparation for war, but Stalin did it as an ideology.

20 years earlier the German Kaiser Wilhelm II had failed to take Paris so with Germany's 2nd attempt, or historically 5th attempt, Hitler went north of France and circumvented the Maginot line protecting the east side of France. His miles of tanks blitzed through the Arden Forest in tiny Belgium and headed straight for Paris. Belgium has great farm land but the low country is often pure mud and entire armies would get stuck. This time the Germans raced through a dry Belgium for their first stroke of luck. Joris, a Belgian friend of mine, has a very funny line he attributes to Hitler: Adolf told his generals, "the Belgian army is very dangerous because you can't see them coming." If Hitler said it, I'm pretty sure his obsequious generals got the joke but knew not to laugh.

German soldiers and citizens were always told they were "protecting" the countries they were invading from Russian and British imperialism. This was a fairly easy sell, with a quick glance at history, because Britain and often Russia were always invading somebody. And the Japanese soldiers, with equally high IQs, were spoon fed similar propaganda. The conquered locals laughed at their gullibility but no army fully knows why it's fighting and the citizens back home are clueless yet. The dictators would lie to keep the spirit levels high and laughingly remind the soldiers of all the unconquered girls on their horizon.

After taking Yugoslavia, the Balkans, Greece and just about any European country Hitler wanted—his soldiers were on amphetamines—writer-historian Max Hastings tells us about the women of occupied Europe. They were victims of any teen meth head with a gun while the civilians in Britain, coffers empty, had it pretty good, safe on the island.

Winston Churchill, born and burned into history, would not have been voted most likely to succeed. His dad Randolph was less than enamored with his son's school years and lackadaisical attitude though as a young military officer Churchill surprisingly led military campaigns almost worldwide. Everywhere Britain wasn't supposed to be, he dodged bullets and came home a hero. In 1939 Winston Churchill replaced Neville Chamberlain as Prime Minister (Neville's cancer was fast; he would die a year later) and the new baby-faced Prime Minister went on to win WWII and produce more material than Shakespeare and Socrates combined, in his "not entirely uneventful life."[25] The common British heckler didn't shake the Nobel Prize winner, he fielded their hits like a seasoned shortstop and tossed them out at first base whether he was drunk or just a bit drunk, AM or PM. With those long British pauses and not as many adjectives as we might expect, Churchill was the 20th century's best speaker and a decent General or even Admiral when he had to be, because majority opinion was only one of the cigars he pondered.

The Brits were getting shiploads of US war machines which Roosevelt supplied for gold on the spot as the US had done in WWI. When Britain's supply of gold was exhausted, again, in late 1941, the US passed the Lend-Lease Act which allowed the continued shipment of armaments to Britain in trade for new US military bases on the island.

The pact between Hitler and Stalin ended abruptly in June 1941 when Germany surprise attacked the Russians in northern Poland (operation Barbarossa) and kept going north, fast. Max Hastings also informs us that in the 2-year German siege on Stalingrad Russia, 800,000 people starved and the living resorted to cannibalism.

The millions who lived in the path of the Blitzkrieg or the retreating Bolsheviks were in the wrong place at the wrong time. In southwest Russia and the Baltics, millions of men on both sides committed murder and entire villages ran into the forest with a baby and a blanket, and got pneumonia or froze or starved. Torn apart, Belarus, Poland, and Ukraine were slaughter houses. With German tanks on Moscow's doorstep, the heavy snow in late 1941 spelled the winter of Hitler's discontent—Stalin's too—but the regrouping Russians had more tanks, soldiers, and guns than Hitler had guessed. With Nazi resupply units stuck in the snow and mud and the Germans machine gunning down so many Russians they ran out of bullets, the Russians kept coming. It was the most horrible 2 years in history. Stalin told Churchill he was losing 10,000 soldiers a day while FDR and Churchill had not kept their promise of invading France.[26] After the Soviet defenders finally turned the siege all the way around, only to fight room to room through Berlin for months, 29 million of the best and brightest Russians had died. The Russians, who had 2 years of D-Days, won WWII for everybody. The allies would have won eventually but thankfully never got the chance.

We could say the Russians made the supreme sacrifice of modern history and don't think they got much credit for it. In terms of casualties a Russian would say that Britain and the US got off ridiculously light. I'm not saying Russia has been a good actor before or since but imagine growing up Russian during WWII; 100 people you knew in your short life are dead and you have no idea what happened but you fervently felt that your country acted in defense.

The trusted Max Hastings—who probably wrote the best accounts of the 2 world wars—was knighted by Tony Blair. Later Max said, about the late Queen Elizabeth: "she knows she doesn't have any power she just doesn't want anybody else to have it."[27]

Here is an evolutionary angle of what led to WWII and later Vietnam. Raised on Stockholm Syndrome, it takes 20 years to grow a new soldier. A score (20 years) is the typical spacing between wars, so in 1939, Germany tried again, and *Johnny Got his Gun,*[28] again. A score later, the baby boomers changed a few things and we no longer had the kind of boys we did on that day so near the summer solstice, D-Day, who would run toward machine guns. In 1968 the US finally had enough early baby boomers to draft and massively ramp up the war in Vietnam but they didn't want to be there or know why they were there.

The Last Dogfight

WWII pilots had to be young and have cat-like reflexes or they flew desk. Enemy planes would crisscross them at 1000 feet per second. In battle, time slows down for flyboys and they gain the agility of a hummingbird, concentrating so intensely they remember every second. The only glory is inside those seconds and soldiers say, whenever they think about it later, they feel sick. The fighter pilots didn't sleep much and drank to postpone nervous breakdowns. Craig had signed up for 3 tours because he was a badass, stuck to his guns, and loved killing Nazis. Only 4 flyers from his 21-pilot 9th Air Force squadron lived through the war, worse than the average, because of Craig's aggression as a leader.

When you must become an efficient killer, it's hard to go back home and turn your aggressive and risky into funny and frisky, because to be super good at something, even killing, you have to love it. Earnest Hemmingway wrote, "certainly there is no hunting like the hunting of a man and those who have hunted armed men long enough and liked it, never really care for anything else thereafter."

What happened was, on the way home after a bombing mission Craig saw a formation of ME-109s against the blue sky high above him and led his smaller group of Thunderbolts up into the attack. With no radar or defensive weapons yet, climbing into the attack was a surprise to the Germans because Craig's thinned out squadron was obscured by land. The German pilots absorbed the first strafing run, instantly snapped into a higher state of consciousness, and peeled off in all directions. It was a long, ultra stressful dogfight that day in June 1944, with a handful of planes lost on each side.

I researched ME-109 pilots who shot down P-47s and the closest I could find in the US records was 2 kills over Italy 10 days after Craig's plane was hit. I went on an exhaustive internet search to find the pilot who damaged Craig's plane.

The German aces (5 or more kills) were the deadliest pilots, with 6 or 7 of them shooting down hundreds of allied planes each. Wilhelm Balthasar, who commanded the Me-109s flying with the JG-27 German fighter group stationed in France in June 1941, was a veteran of the Spanish Civil War and the Battle of Britain. His group had hundreds of kills over France—most Balthasar's—but he was killed in action earlier that year. Aces like Balthasar shot down so many American planes compared to the rest of the Luftwaffe, there's a pretty good chance 1 of these German aces killed Craig: Erich Hartmann, Gerhard Barkhorn, Gunther Rall, Wilhelm Batz, Erich Rudorffer, Otto Kittel, or Theodor Wiessenberger—most living to a ripe old age. With 90% of Nazi airmen dying in the war, we can know the decoys protected the aces.[29] Erich Hartmann, with a world-record 352 kills without losing a wingman, fought on the eastern front. Few American planes had rear view mirrors yet and Hartman wouldn't fire until the plane in front of him filled the windscreen so he lost 3 planes from the debris using this tailgating tactic. They worked as a wolfpack and the alpha-male got the kills while the other flyers were trained to distract. When opposing fighters approached the German strategy was to send the wingmen speeding off to the left and right so the allied planes would pursue them and that's when the German ace, with a faster plane than any allied plane at the time, closed in directly behind the allied fighter. Gerhard Barkhorn, the only other ace to surpass 300 kills, did join the flight group JG 6 in France but was permanently injured testing experimental jet planes in 1943.

After reading what seemed like half of the Nazi's online documentation of their dogfights—much more than the US made public—I ruled out all but one ace from the list above. I was left with Theodor Weissenberger, the last pilot on my alphabetical list. On his way to his 208 kills, he was awarded command of the JG 5 group *defending* France in the early summer of 1944. 5 is a very low number for a flight group, meaning most flight groups were in Russia having a turkey shoot with Russian pilots flying American P-41s. More telling, is with 208 kills, Weissenberger wasn't the top ace but is considered the best by Germany because his kills were earned dogfighting British and American pilots.

In the weeks following D-Day he recorded 25 more kills and by Theodor's own telling of the story, after shooting down 8 P-47s in early June……on 12 June 1944 (the way a European would write it) he shot down 4 more P-47s that were attacking in a squadron of 15 or 20 Thunderbolts. My heart started racing because Jim wrote about this same dogfight on that same day. Theodor's account, with similar numbers of planes on both sides, sounded like Craig's attack. In the battle Theodor lost several pilots including his wingman Alfred Tichy, as Tichy was a decoy, and 4 other P-47s from the 9th squadron went down too.

It was a dogfight that movies are made of and Craig died in his P-47 on that June 12th, almost certainly shot down by Theodor Weissenberger. Late in the dogfight, Theodor—the best fighter pilot in the world—also got hit and went down though he bailed out and survived.[30] Theodor was killed in a car racing accident, almost exactly 6 years later, on June 11th, 1950. Other than Theodor's 4 kills, I could not find any other P-47s lost on June 12th, 1944.

Later that day Craig and the Jolly Roger plummeted into a French farm field and nobody knew but the farmer. No one knows why he didn't bail out. It was his 82nd mission, though some said he flew more than 100, and he was simply listed as missing in action. He was 24 years old and Craig's unique set of genes, about half identical to Jim's, ended the same day Jim was sworn in as a West Point cadet.

During WWII Jim almost received a degree in Electrical Engineering in 3 years at the Missoura School of Mines but after 2½ years he had to join the army for basic training or be drafted. The US government was rushing people through the school and cutting soldier training in half to stop Adolf Hitler. The army still gave Jim credit for his Electrical Engineering degree and gave him a chance to go to prestigious West Point. After taking a few IQ tests, then studying at Amherst college for 9 months, he was allowed to take the more difficult West Point test and scored high enough to be among the 120 men out of the 400 invitees nationwide who were accepted.

The 1st year at the Citadel you are a Firsty, and must scrub bathrooms with a toothbrush. Don't ever do anything to be called the Goat—those punishments are off the books. The 2nd year you are a Cow and have to do 20 pushups on the command of any upper classman. The 3rd year you are a Yearling, the 4rth year a Pleabe, and you get to tell the new recruits to scrub bathrooms with toothbrushes.

Jim graduated as a 2nd Lieutenant in 1947, ranking 12th out of 310 graduates. With no glass jaw, he was a feared boxer in gym class and with that Penhold grip he was the ping pong champion of the college. His roommate was Glenn Davis, a famous running back for West Point's football team. Known as *Mr Outside,* it was not a secret among the cadets that Glenn Davis was dating 16-year-old Elizabeth Taylor, who had just finished filming *National Velvet.* Jim knew classmate Doc Blanchard too, a famous power running back nicknamed *Mr Inside,* so the West Point attack wasn't exactly an arial bombardment. The Black Knights had college football's best teams back then because they could draft everybody except the "fortunate sons" of senators, as *Proud Mary* writer John Fogarty called them in 1969. Doc Blanchard and Glenn Davis were no fortunate sons but like Jim, had no complaints.

While at West Point Jim learned to fly army Trainer planes and his mother Laurinda insisted that he didn't pursue flying. He obeyed. After graduation the army sent him to the University of Illinois in Champaign Urbana where he completed his Master's Degree in civil engineering. At that point he had about 3 engineering degrees and a degree in physics.

The Daughters

When WWII had first broken out the veteran pilot/patriot Walter tried to sign up at age 47 with the army air corps again! No wonder the Scots won the American Revolution (Chapter 8). He was turned down because of his age but all his children were ready and Andrew County, where they hailed from, was fertile for recruitment, as if they knew the farm kids were more than ready to never farm again. Not only did Craig and Jim join the military but Marjorie and Jean did too. The *infamy* of the Pearl Harbor attack on December 7th 1941 made everyone feel an invasion was possible. Everybody sacrificed. Every family got stamps to buy the rationed necessities as FDR turned the economy from butter to guns.

The oldest girl Marge graduated Valedictorian from her 13-kid high school class, won a scholarship to Chillicothe Business College in Missoura and became an expert typist. She joined the navy as one of the WAVES (Women Accepted for Volunteer Emergency Service) and served during WWII at a Navy hospital in Memphis Tennessee where she met her future husband Ed who also served in the Navy Medical Corps. Soon Ed was in the pacific theatre treating wounded soldiers coming back from island combat at the Pearl Harbor hospital he had helped build. 4 years later they got married, had 3 children, and after treating the US wounded the only advice Ed gave his sons was "don't become a marine," diminishing their already waning war gene.

In 1940 Jean started on her nursing degree. As good as their previous education had been the Missoura girls were not ready for Bacteriology or Organic Chemistry, so at night, if one student had previously taken the course, she taught it to everybody else. Everybody helped everybody study and even so, half the girls dropped out. Jean graduated and immediately joined the army nurse corpse, treating soldiers with traumatic injuries or mental stress, called "shell shock," back then. The doctors gave boys sodium pentothal (truth serum) to get them to relive the war horrors they had gone through and suppressed like a nightmare. Jean witnessed lobotomies that turned men into zombies—a procedure that oddly, Dr Antonio Moniz got a Nobel Prize for it. She took care of extremely stressed-out soldiers by tightly wrapping them in ice cold sheets which calmed them down.

Next it was flight school, parachute training, and off to Italy. The combat flight nurse flew many missions with the 802nd Air Evacuation Squadron. They would fly close enough to the action to see explosions, bumpily land in a flat grassy area, and fill the plane with wounded soldiers. The allied invasion of Italy would have been rather uneventful if the German's hadn't come down to help. The allies took Rome 1 day before D-Day.

Jean penned one story of a harrowing rescue while the Germans were stalling the invasion of mainland Italy. On one cloudy flight back to US occupied Rome with a plane full of casualties, the pilot informed the flight nurse that he couldn't see anything. Flying high to avoid mountains and running out of fuel, he instructed her to strap parachutes onto everybody, even the wounded. Finally, some light broke through the clouds and the pilot saw a flat meadow near Rome to set the plane down. Bouncing their way to a stop, a cheer erupted inside the plane. Out of nervousness maybe, with her heart rate at 150, Jean started opening up some of the parachutes and the backpacks were stuffed with army blankets. Nylon was a hot item on the Italian black market and the parachutes had been sold. That little opening in the clouds is how close her 7 kids came to never existing. Jean stepped off the plane into the grass, her knees buckled and she collapsed.

Jean, the 1st Lieutenant, dated other officers here and there, and when she got back stateside, she met a Navy pilot named Smitty who asked her to marry him after a fortnight. She married him less than 3 months later and felt obligated to inform Walter that he was catholic. They went on to have those 7 children, made possible because Smitty had also escaped death on that Sunday morning when the Japanese hit Oahu. Smitty and Ed both may have been at church with most of the sailors, and historians tell us that the Japanese didn't know enough about us to bomb them.

Empty Nesters

"Here's a rabbit's foot......take it when you go,
so you'll always know....... you're safe from harm"

—Lyrics by Mark Knopfler, 2006

Walter had brought along a lucky old silver dollar—a *talisman* or rabbit's foot—when he went to WWI and he brought it back with him. He gave the silver dollar to Craig to take with him to WWII. Craig did not come back and they found the silver dollar still sitting in his college trailer that he shared with Jim—Craig had forgotten to take it with him. 25 years later, Jim took the same silver dollar to Vietnam. A year before Jim left for the Vietnam war, Laurinda wrote a letter to the Department of the Army, reminding them of Craig's sacrifice and begged them not to send Jim to Vietnam. The army didn't write back.

Craig and one of his pilot buddies had torn a 5-dollar bill in half, each keeping half, and promised to tape it back together after the war and have a couple of beers together. Craig got the bigger half with Lincoln's picture on it. The army mailed Craig's personal effects to Walter and Laurinda, including his silver cross, the air medal with 4 silver oakleaf clusters, the purple heart, and the torn 5-dollar bill—everything but the lucky old silver dollar.

Listed only as *missing in action* until the war was over, Walter and Laurinda hoped against hope that Craig was in a German prison. After the army changed it to *killed in action*, Laurinda had a nervous breakdown and couldn't function for weeks. The doctor prescribed her valium which she remained on for decades. The pills numbed her enough to function, and her only excitement was when she got a letter from Marge or Jean, or better yet a phone call. Those were her only hints of emotion, save for never having spanked the kids herself. Laurinda lived to be 101 and Walter died at 69.

Saving Jim's Privates

After FDR had navigated us through most of WWII, the next president and the most unlikely, was this plain spoken, "just the facts," Missourian, who also never used his status to get rich. Truman did what he had to do, nuking Japan on Monday and again on Wednesday (2 bombs called "Little Boy" and "Fat Man") and maybe saving the last one for Friday, they won't say. Emperor Hirohito had to secretly record a surrender on a phonograph disc deep in his bunker. His men snuck it out of the palace to avoid getting caught or killed by rebel military forces and snuck it into a radio station where it aired the next day. Japan adapted to peace and free trade as General MacArthur rebuilt their tattered society in our image.

Right after WWII the US changed the *war* department to the *defense* department and ironically went on the offensive. Jim was a class of '47 West Point graduate and as fate would have it, he could have a 4^{rth} child because the army didn't send him to the Korean War (34,000 US dead) because his only brother Craig was killed in WWII. The 1950 West Point class, for example, had suffered 20% killed, wounded, or missing.

In 1950 the North Korean army (aided by China and Russia) invaded Japan's former *colony*, Korea. The US was well militarized in Japan but defended South Korea late and the reds pushed the South Korean troops, along with many US soldiers to the southern end of South Korea. It was Dunkirk all over again until the US counterattacked and heavily bombed every North Korean city as Eisenhower silently dangled the nuke option in front of the invaders. At that point China sent in a wave of troops to the middle, creating a stalemate at the 38th parallel, and left South Korea as an *island* that borders only the sea and North Korea. After the tie in Korea, the never daunted US went south to the other peninsula jutting out from China—Vietnam—where the army did send Jim, despite the letter his mother sent to the army.

Orientals had long been barred from US immigration so in 1937 FDR-Congress sort of reversed this but also banned marijuana, partially to curb Mexican immigration. Republican President Chester Arthur had signed the Chinese Exclusion Act and FDR began allowing 105 Chinese people in per year. As a farmer and a democrat, unhappy Walter had become disillusioned by 5 democratic administrations in a row, a depression that lasted way too long and became a republican.

After WWII Walter remarked, "my daughters married a Catholic and a Jew, and Jim will probably marry an Oriental." He meant, a *female one* but back then few batted an eye at irrational phobias. In a quick, silent generational switch all of Walter's kids threw out his outdated thinking and Jim never made a racial slur in his life. The war had brought everybody together. Walter also said, regarding his daughters' choice of husbands, "I s'pose they're democrats too, there's one in every family."

By 1948 Walter's surviving kids were married, and Edith, the wife of his only surviving son, seemed a *vague* democrat, but hey, she was protestant. It seems Walter was the only diehard republican protestant in the family, at the time, and his anti-new deal attitude would permeate the south from its northwestern corner where his farm was all the way down and across the south.

Laurinda quietly put up his comments and was proud to hang the war emblem in her window with 4 stars on it, showing that all her kids were active in the war effort—3 of them officers. None were drafted. Of Walter's and Laurinda's 15 grandchildren only Jim's oldest daughter Captain Rachel went on to serve in the army nurse corpse. And with all those pilot genes in the family no grandchildren went on to be pilots. The war gene lost hutzpah from the greatest generation to the boomers, contributing to the tie in Korea, the unspoken loss in Vietnam, and we don't talk about the next 2 losses in the Middle East either, or what our goal was.

Years later Jim would occasionally tell the hotdog story to the kids on those rare nights when he had more than 2 beers. He told so few stories compared to his father Walter, who often told tall tales and made up long rhyming songs, that Jim's kids clung to every word. They knew he wouldn't lie. When he started talking slowly and his voice got lower, the kids moved in a little. You could hear a pin drop in the room and with 3 adoring daughters who never stopped talking, that was a miracle. Everybody talking at once drove him batty anyway and even when 2 people were talking at the same time it was all he could do to contain his anxiety. Sadly, none of the kids ever asked him what his childhood dream was or what fantasy career he had tucked away in the back of his mind. After one of his rare beer stories, it would have been the perfect time to ask him what he dreamed of doing before WWII was dropped on his head. He never had half a chance to be himself and maybe didn't even want to be a military engineer.

Because his brother flew a P-47, 47 became Jim's favorite number. His kids howled when he'd say "fordy sebm," (47 in Missourian) and especially enjoyed that he wasn't keen at getting jokes. His kids would ask him, "birds fly in a wedge but why is one side of the wedge always longer than the other?" They had to tell him the answer: "because there are more birds in it!" Jim never let on that he got the joke, he would say, "there must be 46 birds on 1 side and 47 birds on the other, which made everybody laugh even harder. "Why do white sheep eat more than black sheep?" the kids continued. Jim just stared straight ahead. "Because there are more of them!" they screamed, dying of laughter. The best jokes are about animals because they are our ancestors.

Jim's generation wasn't a barrel of monkeys because they had the hard life and didn't have the time or the choice to learn frivolity and save the world at the same time. Who else can say that?

CHAPTER 8

Saturday Night at the Officer's Club

"Oh my God that man should be taken out and shot." That's what Edith would say when some idiot politician said something idiotic on the idiot box. Edith occasionally fantasized about killing somebody, maybe even Jim after an argument or some loveless sex. She hated the *Ballad of John and Yoko* when Lennon sang, "we're only tryin' to get us some peace," because she thought *peace* was a pun. Like so many women, she even fantasized about cutting off Jim's thingamajig with a paring knife (Bobbitt vs Bobbitt 1993) or removing his spleen with an oyster fork but those were minor compared to her macabre fantasies about torturing and dismembering someone who tried to hurt one of her kids, then sticking everything into one of Jim's army footlockers and burying it in the El Paso desert.

We all fantasize and even rehearse mortal revenge. Killing is in our DNA but it isn't kosher to go around talking about it so Edith didn't know she was normal. If you've ever thought about suicide then you've thought about killing somebody—that's a hate crime if there ever was one. Edith didn't feel guilty for entertaining a little violence but she kept those thoughts to herself except when she told her family: "If somebody tells you I committed suicide please go look for the killer." Edith thought she was inherently good and that helped her through her all too human thoughts. She had little guilt because she hadn't hurt a fly in her life except her high school boyfriend, and almost guiltless 40-year-olds are scarce. Edith was happily in the prime of her life watching her children become teenagers, way too fast, and was dreading the aftermath when her days would last forever while the weeks flew by. She started telling them stuff they would soon need to know, starting with a date she had back in high school.

Miles' dad was the go-to electrician in Alton Missoura so Miles borrowed his dad's 1937 Model-T Ford (the first one with 8 pistons), picked up Edith, and proud as a peacock he almost burned rubber on the way to the school dance. He was trying too hard because she was one of the sought-after girls in their little high school and Edith expected him to act that way. They had grown up together but suddenly they didn't know each other. They didn't know a ton about the birds and the bees either, like most 16-year-olds, but evolution had taken care of all that. Plus, Miles smelled pretty good and he could dance. As their first date smoothed itself out his nerves subsided and they started having a great time. Long story short, Edith let him French kiss her on her parent's front porch at midnight, he hurriedly said "goodnight" and as he limped away Edith asked, "do you have a gun in your pocket?"[1] At the time, she didn't know what she had said.

Much later she would always burst out laughing after the punchline. That's how her 4 kids learned something of great import in life; not about erections but about laughing. Edith's younger 2 even burst out laughing with the older 2 though they didn't get it. Her kids might have missed the gift of unrestrained spontaneous laughter, as many did, and even Jim, who was always gone when Edith told the secret story, was trying to learn how to "bust a gut" after 1730. Though they were both Virgos, he never quite got it down and instead of laughing with everybody he would grin, "that's a real thigh-slapper." *You gotta have the star-dust in your blood.*[2]

After all that nightmare spanking from Jim, the stillness of the afternoon was routinely snapped with bursts of laughter and Edith was pleasantly surprised she'd had an impact. When the kids needed a little rescue from the melancholy, she started buying vanilla ice cream and used that to start the laughter up again. There was never any ice cream left when Jim got home and he wasn't supposed to know about it anyway so Edith always hid the box at the bottom of the bin. If she had been a little more European, she would have mixed them all a stiff little drink.

Edith cried when she told her kids about breaking up with her boyfriend Miles after senior graduation. They were in love—him more than her—and it was still the hardest thing she had ever done because there was nothing bad about him. She wanted to see the world and he wanted to stay in Alton Missoura. "And then the bastard moved to New York!" Edith told the kids, wide-eyed. The kids squirmed at the cussword but more because they were starting to think they were getting too much information. Their father never told them about previous girlfriends or if he'd even had any. If the kids asked him anything along those lines he'd softly say, "get your mind outa the gutter." They accepted his answer not consciously realizing the gutter was their favorite place—another rarity they all had in common with mom. After Edith heard Miles had gotten married, she often thought of him and what could have been. It seems we all have somebody from the rough and ready years we can't get out of our heads unless we become one who stops looking back. "The first cut is the deepest,"[3] because we may never fall in love so fast and so far after that.

She *didn't* tell her kids about Miles and her having sex during their senior year. Edith only wrote about it to her mother, long after the fact, and assumed her father wouldn't bother reading it. The 2 teenage lovebirds had even driven to the beach in Louisiana, the closest one to Missoura, for the weekend. Edith remembered the long French kisses the most. Her girls were approaching the age when they might start "necking" as Edith called it, with boys in cars, which she said meant you were "goin' steady," so she had held back on the gory details. She kept reminiscing back: "we could have been the all-time love story of Alton Missoura and forgotten about the rest of the world." "We wouldn't have missed much," Edith thought, "just those stupid ruins in the Middle East." "Anyway," Edith chirped, "time to go pick up my own kids," and she pulled the curlers from her naturally curly hair, grabbed her cigs and keys and headed out.

Jim is a late model of the always rough and ready Scottish Highlanders. His recent roots are the Appalachian hillbillies, coal miners, rough riders, rum runners, and moonshiners.

For starters, let's bring out the irony of the Scottish people settling both the Highlands on the British Isles and the other Highlands in West Virginia, because nobody knew they were the same mountain ranges! 200 mya, when little mammals appeared and Pangea began breaking apart, the North America continent was jammed against Europe and touched what is now Britain, Spain, and West Africa. The indominable Robert Falcon Scott was found frozen in 1913, near the south pole, bringing back plant fossils in his pockets from hundreds of millions of years prior, that would prove Antarctica was once a timberland connected to Pangea.

The immaculate conception, only 100,000 years ago, finally separated the UK from Europe after ice and tectonic events had gouged out the English Channel and connected it with the North Sea. By then a good raft was required to get to the 2 big islands and the inhabitants gradually mixed with more and more adventurous raft-making strangers. All of them were black until their skin began lightening up only 8,000 years ago in order to absorb more of the sun's vitamin D (Chapter 22). 500 years before Christ, these islanders were discovered by the Greeks who called them the "Albion" (white). In one of my favorite books, *How the Scots Invented the Modern World* by Arthur Herman, we learn that 2000 years ago the Romans invaded the closest island and named the inhabitants "the Scoti" (*bandits*). But they were rafters from Ireland who called themselves "the Gael" and this was the rough start of the Scotch-Irish mix.[4] It was the Italians who first gave the islanders the Latin names "British" and "Great Britain" from their phrase *Noble Isle* (Gret Britanee) so Britain means *island*. The word *Anglo* came later from Germanic tribes who used a triangular geometric symbol called "the Angle" for their identity, and 1500 years ago the islanders battled with these invading *Germans* from the mainland which is how the term *Anglo-Saxon* came to be. As those genes mixed heavily these now island inhabiting barbarians named the islanders the "Englisc" so the name "Britain" preceded "England" by about 500 years. The warlike Germans, with Teutonic or Aryan blood, wouldn't be called "Aryan" for another thousand years and that blood mixture helped spur the royal craving for imperialism.

With countless invaders the Noble Isle became the unlikely 2nd melting pot of the world after the earlier and endless genetic mixing around the Mediterranean Sea. For nearly a million years the mysterious, rainy UK had hosted violent phenotypes from Europe, ironically creating some of the smartest people in the world.

1000 years ago, the Scottish had dark hair and eyes. The story of how some got blonde hair and most got blue eyes is a long one so I'll turn it into one sentence. Before the *Norse* Vikings (shortened from *Northman*) were the first Europeans to reach the New World with a small expedition in the 11th century, they invaded the top of France in 853, assimilated into the French and became the *Normans*, who, unlike the unsuccessful 878 Danish invasion, successfully invaded the British Isles in 1066, won the battle of Hastings and eventually worked their way into the Highlands of Scotland, assimilating with those mountain people. Previously known as the Picts, the term *Scots* truly began with the *Scottish Highlanders*—the poorest of the poor—who didn't hobnob with the slightly less poor Scottish lowlanders.[5]

The Scots still worship their real hero William Wallace from 1300 who stood up to King Edward I. As Genghis Kahn had done,

Wallace made circular battle formations and chopped his way right through the larger, frustrated British forces, forever making him the George Washington of Scotland.

Let's fast-forward to 1700. The Scottish population consisted of the Ulster Scotch-Irish (half of them originally from Northern Ireland), the Lowlanders from Southern Scotland, and Jim's Northern Highlanders who tended to be tall and still in the hunter-gatherer stage, historian Arthur Herman tells us. Even 300 years ago, these relic foragers didn't live in what we'd call houses. The Southern Scot lowlanders followed Martin Luther and John Knox in the protestant reformation, bringing them one step closer to the natural philosophy brewing in France.

Arthur Herman goes on to insinuate that the Scots were the 2nd best immigrants a country could get, behind the Jews, as Europe covered the world.[6] Scots brought the brain, brawn, and gutsiness along with that redneck piss and vinegar, while the Jews—only allowed a toehold in London in fairly recent history—brought a deep, acquired knowledge from their education, family cohesiveness, and resilience to Stockholm Syndrome. The few Scotts who got to America clung to their identity and changed the zeitgeist of America from a tiny European population of less than 1 million in 1625.

Prior to the American Revolution, the British designated east of the Appalachians as Indian territory—the Proclamation of 1763 proclaimed "don't cross the wall"—but the Scots had a habit of not only ignoring governments but doing the opposite thing. They fought their way to Missouri, creating the *how to do it* handbook for settling the west all the way to California, and brought thousands of slaves to the western states long before the Civil War.

The Scotch-Irish founded Nashville and Memphis Tennessee before the American Revolution, historian Carole Bucy tells us, creating a trading hub with cotton and tobacco, and permeated the entire south from there—along with their black slaves. Still bitter about losing their revolution across the pond, these stubborn Scottish pioneers had more than an influence on the American Revolution, as many who fought against them attested. Some diehards fought with farm implements but most of the Scottish musketeers were long-trained with smooth bore muskets from hunting game and Indians.

Using *illegal* guerilla tactics—not in harmony with British military *rules*—the revolutionary snipers would pick off British officers from up to 300 yards using their new Pennsylvania Rifles with long barrels and grooved rifling to put some *English* on the bullet. One Irish lad, Timothy Murphy, led a team of snipers who picked off Brigadier General Simon Fraser at the 1777 battle of Saratoga.[7] Since the British would bayonet prisoners, I wasn't too shocked at what they did when they occasioned to catch an American sniper. They tied the young man to a tree and chopped him into pieces—hands, feet, then limbs—with an ax.

King George III—the too long as King King—went certifiably insane in 1810 and that quick, parliamentary cane came out and yanked him offstage. Even a normal person would have gone crazy if he'd killed thousands of people on every continent but Antarctica. George's prince regent of Whales (eldest son, later named George IV) took over the insanity and restarted the Revolutionary War in 1812—the crown's 2nd attempt to own all of North America. The new Americans had similar ambitions: they eyed the west, Canada, Mexico, probably Cuba, and Alaska, where Russia already had small settlements stretching almost to the barely populated San Francisco.

Britain's first war move was to again embargo trade to and from the Americas with draconian navigation acts. The American colonies responded with an attack on British Canada in 1813, setting Little York (now Toronto) to the torch. Some Canadians switched sides but not near enough and the rest fought tooth and nail for the winter side of America. The Canadians were only repelled in 1814 at the battle of Lake Champlain in New York. After that we know the relationship turned amicable because the 2 countries split up the Great Lakes affably and the long stretch of the US-Canada border is a shotgun straight line all the way to Alaska.

Down south in 1814, with no Paul Revere to warn the colonists, the British landed near Washington DC when James and Dolly Madison (no kids) were eating dinner. The 4rth couple suddenly had to pack up the staff, some art, the black servants (James fathered children with at least one of them[8]) and abandon the capital. The British proceeded to burn down the White House and most of Washington DC including the Library of Congress. America lost all those enlightening French books, almost forcing DC to buy Thomas Jefferson's devilish library at $4 per book, inching the rich man out of miserable debt.[9] After heavy fighting (armies and navies) the British left the next day.

The new republic was on the brink again in 1815 when the British attacked New Orleans—a good starting point to grab the whole Louisiana territory. A rag-tag militia from Tennessee gathered up their rifles in 1814, floated down the Tennessee river or took a newly built American steamboat and fought off the ongoing 66-ship (some say 50) British assault on Fort Saint Philip, protecting the city.[10]

The Tennessee Scots helped the Louisiana locals win, gave up no land to the disembarking British infantry, and it ended in 1815 with Major General Andrew Jackson—a Scotch Irish American—defeating the imperialists on the Chalmette Battlefield 6 miles east of New Orleans. The US and Britain had signed a peace treaty in Ghent Belgium a month earlier but the news had not reached the New World yet or Francis Scott Key (Scottish slave owner) may never have written about the bombs bursting over the Big Easy. The Secretary of War James Monroe gets credit for the win and Andrew Jackson, who had lost 3 members of his family in the 1776 revolution, did the tactical work, clearing out the Creek Indians from Alabama. Jackson invaded Florida next, the Spanish had to reconcile on places west, and eventually New Spain had to move out altogether, even from Oklahoma, and settle everything south of Florida and Texas. Still, the unsung Spanish triumphed over all other nations, settling over half the New World by using sex more and guns less, and they accomplished this right after an 800-year Muslim occupation.

The Treasury printed money for the War of 1812 and by 1818 the 2nd federal bank had loaned out 10 times more money than it had on deposit,[11] which sprinkled America with inflation. Andrew Jackson's war fame helped him beat John Q. Adams in the presidential election 11 years later and Jackson vetoed the re-chartering of America's 2nd federal bank, saying, "if they wanna kill me I'll kill them."[12] Jackson, who thought he could see the future, was correct this time because his veto ended inflation in America for almost the next 20 years. Inflation wouldn't sting again until the 1850s when the state-chartered banks more than doubled the total money supply between 1849 and 1854.[13]

The great unwashed Scots had a real economic impact with their war and work ethic. They subsisted on innate common sense and were quick to get "bowed up," even into a gunfight. "And oh, the smell of the black powder smoke and the stand in the street at the turn of a joke."[14] If you nicely tried to tell them how to do something, they'd say "listen junior, I've been doin' this since you was knee high to a warthog, and it costs double if you watch and triple if you help." They wouldn't take the bait for any assumption imbedded in a sentence so experts couldn't even slip a lie past them because if your lips were moving, you were lying. Using fists and guns for government, the hardscrabble rascals owned whatever little piece of the south they could populate and defend. They didn't invent that rule, the unwritten code for the world at the time was that you owned however distant your musket balls would sail.

The Scots settled from Virginia mining country to the Shenandoah Valley to Butcher Holler Kentucky to Rocky Top Tennessee. They created 2 landlocked towns in West Virginia and Georgia—both *islands called "Liberty."*[15] The Scots in Tennessee had bloody battles with the Cherokee, Chickasaw, and Choctaw Indians (each Indian nation had some black slaves of their own[16]) forcing the volunteer state to beef up their military. 16-year-old boys went right into the state militia, historian Carole Bucy tells us. As commerce heated up, the Scots brought in more black slaves, and more Scottish women went with them into the wilderness.[17] They were proud to have *coal-miner's daughters* who passed along that mole under the left eyebrow—a mark of the Scots.

When the Scotch-Irish had first landed in New York nobody would give them a job unless they joined the NYPD. So, they drank until the police took them away—in what would later be called the "Paddy Wagon"—to a cell, a meal, and a real bed. Most of them gave up on the Northeast and settled in farm country or coal country, eking out a living with a shovel and wheel barrow between the Allegheny and Blue Ridge Mountains. Many Scots like Jim's parents settled from Illinois to Missouri where they re-earned the Highland title *suspicious* and Missouri became the "the show me" state in 1821.

Tennessee didn't have a capital until 1843 when Francis Scott Key died. For decades the hunter-gatherer-farmer economy was spread out and there was no government, no roads—it was hard to find a church—and activity flourished, maverick style, in the volunteer state on the edge of civilization. [18] The Scottish Highlands were still Scot territory, by virtue of reinhabiting it, when the peaks were renamed the *Appalachians*. Shortly thereafter, Washington DC endeavored to manage the area and 5 fat cats from the northeast talked congress into selling them a string of these coal filled mountains in West Virginia. The 5 businessmen took a coach all the way down there to see what they had secured. When they finally got there, they announced to Jim's ancestors they had bought all the land—everybody was working for them now—and the Scottish coal miners shot all 5 of them on the spot.[19] They were not to be trifled with, or robbed, and went right back to their wheelbarrows with those bored Scottish looks on their faces.

After the Volstead act of 1919 and women's suffrage in 1920, the

Scots moonshined in the backwoods and came into the cities to sell it. Things seemed oxymoronic to the democrat Scots: "How can they give our women the right to vote and outlaw our liquor at the same time?" That double whammy was a jolt for a tight, hard-drinking, sexist Scott, so they made their own liquor and told their wives how to vote. Here is my Scottish accent: "When the goverment bans sumthin', it doesn't get red of it, it just reezes the prace."

Ironically, the dry state of Utah cast the deciding vote to end 14 long years of prohibition. Even after prohibition was repealed in 1933 the Scots continued competing with the *good ol' boy networks* using souped up cars to outrun the liquor-connected cops. The fascist state regulators protected these networks from competition, for a fee, back when politics *was* all local. We now think of those as the good ol' days. The rogue Scots eventually got so good at making rum runners they raced each other on public streets and started the #2 spectator sport in America: NASCAR.

Jim's Uncomfortable Evening at the Officer's Club

It was late 1967 in Fort Bliss Texas and Jim was readying his engineering combat battalion for Vietnam as well as anticipating his promotion from Lieutenant Colonel to Full Bird. In the evenings Edith and Jim would often go to the officer's club for parties and ceremonies, her dressed to the tens and him in his light dress blues—not yet colored with much military splash for a man two steps away from General. The alcohol flowed downhill and the big dining hall always had a mushroom cloud of cigarette smoke, making a donut around the stately chandelier, 20 feet above them.

Edith went to the bar: "2 vodka tonics, shaken not stirred please." She didn't whisper, she always talked too loud and never noticed the ears and eyes she captured. Jim would take a stallion stance and repeat it a bit louder saying, "shaken not stirred!" then push his chin up. He always kept his chin up—it was his *I'm in charge* quirk. Edith turned and bumped into one of the generals, spilling a couple drops of her drink on his darker blues (for the top brass) and instantly introduced herself with a big smile in that tight dress. Jim was watching as the general, who had manufactured the collision, spoke with her a little too long.

As proud as Jim was, he was deferent toward the Generals while Edith, who had maintained a life of deference, talked to them like they were neighbors. She never got intimidated or embarrassed, having never learned how in Alton Missoura. She might have even been flirting a little in a natural smalltown way but her countenance was uncontrived and the randy general, an idiot genius with too much power, was more than ready to assume she had affectations. Being ahead of her time confused Jim because his he didn't know the difference between flirting and engaging, while Edith was oblivious to the Stockholm Syndrome the general wielded over him, having never learned that either.

On the way to a table Jim gave her a quiet lesson about respecting the top brass. Edith mistakenly thought she was supposed to give the general *more* respect when simple Jim simply wanted her to talk lower and talk less. She quietly said, "Jesus Jim, what do you want me to do, kiss his Goddamn ass?" He wasn't expecting a comeback that terse and was really confused now, mistakenly thinking she had gotten the hint. He didn't answer. It wasn't often Edith would give somebody an earful and the nearby Generals strained but couldn't hear the whispering. "I'm not kissing anybody's ass, ain't gonna happen," she whispered to herself, still misinterpreting Jim. "There isn't a hierarchy of people in my world," she assured herself, "one life isn't more important than another."

A few officers and their wives took a seat at the large table in the middle of the dining hall. Jim followed Edith from their table to the half-vacant main table as a couple of generals and their wives grabbed the last seats. Jim found himself stuck at this table with the top brass. He felt like the whole "shootin' match" was "goin' haywire" and tried to not let it show on his face. Edith was unmindful and was never crazy about people having titles anyway. Jim had never thought that way and was attempting something more difficult: he was trying to get Edith to listen and smile naïvely like military wives are supposed to. But at a pretty young age, Edith could do what few could: she could fly up out of her head, look down, and see what a bird sees. At her best she could see the colorful middle and the big picture—her family and the world simultaneously—without conflict.

Jim took a big gulp of his vodka as Edith chatted away and continued derailing Jim's train by telling one of her favorite jokes. Oblivious that she was stealing the whole show, a hush fell over the table as she began. Nobody cared if the joke was funny or not, they just wanted to hear her talk.

> "This old washed-up sailor was walking through this dark port town looking for work. He couldn't believe his luck when he seen a sign in a tavern window that read: *Piano Player Wanted*. The sailor walked in, went right up to a man who looked like the manager and said, "I'm your piano player." "O...........kay," said the dubious manager, "go play a tune or 2 and we'll talk later." The old sailor knocked out a pretty good original instrumental at the piano and after some polite applause one guy asked, "what do you call that song?" "I call it, *Nancy sure was easy but she sure was fun*," the sailor replied. "Oh," said the guy with a half-smile, "play another song?" At that request, the sailor played an even more beautiful song that captivated more the diners in the room. After more applause another brave diner asked, "what do you call that one?" "That one's called, *the sailors were playing grab-ass on the upper deck so the skipper angrily ran up there, slipped on a banana peel and busted his ass*," he replied. (The generals burst out laughing, thinking that was the punchline.) "Oh," laughed the diners in the old bar, a bit amused, "play another one!" "I will," said the sailor, "but I have to pee

> first." The sailor, with a slight limp, made his way down the narrow hallway to the bathroom, so the manager headed that way slowly, to offer him the piano job. The manager was shocked when he entered the hallway and saw the sailor coming out of the bathroom with his zipper down and his dick hanging out. "Do you know your dick is hanging out of your pants right now?" queried the manager. "Do I *know* it," the sailor grinned, "I wrote it!"

The whole table roared with belly aching laughter for what seemed to Jim like 2 minutes. Jim joined in, so relieved that the joke—unbecoming to an officer's wife—was over. Everybody in the club was staring jealously at Edith's loud table. She sat quietly for the first time and took it all in of course, smiled broadly, and laughed at her own pianoplayer joke as always. She glanced over at Jim who was still smiling as if he had a coat hanger in his mouth. He didn't glance back.

The conversation turned to the Air Force and how well they were paid, plus, they got flight pay. "Why don't we get that Jim, you fly all the time?" The Generals looked at him. He pursed his lips, still cringing inside and said, "this is the army, we are underpaid to do what we're told." The whole table burst out laughing again! All Jim could muster was a grin because he didn't get it and was hoping to God joke time was over. His best jokes were unintentional anyway and he lit a cigarette, not realizing he had one already going in the ashtray.

Jim didn't know Edith was his *Funny Valentine*—"his favorite piece of art"[20]—and a feather in his cap at the officer's club. God was in a good mood that day, 8/31/1927, when he came up with a dish and a personality to match. Jim occasionally wished he had a great personality then brushed away that meritless thought. Jim finally looked at her and said softly, "the military must be run like a dictatorship, that's the only way it can work." "I understand that part Jim," Edith said, "but after 1730 hours, can't everybody just have fun? Isn't that why we're here?" "Fun?" Jim thought, trying to grasp its essence. He knew contentment but when he was having fun, he felt guilty.

Edith's comportment was their impasse and it smacked of passive aggression too because she had found the chink in his armor. A big fight ensued when they got home. Jim—hard-headed but soft-hearted—finally caved on the argument but Edith didn't. She wanted to go 12 rounds. The kids weren't asleep.

Since Jim allowed no sweets in the house, as soon as the parents had left for the officer's club, one kid took a bike to the 7/11 and loaded up on chocolate, and they'd all gorge on it in front of the idiot box. Maybe TV had more to do with obesity than we give it credit for. Anyway, the sugar buzz and the tummy ache kept them wide awake in their beds, and they lay there still as a mouse, not to miss a word. The knots in their stomachs tightened as the argument got louder. There was a volley of real loud talking, followed by the crack of a cigarette lighter hitting the coffee table and a door slamming. In later years there would be yelling, plates hitting walls, and threats of divorce. As for divorce, Jim was too loyal for that, and Edith……well, I'll get to that later.

CHAPTER 9

Free Will, the Big Hail Mary

I'm a fan of Deepak Chopra, the sensitive, transcendental philosopher who talks calmly and broadly about our infinities. With no competition, he's the best motivational speaker— without effort— and says the only thing constant in our lives is the "I." This one method we each have to experience reality adds up to an infinite free exchange of individual ideas we all tap into, which he calls "awareness."

There are countless infinities, some with borders, some without. There are an infinite number of fractions between the number 1 and the number 2. Infinities are ubiquitous and many physicists assume the universe is infinite. How else can we describe an expansion that never stops? We are in search of the god particle (if there does exist a singular "brick" or basic building block of all subatomic particles) and in the hunt for the farthest galaxy, but as soon as we find them, we will search deeper, so there are an infinite number of infinities, micro and macro. Knowing infinities are everywhere is a nice pep-talk for our doubting brains because it obliterates the mathematical limits we are taught, though the perpetual motion machine of life keeps reminding us these limits don't exist.

The human brain contains 85-100 billion neurons. Each neuron is an octopus-looking cell with about 10 legs (synapses) that multiply our conduits into trillions of connections, and we keep adding connections as we think, dream, observe, exercise and travel. If we ever max out on these connections, it's possible we may run out of disc space but if prehistory tells us anything it's that our brains will be bigger by then. Although most bodily functions are automatic, i.e., heart, lung, healing, etc., the volitional brain is not—it does what we tell it to do. Stephen Hawking, escaped from his wheelchair, went inside a black hole and told us how it gives and takes. He didn't get all that from nature and nurture.

Determinists says everything an organism does has a previous cause. I can see *probable* cause, but it's not proof of determinism and likewise, I probably can't prove free will because it's my emotional religion and the intangible we will eventually find. I'm not an idle worshipper. The big Hail Mary is what free will is for now but in the future, it will be science because there is something about life that's not digital. Our emotional hope for the future lives outside and beyond the discipline of math.

In the book *The Second Mountain* by David Brooks he ventured that "emotion drives reason." This oldfangled theory, profoundly echoed by many including David Hume, born in Scotland in 1711, supports the model that *emotional hope for the future* drives us north. We are born with passion; reason comes next—thank God evolution didn't get that backwards.

If we didn't deeply desire unlikely futures for ourselves and families our logical cognition wouldn't automate them without that foreign aid from heart and soul. The philosopher David Hume said "our reasoning faculty isn't ever really in charge; it's agenda—what it reasons about—is set by feelings."[1] "Cause and effect" he added "is but a [1] sequence of events." Cause and effect contain an infinity of mathematical sequences and Galileo wrote "the world is written in the language of mathematics," insinuating all things are absolute, knowable sequences.

However, math only applies to dead things, and it cannot fathom sacrificial selfishness or predict the future of living things. If math or AI could predict the outcome of individual risk, which it cannot, that would prove we were just nature's most complicated machines, but AI can only calculate the future of unliving, hopeless, deterministic, inanimate objects. Humans are not about evolution anymore and are not predictable.

In a quip about determinism's cause and effect diktat, Voltaire wrote, "yes, we grew noses to set our spectacles on." More precisely, in that old-timey way of writing he wrote, "observe, that noses have been formed to carry spectacles, so we have spectacles."[2]

Now that we know how we got here the next question is: are we biological machines or do we have free will? Free will is defined as making decisions that are outside the purview of and uninfluenced by nature or nurture. So how can I describe an ingredient of the human mind if it wasn't an original ingredient? Humans have always wanted more but what does *more*, mean? It means whatever the "I" dreams it to be, without taking the "I" away from anyone else. As soon as I defraud another person, I've injured my free will.

Brandon Flowers askes the free will question beautifully in his song, *Human*, where he sings, "are we human, or are we dancer?" What I gleaned from his great pop song was this: do we have free will or are we simply dancers, dancing to the beat? Is it a journey we are creating or a predefined journey we are catching a ride on? "Is that all there is my friend?" Peggy Lee sang in 1969, "then let's keep dancing." [3] Flowers continues, "and sometimes I get nervous, when I see an open door…close your eyes, clear your heart…cut the cord." We fear cutting the cord and trying to become autonomous, sentient beings. Flowers has more: "and I'm on my knees, looking for the answer, are we human or are we dancer?" Free will may be his religion too. Even creative geniuses wonder if they have free will.

The Exertion of Free Thinking

In so many ways our psyche is vastly more complex than our simple, recently evolved, language can describe, but I'll try: No individual will ever exhaust all *options*—every life is an unfinished life—and a minority of individuals do choose to change their lives in original ways and the ripple-effect is infinite. Free thinking can be rather disconcerting because a truly new thought can be maddening to come up with, so free will might begin with the simplest question: "should I think beyond my programming or not?" If we don't ask the question we'll never know. Evolution does not demand we start driving our self-driving car and give free will a spin; it may even be against the idea altogether. Evolution gave you a body and brain that will take you to 85—in blissful torpor—without there ever being a *you*. But there will never be another you.

To start a war for example a government must first remove the concept of the individual, then work people's minds in clumps for prolonged periods. If a country is under attack the government doesn't have to motivate the population at all. Although I've never heard it said, the *ultimate* duty of an individual in the US military is to point out when a war is a bad idea. We aren't supposed to but any command we get in life must pass through our moral filter first. Philosophy precedes any important endeavor, especially with Us vs Them, and the war movie *Catch-22* shows the verbal trap of determinism—damned if you want war, damned if you don't. Determinism even increases cheating when we see our future as a determined one,[4] so if "all you are is dust in the wind"[5] try not to get into everybody else's eyes.

Determinists sacrifice their spirit, their individualism, and negate their very being out of an unseen fear which leaves them with the groupthink option. They suffer from *Homo emphaticus* and overvalue what others think (averaging out the mundane) because they have no self. They might have a dream that homicide detectives are investigating them because they *did* kill somebody long ago—themselves.

In the book *NOW: The Physics of Time*, Richard Muller defended free will by saying, "we can either make a teacup or we can break a teacup." Buddha would say the teacup is already broken. Inevitability (entropy) for this pessimist was universal but we do have the moral choice to make something or break something. What makes free will an uphill battle is that entropy, like crime and war, can break a teacup in a second while it takes willful work to make one. Bob Dylan saw this duality, saying "we're gonna have to serve somebody"—either the Devil or the Lord, it depends on which one we feed—but humans have gone way beyond this binarism. (I much prefer his *Brand-New Leopard Skin Pillbox Hat* song.) Figuring out our natural origins enabled us to blend the sacred and profane into an infinite number of teacup options.

Our esoteric spirit does exist in my humble to veto or affirm our wild emotion and ambitious cognition. Freud called our spirit the "superego," and once nurtured, our spirit hopefully takes as much of existence into consideration as possible. This doesn't mean value and risk are uniform, quite the opposite. *Because* our ideas, values and risks are individual concepts, they need personal edits—spirit—and maybe some karma from a few close friends. After a new idea, it's our metaphysical spirit ego who chimes in, "curses, I think I see some unintended consequences." This was the latent spiritual reaction of the great physicists after the first nuke was tested but many more people died in the 3 years before that than since……so far.

Heavily subsidized mega tech companies speed up technology faster and faster as if we're in a perpetual emergency. They force us individual spirits to live in an alternative future and we don't want to—especially someone else's— but, "time keeps on slippin', slippin' into the future."[6] We want to slow AI down to a natural pace and each have a say starting from the ground floor where everything good evolves. Washington DC is pouring money into perfunctory information which is blotting out our common sense. We will improve the archetype of society on our own, very slowly, thank you.

We don't really like to listen to computer music either, written or played, because it sounds like Twilight Zone music and our subconscious minds are telling us something. Grotesque digital monuments that change us in clumps are their answer and apply less and less as free will and complex individualism increases. "The human species *is* the human predicament," Robert Wright pens,[7] and I would evolve that to, "the individual is the individual predicament and groupthink leaves that predicament unsolved." Humanist Jean-Paul Sartre said "man exists only to the extent that he realizes himself," and "man is nothing other than his own project."[8] "Man" loosely meant "everybody" back then and this existentialist never arrived at the concept of the "individual" either.

Some determinists and existentialists like to pickpocket the individual from the equation and say, "there is no such thing as a new idea." That was true until Cro-Magnons arrived on the scene sporting that new pre-frontal cortex and saw themselves as separate from their environment—the first animal to do so. This was an assumption because the brain is a gift from nature, however, evolution's secret ingredients became greater than the sum of their parts. For the first time in nature's epic journey ancient humans had an ontological idea—I own my own body. That was our first baby step towards free will and the second step was realizing we owned the products of our work, which created the incentive for vast wealth we see today. If new ideas aren't the path to free will is having *fewer* ideas the path?

We can't define a brand-new idea as something that's impossible for a human to have because that's another Catch-22. It's like saying monkeys would have eventually written the Bill of Rights. No. Monkeys are limited to stealing bananas and throwing poop. All the Catch-22s are veiled threats or at best either-or traps to fool us into thinking we have only 2 options. Even the binary trap of *either* a life of free will *or* a determined life is a distraction because there are infinite variations betwixt. Countless new ideas are everywhere so if those don't exist then this beautiful modern world is a hallucination.

Charles Darwin had an original idea and invented a brand-new science. Albert Einstein worked miracles under the preposterous assumption that gravity travelled at the speed of light. Archimedes came up with the screw, which we adapted to everything. Long after we heard new ideas from Buddha and Carl Jung, we are still cultivating our subconscious minds. And if apophenia means what it means (making connections in our heads that have no counterpart in reality) we all give birth to thoughts that never existed before.

Unfortunately, most of our thoughts are the same ones from yesteryear and some of us creatures of habit eventually get called "one-dimensional." A great catalyst for breaking out of the doo loop is to intentionally create new thoughts, which will change the future. New thoughts are very hard to create(!)—try to come up with one today, it's difficult—and if a new thought makes you a little nervous you may be onto something. I've said that no animal changes physically in one lifetime, however, humans have yet another superpower: "As soon as you think a new thought, you become changed—neurologically, chemically, and genetically."[9]

> Notice Descartes didn't say "we think therefore we are," because by speaking for himself ("I think therefore I am") he was speaking for each thinking individual. Back in his day, there weren't as many, now there are billions of us. Over time the "we" of tribalism became the "I" of individualism and the butterflies we got in our stomachs about our relationship with the tribe became butterflies about our relationship with a lover. Individual free will is still pecking its way out and the current literary war on the vertical pronoun "I" is part of the pushback. The philosophe Ayn Rand said that we each know we're conscious and have free will because it's "axiomatic to the nature of man." I'd say, "human

> consciousness and free will are obvious," in my blue-collar speak and Thomas Jefferson, in his white-collar speak, might say it's "self-evident," after Benjamin Franklin shortened his phrase up for him. All 3 say "we have free will because we think we do." This axiomatic assumption could be a copout or may have legs because if an animal has the brain to ask the question, the animal can ultimately get the answer. The discerning Carl Jung said, "I saw how a keen intelligence grasped the problem and formulated the questions which in themselves were half the solution." [10] Although we are using ourselves to define ourselves, lower animals cannot contemplate the concept of free will, so *cannot* have it.

Still, we look directly into ape's eyes as they do ours and both animals know that a conscious being is recognizing another. We see the intelligence there and know that they can contemplate the near future well, however, we can see farther. We archive priceless information from the past and apply it to the future, while making subtle changes based on what we've just learned. We later learn whether we were wrong or right and make more updates and changes, which is the conceptual quantum leap from the ape brain to the human brain.

Animals can't make many mistakes either which is a curse because that's the best learning tool. An unobserved mistake gives entropy a permit to destroy; an observed mistake can both stop entropy and open the door for a solution. If humans were programmed not to make mistakes, civilization wouldn't exist. The instinctual lower animals have an angstrom of free will, or the evolutionary potential for it, whereas humans are in position to identify more instincts and plan on doing other things which is the *only possible path* to free will. Crocodiles have lived the same way for 200 million years and humans change everything they touch. The difference in choice is staggering.

"Beyond our control," is our history and initial biology, which summons us to look at everything beyond those givens—an infinite future—as within our control. If an all-knowing God knows what you'll be doing 10 years from now, then we must do that or he is wrong, and not omnipotent, so religious free willers are caught in an invisible logic trap. If we have to follow God's foreordained plan, which he decided before we were born, we have no choices. Convincing ourselves that Gods are unbreakable is the loss of free will and Shirley Manson sings in her song *Stupid Girl*, "I don't believe in anything, that you can't break." A breakable brain that we own and operate is all we've got and like the infinite fractions between the number 1 and 2, there are an infinite number of options between age 3 and 90.

Free will is blossoming fastest inside those who are casting off their last societal chains. We are replacing the instincts we've robotically followed—anxiety, fear, Stockholm Syndrome—for thousands of years with individual choices that are independent of nature and nurture. Nature is the modus operandi influencing us from the outside and our 8 billion brains are 8 billion experiments pushing back from the inside. *Why* we are here can have 8 billion answers, and they all point to individual happiness. The radical philosophe Epicurus told us of the good side of hedonism which reminded us of what we already knew we wanted, subconsciously. Epicurean happiness is atomistic too, meaning, it has more influencing souls than we can count and adds up to more than the sum of its parts.

If we cannot influence ourselves then we cannot have free will, so we have no agency. It's incumbent upon us to know our agency and close the gap before the pyramid convinces us again that we are not individuals. This has been our repetitive blunder throughout history and it's time to permanently snip the cord and unredact a few amendments.

Brian Greene, in his awareness raising book *Until the End of Time*, argues we have a freedom of thought and have a larger degree of this freedom than lower animals but says this freedom is not free will.[11] "Learning and creativity do not require free will," he writes.[12] Greene put much thought into explaining this freedom while lamenting its limits but we may be fencing with parlance again and showcasing how our sentences aren't precise enough to create a conceptual, universal schematic. We can't even agree on the difference between sex and love, plants and animals, cognition and emotion, a cup or a glass, or dead things and living things. Further, each brain has a different concept of words, learning, language, and future. Our complex speech is but a 200,000-year-old child[13] so our communication is playing catch up with our state-of-the-art conceptual abilities.

Greene doesn't get into what happens when this learning and creativity grows inside the illimitable free will brain forever. As it expands, we can conclude *more options* will be exercised each generation from a zero to an infinity you and I may never see. Greene calls my infinity, "a diverse set of behaviors," or "*innumerable* strategies an individual may pursue (my emphasis)."[14] Greene's word *innumerable* is the spot-on word for describing our infinite, planned future, and determinism might be correct if there existed a ceiling to human learning. Only humans entertain the idea to go beyond the diktats of nature and nurture with peace, reproduction, innovation, and charity. There is a profound, difference.

Brian Greene is also hilarious in a subtle, endearing, almost apologetic way, because he's truly a scientist. He wrote about going on an African safari with his buddies and I will greatly shorten his joke. They headed out into the Savanah with a guide who went over the safari rules, and he ended with this: *if you see a rhinoceros, lion, or even an ape, stand perfectly still,* then he lowered his voice and said, *if you don't…you'll be running for the rest of your life.*

Maybe a joke I told when I was 10 will help illustrate where our free will is: there was this guy walking around with a tiny little green man growing up out of the top of his head. No one would say anything because they could barely see it under his hair. As the tiny little green man grew and became more visible to others, the guy kept walking around till somebody finally asked, "what happened to you?" The little green man said, "would you believe it started as a bump on my ass?" Free will is not a dominant actor, it's the little green man—the needle in our haystack. Our free will may be somewhere inside this Steven Wright joke: "I've got a great seashell collection—it's scattered all over the beaches of the world." The world is our *oyster* and as we learn its secrets, we will one day obliterate poverty with a radical idea that doesn't involve money, refine our language with new words, and define free will.

As you can see, I've defended free will just a bit better than one would defend the existence of a supreme being who created himself.

The Oxymoron of Profit

We live better than any humans before us—every generation knew that—however, we the living have innovated our way to a unique position. We live better today than the Kings of Europe did in the 1800s, Deirdre McCloskey explained in her 3, 500-page books under the umbrella name, *The Bourgeoisie Virtues*. There were no antibiotics or anesthesia until long after those kings had died young and gone to heaven in chariots of gold. Today, we have almost everything we could imagine and more free time than any before us. Where did all this come from? Profit. The vast majority of innovations came from individuals too and the incentive was money.

McCloskey's 3 books show us how the proletariat *became* the bourgeoisie by ignoring the *clerisy* (her outstanding obvyism for the pyramid) and learning buy-low sell-high. The proletariat infringed on the bourgeoisie by trading sideways with their peers instead of selling their stuff to barons for almost nothing. This brought more food, time-saving devices, and economic freedom to a much broader base of people. Buying and selling among commoners gradually rid them of the king's middle-men, never knowing that they were practicing *creative destruction*. To help you, creative destruction means to get rid of junk in your house, or trash an outdated corporation or a bad government agency, and when that's not allowed, we drown in the trash and slowly go broke with negative profits.

The kings never could understand the free division of labor so they overlooked a fortune in taxes but those were hard to tally and collect until the electronic revolution (no moving parts) evolved. The idea to skip past the king's middle-men occurred to so many peasants at the same time that artificial management by edict couldn't be enforced anymore. As McCloskey says, "the people gave themselves *permissionism*," by giving the market back to themselves when the clerisy wouldn't, as women did later with marriage too. The new privateers walked straight through the invisible walls of the caste system, replaced the olde school of facilitators, and economic justice prevailed as more profit trickled down to those who did the actual work. The new farmers and manufacturers began loading up their carts with produce and textiles, taking them to town center, and selling it themselves—without a permit. Cutting out the middle man by becoming both producer and seller made food cheaper for the buyer—minus the baron's absurd markup—while the farmer got a raise. Europe gradually lost the demagogues: barons, earls, dukes (who made rules for "thee, not me") and the proletarian wages from every region, rose.

Trickle-down economics worked and kept working, as it did in Europe and the US, until the facilitators figured out how to manipulate money itself. Covered in Chapter 28, the pyramid readopted the economics of the dark ages and simply changed the chariots into Learjets. They fortified the economy with financial middle managers and the new paper assets became more lucrative than income or work. As the money began flowing uphill again, the robust middle class began thinning out. Historically, economists could never shake the feeling the great unwashed had to be managed, but the great unwashed evolved and the economists didn't. Today's economists have manipulated the numbers so, that the economy is plotting graphs they don't understand themselves, so they remedy that by explaining the graphs to us on the idiot box.

How is it possible that more people buying low, then selling high, lifts all boats? Doesn't it sound counterintuitive to you as it did to some of the most brilliant economists in history? It lifts boats, except for the boat the King, Pope, and their cronies are in, because fair competition plus incentive (minus controllers) brings down prices and raises pay simultaneously. After cutting out the windfall profits of the clerisy there was more wealth left for everybody, and with real competition profits kept getting smaller. A thousand workers now had the money that one greedy, corrupt baron once had. 100% free trade is what we would all do if not forced to do something else and the laborers ultimately swapped *His Eminence* for a prime minister.

Value is personal to each individual so *universal value* is a shot in the dark—societies have long tried to define things that don't exist. If a king sets the price for vegetables for example, he will create shortages or rotting surpluses and destroy the vegetable market. A free market will hone in on a price point, then customer sentiment will change, and the self-correcting market will adjust again. Each consumer has precise needs that change over time and it's absurd for anyone to regulate that which he knows nothing about. Value is subjective and cannot be measured.[15] Who are we to intervene when the market adds up all of our points of view for us?

Passing judgement on other people's buying and selling habits gets murkier: Dierdre McCloskey says, "both have the sacred and profane in mind."[16] Even the facts of life get involved. No nosey do-gooder could sort all *that* out because some want to buy something to impress a lover, some want high quality products, some are concerned with quantity, some yearn for yesteryear—machines that work for a lifetime—and some just crave the feeling of purchasing something. A few years ago, I cleaned out the garage and I had 13 flashlights. A rich friend of mine was looking at yachts online and found a nice one for a million dollars. He said, "this is a great buy!" and I said, "then you should buy 2 of them." When we're impulse buying, we don't want an economics lesson.

Some buyers are looking for provenance or intangibles, sometimes nobody is selling what we want, and economics goes on into infinity. Dierdre adds, "we don't want to work ethics down to a formula," meaning, everybody's formula is different—there's no accounting for taste.

"Wealth only comes from intelligent work," is an axiom. Work plus profit incentivize us to make more goods and services—suddenly there's more of everything for everybody—which inspires more people to work more intelligently, creating ever-expanding wealth. The word *wealth* can also mean anything because it's a synonym of another undefinable word—*happiness.* Wealth, happiness, profit, value, salary, time, or simply more *free* time to create art (all synonyms) tells us something new: there's really no such thing as a nonprofit organization. Our goals are too vast to explain away with money and can only be understood using the broad brushes of *happiness* and *intelligent work.*

Western Europe began wiggling their way out of this dilemma in the 1600s as the competition killing, sanctioned monopolies slowly shrunk and the little companies grew. McCloskey plots this early modern era as the "hockey stick graph," as wealth shot north and monarchies slumped south. The history of continuous wage growth, at least on the west end of the world, until 1969, is the empirical evidence for the necessity of the unhindered and un-helped, profit motive.

I loved McCloskey's theme of *hope,* which she weaved into her books, so I stole it. I'll pay her back one day if I can. *Hope*—our driver—was the missing word for describing sacrificially selfish behavior. I'll give you a counter example to hope: the western world is still a pretty good smorgasbord of goods, services, and psychological epiphanies—it's hard to miss out—yet so many go for get rich quick schemes and state lotteries. They've lost their hope for the future and when one of them gets astronomically lucky the unearned money usually destroys them. If you're rich, a morbid experiment might be to send 3 random 20 somethings 10 grand a month for years—you'll destroy 2 of them. If we know anything it's that personal struggle keeps us in evolution's favor and when that is removed for free, we atrophy.

Another Long Walk off a Short Pier

Charles Barkley (basketball great) is a philosopher who doubles me over with laughter with his honesty which is what gets him into hot water as a sports commentator. He's politically incorrect and irreverently entertaining, on national TV. He jokes about fat, blonde, cheerleaders just because he doesn't like their sports teams. Imitating how we transfer and project our biases, he makes sports fun with lines like, "you know things are going to hell when the best rapper is white and the best golfer is black." Go ahead and laugh, it releases magic endorphins that add heartbeats to your life.

My wife and I still love retirement in West Georgia, living slow southern lives, and most of our friends are lazy, fat, white, Christian Republicans. I get away with that joke, I hope, by referring to myself as that too—at least the first 3 parts are true. It's my version of *Crazy, Rich Asians*. They say "when in the south do as the south does" and with a blue-collar heart and a white-collar brain I've probably voted republican half the time. We heuristic humans can't help but be influenced by our peers and I love their republican white bread too. There are rednecks all over the planet; we just happen to know some cool ones here in West Georgia, but I can't convince them that our 2 political parties are depressingly similar. I can't remember which author said this, but when asked if she was republican or democrat: "well, I've been called a lot of things."

I'm not being derogatory about our West Georgia friends—these are our people and we love them. If you are a left winger you can read between the lines here. Some of our friends are whiter than they are fat and the reason I say "lazy" is because most of them don't qualify as golf cart republicans but do have a little money to relax with. I guess the weight problem is because we are American by birth, southern by the grace of God, and we avoid food insecurity with the anti-starvation gene which is selected in the south. God is who we worship but he's truly 2nd in command to the Earl of Sandwich. "Don't laugh at my jokes too much, people will say we're in love."[17]

I am prochoice and in spite of the legal merry-go-round I'm not worried about legal abortion going away. We own our own bodies, this is axiomatic, so we can put anything into them or take anything out of them. It's not even a gender issue, it's **the** basic human right. I call ownership of your body, the "Zero Amendment"—the one Thomas Jefferson and James Madison forgot, or left to the states…or left to us.

Individual freedom isn't always pretty but it's always necessary because if you don't think you own your own body you are putting the rest of us in jeopardy. There are always those waiting in the hallowed halls to tell you what to do with your body, time, and money. After they're done with you, they'll come after me. SCOTUS overturning Roe V Wade is an inconvenience but Americans will still have access—we'll vote it back in state-by-state which is how freedom comes back. Freedom lovers need to be vigilant because states' rights are necessary and intentionally vague subjects—tempting carrots for Uncle Sam too—and we need that balance for when federal laws go astray. The founding fathers created a triple competition of power—the Feds vs the States vs the People—forcing power to have to work uphill for the first time in history. With the exception of banning alcohol and a couple other bad amendments, or a sneaky new law buried at the end of an amendment, notice that the amendments to the constitution are good laws, because they went through all 3 filters.

On the B-side, states are making gambling illegal, advertising for it, and then monopolizing the profits!? This is as bizarre as if a state banned abortion except for state employees, or exempted them from social security taxes. "Whoops, I shouldn't have told you that." States change only the name, from *gambling* to *gaming*, as my state Georgia did, and are flirting with Benito Mussolini's: "everything in the state, nothing outside of the state." Since you and I own our own bodies, there is no victim with gambling—it is a victimless act between consenting adults so there is no one to prosecute. It seems I'm nitpicking with the gambling thing but when the states or the feds can violate their own laws, all bets are off. The founding fathers were well aware of victimless crimes and did nothing about them. Let us not forget the third part of the 10th Amendment: constitutional power…to the people.

The federal government also breaks the spirit of its own sacred documents. It was 1954 when Eisenhower and the federal government inserted *under God* into The Pledge of Allegiance. Because of the brilliant *separation of church and state* clause, that's all the Christian right has been able to get away with unless you consider the 2002 crusade into Iraq, when Texas invaded. The left is correct in wanting to keep the separation of church and state sacrosanct and correct and on the invasion of Iraq too.

On the flipside, the left wins me over with identifying problems then loses me with their solutions. I like their causes until the federal government partners up with them because the cause then leaps from democracy to plutocracy. At that point the catchphrases are concealed inside a broader basket of, "we are all in this together," which would be true if we were being invaded. Translation for catchphrases: "the federal government can solve all our problems……with money." This is the red-carpet mistake and the idealess right wing offers little pushback. Peoria Illinois has no idea how to solve the problems in Greenleaf Idaho—problems are different everywhere and better solved by small communities or individuals.[18] Still, the left always goes national—DC can solve all problems with a blanket of new money—and the lefthanded *newspeak*[19] is beginning to rival the old righthanded hell, fire, and brimstone from the 1950s.

We mistake our personal problems for national ones. Eat more fruits, vegetables, fat birds, exercise, read, and interpret your dreams. That's the sum of my advice. Wellness solutions are inexpensive and don't cost other people money. And reading what we want is more educational than college knowledge because we remember more of it. Reading books at night is cheaper than college too and after learning on our own with no debt, we don't get the impression that our learning is over at age 22. If you want to get ahead of the first hundred names in your phone directory (if they have those anymore) just randomly pick books from library shelves.

To me, the democrat-republican debate on TV is a circus for us to watch because both parties want to accelerate deficit spending, manage a free society, and cozy up to their latest favorite dictator. On TV, they talk about everything but those things. We can switch from left to right, or back, but we'll just be trading cabins with each other……on the Lusitania. And when the west transitioned from belief to nonbelief—Europe traded in religion for government first—we were simply switching beds on the Lusitania again, because religion and government both attempt to manage a society that doesn't need to be managed.

I'm about 50% leftwing (minus the red-carpet mistake) and the left did go to considerable trouble dragging us white folk kicking and screaming to introduce us to the other people in this country, reversing the momentum of the psychological arms race. What I mean is, the greatest generation was violent, the baby boomers psychologically pared that down to verbal schadenfreude, and gen X women killed that schadenfreude and elected Barack Obama, twice, to put an exclamation mark on this evolution. The psychological arms race was so lopsided the Xers defected and even many of those fat, blonde, cheerleaders voted for Obama. Empathizing with racism victims, the sexism victims remembered the locked doors they had gotten to in life and how they'd figured out how to open some of them. Next, they imagined how many African Americans never got to those doors and never had a chance to find the combination. We've still never had a female president which means sexism runs deeper in the subconscious than racism, but we never stop building and the gen Xers—whose mothers didn't smoke and drink through those pregnancies—have the strongest duality of mind so far. (Duality of mind is not when you personally relate to another person, rather, it is when you empathize with someone you can't personally relate to.)

Because of these pioneers, sexism and racism are receding faster than ever "but I think it's gonna be a long, long time"[20] as Bernie Taupin wrote, because archetypes change slowly. I will take another risk and say if African Americans were as bad off as the far left tells us they would be migrating to other countries. Most black Americans know first when an interloper is crying wolf, or not. And I'll also risk a cliché: We have many Asian, Black, and Latino friends and when they're over at our house, I don't bring up religion, because I'd get that thigh pinch under the table from you know who, that I forgot to tell you about earlier.

Here in West Georgia, the smalltown republican husbands tend to think they're in command but they are usually 2nd in command. When I bring up institutionalized racism or institutionalized sexism the couples get monkey faced—even the republican wives who still leave the toilet seat down. Having heard the republican talking points I know them by heart. The good ones are about family and free markets, or whatever you want to call those 2 evolutionary mechanisms that never stop humming and never go out of style. The best republican talking point is love of family and if republicans ever drop this gem they'll never win another election. If they become prochoice it'll be hard to lose one but their bigger problem is that they get tongue-tied when defending capitalism because they don't know what it is. Like the democrats, the republicans can't seem to separate capitalism from the government-religion-banking pyramid.

A capitalist friend of mine who built up a tiny gas station into a large convenience store by working 12 hours a day said he has no problem with governments starting businesses everywhere, as they are doing now. "As long as they make money it's fine with me," he said. I asked, "it would be fine if they started a gas station right next to yours using taxpayer money, some of it your own, and charged less?" He stared at me with that waking up look and I told him about the thousands of GSEs (Government Sponsored Enterprises) that state and federal governments launch that compete directly with private businesses, built from scratch. "Fair competition increases the general wealth and unfair competition decreases it," I added. A new began gear turning in his head.

The only way capitalism can go majorly wrong is if it gets help, you know…from above. The help usually came from religion, now it comes from government, and these overseers pick economic winners and losers *for us*. Some companies and some economic sectors are punished while some are helped and the purchasing public doesn't get to make those decisions. This is not capitalism, in fact, it is closer to fascism.

The French wine industry, for example, will continue to decline because they are spoiled by their own government. When an industry becomes special—protected and subsidized—that industry gets lazy and rugged competitors, if allowed, leave them behind. The sum of 8 billion palettes is a *many splendored thing*[21] and the French wine makers have lost some embarrassing blind taste tests (overpriced for quality is the market's response) which slowly funnels money away from other French industries as trust degenerates. If Europeans had their choice of wines of the world without those heavy import taxes, they'd have money left over to buy other European products. With no import taxes more European companies would evolve than de-evolve because competition forces improvement and the same logic applies to the automobile industry.

Cars made outside of Europe are heavily taxed—it's hard to find a Ford or Chevy there—so the EU helps decide which car a European will buy. Adam Smith might suggest the EU thinking exactly backwards indeed: protecting their sellers (the few) at the expense of their buyers (the many). In the US, DC allows foreign goods to come in almost untaxed, however, they loan trillions of dollars to select US corporations that they like. It's the same thing.

As We Unsubscribe from the Issues of the Tribe

"Ain't no angel gonna greet me, it's just you and I my friend," I sing as a mere mortal, thieving Springsteen's line. I don't mean to sound immoderate—this is what I've come to believe by the weightiness of the natural evidence—and occasionally I just tell people I'm "nondenominational." Nonbelievers are still pariahs in the south and there's lots of lightning here you see, but if it's any consolation I don't believe in the Devil either. We each have good and evil tendencies which infinitely vary from person to person. When John Denver sang "you might say he found the key to every door," I think he was offering false hope. There is no key like that, and when an atheist tells you he's a "secular humanist" he is simply cozying up to groupthink. He's saying "everyone is right," which isn't a stance on anything.

The archetype of our previous 40,000 generations still sticks to our ribs—their dreams, fears, losses, beliefs, victories—because they were always *bringing in the sheaves*. It'll be a while before we discover how this encrypted innate knowledge gets passed down but wherever we grow up that religiosity is in our DNA and we don't want to change it too fast. Isn't it weird that almost all the murders in the 20th century were executed by countries that pushed atheism? Prior to Germany, Russia, and China, the enlightened in France tried to alter the alter and ended up in a European bloodbath. As we tepidly modify our metaphysical archetypes and teach those alterations, we might remind ourselves that we are changing the future.

For over half the planet, mysticism remains a superpower. It extends our lives and astonishingly defeats addiction simply because we believe it can. It enables us to venture where none have trod or go completely off the grid. Mysticism can train our forever young brains to ignore our own psychological introspections and feel magically, suddenly cured. That's simply positive thinking which will come and go. Let us not fill in the blanks with our #2 pencils just because we children love to color in those squares, but without childlike wonderment we would be computers and keyboards that any flat earther could type onto as they wished.

Existentialism rejects mysticism and is an endearing philosophy up to the midpoint. "Humanism" is their philosophy and, as evolution also thinks, existentialists see an individual life as a part of the whole. From humanism they next slide us into collectivism, which, like old time religion, can only be administered from the top down. Their philosophy is existentialism = humanism = collectivism = communism. Minus the last word, professors teach this equation as the best philosophy (I've sat in the classrooms) though they are rich and living in the west. Communism keeps the throngs commensurately fed for their hard work—a small bowl of rice with bits of chicken. This philosophy is called "asceticism" and existentialists are minimalists which means *to under consume*. Humanism had no *renaissance*. Empirically we can see the results of their equation and that's why people quietly unsubscribe and choose individualism whenever they have the choice. Individualism makes us happy and independent however with humanism being the placard that the pyramid not-so-subliminally presents to us—yet doesn't follow itself—most of us leave the philosophy of individualism as a private thought.

Imagine a dolphin swimming up to a pod of dolphins and saying, "I found the answer for all of us—dolphinism!" "What?" offer the others, "isn't that what we already do……in various clever ways?" Humans don't live in tribes anymore, we specialize, and any existentialist is free to go live in a commune but why do they insist everybody follow them? From Chapter 2, "advice is a gift from the advisor back to the advisor."

There is nothing more prevalent than *individualthink* (not a word yet but groupthink is) but some still hand over their trust and power to the tribe. Eric Hoffer wrote *The True Believer,* explaining the "Madding Crowd" to us. His take is that we emotionally cling to groupthink movements, from fear and self-loathing, as if we detest our unique selves.[22] Some see that person in the mirror and don't stand there long enough to recognize them. The genius of the masses is a different concept from the Madding Crowd because the former is a slow mathematical compilation of individualthink, long called "citizen science," and the latter is a frantic gathering, confused about the slow, creeping change of humanity.

When Possible, Think Slow

If you've discovered the author Daniel Kahneman—the current grandaddy of statistical analysis—you already know thinking slow is better than thinking fast. Although mother evolution has empowered us to make incredibly accurate, fast, intuitive assessments, she has also given to us the patience and cognition to ponder them longer.

People who *always* think fast have distilled complex reality down to a small set of simplicities which catalyzes some good answers but creates the same wrong answers over and over. The cave people had to think fast, giving us the habit. Daniel Kahneman won a Nobel Prize for his groundbreaking research in d*ecision making*, informing us that thinking fast short circuits the modern brain. A personal injury lawyer entertains the premise that a quick answer is better than the right answer and knows that the captive *audience*, sorry I mean the *jury*,[23] naturally responds to emotional evidence. Quick answers are employed to win debates by intimidation and we are attracted to these showstoppers because we'd rather be entertained than educated.

Kahneman teaches us to take our far-flung beliefs and *regress to the mean* which is an age-old method of statistical analysis first invented by Charles Darwin's cousin Francis Galton.[24] As with Edith's colorful middle, we can toss out the emotional advertisements—the highs and lows—and see what's really there. Every culture has a *colorful middle,* with the strangest of oxymorons. Here are 5 examples: more less (US) mas o menos (Spanish), yin yang (China) elevated valley (Arabic), full empty (European). Isolated groups separately came up with these polarized, colloquial, medians.

Since I'm a *hoopaholic* (basketball nut) and always look forward to March Madness, I lost my colorful middle on a sports statistic. The tournament is a thrill downsouth and I've always been proud of how southern colleges have dominated the NCAA basketball championships, including 3 different teams from North Carolina. However, when I added up the wins north and south of the horizontal population line across the US—putting University of Kentucky in the south and UCLA in the north—it was even. I was wrong. It was my southern pride making up another apophenic statistic.

I'm not an expert on statistical analysis at all; I find it a fun subject with lots of room to play, so I'm offering ways to reanalyze situations before we leap to conclusions. My favorite statistical fun is to joke with brevity and poignancy, and toss in a hook. For example, when people are in our pool and hear distant thunder, some get freaked, so I tell them that in a pool they have a higher chance of having a heart attack than getting hit by lighting. The funny part is, with 2 worries now, they keep swimming. For some reason that reminds me of the Peewee Herman joke: can you name 2 people who were shot in the back of the head in a theatre? People are more horrified when they picture the guy sitting in front of Peewee Herman, than picturing Abe Lincoln getting his brains blown out, illustrating some of the peculiar ways we process information.

TV is also designed to destroy our ability to make statistical common sense. The funniest of riddles is presented to us by the old westerns. There's always a guy riding the plains alone with a rifle and a little roll behind his saddle, then at night he's got a big fire, a coffeepot, cooking pans, a clothesline full of laundry, a sleeping bag, and sometimes even a dog named Cody. Where did he get all that stuff? Why is it that at the end of a new drug commercial by mega pharma, the couples who take that pill are always watering their garden using that handheld spout with flowers painted on the side? And why are they aways grilling vegetables in the backyard and grinning at each other like idiots?

The only common side effect with placebalimumab is difficulty breathing. Westerners are raised on the TV reality makeover which has transformed the American CEO from a leader into an onscreen public relations actor. Our perception of the company is now the CEO's personality instead of the quality of the product and watching the news will make us overall terrible statisticians.

The most difficult statistical analysis is measuring how happy people are and Scandinavians often win. Happiness is a synonym of longevity and an antonym of depression. People get depressed in areas where it is overcast but why not in Scandinavia where they love the outdoors? The stock answers rush to environmental factors (weather can't be the answer) as if the individuals there have nothing to do with it! Another way to say it is, if Nordic people are in fact happier, if they moved to a different area of the globe they'd be just as happy and live as long. And I'll contradict myself again and say that happiness and longevity sprout more in regions with colder weather. It keeps our metabolism higher and these non-religious, happy Scandinavians bundle up their newborns like Eskimos, and take them out into the deep freeze.

"In olde England they bequeathed centuries of prayer to the longevity of their Monarchs, their sovereigns," Francis Galton wrote and he "statistically calculated that these conduits of God were the shortest lived of all the rich in England."[25] The Lords had everything money could buy and still weren't happy. Pyramidal thinking corrals us into believing that happiness and longevity are external gifts and if that were true, individuals would be powerless robots. We *Kahn* ourselves right and left.

Daniel Kahneman was a child walking through Paris in Nazi occupied France when he was stopped and questioned by a secret service officer. Wikipedia tells us he had covered up the Star of David like his mom told him to and the officer let him go or we may never have had the pleasure. If Daniel Kahneman or Francis Galton had died young, we might not know to this day how we love coming to irrational conclusions, accidentally on purpose. I especially enjoyed Kahneman's book *Thinking Fast and Slow,* where he lets his 1 hair down a little. He found that professional golfers hit more 11-foot birdie putts than 10-foot par putts! Making a birdie is a dynamic that excites pros, so the anticipation of future rewards releases endorphins that enable them to make more longer putts than shorter ones.

I often thought the republicans were more warlike than the democrats but when I added up presidential decisions it was yet another tie between the 2 parties. From golf to politics, we can temper our eccentric thinking and *regress to the mean* to hone our emotional observations. On the other hand, we love the outlandish. When we go out into the world of goods and services we want to be impressed. We want to see bizarre variations in our stores, institutions, and life options.

It's *mean* to say "all kids are above average." That's how I felt during my school years, though nobody specifically said it. This isn't the fault of the great teachers, it's from the 1-size-fits-all philosophy of our school system. Everybody gets a trophy and the children themselves start seeing through this. Western education isn't bad at all but it has been in a static state since 1950 while all other western institutions have evolved along with us. James Tooley, an education author, says if you "search for something mythical, something people deny the existence of, you might find it." He's talking about innovative schools. 90% of US schools have the same curriculum and Tooley doesn't mince words about how damaging this 1-size-fits-all prospectus is.

I'm prochoice on everything but whether we lean left or right our kids go through the same academic stanchions as if they were all the same person. "All in all, you're just another brick in the wall," is how Pink Floyd puts it. With what we now know, boys and girls should be in separate classrooms at least for the first few years, because they are different species. Wildly different schools for artisans, athletes, and artists will create cracks in the wall by finding where each student excels. It can bring boyish normalcies like ADHD, anxiety, autism, and agnosia into a world of individual innovation because it doesn't matter what we learn as long as we are making more synaptic connections. And as we know from the old farming educations Jim and his siblings got in Missouri, these schools can be tiny.

Here's the irony of national education: If all the restaurants in your city had the exact same menu you would be horrified and think you were in the Twilight Zone or on the wrong planet but we send our kids to a place like that for 12 years. Consumers want and need more variety in education, so do the kids, and the economy wants more variety too. It's bizarre to me that 90% of western schools have the same menu and more bizarre that half the parents aren't phased. Whatever we don't like about a school is usually a symptom of a much bigger problem: monopoly. Monopolies always, and deceptively so, turn into self-serving beasts which can't be fixed without creative destruction.

For a counterintuitive statistic, Olivier Sibody tells us in the book *NOISE* that the rampant male sexism in company A results in almost all male hires. If the bias in another company, B, is half prejudice toward men and half toward women, we get a 50-50 male/female hiring pattern and we think that settles it. But both companies have the exact same percentage of irrational bias! Both companies have about a 50-50 chance of hiring the best candidate, which is no better than random luck, so they may as well skip the interview process. Daniel Kahneman, another coauthor of *NOISE,* finds that judges, parole boards, and doctors make creepy errors in decision-making, and too many of the verdicts depend on when they last had a meal.

We run across many psychopaths in our lives and the most difficult statistical assessment is knowing when we meet one because they are so clever. My wife and I had a haunting experience: we had a good friend, 10 years divorced, who met this guy, married him, and they drove down from Wooster Ohio to West Georgia to visit us for a week. He was perfectly nice but had no spontaneity, like a politician. He would smile politely at appropriate times but wouldn't laugh and I noticed his car was immaculate and even his CDs and mirrors had no smudges.

Everything about him seemed flawless as if he had some other agenda and I told my wife that he gave me the creeps. A year later, he had gotten his name onto all his new wife's accounts and while teaching her target shooting, held a pistol *in her hand* and shot her in the temple. The smalltown cops knew, because they knew her, but found zero evidence and had to file it as "a suicide."

CHAPTER 10

Marriage Is What We Came Here For

During Edith's courtship with Jim, she made a big decision based on what she thought her options were at the time. Love, honor, and *obey were in Edith's marriage vows and she didn't flinch or even hear much of what the preacher said after that. Jim and Edith were both in a trance as she ceremoniously lost her last name as if she was a pet—once removed. Mulling over it later she did recall one thing: Jim had been commanded by the church to provide for her and she liked that part. In marriage vows from 1500 A. D., sex was redrafted into an almost palatable form of trade. Consortium was painted over as a duty, needing an attorney to shirk it and the quid pro quo—an exchange of services for goods—was the man supported the wife. "Hey big spender......spend......a little time with me."*[1]

Marriages were "legally and regally prepared,"[2] *and still are. We must bite our lip and think of it as an historic improvement, as women, 1 by 1, break the chains of fealty. We sometimes forget that nature doesn't care what predicament we are in or where we are in the power struggle, because evolution never fails to accomplish what no pyramid can turn asunder—reproduction. As Voltaire said, "God created sex, priests created marriage." Gary Lightbody of Snow Patrol said, "forget what we're told, before we get too old, this is my garden that's bursting into light."*

Bella, from Disney's *Beauty and the Beast,* whom the villagers figured would marry the boorish Gaston, sang, "there must be more than *this* provincial life." *Provincial* means pastoral, slender minded, or old-fashioned and Bella had a little Stockholm Syndrome from that bonjour little town.

We all strive for that picture-perfect marriage Disney put into our heads. *Happy ever after* is a mythical creature and we began the search for this unicorn 700 years ago in England when arranged marriages were all the rage. We can't pinpoint when this archaic tradition began its slow death so I'll give the credit to the iconic Romeo and Juliet because they became European symbols for freedom, though they were semifictional. The famous story is loosely based on an Italian pair who met in the city of love, Verona, and died together because their parents didn't approve of their love. The double-suicide heard round the world; well, William Shakespeare heard it 2000 klicks away in England and it started a ripple effect because we're never satisfied with the status quo.

Semi-modern marriage has its earliest roots in 12th century England followed by Shakespeare's play in the 14th century. In 1140 Benedictine monk Gratian wrote "verbal consent of both partners" into English law, a nice springboard for freedom of speech and marriage, but consent wouldn't truly be realized for 800 more years. Like free will, it's a process, and the big shackle only came off in 1967 when English women got the right to legal abortion—finally owning their own bodies.

The average lifespan in 14th century England was 30-35 years and when a British child became 18 their lifespan went up to 40-45 years. Everyone had accepted this pensive sadness and married off their teenagers, so they'd have time to raise the next family. The English felt lucky to live that long, not knowing life expectancy had not changed much for the last 7000 years. With agriculture in full bloom, they also didn't know that their height, lifespan, and brains were shrinking, and falling behind the meat eaters of the world.

After the pope was demoted then laid off during the violent 16th century Protestant Reformation, mutual attraction was gaining favor in the minds of all religions. Professor Frances E. Dolan's study of this period concludes, "a living partnership between equals found broad dissemination as early as the 15th and 16th centuries." I think she's being optimistic but what's hard to imagine is the rest of the world enjoyed none of this freedom. Marriage had been about class, business, money and power but with common women gaining a modicum of choice in these 4 institutions English culture blossomed. Olde Europe should have gotten the 16th century hint of what women were up to when Leonardo da Vinci painted that quirky, clandestine, half-smile on Mona Lisa's face. Most men didn't think women had a sex drive back in the days of yore, now they're jealous, knowing they can have an orgasm whenever they want.

After the 2nd English Civil War the Marriage Act of 1653 set a new minimum age for marriage: 16 for males and 14 for females.[3] The official state sponsoring of marriage, with the church calling the shots, officially went into law in England with the Clandestine Marriage Act of 1753, which was essentially a life sentence even with the Divorce Act of 1857.[4] Although marriage was sanctioned by the Monarchy, who technically owned everything too (communism), it was a step up from how females had lived in the past and still do in Saudi Arabia where women are just a stone's throw away. Powerful Saudi men have mansions with vast, dimly lit basements underneath, full of blondes trafficked from the Baltics. After centuries, Britain finally ended the trading of slaves in 1807 and freed their own black slaves in 1833. The notion of societal choice had begun in the 14th century when 2 individuals demanded individuality and a different fairy tale came to life.

Once there was a couple whose hearts, hormones, and imaginations cared not of English law. At age 13, as the Shakespeare play goes, Juliet Capulet fell in love with 16-year-old Romeo Montague, or, as Jimmy Carter might say, "she lusted in her heart for his immune system." Albert Einstein said, "imagination is more important than knowledge," imploring us to think beyond the status quo. Julie Delpy took it further, insisting in a movie with Ethan Hawke that Einstein said, "if you don't believe in magic, you're as good as dead."[5]

Other girls overcame their eleutheromania and got curious about all those single males walking around with those opposite immune systems. They defied society, tradition, religion, and their parents by picking a boy. Shakespeare was way ahead of his time but never knew he fired the first shot of the European sexual revolution. "Marriage is what we came here for," is from the classic *Princess Bride* movie but marriage based on mutual attraction, for us westerners, represents .04% of our million-year history! Maybe we get married because everybody else is doing it—"it's a story we take on," as Deepak Chopra might say.

Marriage is still baked into the cake of the legal system in the west so the next step is to remove lawyers from the equation because they are unnecessary middle men, unless children are involved. People who live together amicably split up estates all the time and go their separate ways without hiring over-priced strangers to represent them. There should be no legal stipulations on relationships between consenting adults whatsoever because it easily falls under *pursuit of happiness*. In 2015, the US Supreme Court legalized same-sex marriage which seemed fantastic but it was a mistake! Were gay couples who were already happily living together supposed to do quadruple axles in the living room? The court should have thrown up their hands and said, "anybody can get married to anybody in America the beautiful, anybody can divorce, and the risks are all yours." The litmus test for a law is whether it applies equally to everyone and SCOTUS was stuck in groupthink instead of interpreting the constitution.

If the court gives a damn about who marries who or how many, or how anyone defines a *relationship*, they are shallow and neurotic. Regarding benefit of counsel, we should refer to a relationship as "marriage" only when they have children and let us not let the pyramid raise the kids during those first 5 years. Evolution has a little experience with that.

The King's and their fellow mystics believed human nature was depraved—they were accidentally peering behind their own firewalls—and Shakespeare agreed: "the good men do is oft interred with their bones but their evil lasts forever." "All things pass into the night," the band Q Lazarus sang too, but then their backup singer said, "Oh no sir, I must say you're wrong." [6] Humans are born basically good and without a king mucking everything up that goodness spreads like ripples in a pond. Shakespeare, an elitist protector of olde England and a weak philosopher, didn't understand that.

Individual choice in relationships and economics eclipsed evil but for half the planet it remains the most difficult thing to demand. Socrates didn't see us heading north either, typically thinking the new generation coming up was weak-minded and irresponsible. Old codgers think this way though it's observably impossible and almost evolutionarily impossible, for generations to degrade. It's tantamount to saying "all the new baby birds are so feeble and clumsy, that the birds will go extinct." Thomas (Robert) Malthus too, couldn't have been more wrong, though these thinkers appeared to have their fingers on the pulse. It's hard to see sacrificial selfishness when you're above it all—we fooled them posthumously, all 8 billion of us with belly buttons.

One of the overarching deal cinchers for modern marriage is similar IQs between lovers. Murray and Herrnstein crunched the stats on that for us in their book *The Bell Curve* and I would add that height and similar upbringings of Stockholm Syndrome match up couples too. Obviously women pick husbands for earning power and IQ but there is no real definition of IQ which they neglected to say in the book. Those tests are to see how valuable we might be at slaving away *inside* the pyramid while I see intelligence as how much happiness we can find *outside* the pyramid. A sickly child, Ringo Starr was dubbed a dunce in the 60s—with an IQ of 68—yet he's always been the best interview of the Fab 4—always confident and relaxed. Michael Jackson barely made it out of high school but later learned to write hit songs—one of the most difficult, complex, and sophisticated of endeavors. I would know, I tried to write a chart-buster for 12 years.

I have a basketball buddy, Lonzell, and he went to high school with Michael and Janet in the "great state of Chicago."[7] He said the Jacksons were ushered through high school and at graduation they got new TV outfits while Lonzell's dad, who was in the cleaning business, gave him a mop and a bucket. Although Lonzell was a good student he went full bore into the business, running crews every night cleaning hundreds of offices, and he's makin' scratch……and still alive.

Back in the day me and full-court Lonzell would scout out different gyms for a good pick-up game. One day we went to a gym near his crib. We sat on the bench trying to get into the next game and I said, "it's dark in here." He thought I meant everybody in there was black and what I meant was the overhead lights were turned way down. We both got a big laugh, and another laugh when I reminded him that "the white gyms are always lit up like Christmas," which takes me back…….to slavery and free speech. Free speech was the sound that broke the slave barrier for women and African Americans alike.

The Evolution of Belief and Law

Free Speech

Cognizant of the painfully slow creep of British law the founding fathers of North America took a leap past them toward equal rights, making all white men, rich or poor, equal under the law. Men ruled every country at the time and offered their people no rights, so we can be optimists and at the very least think of the first constitutional republic as a good start. The historical weight of the ideas forged from 1770-1820 created America and somewhat the world, yet were alone in the US with "congress shall pass *no law* abridging freedom of speech or the press," and still are. All forms of speech were protected—ideas, inuendo, images, irreverence, intellection, insults—including the inalienable right to be wrong or even lie, or the 1st Amendment was meaningless. If politicians can decide what a lie is, what if some of the founding fathers had been atheists? Some of them were, so should they have been able to censure or prohibit any number of beliefs from being taught?

Is a comedian telling the truth or not? It depends on who you ask and Pink Floyd asked, "so you think you can tell, heaven from hell?"[8] Many icons in history have tried to define the difference between heaven and hell for everybody, and the very 1st Amendment bypassed the graveyards of history and left heaven and hell to the individual. The catch for liars was that they can be sued for libel (written lies) or slander (oral lies). To win, the plaintiff had to not only prove it was a lie, he also had to prove that the lie was intended with malice and was injurious to the plaintiff.

The first near infinite tolerance of free speech by congress in 1791—first in millenniums of written law—hurled simple conversation to its most productive level. Every transaction begins with a conversation. We have James Madison (main author of the 1st Amendment) and Alexander Hamilton to thank for free speech. Thomas Jefferson—an avid reader with an enviable vocabulary—was even freer from the handcuffs of church and state, putting him in poll position to see how free speech would grease the gears of the economy. The founders had help during their adolescence from the old and wise George Mason (slave owner) who had led the initial philosophical fight for individual rights long before the Revolutionary War and died in 1792.

However, when I read that Mason wanted "control over commercial actions" in the Virginia constitution[9] I smelled the blood of an Englishman. This is the worldwide mistake because politicians happily become partners with landowners and businessmen who shake hands, mutually profit, and spread corruption. Since the backroom players garner government power for personal gain, we rarely find out about these secret conversations. Unseen mafias pop up here and there and the series *Yellowstone* showed us in red how these secret partnerships end up in murder for money, and they rarely get caught. Even the good guys end up having to murder just to live.

If the US had left the government out of private business like they knew they were supposed to, we'd be looking at a much better economy. In the constitution, the founders watered the business question down to: "the congress shall have the power to regulate the commerce among the several states." They might have added "during emergencies, as in military war" because congressmen can be nepotistic like all of us and have no problem helping certain companies over others, even during peacetime.

Getting back to the untold benefits of free speech, John Adams and his Vice President Thomas Jefferson grew alongside each other through decades of arguing and correspondence and Jefferson finally convinced Adams words are not guns. Not originally twin-minded, Adam's last dying words were "Thomas Jefferson."[10] Initially, the federalist Adams was not a free speech absolutist and thought the government's job was to bring the most happiness to the most people.[11] If I may speak for the states' rights man Jefferson for a sec, he might say "freedom is everything for a people who can forge a contract which restrains their own government, as happiness *is* freedom, nothing more." If the government's job is to provide happiness, which often prompts verbal policing, then *they* must first define happiness and free speech, and they'll eventually want to decide what emotional security is too. The long arm of the law shouldn't be that long because everybody has a different characterization of all these things and Jefferson knew that intuitively.

Jefferson *did* say, "if you trade in your freedom for security, you'll end up with neither." He was looking out for us, meaning, that the proverbial "better place" politicians love to talk about can mean anything. The founders contracted to protect citizens from enemies and the *enemy* meant violence and fraud. For the government to get involved it had to be an overt hostile act—someone had to be defrauded or accosted—which didn't include any likes or dislikes a citizen happened to have.

Most founders knew that these matters weren't in a republic's purview and, in a pragmatic sense, would be astronomically expensive to sort out anyway. People could do as they pleased as long as they didn't violate the individual rights of another. The founders were well aware of marijuana, gambling, homosexuality, prostitution, and atheism, and chose to make no laws for, or against, or about, any of it. There were no victims. The most brilliant of phrases, *pursuit of happiness*, meant that whatever was not illegal in the new world should stay that way. The aging founders were worried sick about their simple, abstract revolution getting dissected by future governments and were long dead when the US government started legislating our lives.

Prior to Thomas Jefferson's successful tutelage of John Adams, the first free speech shock was when Adams signed the Alien and Sedition Acts after congress pushed for the censorship of incitement, and passed it. John the freedom fighter goes down as having jailed publishers of newspapers with the ink still drying on the 1st Amendment. The press called John Adams "blind, bald, crippled, toothless, and a closet royalist who would start another British monarchy."[12] Adams handed the free press the reason to fear that last charge by stomping on the first sentence of the young 1st Amendment. Hamilton, the most innovative protector of free speech as a defense attorney, oddly went along with Adams and called the democratic republicans (the states' rights party) the treasonous "French Faction."[13] Perhaps these *federales* were *too* federal and were steadfast about words not being guns until the words were pointed at them.

Republican newspapers, the focus of federal prosecution, doubled during the 2.5 years of the Sedition Act.[14] When we ban something we promote it. The old neighbors Jefferson and Madison hip checked the hubris of Adams and Hamilton on restricting speech and won the day, not to mention a power changing, razor-thin election. When the dust had cleared, the tripod holding up fledgling America—free speech, equal treatment under the law, and the 10th Amendment—still stood for white males. These were ideals to strive for (virgin territory with no historical precedent) and it would end up costing 580,000 white lives and 40,000 black lives to begin assimilating everybody into this great experiment.

Sally Hemings

Long before Thomas Jefferson was president, Sally Hemings, with whom Jefferson would have 6 kids, was 1 of his 140 or so black slaves although she was the granddaughter of a white slave owner. She was, one could guess, 3/4ths white (*a quadroon*) because she was also the daughter of Jefferson's father-in-law—John Whales—the baby daddy. So, Jefferson's wife Martha Whales was the half-sister of Sally Hemings who, after Martha's early death, became the governess of the surviving Jefferson daughters.[15] Many slave women would raise the master's kids and their own kids while buttoning up with 2 coats to make themselves less accessible to froggy white men.[16]

Martha was a young, rich widow when she married Thomas, bringing along the Hemings slaves and doubling his land holdings to 10,000 acres. They had 6 kids, 2 of whom died young, and Martha died too shortly after their last child was born.[17] Jefferson felt the loss of something precious and found a deep depression after her death in 1782. As luck would have it, America needed him in Europe so off he went to France in 1784 for 5 years. There he was smitten with a married English woman which didn't work out.[18] He worked and travelled Europe with Martha's surviving 4 children who were taken care of by their governess, the 14-year-old Sally Hemings. We know the gist of the Sally-Thomas story and though their first recorded birth was 1795, the start of their relationship is presumed to be 1788 when she was 18.[19] The details however are highly disputed *and* confirmed by historians, including 1 DNA match,[20] plus Thomas was in Monticello for the conception of each of Sally's 6 children. The comedian Eddie Griffin might say "he creeped up into the black forest and got lost." Fast forwarding a few years to these start-over babies, 4 of Sally's and Thomas's 6 kids survived too, and from all accounts, any of Thomas's living kids could have sung, "my daddy's rich and my momma's good lookin,"[21] not knowing dad was heavily in debt.

Before Jefferson was president, he did stop growing work-intensive tobacco, built little houses for many slaves, and gave each a tiny plot of land on his property from which they could personally engage in the economy. He never publicly acknowledged his own slave children, or campaigned against slavery, or he never would have made it to the White House.[22] It wasn't until the last month of his life, June 1826, when the bankrupt Jefferson finally released all his slaves including his own children with Sally Hemings. Jefferson loved them and his view that black people were inferior and the races could not intermix, cannot be explained,[23] except by the woeful state of science of the time.

The contradiction of Jefferson was his unbending belief in limited government and central banking, alongside his perseverance for public education, on the state level, and straddling the fence on slavery. Kris Kristofferson would say "he's a walkin' contradiction partly truth and partly fiction, takin' every wrong direction in his lonely way back home."[24] Jefferson's contrary ghost haunted the commonwealth of Virginia for 140 years—it would be 1967 when SCOTUS finally struck down the ban on interracial marriage in *Loving vs Virginia.*

The tobacco plantation owners and many other croppers were funded by British credits called bills of exchange which were fancy paper banknotes that bought shiploads of crops. Britain was slightly inflating the New World with printed paper while trying to tax the colonies for printing stamps.[25] Xeroxing money is now off the charts—it's the national sport everywhere—and back in the day Britain enforced what monopoly on value they could across 3 continents.

Sailing under the boot of the red cross unfurled, England forced the world into using *credit* and while they spirited away with the spoils few knew that most everything the Brits imported from the 4 corners was free to them save for the cost paper and ink, plus shipping. Mark Knopfler writes, "I have legalized robbery, called it belief." There was a big red X, you see, through the red cross on the billowing sail.

Money

Prior to the American Revolution the individual states weren't allowed to coin money although they did occasionally because coins were in short supply. Most of the coinage came into the colonies from outside traders and buyers. In addition to the weightless British pounds circulating, other European paper money mingled, and by post revolution, each colony was issuing paper too. Some states would simply print up enough money at a fairly low cost to pay off their debt to a neighboring state. This printing was held in check from becoming a blank check, by competition, because if one state printed too much, word got around and other states would refuse that devalued paper. It was somewhat self-regulating and the same logic applies when a country prints too much money today.

Coins were preferred by the colonists—Italian and Spanish coins had the most consistent precious metal content—and the Spanish gold reale was the unsanctioned colonial dollar before and after the British occupation. Pirates and Caribbean traders brought in gold and silver "pieces of 8" to spend in the cities; they didn't tarry much with paper money. Late to the paper money game, Spain started their first central bank in 1782, which is why their metals traded worldwide, 1:1, until their paper money began metaphorically shaving their coins.

The currency that spiked inflation in the 13 colonies, for a spell, was the continental currency printed to pay soldiers and the like in the 1776 revolution. Unlike today, sellers weren't always required to accept these continental dollars, which paid for 2/3rds of the war. 1 continental dollar would buy 50¢ worth of goods by 1777 and by 1779 it would buy 6¢ worth, and by 1780 it would buy 2¢ worth of goods. [26] Inflation from this currency vanished because the people had the choice to use it or not and the continental congress ceded the power to print currency back to the states.

Alexander Hamilton started the New York Post, the State Bank of New York in 1784, and was the New York delegate to the constitutional convention, endorsing it against the wishes of his constituents. The bill of rights was yet to be written. He lost his seat, rebounded and formed the federalist party as George Washington's first cabinet member. Hamilton detested the concept of competing parties and wanted the smartest to run the country.[27] Hamilton thought the bill of rights was unnecessary too [28] and said "the greatest man that ever lived was Julius Caesar."[29] Caesar was also 5′ 7″.

He also wanted to consolidate the never-ending debt problem in 1790 by starting a central bank that would replace the modicum of paper money each of the 13 states printed and make the US dollar the only legal *paper* tender for transactions. Jefferson was opposed, saying "it would be more dangerous than a standing army [probably referencing the British occupation]." James Madison was against this too because it would devalue everybody's money and amount to the forgiveness of debt to a tiny number of debtors. Devaluing money = devaluing debt, which Madison said was "unjust."[30]

Jefferson and Madison saw Hamilton's paper money as benefitting a chosen minority—the few who could get loan money fashioned from nothing—and equality under the law was inviolable to them. But there was another problem: congress could not tax the states with much success so had almost no money. The constitution allowed the federal government to "coin money," and the 10th Amendment ostensibly prevented them from doing anything broader. Alexander Hamilton's reasoning for a national bank hinged on the constitution's *implied powers* clause which he used to establish the Bank of the United States, defeating the states' rights coalition. The first supreme court justices, all Geroge Washington appointees and therefore federalists, were on Hamilton's side. Modeling the bank after the British bank, the government could then print and borrow money from themselves, and for extra cash established the first Federal Excise Tax.

So, Attorney Hamilton got his central bank in 1791, cheaply paying off some mounting national debt and the debt of each state too, but ended their privileges to print. In 1792 the American Stock Exchange opened, Hamilton's New York bank stock was the first paper traded on it, and Hamilton's good friend William Duer (a wealthy politician) immediately began speculating with insider trading. The funny business started right off the bat and the American Stock Exchange crashed the same year. In 1794, Hamilton then engineered the first US bailout of bank stocks and securities—$3 million[31]—which kicked off the now infamous American boom-bust-bailout cycle. Only Thomas Jefferson voted no on the bailout.

Bear in mind that these *securities* were inflated pieces of bank paper no one had worked for or earned but a privileged few got to spend. These securities were hardly part of the *general welfare* or *necessary and proper* for the country. Hamilton experimented with this financial federalism together with urban bankers and business leaders—modelling it after the British system—and used the *implied* powers written in the constitution to implement it in America.

This is why, and it's in the realm of historical acceptability, that Jefferson had Aaron Burr duel and kill Alexander Hamilton. Jefferson murdered the Hamiltonian financial oligarchy, fearing that the US would turn into another Britain. After 20 more years of this type of banking, the charter of the Bank of the United States was allowed to lapse, having loaned out much more money than it had on deposit.

Hamilton was heavy into the insurance business too, and Hannah Farber tells us about it in her book, *Underwriters of the United States.* He litigated hundreds of shipping cases between shippers and fledgling banks in New England, believing they were covered by the Bank of the United States. This mother bank was a tiny version of today's central bank, with a big "maybe" surrounding its carte blanche powers. The colonies were still heavily split on this issue. Little banks were covering maritime shipping on margin, because they couldn't float the whole risk. To attenuate risk and payouts, insurers had clauses that rejected claims for shippers who engaged in smuggling, war, or running blockades.

This insurance-banking partnership was already using paper IOUs (derivatives) that had risk but no value, which I call "overwriting" instead of what they called it: "underwriting." It was a betting game for the 4 political allies—banks, states, shippers, and insurance entities—because insurance risks exceeded the money the banks had to cover them. Copying Britain, one of the first US financial instruments was called "a bill of exchange." These pieces of paper allowed merchants to buy more, make more, and if the whole deal went sour, bankers didn't lose because the bill of exchange was created out of nothing. The insurance paper was often a moral hazard though because the banks sometimes had to print up some real money in the backroom to cover the loss of a ship.

Working with the banks they had chartered, the state governments lived off this money creation process by taxing it and as Hannah Farber says, "this funded the majority of state government operations throughout the 19th century!" That's a lotta tuna but these increases in the money supply were at first tiny, per capita, and it would be the 1850s—50 years after Hamilton's death—before Americans even learned what inflation was. The gold coming in from the west was most of that inflation but not all of it.

States' Rights vs Federalism

In the 1780s when our founding fathers were endlessly hammering out the US constitution, they decided to omit the words *capitalism* (not used much then), *slavery, democracy, God, executive privilege, civil rights,* and *bank*. Federally establishing a church was still a popular idea but the leading founders were intent on emphasizing what the federal government *shouldn't* be allowed to do. A constitutional republic was radical because strong federal governments had been the norm throughout time and momentous, battletested arguments persisted to keep things that way.

The usually affable afterwit, slave owner Benjamin Franklin said, "it's a republic if you can keep it." Though this quote may be apocryphal he knew the republic could slip back into a monarchy or a banking oligarchy and he was leery of the designs of men. John Adams wrote: a republic is a "government of laws and not of men," [32] and both men knew that a constitutional republic meant a majority of lawmakers, churches, corporations,[33] or people could not vote away your rights. Unlike Britain, the founders placed the constitutional restrictions in 3 competing, separate departments: congress, the presidency, and the courts. This triopoly of democracy placed all politicians—appointed and elected—below the law. They had to be weary of the other 2 branches, so this first constitutional republic went beyond the Magna Carta and drew the first straight line in the shifting sands of political history, for white males.

The Federalists opposed slavery more convincingly than the states' rights advocates did, however both factions were for the freedom of African Americans, eventually, and at the same time would have hated to be mistaken for one. In a nutshell, John Jay (slave owner and 1st supreme court chief), John Marshall (slave owner and 2nd chief) and Alexander Hamilton (not a slave owner) were the leading federalists. None got to the top office. Thomas Jefferson, James Madison, Patrick Henry, and Samuel Adams (only Samuel didn't own slaves) were the leading anti-federalists.

A *republican* form of government was their word even back then and states' rights would prevail for almost a century because of James Madison's 10th Amendment: "the powers not [expressly] delegated to the United States by the Constitution, nor prohibited by it to the states, are reserved to the States respectively, or to the people." Marshal and Hamilton won the battle to take out the word *expressly*, leaving the 10th expressly unspecific, while Thomas Jefferson wanted to restrict the federal government to "certain definite powers."[34]

In his 2005 book *Thomas Jefferson: Author of America*, Christopher Hitchens paints a heart-felt, cogent portrait of the man who used to be our most remembered president. I'm bias toward both of these thinkers so I as soon as I heard that groups were trying to ban his book, I bought a copy. I loved it and 2 years after publishing it, Hitchens became an American citizen. Hitchens lists the methodical yet unsuccessful steps Thomas Jefferson took to gradually phase out slavery in his home state of Virginia as well as parts south. Not the words of the usually quiet, measured man, in 1784 Jefferson said, "after the year 1800 of the Christian era, there shall be neither slavery or involuntary servitude."[35] These were the words of a nonpolitician becoming a politician but Hitchens leaves us believing Jefferson's intentions. The federalists agreed with Jefferson's iffy soundbite but remember they'd held power for the first 12 years, and had the supreme court, without putting a dent in southern slavery. Jefferson was conflicted and heavy-hearted about ending slavery because he knew it would mean another war, plus, he had his eyes on the Presidency. He needed the southern votes so he could diplomatically juggle the precarious relationships with Britain, Spain, and the Indians...and go down in history.

The 3 checks and balances—executive, judicial, congressional—weren't enough to maintain a republic. The true balancing act was written into the 10th amendment, ostensibly giving the feds 1/3rd of the power, the states 1/3rd, and the people 1/3rd. These were the 3 speedbumps Jefferson and Madison set in place for the philosophical blunders that would inevitably follow. Jeffersonian democracy was intentionally far from a real democracy though (tyranny of majority) because he was trying to goofproof the process for if and when the federal government, or a state, or the people, inevitably went too far. If one state started bullying its citizens, taxpayers would move to another state.

Jefferson had tried to put a fierce denunciation of the "British Christian King's slave trade" in the Declaration of Independence, got voted down,[36] and in 1780 he tried unsuccessfully again to ban slavery from all western states. In the 1820s he all but predicted the bloody Civil War, dreading but not knowing it would be fought in his swing state of Virigina or that more Americans would die than in all our other wars combined. The historical notion has persisted that a states' rights position is untenable because its supporters wanted to keep slavery and this is half true. To avoid war, the majority of states' rights politicians and federalists were trying to end slavery state by state, with 50% success.

Under pressure from James Madison, the states gave up their claims to western territory. Madison hated fraudulent land speculators with real estate in their bags and in 1783 the federal congress assumed ownership of the west, including the admission of new states.[37] The 1st problem was that the west was settled chiefly by southerners who brought their slaves with them and the new state governments sorely needed that tax base. The federal government was too weak—couldn't or didn't try to stem the tide—and Madison and Jefferson had a 2nd problem. They knew people were inherently selfish and would sometimes vote too selfishly so the solution was for the federal government to give no favors or hinders. Leaving aside slavery for a minute, these founders didn't favor one state over another, didn't dangle money in front of the voters, and didn't marginalize businesses they didn't particularly like.

The US had a good start. None of the founders said "you own your own body" that I know of but they certainly *spirited* it into the

Constitution. Written by farmers, the first 10 Amendments were the greatest gift to the world and it is arresting that countries all over the world didn't adopt them, and still haven't.

The balance of power between the people, the states, and the federal government hammered out their differences until the republican Abraham Lincoln won the Civil War. Lincoln painstakingly solved the most formidable problem, slavery, and evolved the constitution out of its hypocrisy. Lincoln then saw it *altogether fitting and proper* to absorb almost all state rights into Washington DC, which can easily be argued as having usurped the 10th amendment. Author Kevin Waite said, "no president ever wielded federal patronage so aggressively," and I might add, "up to that point." The 10th Amendment, which could today be giving the people much more input about the powers intentionally *not delegated* to the federal government might as well be redacted from the Bill of Rights.

Few wars can be won without the federal government seizing too much power but after eliminating slavery, the US government didn't relax back into the triopoly of checks and balances—the feds, the states, the people. After the assassination, the republican federal government engaged itself in economic activities they never had before, which ushered in the corrupt Gilded Age.

The republicans, after holding out for 100 years, had become federalists too and the 10th Amendment was eclipsed, in the minds of those who used to be statesmen, by the old, unofficial Federalist Papers. The old Jeffersonian political party, the *democratic republicans* (states' rights advocates) had morphed into *the republicans,* and their ending of slavery was such a milestone most didn't notice a chunk of democracy died with it—states' rights.

Inflation

Thomas Jefferson doubled the size of the United States with the 1803 Louisiana Purchase but nobody knew what was there, or, that it would produce 13 new states. Bought from Napoleon for $15 million after Napoleon annexed it from Spain—3 or 4 nations traded half of the Indian land around—Jefferson finally bought it from France for 4-5¢ per acre.[38] Jefferson and Madison paid the debt partly in gold and partly with bonds (borrowing) issued by Hamilton's bank, i.e., paper money created simply to pay down foreign debt. The new money caused inflation in France more than it did the colonies, where there was almost no inflation until 1850. In 1867 the US bought untravellable Alaska for almost the same price per acre, meaning, that there was a heavy increase in the money supply from 1850-1867.

Long before 1801, most European governments had understood how to use paper money for freebees and likely divined that the nonelites pay the inflation bill. To pay for the Lewis and Clark expedition Jefferson again used the central bank, getting $2,500 from the explorers, to find out exactly what he had acquired.[39] Jefferson had compromised on his anti-central bank principles twice but in his defense it averted war with Napoleon.

Inflation stayed low until the Civil War. Abraham Lincoln printed up Greenbacks to pay for the war and the inflation from that new money subsided by war's end. The western US basically ignored the civil war while the south was melting, ushering in the Gilded Age (1870-1900) as well as the so-called "Reconstruction" in the south. What followed was a dynamic transition from an agrarian to an industrial society, everywhere but the south, and the industrialists lobbied for more capital.

The oddity of it was that the money printers were not saying they were creating money out of nothing, they just called it "banking." For many decades after the Gilded Age, maybe until now, most Americans assumed banks were loaning deposit money or private investment money.

Along with increases in the money supply, poor immigrants were pouring in which helped slow inflation because more people using money brought down prices a little. Much of the money vanished into the northeast and into the west, and into estates of corporate legend, so America could expand to the Pacific Ocean. The Gilded Age (meaning to gloss something over with a thin gold plating) was a concerted, subsidized, corrupt, mid-industrial revolution extending from post-Civil War to 1900.

When African Americans were freed by the 14th Amendment the government put a 4rth clause in that 1868 law legally sanctioning debt and borrowing. Washington DC pumped new money "from California to the New York Islands,"[40] and what *Reconstruction* really meant is that they forgot about the Gulf Stream Waters. Naturally, there was plenty of fresh water in the south so getting water and goods to places west was the priority of the new republican federalists. No sooner had reconstruction started in 1870, in the war-torn, charred, hayseed hinterlands of the south, it ended in 1877, but the white southerners hadn't exactly been cooperating. With precious metals coming in from California and the Yukon, spending rose everywhere except on southern farms because the price of cotton and tobacco stayed low.

Free southern blacks were finally getting paid a little to pick cotton and work textile jobs, but the whole place was so depressed it lacked a chemistry, to say the least. Almost nothing there changed except for a small boom in textiles, while both coasts were booming by 1878, with boilermakers and bankers in the northeast, and 80,000 miles of rail laid out to California, which would soon double.[41]

Western towns wanted the irrigation and train tracks to run through their town, not the next one over, and money changed hands. Businessmen began realizing more than ever that Washington DC was the place to start if you wanted to go big. In a switch of policy, the free-trade US became protectionist too and slowed foreign imports with high tariffs in 1890, partially so the newly mined gold wouldn't sail away. Rapidly growing DC was finally thriving from these tariffs, insurance-banking taxes, and printing.

Along with the industrial progress, a small wave of speculation with new financial instruments came to a slow boil. It was a little mess with state banks printing money, big city banks printing money, rapid financial expansion, and risk-takers winning big or losing big. Clamoring to invest in the railroads or along the 2 coasts, speculators created banking panics but with no real central bank to bail everybody out the lemmings followed each other off the cliff. Little banks were loaning new money to lazy dreamers who overinvested, the bubbles popped, and they couldn't pay the loans back so the New York banks tried to shore up the little broken banks. With no real safety net and no idea of how much inflation was coming NY banks rightfully tightened up money creation.

Juggling paper is not real work, more like betting, and as usual the gamblers lost and so did the banks. Investors found themselves trying to get rid of their bad investments as fast as they could, not unlike 2008 when paper-pushers were trying to get rid of their mortgage paper before the price dropped again the next day. Finally J. P. Morgan used his own money to save the banks and that prompted the embarrassed US government in 1900 to report that they were going back to the gold standard. That should have stabilized prices, which didn't happen, in fact the cost of living shot up after 1900. Morgan had bailed out the banks (he would eventually make a huge profit) and the banks had a nice cushion to start printing and loaning again which is how they paid Morgan back, bringing in the Progressive Era. The banks would only have to wait until 1913 to begin getting more stocks, securities, and loan money from the new central bank.

To give you an example of inflation *after* the Gilded Age, $30,000 in 1890 would buy $1000 worth of stuff in 2003, 113 years later.[42] Keep in mind this is using the government's *conservative* inflation calculations and I will explain the 100-year growth of banking, mega corporations, and insurance, in Chapter 28, entitled *The Best Kept Secret in the World.*

Religion and the First 7 Presidents

At first, the founding fathers happily proclaimed that Americans could be any religion they wanted as long as it was Protestant. Little did the world know of secularism except for a tiny percentage of Unitarians, and most of the founders, we will soon find out, didn't really care about religion in general.

Historians tell us that the Protestant Churches in the original 13 colonies collected the state taxes, the all-male preachers were paid by each state, and of course black slaves had little choice in how they were taught. If they wanted to learn to read, they were handed a book on Protestantism. On paper, white women had no rights either but they weren't treated like animals. If they had a respectable churchgoing husband or a rich one, they had standing, and that served as kind of a right.

The very religious John Adams wrote it was the "duty" of all to worship.[43] For the first repair of the protestant monopoly the founding fathers penned "Americans have freedom *of* religion." Some European countries had already gotten that far so they elevated it to "freedom *from* religion." Most of the founders helped with the wording of this radical, first of its kind movement, and the brilliant young John Quincy Adams had a hand in this too. These disestablishmentarians (those against the official sanctioning of a church) also gave the same freedom to people like me and called us "the others."

An antidisestablishmentarian is someone who wants to take a secular country back to the old ways, where the government established an official church—as European countries did—and surprisingly, John Adams originally wanted a state church. 100 years earlier, the semi-naturalist philosophe John Locke, who warned of religion's "intemperate zeal," had been an establishmentarian too.[44] And he thought a baby was born as a blank mental slate which we now know is far from the truth: we are born with long-honed instincts, fears, and mental proclivities to survive.

The US government has finally released the founding fathers' personal correspondence, and great historians, who get to read the letters with plastic gloves on, are telling us stuff we've never known: who these people really were. 6 of the first 7 US presidents were slaveowners and 5 were desists, or borderline atheists, but "deist" was the world back then because the A word was left unspoken. I have the evidence. A deist might say that "God kick-started humans but we are on our own now," which is a northern turn on the long and winding road to free will. This was peculiar too: unlike the castle dwelling British sovereigns, all 7 founders lived surprisingly long lives, spending their days out in the countryside, walking and thinking.

The final constitutional version of the government's relationship with the church was "congress shall pass no law respecting the establishment of a religion." It would be later in life when John Adams—waiting until his parents Deacon John and Susanna had passed—softened his views on religion and controlling free speech. Raised on religion without slaves, John Adams was a virtuous, rum-drinking, round-faced, nonviolent, short, high voiced, shockingly hard-working man and Adams resisted sex, keeping his virginity, until finally marrying Abigail.[45] Prior to his Sedition Acts, he was the most introspective founder, always questioning himself as if he knew what apophenia was, before it was a word, and he gets my vote for *most improved*. Adams stayed sharp by routinely walking 5-10 miles to "rouse the spirits."[46]

Alexander Hamilton, an attorney of Scottish extraction and a Love Child born out of wedlock, went to church when it was convenient. John Adams was Washinton's Vice President and the philosophies of these 3 men usually coincided, except that Adams was very religious. Publicly, George Washington was a promotor of faith but never knelt in prayer.[47] By Washington's 2nd term, George himself sported 200 slaves and was a federalist too—sold on Hamilton's capital-centered ideas.

Some historians tentatively place James Madison, father of the constitution and Jefferson's close friend, in the deist camp too, citing his effort to disestablish the Church of Virginia in his home state.[48] James saw religion as a social utility and usually stayed private with his personal beliefs save for a few choice criticisms of religion in 1-on-1 conversations.[49] Indeed, someone publicly saying "there is no God" would have been eerie. James Monroe (slave owner) was maybe the least religious of presidents after Thomas Jefferson, despite historians claiming the opposite and accusing other historians of egregious exaggeration. Being from the magic state of Virginia, as Jefferson, Washington, and Madison were, Monroe played hooky from church, never took communion, and was never confirmed.[50]

It seems odd now that America was founded by so many non-believers. They were bolder than politicians are now—had better vocabularies—and it was a very, very different time. In a way it was more open, freer—the colonial governments and churches weren't eyes in the sky—and in another way it was less free. Almost 2 dozen "witches" (rather common young people) were hung 100 years earlier right up the road from Boston. With another British invasion coming before James Monroe would leave office the colonial army was still weak too. Every commoner had to be ready to defend themselves, stay tight-lipped, appear ordinary, work like dogs, and not fish in other people's ponds. The people governed themselves.

Federalist John Quincy Adams—middle name from his mother's maiden name—was leery of the first drafts of the constitution, slowly became disillusioned with Hamilton's federalism, broke with the party and lost his senate seat. Years later he would bounce back, become a US president—sworn in with his hand on a law book instead of a Bible—and John Q sported the highest IQ of any president by 20 points, at 175.[51] The average IQ back then was below 70. Maybe his high intelligence came from the loving relationship John and Abigail had, combined with being born in a little town outside of Boston called "Braintree!"

The Unitarian attorney John Q Adams hated slavery and served as a pro bono legal advocate for Native Americans and blacks. He wasn't as religious as his parents were and the Unitarian "anybody can come" churches were not considered Christian to say the least. John Q is referred to as a *devout* Christian like his father in some texts but he rejected the holy trinity saying "God did not make himself." Ironically, John Q Adams was a lifelong Bible reader and in a letter to his 11-year-old son George he wrote, "the Bible is about morality but faith must follow reason," adding, "there is no possibility of salvation."[52]

John Q is where the run of deists-atheists ends, as Andrew

Jackson—the bare-knuckled, slave owning, Indian hating frontiersman—was quite the religious Scotsman and fancied himself as a prophet. Thomas Jefferson made one stab at prophesy too, saying "the day will come when the virgin birth of Jesus would be classed as a fable."[53] Jackson also used the US Post Office, as many administrations have, to shelve certain publications, squelch free speech, and rid the mail of anti-slavery rhetoric.[54]

Unitarians believed Jesus was mortal, they taught natural philosophy, and Jefferson resurrected this science revolution at his new, personally crafted, University of Virginia. This caused heavy unrest from the Virginia Presbyterians who were already busy prosecuting the minority Baptists. Jefferson told the Presbyterians that they "dread the advance of science as witches do the approach of sunlight."[55] He even taught his daughters in the natural sciences, reasoning that the chances were quite high they would marry a "blockhead," as he put it, and his daughters could then teach their children philosophy.[56] With so many early presidents exhibiting signs of deism, they would probably be considered atheists now? It's a grey area but listen to their words.

Never quite an atheist and ever tactful until his death, Benjamin Franklin said "a virtuous *heretic* (one who makes choices) shall be saved before a wicked Christian." Historians tell us that as a small boy Franklin read the bible at 5 but grew weary of his father's incessant prayers and suggested they say grace once for the entire winter—to save time.[57] My impression of Franklin is that he didn't preach and would agree that if one is giving advice, they're not doing their own work. A copper penny designed by Benjamin Franklin in 1776 was engraved MIND YOUR BUSINESS, reminding the colonists that the close-mouthed middle class was the backbone of American society. He lived his own philosophy, chasing prostitutes of all classes on both sides of the Atlantic.

CHAPTER 11

Edith's Childhood: Helen, Jesse, and Magic

"In my little town, I grew up believing, God keeps his eye on us all." —*Paul Simon*

When Edith was 5 years old (1932) a neighbor told her that way up in one of her parent's oak trees was a magic box. Edith loved the word magic and noticed people's eyes lit up when they heard it. "I always usually like that word sometimes," Edith said to her mom, gently prying her for information to see if she might know something about that magic box. If Helen knew, she didn't say. "I can do anything I want if I can find that box," Edith dreamed as she ran back outside, "I think I see it way up there." The magic box was the only thing she thought about for a week. Her parents didn't like her climbing the 400-year-old black oaks in their front yard so told her they had poison caterpillars in them. Edith borrowed that lie and manipulated her 2 kindergarten friends, Andy and Miles, into staying out of her magic tree.

"Ya know those caterpillars up in that tree up there?" she said, confidently pointing up and trying to look away from where she thought the magic box was, "they'll kill ya." "Oh wow," said Miles, "you know I'm double-jointed right?" Then he showed her, moving his thumb weirdly. Edith said, "wow Miles," relieved that he had changed the subject. Then Edith noticed Andy had disappeared off somewhere and she asked Miles, "where'd Andy go?" "He went around back to pee," Miles said. Edith responded, "he went to Pete's house?" "No," Miles said, "we say *pee* if somebody needs to go pee-pee." "Oh," said Edith, "we say *tinkle*." "Anyway," Miles said, "how do those caterpillars up there kill ya?" She paused, stuck for just a second, and said "they pee on you," squinting directly at him. "Oh," said Miles. If anybody was going to find the box it was going to be her.

Edith learned to lie, the way we all do, from our parents. And most good things come to an end and she finally realized at the tender age of 6 that she had been tricked—there was no magic box in that oak tree. Worse, she started thinking there was no such thing as magic. She would need it later. "Goddamn it," she said, for the first time in her young life, with many more to follow.

To keep Edith out of the forests too, Jesse told her that the most poisonous snake in the world lived in the woods surrounding Alton Missoura. He called it a "kate snake" and 1 bite was all it took. He made it up (or he was thinking of the Krait snake) but the internet was 70 years away and the encyclopedia salesman hadn't gotten to Alton yet. Edith believed in the kate snake for decades and later put the fear of God into her own kids about the damn kate snake. They looked it up in the encyclopedia and told her, for the first time, the kate snake didn't exist—and neither did poisonous caterpillars. Edith was quite surprised, at least about the first part.

Jesse was a nice, apolitical man who started 3 businesses in 1920s Alton: a pharmacy, an ice cream shop, and an insurance company. If he hadn't read about America's Great Depression in the Alton Telegraph, he never would have known it had one. Jesse hired young people to run his ice cream shop/pharmacy—both in the same store—and never had to worry about them stealing from him. He hated thieves, saying "them's just heppin' themselves." Throughout Edith's childhood she would prance down to the ice cream shop whenever she wanted, plant herself on one of the round red bar stools, and order different flavors for free, with those black ceiling fans spinning slowly overhead, connected by room length black belts. She never gained weight.

At 6′ 2″ Jesse married the 5′ 2″ (eyes of blue[1]) Helen in 1925, and they had Edith 2 years later. She got Jesse's green eyes. He looked like the actor Rex Harrison. Edith's Irish lineage had come to Missoura from Kentucky and Indiana and Helen's grandmother still lived in Ireland. The 3 or 4 historical letters I found in that trunk were nutty and I could see where Edith got her Irish funny. Her ancestors were a feisty bunch for their time but Edith was the first interesting writer. She was a mix of Irish, German, English, Scottish, and Scandinavian, however, Jesse and his father, one of whom may have been adopted, didn't leave any family history. Jesse had a cream-colored British face and sheet black hair which hung on tenaciously until his death at 77.

Jesse would affectionately call his little daughter "Edith Virginia" and she loved it; she loved his deep voice and those 5 syllables. At her 7th Christmas, Jesse—a terrible gift giver—surprised Edith and Helen with diaries. Helen probably never opened hers but Edith started writing almost daily (mostly girl talk) and by the time she was 16 she was on her 3rd diary. That diary was all about her new kitten Spotty Ann Feisty. In her 2nd diary, when she was 10 years old, she told a story of Jesse not coming home from work one evening.

That winter night the nondrinker hit a patch of ice and flipped his no-seatbelt car over and the trauma to the top of his head put him into a coma. Helen and Edith would visit the hospital every day after school and pray. As the weeks went by Edith felt her little heart turning to stone and wondered what had destroyed half her world. A month of Sundays went by with no improvement and as the doctors reluctantly discussed saving money, Edith leaned over and kissed him goodbye. He opened his eyes! Edith's face lit up like Christmas and by the next day he was talking to her and Helen. Nobody learned anything at school the next day except that her dad came back to life. Jesse's recovery was the talk of the town and Edith the chatterbox couldn't stop laughing and crying at the same time. She might have capitalized on the magical event to recapture her *own* lost magic from 5 years prior.

Jesse recovered and went back to work but he was never the same. Edith's father became more distant and spoke few words after the brain damage. His smile was gone. While Helen practically lived in the kitchen, Jesse would sit quietly in the dark living room and smoke his cigarettes. Later in her teens, Edith would steal a few cigarettes and go behind the house to smoke with her friends. Jesse didn't notice much anymore and the cigs she snuck from her dad became her lifelong friends, friends who wouldn't go away.

Her father, who'd always had a weak love gene, could not love anymore. Edith felt a tsunami of chill as if a murderer was in the house and touched her heart like there were a hole in it. Later in life she hated Archie Bunker (wife's name Edith, he pronounced it *Edut*) and Fred Sanford, to give you an idea what Jesse was like on a bad day. Edith had lost something precious but couldn't help feeling at age 12 that she had something to do with it. She wasn't old enough to simply conclude that men and women were 2 different species. Searching for answers, she fantasized that if her parents had had a boy that Jesse might have been able to love that child.

Her mother Helen was a simple person with no pretenses: a cooking, smiling and listening person. Edith picked up the last 2. Helen would try to make people feel good no matter who they were or what they said. People back then, much more than now, loved to announce the most interesting new thing and Helen would smile and say, "why, I'm flabbergasted!" Since old General Sherman had burned Atlanta to the ground, the staunch southerners Edith and Helen would sing *Dixieland*, in the house. They *felt* the song. It *is* one of the most beautiful songs ever written (unknown author, possibly Daniel Emmett) and Helen would harken back to what these haunting words meant: "look away, look away, look away, Dixieland," as Atlanta burned. But the song was written *before* the Civil War.

Helen died of uterine cancer when Edith was 35 and the doctors in 1962 said it was from the tearing of her uterus. Helen's cancer, like so many cancers, could have been simply bad luck as she had no risk factors save heredity—and a little depression. On her death bed, Helen made Edith promise to resume taking the kids to church every Sunday, knowing that practice had lost its luster. "I'll try, momma, I promise I'll try," Edith said. Edith was emotionally devastated by her mom's death while nothing seemed to phase Jesse. He *was* sad about Helen's death, which we'd think might bring him much closer to Edith, but it didn't.

As Jesse grew into middle-age, alone in his head, he would occasionally wave his gun around at neighbors. People avoided him. He still wouldn't fly ("too many planes hittin' the ground") and drove down to visit Edith and her family about once a decade. He carried a baseball bat in his car for "hammerin' in hubcaps" but his grandkids knew it was for protection from "culprits," as he called them. In his deep voice he told them the Russians were behind the latest market crash and even the 1977 power blackout in NYC. He once said, "education causes inflation."

As Jesse went further downhill, he stapled fliers on Alton telephone poles announcing his first upcoming sermon at the town church that next Sunday night. He even cc'd the pastor and Edith heard from her cousin Lucille that nobody showed up. Jesse had a stroke at 73—couldn't remember the previous day—and Edith put him in a home near St. Louis, far from Atlanta, where he died alone a few years later. Edith the only child got his $24,000 house and $24,000 in cash in 1980.

Let's go back in time to 1968, when all Edith's kids were teenagers.

CHAPTER 12

The Indefatigable Jim

The year All the Kids Were Teenagers

There was a height limit on how high above your plate you could shake the salt and pepper—3 inches. "Yeh high," as Jim showed the kids with his flat palm down and his furry arm up. He was also serious as a heart attack about how to get ketchup out of a bottle and taught all the kids his patented method. This is what a Missourian was like—you had to be there. If it was sprinkling outside his kids couldn't say, "it's raining," knowing they would be corrected, Missoura style. "What with all the rain we've had recently," Jim instructed, "that isn't rain." "Now, yersty [*yesterday*] it poured like the dickens," he continued, "and that's what we call rain," as Edith rolled her eyes.

When he got home from work, he walked around shutting all the lights off, yelling "do you people think I own the electric company?" Everybody prayed in the dark that would be the end of it, but it wasn't: "will it take a Goddamn act of congress before any of you people turn off a light?" Nobody in the house could think until he finished and with a straight face he barked, "I've told you people elebm hunerd [Missourian for *eleven hundred*] times!" The kids were not worried about the damn electric company, they were hiding in fear because of the minor crimes they'd committed that day and cringing, hoping mom wouldn't bring it up. "Don't piss mom off tonight," they reminded each other, "or she might flip out and say something."

Jim picked Ford over Chevy and the kids followed suit picking The Beatles over The Stones—everything had to be compared to something else. Jim graded the Beatles songs C or C- consistently—art was silly to him, even Edith's art. Living in an artless world, he never saw that aesthetics could have a frivolous, rich efficacy.......and offer nothing else of value. "Why don't those hippies cut all that Goddamn hair off, they look Godawful," he winced, pursing his lips with pride and disgust. "They'd look a damn sight better'n that with hair like mine...I mean with a crewcut," he corrected himself. Once a dashing young man, Jim was getting bald very early (from his mother's father) and nobody could say it bothered him because his pride was all in his character. Edith was back in the painting studio, listening to the distant barking, and getting a slight headache from rolling her eyes. Jim would mess up the names of bands and call them, "Fleetwood Brougham and Red Zeppelin," adding, "they should all be in Vietnam."

Jim considered everything he heard a lie until further notice. Even if he hadn't been from Missoura, the *show me state*, anyone would have assumed the buck stopped at his desk. If his kids said something delightfully new, he wouldn't say, "is that true?" He would say, "balderdash, ballyhoo," or "hooey!" If one of the kids made up a story, usually Miles, Jim would say "I bet you my eye teeth that's not true." Miles, rhetorically challenged, could make the truth sound like a pretty good white lie anyway, and in a nanosecond Jim called it a "cockamamie story without a kernel of truth." When one of the kids did miraculously teach him something he'd acknowledge it and say, "I'll be damned," and ask, "what's the upshot of that?" The kids relished his rare compliments and would glance around the room to make sure all had witnessed the miracle.

I'll be damned was not a reference to hell because Jim never referenced the up above or the down below—the meaning of life was all in your elbow grease. Strangely for a man, scrubbing off dirt was almost as important as exposing lies. Jim needed proof positive—he didn't lie himself, if rarely, or believe he did—and almost never talked about himself. When he did talk about himself, he felt guilty and would dissipate that energy by adjusting his dinner napkin geometrically to the edge of the table. Or he would keep nudging his glass of milk until it was perfectly in the center of one of the table tiles—back when everybody had a glass of milk with dinner.

Jim gave his children scheduled character talks. With his bullet eyes aimed at their little peepers he'd say, "there's no difference if you steal a penny or a million dollars," as he set his jaw back with a click. The kids were trying their best to process that strange statement when he repeated Walter's line, "I'd rather you kill somebody than lie to me," with his bottom lip trembling and Edith's eyes still rolling in the painting studio. She knew a lie when she heard one and knew how easy lying and stealing were after sneaking cigs from her dad since she was 15. "I've told you people umpteen times to never lie," Missoura Jim would say but Miles was so naughty he had to lie about what he'd been up to, and Electra elected to lie by omission. Jim *failed* with behavior modification and didn't notice it *had* worked with Mary, and somewhat with Rachel who only lied by exaggeration. Mary had completely rejected sibling rivalry, didn't learn to lie, and Jim didn't notice. He hadn't taken a shine to his son Miles, Rachel or Mary—only to Electra.

The shamans Electra and Miles became the best liars because Jim's punishments fit the crimes. Edith was ahead of Jim. Only a mom will defend a child's honor before they've developed any, and she decided she wasn't going to try and solve the lying problem 200,000 years after it began. Nobody could reckon with Jim save for Edith, the 2nd banana, who knew he wouldn't lay a hand on *her*, so she hit above her weight and kept her big girl pants on.

Edith protected her last child from physical abuse and Miles was glad for this protection but resented needing it from a woman. Miles had been spanked much less as a toddler than his sisters did, they noticed, and they subconsciously resented that too. Jim made up for it later when the troublemaker was 9-13 and the only good part was that he wasn't a small child, but Stockholm Syndrome had become a proud badge for Electra, and sometimes Rachel, to wear. They had earned it and wondered why Miles never had to pay his dues in his toddler years. Life was unfair, sexist, and on top of that the girls had to help with the dishes while Miles didn't.

So, there was Jim's whole "caboodle," 3 daddy's girls and one cosseted momma's boy. For all the kids to go psychologically opposite sex parent is textbook (the rare kind of textbook) and worthy of study.

Edith's live and let live philosophy kept a toehold on the family, Electra felt a glitch, and began marginalizing Edith subtly and Miles not so subtly. Electra kind of *put up* with those who hadn't acknowledged her as the vice president of the family. 5 years younger, Miles marginalized Electra as best he could but Electra and Rachel, who always had to share a bedroom, held the narrative. That's the gift of transgenerational Stockholm Syndrome—the SS hierarchy is always in the right—and their motivations are not to be analyzed.

Jim the fundamentalist considered all of this as somewhere between normal and superfluous. He clung to his old farm thinking, knowing that every day brought bad news and good news in tandem. He had the good life now but didn't trust it so minimizing risk and giving advice was his schtick. "Never put off till tomorrow what you can do today," Jim would always say, but contrary Miles had a "devil may care" attitude which irked the hell out of dad. "And on the 7th day, Sundy [Sunday], you can rest......*if* you finished all your work," Jim warned him and added, "the 2nd half of that sentence broke off the engraved stone." He never cluttered his sentences with needless words—Miles did learn that—and all the kids were immediately corrected whenever they mangled a sentence.

"What's on the slate for today?" sayeth Jim on Saturday at 8am. The kids hated that question because it wasn't a question. He always found supm [Missourian for *something*] for them to do on the weekends. They got their "marching orders" and they had to do everything well without complaining or he'd start pourin' the coal to 'em and say, "you have failed!" You might end up being an "also ran," meaning, you were in the race but came in last. The kids bridled at the draconian question, "you have failed, did you not?" because all they were doing was cleaning up their room. When they were done, he'd say, "ready for inspection?" His kids were well versed in rhetorical questions by then, and they'd say "no, duuuh……not ready," but he was already at the bedroom door yelling "if I flip a quarter on your bed, it better hit the ceiling." The kids' hearts would sink when he would look under the bed and find all the toys under there. Even the toys flinched, knowing they were "a day late and a dollar short." The kids made sure not to look like they were having fun while working either because Jim and the Catholic Church, which he knew nothing about, were both in constant fear that somebody, somewhere, was having a good time.

Jim called a corporation an "outfit" and when a distant relative flew in, he'd always ask about work. "What kinda outfit you workin' for these days?" Jim would say, looking at him and expecting a quick answer as Americans did back then. When the man told him what company he worked for Jim would snap, "how many people you got workin' in that outfit?" One clever cousin said, "about half of 'em." Jim wasn't pleased at the following laughter because he didn't get the joke, and his lips pursed up—these were serious questions.

All 4 Scottish kids developed regulation stolid faces like Jim—only Edith braved the face that disclosed how she was feeling. Jim didn't notice either one but he did note the kid's bad posture and made them walk around balancing books on their heads. "Backs straight, shoulders back!" he would bark, as everybody flinched and 20 books hit the floor. Behavior modification was the sum of his psychological education—that ancient conditioning had worked ad nauseum—but by 1969 Americans were beginning to reject violence wholesale, pushing psychologist Dr B. F. Skinner's behaviorism into the dusty shelves of history. Edith, the unnoticed bass guitar player of the family said, "doesn't everybody know all this already?" Jim didn't get the memo as spanking declined and Dr Benjamin Spock filled the utopian void left by Skinner, advocating for more nurturing. America got a speck less neurotic. Undaunted, Jim stayed true to the beaten path and repeated his Skinner lessons over and over—skipping the positive reinforcement part—to engrain the work ethic into the kids as a panacea cure for all that ails us.

After Jim's initiations all the kids came away with their own version, scrutinizing and evaluating people with lifelong confidence—never missing a beat to point the finger. The band Bush wrote, "nothing hurts like your mouth," and everybody's words hurt until they heard Electra take the game to a new tier, followed by her patented "silver grin" and hate laugh. Prior to that innovation, no one in the family had ever smiled when they were angry.

Jim had put the fear of God into them from toddler to teenager, and Electra, after filtering that through her Stockholm Syndrome, sprinkled some wicked wiles on his rectitude. Almost as well as Jim, Electra would stare like a statue after delivering an affront and squint a little to get the victim's fear in focus, savoring every second. She failed to bully Miles which irked her to no end after he'd gotten the Y chromosome she had always wanted. After Electra successfully bullied Rachel for years, giving her a 2nd dose of heavy Stockholm Syndrome, Rachel obediently backed Electra's premeditations. Rachel became an accomplice, never opting out as Mary had, and followed the Jim-Electra power play as the 3rd wheel.

Mary, one of Electra's easy targets, didn't fight back so Electra used one of her verbal body slams and told Rachel that Mary had "dead eyes and a lifeless face." Then Rachel told Mary what Electra had said about her. You either fought dirty in this family or you were crushed which was a new twist neither parent had taught. Mary was the Switzerland of the kids, but to the other 3, the concept of neutrality got lost in superfluity. Jim and Edith too, didn't notice that quiet Mary was the only child unsullied by hate.

During Jim's next pep talk, with his ducks arraigned in a row on the divan, Edith snuck from the painting studio into the kitchen and whispered, "please steal a penny before you steal a million dollars," and finished wrapping 6 potatoes in tin foil. "And please lie to me before you kill anybody," she added, laughing softly at her own jokes again. Miles asked "when's dinner," and Edith said "soon." She would never give a time. "Dinner is served," she announced an hour later, like Lucille Ball, making her entrance again with her usual flair.[1] Since the pantry was devoid of snacks and always had been, the kids came right to the table.

Cooking was not Edith's forte but with *some* dishes she had no equal. Jim loved the young sweet corn from the farm days, knew it by smell, and would comment on whether Edith had bought the right corn or not. Edith had the right corn that night and was bringing in her signature smokin' baked potatoes while hungry Jim was adjusting his fork perfectly parallel to the table tile. At 450° for 1 hour, her baked potatoes were the best, east and west of Texas, with crispy thick skin that crunched like a hot Pringle.

Her cooking was simple, like most men cook. She was androgynous in that way because her evening time was too precious to labor on and on. It got in the way of her cig and dirty martini (light on the vermouth) in the left hand and paintbrush in the right. Edith was so efficient there were never any leftovers. For a *nothing wasted* cook, Edith's fortes were borék and Chicken Kievsky (Kiev). Edith had learned how to prepare both from their houseboy Durmuş, who had worked at their apartment in Turkey 5 days a week for $50 a month. It had taken him, and later her, all day to make her mouth-watering butter filled Kiev and people would fly in for a seat at her Kievsky table.

Besides Jim's method of getting Ketchup out of a bottle Missoura style, he had another patented, scrumptious way of fixing the baked potato: he'd cut it in half, dig out all the stuff, make mashed potatoes in his plate with tons of extra butter and salt, and mash it back into the 2 crusty halves with a determined look on his face. He munched it like an ice-cream cone, his hairless temples pulsing in and out, and the kids started fixing theirs that way too. "Chew each bite 32 times," the parents commanded—to maximize surface area—so the kids did that with the mouthful they had and never did it after that. They noticed their parents didn't chew each bite 32 times either (everybody but Edith counted everything) and the kids were bursting to comment on Jim's jaw-temple rhythm. Once Miles started imitating the way Jim chewed, so Edith, standing behind Jim, gave Miles the wide eyes and shook her head.

All in all, their dinner table was a free speech zone—it didn't have to be—and no one's opinion about the world was derided unless it was just stupid. If the kids complained about the things the neighborhood kids were allowed to do, the parents answered "we don't care how other people raise their kids!" That was Edith and Jim teaming up for a philosophical clencher and the young'uns almost understood—*don't compare anyone to anyone else*—but the parents weren't consistent with their own philosophy. Sometimes Edith would lose her feng shui and compare the bodies of her 3 daughters, perplexingly ridiculing them as if a teenage body could be changed. She cast aspersions on Mary the most which ended the chance of Mary adopting Edith's free-spirit philosophy. She had put Mary (normal weight by today's standards) on diet pills. Edith wasn't Twiggy but was tall, slim, and proud of it after having 4 kids.

When it came to clothing, she was a fashionista without the bank account and when the kids tried on clothes in stores Edith talked too loudly, embarrassing them to death. She made a spectacle of it not realizing that the last thing any of Jim's kids wanted was to be the center of attention. She did have the effect of dressing them well and in that little way she *owned* the kids. Not caring much for math and science or impeccable character, she pulled what strings she could. She would make Miles try on new pants and if the material stuck out a little in the crotch, she would try to push it down with her hand, right there in the store. If 13-year-old Miles was playing with a 12-year-old, she'd say "what's a'matter, you can't find anyone your age to play with?" If he told her anything personal, she would be on the phone later in the kitchen—the only phone—telling it to another military wife.

"Don't waste other people's time" Jim grilled into the kids. Even his 3 daughters never used "female time" if you'll excuse Jim's expression and one person in the family did use it and you know who that was. When Edith wasn't in a time machine (Chapter 15) she was her own time machine, and often picked up the kids late, especially for after school stuff. "Hop in," she'd smile. The smile had no hint of culpability as she happily navigated the boat (1965 Chrysler Newport) back to the crib, only looking down to push in the cigarette lighter. Back in her day, nobody said anything if you picked up the kids late, not even Jim—the military bases were safe places.

Jim's Sense of Humor vs Edith's

Jim used to tell this long joke about a dog chasing a rabbit. Long story short, the dog suddenly stopped in a cloud of smoke because he almost went over a cliff. Jim didn't explain what happened to the rabbit (that wasn't germane) but there were these 2 guys standing nearby who saw the near death of the dog. "What's that red collar doing around that dog's neck?" asked the 1st guy, and the 2nd guy said, "that's no collar, he's just not used to stopping so fast." That was Jim's punchline. The kids were asleep on the divan by this time, so Jim explained it to Edith: "When the dog saw it was running straight towards a cliff and had to stop on a dime—front feet out, butt up—the sudden change in momentum rolled the dog's rectum all the way up its body to around his neck." Jim's jokes always broke Johnny Carson's *too long* rule. "What happened after that?" Edith asked sarcastically as the kids were waking up. Everybody chuckled as Jim stared straight ahead.

He did tell 3 good jokes, but only 3. Miles' friend said he was first in the state in table tennis and after Miles crushed him Jim said, "maybe you are the first in the state of anxiety." Miles and that friend were in a band too and somebody asked Jim if they played electric guitars and he said "no, they sound more like gas-powered guitars." His famous Scottish Limerick was: "There was a young lady from France, who hopped on a train by chance, the engineer fuck'd 'er and so'd the conductor and the brakeman went off in his pants." Edith hated that one.

Edith would joke about this southerner who got stranded on an island for 20 years somewhere in the nether regions of the Pacific. Finally, he saw a ship on the horizon and built his biggest fire yet. He'd been preparing. The ship anchored and a sailor rowed to the island in a little boat. "I'm so glad to see you!" yelled the guy and the smiling sailor said, "hop in, we'll go back to the ship and get you a hot meal and a physical. "Can I show you my island first?" asked the guy, "it's been my home for 20 years." "Why not," said the sailor. The guy pointed to a little structure and said, "that is my home and that other little building over there is the church I go to, and that little shed over yonder is where I keep my food and supplies." "What's that other little building way over there?" asked the sailor, pointing at the other side of the island. "Oh," the guy said, "that's the......church......I *used* to go to."

Sometimes she accidentally told jokes in the present tense, which is how they're supposed to be told. Edith's 2nd favorite joke was about this little polar bear who walks home from school every day back to his parent's little ice cave. His dad is there. "Are you sure I'm a polar bear?" he asks his dad. "Of course you're a polar bear," dad says, "now go do your homework," and he turns away. The next day the son again walks a mile over the glacier back to his igloo and his mom is there, happily getting everything clean as a whistle. "Are you sure I'm a polar bear?" he asks his mom. "Of course you're a polar bear," she says, giving him a weird look, "now go finish your homework so you can play outside before it gets dark." The 3rd day he walks the glacier and finds both parents there in the ice cave. "Are you guys absolutely sure I'm a polar bear?" he asks with pleading eyes. "Yes, you're a polar bear," they say, "we are all polar bears, why do you keep asking us?" The little bear looks up at them and says, "because I'm fucking freezing."

Edith had no idea she was a joke fashionista too and would laugh so hard at her own joke that the people who didn't get it started laughing. When she couldn't stop laughing, she'd apologize, "I'm sorry, I got tickled pink!" I don't think Jim got most of her jokes. For instance, she told her family about a baby born in Oregon that scientists were eagerly studying: "they couldn't figure out if it was a boy or a girl because it had a penis and a brain." She laughed again, looked around at the blank stares, and covered her mouth like a schoolgirl.

Her family was her full-time job and it fit her to a T: rollers in her hair, vodka stinger in a small glass, a cig hanging—she watched over her kids 60s style. If Jim said anything about her drinking Edith would say, "I would go to the meetings but they're always at night." He got the *meeting* part but not the *night* part, though one of his favorite sayings was, "I was born at night, but I wasn't born *last* night." She had gotten to where she drank "every day that ended in Y," as we say in the south, and Jim wasn't far behind. Scotch was the only thing he bought for himself.......and those ski boats.

CHAPTER 13

US 1969—The Tipping Point

Americans were the first to walk on the moon, setting the lunar module down in the dry Sea of Tranquility. The Soviets had rushed to beat us, and crash landed an unmanned spacecraft into the dry Sea of Crises, or Mare Crisium. Most believed all of it. It was true. The eagle had landed and proud were the Americans, one last time, in 1969. A few years later Don Henley sang, "I haven't seen that spirit here since 1969." As the thrill of the moon landing faded, Vietnam degraded, and Americans sensed the philosophical fabric tearing across the microfibers.

Not a pristine place to start, the baby boomers were the biggest druggies/narcissists the US had ever produced. Out of this slightly altered reality they saw sexism, racism, violence, and war, as the same thing. Every generation sees things a bit clearer, and the boomers noticed that the silent majority was acting like American robots—the machines depicted later in the movie *The Stepford Wives* (1974). They thought that the peaceniks, hippies, and marijuana, with its anti-war effect on the mind, was proof that the America they loved was changing. They were about half right, as every movement is.

The defiant female fight song *"You Don't Own Me,"* came out in 1969—I own my own body—and the movie *Midnight Cowboy* came out of the closet. *Everything You Wanted to Know About Sex But were Afraid to Ask,* came out in 1969 and sold 100 million copies. In the midst of the "crazy Asian war," Mel Tillis wrote the haunting song, *Ruby, Don't Take Your Love to Town,* in 1971 Don McClean wrote *Bye Bye Miss American Pie,* and in 1973 Paul Simon dreamed the Statue of Liberty was sailing way.

Jimi Hendrix played the Star-Spangled Banner at Woodstock. He was a little sharp—it wasn't warm—and his terse 1969 solo perked up ears. The irritated American soul looked inward and the boomers knew something was out of tune but couldn't put their finger on it, as the loud music screamed the stanzas into their ears. The government-religion-money pyramid had crept past the archetype of the great American experiment like a silent glacier. And the band played on.

The Beatles didn't. They played a set on the roof of Apple Headquarters in 1969, made their last photo shoot and broke up, while across the pond Eisenhower died and the US inaugurated Richard Milhouse Nixon. Nixon's opponent was Hubert Humphrey who also supported the Vietnam War, as did Eisenhower, Goldwater, and LBJ, so voters weren't allowed to vote *no.* In Russia they could only vote *yes* too while the Americans sang a Beatles song, oblivious of the pun inside: "We're back in the US, back in the US, *Back in the USSR.*"[1]

Patton won best picture in 1970 as the confused Americans lamented their last romantic war—WWII, the last victory—and begrudgingly started the process of growing a new soul. We heard *Seasons in The Sun* by Terry Jacks in 1974 and we felt a personal haunting. "As if your dog or your best friend died,"[2] the song made Americans aware of how they already felt: the great 200-year-climb for America the beautiful was over, *the age of innocence* was gone, and somehow, they'd become *children of a lesser God.*[3]

After the failed 1968 Tet Offensive, the army sent Jim to Vietnam on a 1-year hardship tour while Edith was loosely herding 4 teenagers alone. It felt natural for Electra, the honey badger, to act fearless and fill in for dad whereas Rachel, like the younger 2, became outwardly worried about Jim and her own future. Rachel would frown and bite the back of her hand while Mary got quieter and read books in her room. Electra would lighten the load and pull out her best joke: "oh my God, Mary's vomiting and Rachel's getting all the big pieces!" Miles had the typical love-hate relationship with dad—Stockholm Syndrome's lasting gift—and had a sick feeling in his stomach for 1969. The kids couldn't really enjoy a year off from Jim's draconian because they worshipped him like an eye in the sky.

It turns out we are all raised in some sort of an insane asylum. "Even if you're switched at birth," as we say in the south, "you're gonna grow up in one and you'll be there all day long." "Believe you me," Edith would say, "and wouldn't ya know it, some insane asylums are better than others." It was a harder 1969 for a 42-year-old single mother because she had never worked for money and the only person who brought in money might not be back.

Edith loved the kids for who they were and Jim loved them for who they might become. The unconditional love was taken for granted and the conditional love wasn't. Even with Electra momentarily in the lead, each kid secretly coveted that they might end up dad's favorite. Jim wasn't the jealous type—1 of the 6 deadly sins after I removed vanity—but that got lost in translation and the kids reinvented it. What stitched them together was the adamant hope that dad would come back into their magic world alive.

Speedy Gonzales

Back in the thriving metropolis of El Paso Texas Edith and her 4 kids were gardening in the backyard—the summer of '69, [4]—with their underwear drying on the clothesline. They were trying not to think about dad in Vietnam when the familiar jingle of the ice cream truck broke the stillness. Edith called the guys in those trucks "creepers." Electra, who could handle any creeper, volunteered to go get everybody ice cream bars and went inside to gather up the coins. Electra eventually came back to the garden with only 4 ice cream bars, 1 short. The other 3 kids greedily grabbed one.

Edith and Electra got into an argument as both wanted the other to have the last ice cream bar—competing for *most adult* status—and it was game on. Edith wouldn't take it, so Electra cocked back her arm to throw it at Edith and the chase began. Nobody knew how fast Edith the high school track star could run until gardening day. Speedy Gonzales had some hustle in her bustle, and she tore across the yard with a 19-year-old in hot pursuit but the gap between them widened. Frustrated, Electra threw the ice cream bar at Edith on the dead run, it flew off the little wooden stick and hit a bedroom window. It was an air ball and then some. The other 3, happily watching and eating their ice cream bars, burst out laughing so hard that Edith started laughing, and a couple seconds later…so did Electra. The short diversion was perfect and the gardening quickly commenced in silence as their collective brain switched back to Dad, and Nam again, ruining their sugar buzz.

"Never Start a Land War in Asia"

After General MacArthur said that, Richard Pryor said, "I would be nice to anybody who's got a billion of anything."

In about 1500, many proud Chinese freed themselves of China's rules, oppressions, and invasions, populated what is now Vietnam, and pushed the Cambodians southwest. In the 17th century the Vietnamese pushed the ethnically different people in Laos to the west, leaving the Laotians with no coastline. The Vietnamese were called the "Lac" people and formed their own country, carved out of China, Laos, and Cambodia, taking the entire, enviable, 2000-mile coastline—nearly as long as Florida's and California's combined. The Vietnamese were used to winning until annexed by France in the 19th century. The French redrew their northern border with China—consumed Vietnam, Laos, Cambodia—and ruled for 100 years. "Oops there goes another rubber tree plant."[5] Ho Chi Minh and his Vietminh overran the final French stronghold in 1954 as the first US nuclear submarine glided down the slipway into the ocean. The toll in the trenches was high and few of the French prisoners lived. Asia was now ahead, with a tie in Korea and a win in Nam, and the "Dragon people to the south," as the Chinese called the Vietnamese, were the tip of the sword.

Jungle Jim

"Soldier boy, kiss his girl, leaves behind a magic world,
but he don't mind, he's in love and he says love is blind."

—Written by Paul and Linda McCartney

Jim was a full bird Colonel now heading up a group (5 engineering battalions) strategically placed at the midpoint of South Vietnam. The large compound and shipping port was in Quin Yon (Quy Nhon)—an eastern coastal city south of Saigon—and a relatively safe area. The vast majority of his men were not engineers, just boys who couldn't get into college, and one young soldier attempted suicide by slicing his wrists lengthwise. Jim used the Catch-22 approach and told him it would be much more effective if he cut sideways *across* the wrist, but the lad did not take his advice.

The army engineers and the multitudes of enlisted men chiefly built roads, bridges, and delivered supplies throughout the south—the dangerous part of the job. His soldiers called him "check your tires Jim" as he was always pushing maintenance and kicking tires—barking out orders in that Missoura accent his boys made fun of on the sly. They filled up the 5-ton trucks with 5-

gallon diesel cans and knew not to spill one drop, while the drops spilled in Washington DC were in billion-dollar pools, not to forget the 4 billion drops of American blood left in Vietnam. 10 pints of blood per person, 7,300 drops per pint, times 58,000 dead = 4 billion drops of blood. For the people and soldiers of Vietnam, 4 million deaths = 300 billion drops of blood.

Jim did everything possible to avoid a truck breakdown in the jungle because his boys had to cross the beautifully murderous vistas of *An Khe Mountain Pass*, 30 miles inland, to supply US bases with critical material and engineering support. By 1969 the Vietcong were pouring into that area through South Vietnam's side door, the Ho Chi Minh Trail, that drew a rough border between Laos, Cambodia, and South Vietnam (the bigger half of Nam). The ensuing ambushes on An Khe Pass and nearby Mang Giang Pass further west—with 5mph hair-pin turns—were getting worse. The heavy, slow trucks ran over mines, got hit with IEDs and machinegun fire, and were so loud the boys came back not knowing their truck was riddled with bullet holes. 6 of his boys died on An Khe Pass, some teenagers, ambushed by the Viet Cong. While driving over the "dragons back" they were riddled with machinegun fire while sitting in their trucks, 2 abreast.

Jim snapped up the radio and got all US forces out of the area around An Khe Pass, called in some C-130 transport planes with those 6-barrel Gatling guns named *Puff the Magic Dragon*—sticking out of a side door of the plane—and each sprayed the mountain with a generous barrage of 100 bullets per second. Every 10th bullet was a tracer, and the gunners could see where the bullets went in the daylight. When the bamboo curtain settled, he sent utility helicopters in to go pick up the Vietcong bodies.

When the high-risk clean-up patrol came back to base unhurt, with the casualties in tow, Jim ordered them to lay the dead Vietcong out in the middle of the base's compound so everybody could see them. There was about 10 of them, distorted from 50-caliber wounds. Jim told his boys, "I want everybody to know there's a Goddamn war going on here."

Jim was Pattonesk for an engineer but he never read the Bible and the Scottish General Patton read it "every Goddamn day." Jim had some Vince Lombardi (ancient coach of the Green Bay Packers) in him too and would have killed to be the first to say, "if you're not 15 minutes early you're late." The Colonel was always a Dallas Cowboys fan though because of the stoic Tom Landry and Jim had the body-mass-index of his Navy hero, Quarterback Roger Staubach.

Jim was the *Great Santini,* in the flesh again, if you saw the movie or read the southern novel by the late Pat Conroy, about his Navy pilot father. Pat's father "ate life" and told his son to do the same, but he chose to write, having more options *because* of people like his daring father. I saw an interview with Pat Conroy late in his life and Pat remarked, "writers just seem to *notice more* than other people do." He then proceeded to tell a story about a writer's conference he attended where he had observed that the lady writer sitting next to him was missing an arm. She had tried to pet a lion through a cage.

Anyway, Jim had no more casualties in his group after the one ambush and they never heard gunfire the rest of the year. Rifling through the pockets of the dead Cong, he kept a crumpled Ho Chi Minh Trail "passport," as a souvenir.

The Pragmatic Psychopath

Nixon's vibrant spirit was mystifying as if there was a chunk missing and he covered that hole with an icy grin. One way to identify a psychopath is to notice they want something but we can't identify what it is because they talk about everything but that. Nixon (the 2nd child) and his 4 brothers (most named after British Kings) were abused by their violent father and for some reason in nature's pecking order the 2nd child seems to weather the abuse better but tends to emulate it.

Uncategorizable, Edith's 4 kids were Republican, prochoice, agnostic, prowar, and loyal. They were in the kitchen one afternoon, Edith was out somewhere, and they were talking about metaphysical teenage stuff. Electra assumed command and staunchly broached *the subject* by announcing "there is no God." The other 3 looked at her and said, "well…okay," as she proudly stepped back to study their eyes. "They had all considered it a possibility," is the way Edith described the strange event after she got wind of it and their decision was partly to piss off the parents which didn't even work. The parents kept a toehold on religion while the now temporal kids ushered in 1969 by abruptly abandoning the whole of spirituality, but at the same time, philosophy starts at religion's end.

When asked why he volunteered for Vietnam Jim said, "to fight for my country." He wanted to become a true war veteran too—get his *red badge of courage*—since the army had saved him from the Korean War. With their own flesh and blood at stake, the 3 kids defended Richard Nixon and America, armed with a few history classes. He's "stopping the spread of communism" they repeated as they stared at the TV, the flower children, the hippies, and the draft dodgers, as if they were watching the bar scene in the first *Star Wars* movie. But Nixon—a "pragmatic psychopath" as one journalist called him—had a charming grin made of dry ice and was toying with a little communism himself.

Nixon was a genius—with an IQ just below John Quincy Adams—and we must admit it took a lot of imagination to do all the things he did. He posthumously ended the gold standard to pay for the Vietnam war, while rationing gasoline, and declared an additional war on drugs. He instituted domestic wage and price freezes while his monetary inflation forced prices up, creating a dyslexic Keynesian economy. Nixon thought he could manage the world like a chessboard and while none of this was particularly new, no leader since FDR had juggled that many balls at once.

The conservative JFK had opposed, at least in principle, the overprinting of money during his short administration and JFK was the last of the Mohicans. Little understood by the public, the momentum for more and more peacetime deficit spending was 2 generations old by then. Like FDR had in WWII, LBJ promised not to send any American troops to Vietnam in 1965, and as the *never back down* LBJ casually stopped making quarters and dimes out of silver, he increased the solder count in Nam by 10-fold. LBJ's 1968 budget deficit was bigger than any of Nixon's deficits[6] but it was too late to stop the cascading money which would lead to America's worst inflation. The post WWII governments had overprinted for 3 wars—the war on poverty, drugs, and the war in Vietnam—all 3 of which they would lose.

Nixon and Federal Reserve Chief William Martin knew they were sitting on a financial time bomb in 1969 yet continued increasing the money supply. It would explode in the 70s with double-digit inflation, double-digit interest rates, and double-digit unemployment—a "hat trick" as they say in hockey. The reported inflation numbers were accurate back then. The consumer price index continued rising up to 6% by Nixon's second year[7] while yearly raises for blue-collar workers were half that. In 1970 Nixon fired William Martin and appointed Arthur Burns as FED chief, who also ignored the inflation he knew was coming. Paul Volker and Jimmy Carter would have to fix it later.

Conservative economists—*monetarists* like Milton Freidman and later Steve Forbes—rightfully put the blame on Nixon and his advisors for the hyperinflation that ensued. Forbes saying the "gold window was still open," and "we don't have to have any inflation at all,"[8] pragmatically meant Nixon could have reset the gold standard at $100 an ounce because the paper money supply had at least tripled since the Great Depression, when gold was $35 an ounce. This would have saved some trust after the wholesale disappearance of precious metals from the people's pockets.

Nixon, not America, was Nixon's #1 concern. No president wants to preside over a healing economy, i.e., the recession that follows any printing boom. They want to put the economy on steroids to make their 4-year-term appear prosperous, and Herbert Hoover, caught in the aftermath of the roaring 20s, had been a great warning to all future presidents. It's the Catch-22 of printing new money—the hamster wheelhouse—still going on today.

Like drug addiction, and I would know after breaking the *white drug rule* (avoid drugs white in color rule), printing money always solves the *immediate* problem. It makes me think back to Thomas Edison's observation of the invention process: "I was always afraid of things that worked right the first time." After Washington DC printed its way out of the jam it had created the future was pawned again and the commercial for the FRAM Oil Filter capped off this retro addiction with "you can pay me now or you can pay me later."

After Nixon trounced George McGovern, the only major figure against the war other than Martin Luther King and Jane Fonda, Nixon reduced the LBJ's army presence in Vietnam but increased bombing. The North Vietnamese smelled weakness and ignored the bombs while the hippies in the US hated Nixon for prosecuting the war as LBJ had done. A statesmen would have known to pull out of the mess he didn't create, salvage some peace with honor, and tighten up the overprinting. Nixon could have listened to JFK and Goldwater, reset the gold standard, ended the absurd war, and gone down as one of our greatest presidents. Watergate blinded us to the bigger problem, oligarchy, as well as to the sensation in our stomachs that America's roller coaster had peaked, and we were in freefall. By the time the pragmatic psychopath resigned the US had lost its reputation as the good example to the world and nearly every government began fast-tracking money creation. Things got worse.

At a time when Americans had a queasiness about the great American experiment, LBJ and Nixon began the 35-year-long process of stealing all surplus money out of the Social Security Trust Fund. They could have sold it as an emergency measure—didn't bother—and kept re-raiding the fund with bipartisan congressional help from Mike Mansfield to Everett Dirksen. Decades later Bill Clinton and Newt Gingrich finally finished the fund off in 1999, neglecting to tell us they had spent our retirement. Their final emptying of the Social Security Trust Fund (nearly $3 trillion total) was the biggest theft in history, so we "partied 'till it was 1999."[9] Everybody knew the biggest generation, the boomers, would need their retirement money in 10 years. The *balanced budget* of 1999 was balanced by snatching the last $270 billion from the Social Security Trust Fund and Gingrich and Clinton were on TV grinning like they had coat hangers in their mouths. Next came an underreported recession, the tech bubble, unpaid car loans, leverage buyouts, and the stock market quit growing. You'll find strange articles on the net saying that social security was always a general part of the federal budget and that they only "borrowed it." But they never paid it back.

After downloading the CBO data (Congressional Budget Office) for the 1990s, it was difficult to find the accounting trick—they tried to hide it. At the far column to the right, the table showed the yearly *surplus* in the Social Security Trust Fund in 1999. If you take that $270 billion number, move it all the way to the other side of the table and add it to the actual deficit they *did have* in 1999, you'll get a surplus! It's magic. In real life, Uncle Sam spent more than he took in, in 1999. Imagine if those 3 trillion dollars had been invested in the Australian Superannuation Fund—a retirement fund managed responsibly—and what it would be worth now. That 3 trillion dollars could have tripled in value. The US central bank would have to create new money each month forever to make it appear that Medicare, Medicaid, and Social Security were not completely bankrupt. When it comes to money, the US has a 1-party system.

The Vietnam war, being a cause or a symptom, paralleled a sharp rise in mental illness, drug abuse, government growth, debt, crime, and a population almost as divided as in 1860. Edith was in her prime in 1969 and had a front-row seat to see America's once proud face now with a diagonal scar across it—in the shape of Vietnam. Starting a war in Vietnam to test our new weapons and get our banking system into Asia wasn't worth 58,000 boys, or even 1. Notice on the map that Vietnam and Korea are the 2, juicy, strategic peninsulas sticking out of Asia—lots of coastal property—and the US had already Americanized the pacific rim so figured they'd try a couple bites from the main entrée. We got our banks and baseballs into half of Korea, as well as Chevys and mom's apple pie. The South Koreans did alright. We did an awful lot of good.

"Let's Go Off to a Sand Dune, Real Soon"

"Do you wanna know a secret…do you promise not to tell?" [10]

In the middle of his tour in Vietnam, the army flew Jim and Edith to Hawaii for a 2-week conjugal visit, so to speak. Edith unpacked his suitcase, as women do, and noticed red lipstick on one of his shirt collars. A big fight ensued and went on and on as Jim was incapable of explaining away things. It could have been a tryst with Miss Saigon or some crazy night at a Vietnamese den of iniquity but we'll never know if his temperance failed him or not. With his farm upbringing and awkward perfection, he felt guilty just being accused of wrongdoing. Edith was convinced of the worst and when she got back home, she took a risk of her own. A family *friend* happened to be in Fort Bliss Texas, another Colonel, and called her. "What's good for the goose," Edith rationalized and went out with him. "Hell hath no fury like a woman scorned."[11] "A writer takes his pen, to write the words again, all in love is fair."[12]

The next night she got smashed drunk. Edith's Aunt Mary, who Edith had lived with in DC all those years ago, was living with the family for that year. As a reformed alcoholic, Mary knew how to handle the situation. Mary knew or guessed what had happened the night before, quieted Edith down, and made the evening look like another hangover. Edith might have even been raped—it's wasn't a night she could talk about, and the Colonel knew that. She wrote a few barely legible sentences about it and sent it off to her mother, thinking nobody would read it, and Jim never knew. "You've got to live a little, love a little, sometimes you've even got to *lie* a little, that's the story of, that's the glory of love."[13] A few years later Mary died from a life of consumption and 10 years later that Colonel had his final heart attack, leaving a wife and 2 teenagers behind.

Edith and her atheist kids did get one prayer answered: before the longest year closed out Jim came back from Vietnam to a grand welcoming with his father's lucky silver dollar from WWI in his pocket. He received the Legion of Merit and the Silver Star. Although he never had to pull out the .45 caliber Colt on his hip, he brought home a bit of PTSD. When he heard a loud noise, he would yell "incoming," and half in jest holler "battle stations," or "hit the foxholes," though no shells ever fell into his compound. So happy to be home, Jim didn't know America the beautiful was rending—it looked the same—but Edith could feel it in her chest.

Acquired Traits

Edith *the more the merrier* Virginia liked going to church but against her mother's dying wish she had stopped forcing the kids to go. Edith replaced the hymns her kids made fun of with popular tunes, she played them right off the page, and the fair lady filled the house with music and color. She painted portraits of her friends, strangers, beggars, and kids, but her still life paintings from small photos she had taken in Turkey were her forte. She had leaned way back when taking the snapshots, as if going under a limbo stick to try and get a bit more in the picture, which always made the family laugh from the car. The laughter, with Electra and Miles usually leading the charge didn't break Edith's concentration. She was an independent cuss who did whatever crazy thing she wanted and the kids didn't know what to make of that.

Schadenfreude, the delight in the perceived or the actual misery of others, was the solitary bond between Electra and Miles. She called him "the family mascot," he called her "Your Insolency," and all they ever learned, as Leonard Cohen says, "was how to shoot someone who outdrew you." The only rivalry in the family was now set. Compliments were almost unheard of in this family anyway, so, on a good day when anybody gave one besides Edith, the kids squirmed.

The kids knew not to make fun of the standard bearer, Jim, who never minded the occasional church visit—it was an obligation and *obligation* was his middle name. He never complained about a life that was "uphill both ways," but he wasn't really a Saint, he was "only a parttime Saint,"[14] as Chet Atkins calls himself. Saintly for 1 hour in church per month, if that, Jim was a typical atheist in an *apatheist* sort of way but his eleutheromania froze him in place, because any hint of radicalism might have pissed off the army. The army couldn't function alongside individualism, neither could a farm, and this anti-individualism that had originated from religion was so imprinted into Jim that saving money was ample excuse for skipping church.

Jim was raised loosely Presbyterian, Edith roughly Methodist, and like Gore Vidal's family, one Sunday they wouldn't go to a Presbyterian church and the next Sunday they wouldn't go to a Methodist church. By the way, I laughed out loud when Bill Maher was interviewing Gore Vidal and asked him if he'd ever met Hugh Hefner. Vidal responded, "well, there are some people you just can't avoid." Hefner was having sex with the peers of his great granddaughters.

Jim was away 50 hours a week while Edith was always home, teaching by example, but the kids were impacted by their father more and considered her the babysitter. "None of them want to be like me," she said out loud when everybody was gone. She didn't overtly demand equal respect—the little unnoticed mistakes in life pile up—and she began feeling miscast in a play somebody else had written. Someone had "put old pigweed in the Mulligan Stew"[15] and something didn't taste right but it was all mixed in, "whadaya do?"

None of the kids grew up to cook, read music, garden, sew, paint, have patience, smile easily (unless something was funny), or assume Edith's sense of life. They preferred Jim's and Alisa Rosenbaum's philosophy: *judge and prepare to be judged*. If there was an event, blame was assigned to somebody. "Are we all on trial?" thought Edith, "I worked my ass off to raise the kids, what was the crime, original sin?"

Work does build every material convenience but the kids never even noticed that Edith didn't feel particularly virtuous when she was working and felt no guilt when she wasn't. "Doesn't anyone see the colorful middle but me?" she wondered. "Miles seems to be the only one who shows signs of my live and let live philosophy," and she had a sad thought: "he might end up a minority in this world, like me, and *suffer for his sanity*."[16]

None of the kids showed Edith's vulnerability either—a very attractive trait for either sex—because there were always vultures waiting in their blind spots, ready to pounce. Nobody made fun of themselves, ever, except you know who. Edith's vulnerability caused her to come in a distant 2nd—an *also ran*—in the competition with Jim for transferring acquired characteristics to the kids. Her traits, being atavistic, would rise from dormancy but for now it was as if someone had taken a baseball bat to a chandelier, or as Christopher Hitchens put it, "an ax to a grand piano." "Maybe that's why I had the affair," she whispered, so, thinking her secret was safe she shrugged off her melancholy face, switched gears, and began conjuring up the courage for another self-portrait.

Jim was building a little family economy based on the value of work, character, money, and abeyance without creativity. Edith had never worked for money per se, and Jim inadvertently trained the kids to forget about that, leaving them to conclude that it wasn't a good life. "The kids are trained to worship their father, lest ye parish," she joked and started singing "they were not listening they're not listening still, perhaps they never will." She put a new taught canvas on the easel, cocked her head to the right—smiling at the blank white rectangle—and burst out laughing at her latest Jim joke. She always laughed at her own jokes and everybody in Alton had laughed too but she was not there anymore.

There would be no homecoming for the Queen. She mixed up a few oils, trying to find the right color, then laid the brush down. She felt inconsequential—a book left unread by the world and her own children. She was the Huckleberry of the family; the bass guitar player in the background who blended the drumbeat with the melody, and she was an individualist, to boot. These gems went right over everybody's head. It seemed to Edith that the whole nation was losing its patience, its individualism, its colorful middle, and losing the Bohemian spirit that had made her love it. 1969 was the death of art, vulnerability, and distinctiveness, as America went full-bore into a race for technology, and groupthink, followed by the flaccid music of the 70s.

Bad Moon Risin'[17]

1969 was the death of the stay-at-home mom too. After centuries the pyramid had abruptly swept lady liberty away and suddenly it would take 2 incomes to support a family. The deep state had doubled the price of groceries in the 60s and few knew that would be repeated every decade. The new American home was soon to be thrice the price as the deep state continued going for broke in Vietnam.

Trying to be *Team America—World Police* was so expensive America couldn't afford to raise their children anymore. "There's somebody else that needs taking care of in Washington," as Pink Floyd put it the song *Nobody Home*. The kids in the families after Edith's were getting themselves ready for school, buying lunch instead of bringing it, and unlocking the front door of the empty house at 4pm. As TV took over the American brain too, fewer and fewer ventured outside save for utilitarian reasons. The sale of children's bicycles radically dropped between 1970-1975[18] and neighborhoods became ghost towns.

After marginalizing Americans who didn't want to interfere in the affairs of other countries, there was no way home for America. To see into the future, they had to understand the past, but

America's free spirit was burned into the back pages. The trail of breadcrumbs got stale. Nobody would bother to go back through the forest of mistakes anyway.

The longest year, 1969, was now finally over. The people got the US out of Vietnam but left the lust inside of the deep state. Like the French Enlightenment, they won the battle but lost the war and the overexposed US remained in a state of monetary and psychological taxation without representation. The power remained with the top 1% who ran most nations no matter what ism they gave it. With military personnel in 150 countries, a central bank to prime the pump, and a welfare state to appease those who fancied they lived in a democracy, *Uncle Same* only gave up 1 thing: Vietnam. And like a squirrel who runs 2/3^{rds} of the way across the street, sees a black limousine coming and runs back, the people just sat there in front of the idiot box as the US took its dismal war record from Asia to the Middle East. The US had a good 200-year run. It would never recover.

Religion and the Psychology of War

> After leading the daylong cavalry charge against the Dervish Muslims of Somalia in 1898, Winston S. Churchill wrote: "Now only the heaps of corruption in the plain, and fugitives dispersed and scattered in the wilderness remained. The terrible machinery of scientific war had done its work. The Dervish host was scattered and destroyed. Their end, however, only anticipates that of the victors, for Time, which laughs at science, as science laughs at valour, will in due course contemptuously brush both combatants away."[19]

Soldiers rarely start a war. Soldiers kill when they're told and obey less every generation. A purgatory of Politicians or a coven of Priests or a covet of Kings start a war, when the young people of the 2 countries hold no grudge. For a strange example, if you want a dog and a cat, get a kitten and a puppy because they haven't learned to hate. If ancient war makers knew what they were doing, modern war makers don't because it is ultimately about sex. Those same ol' genes subconsciously tell them that killing many men, even their own, leaves them with a much greater ratio of women to men. The warlords would cull the herd of dicks and spread their seeds far and wide, obeying their ancient programming.

Sex and killing are two sides of the same coin for a battery-operated war maker because one adds a branch to his family tree while breaking a branch off another man's family tree. Osama bin Laden consciously knew what he was up to, making hundreds of sons with his pick of the most beautiful Arabian women, and killing more western sons. And if a woman's face can launch 1000 ships, that tale tells us the king knew that all men craved her iconic beauty, which is why Helen got kidnapped in the first place. The king used Helen as a trophy wife to laud it over his own soldiers, then defeat another kingdom, so, men like trophy wives because other men want them? Sex can be mimetic? Many idiot geniuses still don't feel like a new sex liaison was really consummated until they tell their friends about it, or film it. Rick Springfield asked, "why can't I find a woman like that?"[20] Like what? Like somebody else's? There are billions of women. Robert Plant sang "a big legged woman ain't got no soul."[21] Since sex devolved to be about power over women, and other men, did Plant mean that she wouldn't drive his friend's crazy?

If a King, a Pope, or Caligula kills a soldier and sleeps with his widow, he consummates 2 birds with one stone. The Japanese soldiers were one of the best at this double trouble but it is common for invaders to kill the men and rape the women, inconceivably, in 1 fell swoop. And these men have the same look on their faces with both acts; they aren't laughing during rape like in the movies because they are affixed on a conclusion.

Serial killers say killing is more intense than having sex. Mao tse-tung, earth's 2nd best serial killer behind Genghis Kahn, was a serial rapist too and knew that if he conquered the men first, the rest was easy. The blood-thirsty war makers had lots of children, including violent sons, and nurtured the war gene until it became *the thing that wouldn't leave.*

The war gene was retriggered for the greatest generation and the "Christian" Germans, as the incomprehensible German philosopher Friedrich Hegel loosely suggested, paid dearly. So did the intriguing Shinto Japanese, who have always worshipped their ancestors, i.e., genes. After losing WWII, both countries adapted to peace and world trade, which hasn't happened in the Middle East where they don't replace their culture when they find a better one. Their thinking is not as plastic and adaptable after a heavy childhood indoctrination into Wahhabism, where a schoolroom full of 5-year-old boys chant and rock back and forth on cue as if in a catatonic stupor.

That Stockholm Syndrome, however, makes them unconquerable, which is yet another reason that the US military shouldn't be in the Middle East in the first place. Let's let Russia and China keep infiltrating the Middle East until the Muslims see *them* as the Great Satan. The Native Americans had an open-ended view of religion and didn't fear Christianity, they feared the *spider*: a duplicitous white man who smiled and talked positively while spinning a web around you.[22]

Shintoism, Japan's indigenous religion, has an interesting genetic turn—they say, "mom will live through me." When they must say "goodbye" (sayonara) to mom or anybody they're saying, "if it has to be that way." Gathering moss before Christ was born, Shintoism has no holy book, designers, or prophets—it evolved from the ground up. My favorite religions, if I had to pick, are Buddhism, Shintoism, and Hinduism, in that order. I like the benign attitudes of all 3 and you can never find a Zoroastrian when you need one. If I've said it once I've said it a thousand times.

The Hindus have 300 gods (but Brahma is the leader) and they don't seem like gods to me, at least in that western way. They seem like unconscious (in a good way) traditions with a gnostic flair who effortlessly blend good and evil like binary stars rotating around each other endlessly. Their attitude is "who am I to doubt those who brought me into this world?" Their superego tames their ego. The 300 gods represent the 300 facets of us, like the infinite nature of the human condition, minus an all-powerful God and Devil. They might want to sit down and have a little pow wow with the arranged marriage God, and, the sexist God because the highest reward in Hinduism is to be reincarnated into a male.

Western religion, going the other way, is Forrest Gump's box of chocolates that we pick from or don't. We combine astrology, religion, and science and choose which teachings to believe by line-item veto. We are questioning tribalism at its core.

Buddha is thought of somewhere betwixt a God and a man but he was a mere Prince who wrote his own riches to rags story and said goodbye to being a god for an all too human enlightenment. The many secular Buddhists in India believe in that man, but they don't believe in the supernatural except for toying with a little reincarnation which we in the west might call "transgenerational epigenetic inheritance." Buddhism represents the other half of Japan's quasi-religious posture too and they get along famously with the Shinto—they don't preach to each other. Their religions are of a private nature—a family thing. Thomas Jefferson didn't give a whit about private religions, saying: "neither picks my pocket nor breaks my leg."[23] Imagine if Christianity and Islam were private beliefs and didn't break legs. Consider a world history where Christians, Muslims and even communists were unconcerned with groupthink. There would be more of us.

Getting back to US wars, the US won for 200 years, tied in Korea, lost in Vietnam, and then lost all the others. Asia and the Middle East hunkered down. When president George W Bush was discovering the "internets," he made a Freudian slip calling the 2nd Iraq war a "crusade" on TV (crusade is a synonym of *Jihad*) and in another TV interview Dick Cheney mixed up Saddam Hussein and Osama Bin Laden. Cheney said we would "find

Saddam" but he meant *Bin Laden* because Saddam had already been tried and hanged. The Fox News reporter said nothing and Saddam never had half a chance to watch George W's head "roll through the streets of Baghdad and be kicked be feet." When we think of everyone in the Middle East as the same person, we aren't thinking at all, and Colin Powell naturally knew that. The Sunnis hate the Shiites but when the Great Satan comes, they fall in love with each other.

The late Colin Powell credits the military for spear-heading true integration and I may convince you soon that if was the African American music renaissance. The military did put together an eclectic mix who learned more in the forces than they learned in high school. Powell told W, "if you break it you own it," and W broke Iraq and later presidents couldn't fix what cannot be fixed. Secretary of state Powell favored a multi-tiered approach to Iraq and Afghanistan but couldn't stop the Texans from invading the Middle East thrice. George W. Bush was trying to avenge the Kurdish Saladin's victories over the crusades from over 800 years ago while the establishment of Israel in 1947 had already done that. W was also finishing what his dad had started in the 1st Iraq war while both ignored our corrupt *friends* in Saudi Arabia. W might have set himself morally equal to Al Qaeda, but it never crossed W's mind that our new soldiers no longer believed dying in battle would ensure them a place in heaven.

I will pick up the story again after a short chapter on Albert Einstein.

CHAPTER 14

Albert Einstein

Isaac Newton treated the speed of light as if it were instantaneous. Though his life overlapped with the Danish physicist Ole Roemer who had discovered that the speed of light was much slower than that, Newton did precisely define how accelerating forces moved objects. To understand force, think how boxers are instructed to hit past and through the opponent's face. In other words, they are taught to keep accelerating through the punch and aim a something behind the opponent's head to greatly multiply the force. With forces between far away objects Newton missed one detail about time, believing that if the sun disappeared, the planets would all start moving in a straight line instantly. 150 years later Einstein upended that theory, not to mention all of physics.

If the sun vanished, the earth for example would keep travelling in the same arc around where the sun had been for 8 minutes and only then would earth take off in what appeared to be a straight line. Why? It would take the last gravitons 8 minutes to get from the sun to the earth so we would keep orbiting from that force field for 8 minutes after the sun disappeared, as if a string were attached. And since nothing can travel faster than light, *Mr Absentminded* simply deduced (assumed) that invisible gravity travels at the same speed as light—3 million meters per second.

Where Newton's earth would be hours later was not where Einstein's earth would be. The difference was crucial for space flight and Einstein explained that spaceships would invisibly curve back and forth through space, pushed around by the whim of every gravity producing planet and star. It's hard to make the sun disappear so it was 2003 before scientists could devise an experiment to prove Albert's brilliant deduction.

Just after WWI, Albert Einstein's insistence that gravity and light-rays bent around stars had been vindicated in a solar eclipse experiment. He even calculated how much the light would bend (gravitational lensing) and the famous British physicist Arthur Eddington confirmed his calculations.[1] Einstein didn't say light rays (photons) have any mass (density)—what we might think gravity affects the most—he simply said spacetime is curved so *anything* zipping through space must follow those invisible, parabolic corridors.

Anything anywhere in space is *falling* somewhere. Even if the object is a heavy moon, "everything falls the same way," says physicist Sean Carrol and "gravity may not even be a force but just an intrinsic feature of spacetime itself."[2] Renaissance man Gottfried Leibniz had similar thoughts around 1700 with respect to time itself. What we call a "force" or a "duration" could be facets of a vibrating continuum that we hope never stops.

Einstein figured out the big picture with his *imagination*, a pencil, and piece of paper. He explained the mysterious Brownian Motion (tiny dead things moving constantly) saying that heat transfer causes molecules to collide millions of times per second. We love Brownian Motion because without it, that would be all she wrote—no more halogen light—and the universe might collapse. Einstein theorized black holes after seeing the faint swirl of a galaxy and scientists found one after his death at the center of our own galaxy (Sagittarius A). The Great Satin's gravity is so horrendous it lives in the future. If our black hole vanished, our solar system would keep spinning around it in an arc for 26,000 years before it floated off down the lazy stream.

Albert contemplated existence without words, often thinking in the realm of pictures or music. He had the fertile imagination of a child and it's funny to me he was not great at mathematics though some say he *was* great at math, citing that at age 11 he proved the Pythagorean theorem. It was his abstract thinking that changed the world, but his wife Mileva *was* better at math than he was—she didn't ditch calculus classes like he had[3]—and maybe better at imagining too.

When Einstein was dating this brown-eyed, mousy-haired girl from Serbia—the only female attending the Physics Institute in Zürich where he was studying—he didn't yet know about this crazy time-space warpage. His parents didn't like his girlfriend: short, with a limp, and not Jewish—they didn't know he wrote his religion on applications as "none." They told Albert he couldn't *afford* the luxury of a wife because he didn't have a job. Albert told Mileva, his Serbian honey, that his parents were saying "the only difference between a wife and a prostitute was the length of stay."[4] I doubt she was Albert's first love though he was probably hers, and it was she who first saw time is not constant—as we all assume it is—and told *him* about it! A female physics student, struggling with sexism, gave birth to relativity and just happened to be dating the charmer, Albert Einstein. I learned about this in Marie Benedict's book, *The Other Einstein*.

Simultaneous Events Don't Exist

Benedict's explanation of how Mileva discovered relativity was short because the Einstein's love letters didn't have *that* much in them about physics. Mileva Marić was waiting at a train station in 1903, excited about visiting Albert. Marie Benedict informs us that Albert called Mileva his "sorcerer" [5] and the sorcerer was cooking up some voodoo spells on that love train. In my imagination, she discovered relativity with this thought process:

She was travelling from city A to city B where Albert was, and the train she was going to board arrived in her city A, at noon, let's say—12 o'clock straight up. She then imagined another train arriving in city B, pulling in at 12 o'clock straight up too. She then realized that the arrival time of these 2 supposed concurrent events would be slightly different and depended on where you were standing and how fast you were moving.[6]

To see the faraway clock in city B (where her train was headed, 1000 miles away) she probably had to imagine it being 50 miles wide. At that aha moment she realized the second-hand of that faraway clock would strike 12 noon a fraction of a second later than the clock she was standing in front of. All physicists knew at the time that light travelled at 3 million meters per second and she realized that the light reflecting off that far away clock would take an extra fraction of a second to hit her eyes. There was no way both trains could arrive at the same time for a single observer.

She excitedly detailed her brand-new thought process to Albert, and he sat silent for a long time, trying not to show his elevated heart rate. "That's very good, Dollie," Albert finally said, using his pet-name for her. Her pet-name for him was Johnnie. I started thinking *Johnnie Einstein* and almost couldn't stop laughing. Anyway, they began writing their first paper on relativity together.[7] Mileva saw the first relativity paper on Albert's dining room table and her name was not on it. Albert stumbled through an explanation about how nobody would read it if a woman's name was on it—probably true then—and he began giving lectures on relativity before graduating.[8]

Noon to you isn't exactly noon to most other people and Mileva noticed tiny difference. It led to recalculations of time and location which was critical for landing the lunar module safely on the moon in 1969. If mission control hadn't adjusted for the spacetime curvature the lunar module could have set down ¼ mile off target and crashed on the edge of a mountain, in a deep crater, or descended too fast.

Mileva didn't want to upset Isaac Newton's applecart, but a shiver probably ran up her spine as she realized he was a hair off. Mileva had read about Ole Roemer who had seen Jupiter in its far orbit, 600 million klicks away at times, and she probably realized that he was seeing it as it looked 45 minutes prior. Concurrent events don't really exist in the fluidity of spacetime. Here's an obvious way to explain it: if Jupiter exploded right while we were looking at it, we wouldn't see that explosion until 45 minutes later. The light from the explosion would take 45 minutes to get to earth and if you were 20 years old when Jupiter exploded, you may even hear the same explosion at age 96. The only *now* is what *your* opinion of it is. Getting back to the train scenario for a sec, how could a person in city A know their train arrived first and a person in city B know *their* train arrived first, and both be right? Well, like Chauncy Gardener, you had to be there.

The Einsteins were suspicious that if spacetime is relative to the observer, then speed, length, mass, and energy had to be relative too. They grasped that everything was relative to the space/time frame an observer was in and any other observer in a faraway frame would get slightly different answers on any aspect of reality. I thought of another wrinkle: nothing in the entire universe, not even 2 electrons, 2 photons, or 2 God particles, are the exact same. Their sameness is our assumption.

Albert Einstein had a unique brain, with quirks to match. He changed the world while getting lost walking to work and he saved every grocery list he'd ever written. He would pick up cigarette butts and sift the remaining tobacco into his pipe—thought wearing socks was ridiculous—while thinking if you shot a bullet through a descending elevator, it would pass through the front and back wall at different heights, author David Bodanis writes his book *E=mc²*. He got me thinking that if Superman shot the bullet through the elevator, he would see the bullet go in a straight line and another Superman inside the elevator would see it curving up as the elevator went down. Whose x-ray vision was right? Both. A single bullet has an infinite number of trajectories depending on the relative speed and position of the observers.

Light travels about 12 inches in 1 nanosecond (a billionth of a second) Dr Robert Mueller calculated. If you threw me an Aerobie

Frisbee 300 feet across a soccer field I would think I caught it 300 nanoseconds before you saw me catch it. We don't pay any mind to these differences on our pale blue dot, but they become crucial when we get into the inner regions of atoms or out in space. We can't contemplate a billionth of a second either but we can contemplate 1 year and light travels 5.8 trillion miles in a year (a light year). It takes 4 years for light from our nearest star (a red dwarf named Alpha Centauri) to get to earth so with this distance paradox—23 trillion miles—we won't be visiting another solar system without a *much* faster propulsion method.

There were no atomic clocks invented yet for Mileva to prove her theory, but she knew about the time lapses because Ole Roemer damn near calculated the speed of light correctly, 240 years prior. The Danish physicist Roemer embarrassed his boss Cassini at the Paris observatory one day. Cassini, who had discovered moons circling other planets, was telling King Loui the 14th when the telescope would reveal Jupiter's biggest moon, Ganymede, coming around Jupiter but the King looked through the telescope and no moon appeared. It came around 5 minutes later as Roemer said it would because Jupiter was farther away than when they had last watched Ganymede coming around. The further distance made it a bit longer for the light from Jupiter to reach earth.

To get the speed of light all Roemer did was simple math: he subtracted how far away Jupiter was that last time he saw it from how far away it was the day the King visited. Cassini had skipped that step and he skipped the next one. Next, Roemer divided the difference in distances by the 5-minute delay in the moon appearing in the telescope (Velocity = Distance divided by Time) to come up with his fairly accurate calculation of the speed of light—2 million meters per second. He would be an old man when his calculations were vindicated and updated to 3 million meters per second.[9] His calculation would have been unflawed if their distance measurements had been better at the time.

Here's a modern example that illustrates how simultaneous events don't exist: imagine you are a spectator behind center field watching a baseball game while talking on your cellphone with a friend in another city. Remember, light travels about 1 foot in a billionth of a second. You see the batter hit a homerun. When the bat hits the ball, that's time A for the batter and only 1 nanosecond away from the absolute, singular occurrence. The sight of the bat hitting the ball hits your eyes in center field (400 feet away) 400 nanoseconds later and that's time B, for you. Your ears hear the bat hit the ball about .04 seconds later than your eyes saw it because light is 9000 times faster than sound, so when you *hear* the crack, that's time C. Your friend on the cellphone hears the crack of the bat a little later than time C; he hears it at time D. Your friend must wait for the sound to travel from the bat to your cellphone, and for the digital signal to travel at the speed of light from your cellphone to his. When did the bat hit the ball, time A, B, C, or D? It depends on who you ask.

For these reasons a baseball umpire might call the runner safe at first base when he is out, because he's *looking* at the bag and *listening* for the ball to hit the first basemen's glove. Standing 10 feet from the first basemen, the umpire sees the runner's cleats hit the bag instantly but the sound of the ball hitting the first baseman's mitt hits the umpire's ears .01 seconds later. This is because sound travels a million times slower than light, so technically, the tie at first base should go to the first basemen.

Time has varying speeds too, depending on how fast something is moving or how far it is from its main gravity field. After the cesium atomic clock was invented in 1949, we could measure exactly how much slower time passes for us when we're travelling in an airplane compared to standing still. A rock at the top of Mount Everest will decay slightly faster than a rock that rolled to the bottom of the mountain, because gravity's hold on the lower rock is a bit stronger. Even atoms want to live longer. As Brian Greene puts it, "in a sense, all objects *want* to age as slowly as possible." A scientist named Ernest Lorentz created relativistic formulas that calculated how much an object's shape will change at different speeds too. The 1-meter platinum rod, kept in a vault in Paris as the world standard, is no longer 1 meter long when streaking through space.

Albert Einstein's crowning achievement was the formula Energy=mc^2 (c is the speed of light). Energy=mv^2 (v is velocity) was known in Ole Roemer's day and Einstein simply substituted the v with a c. 4 decades later this eventuated in 1945 with the nuclear devastations of Hiroshima and Nagasaki while Russia was sandwich-attacking the Japanese in Manchuria. Physicists had long studied Einstein's new equation and knew that when they squared the speed of light (that's a big number) that would release ungodly energy and the Nazi Werner Heisenberg realized that the E in the equation was the path to the nuclear bomb. The Nazis knew they had to make the bomb first and if physicists Leo Szilard and Albert Einstein hadn't written a convincing letter to FDR in 1939, the unthinkable might have happened. Here is the background to the race for the nuclear bomb:

When Hitler had taken Norway in April 1940, Werner Heisenberg was in Austria working toward a nuclear bomb for Germany and he was so heavily guarded that all allied attempts to assassinate him were tabled. He travelled to Sweden to talk to the reluctant Niels Bohr—another Nobel Prize winner—about building a nuke. Bohr put him off, thinking it would take too long but Heisenberg was as determined as Hitler was. They knew they desperately needed *heavy water*—a rare isotope of water with the molecular makeup of D_3O—and unknown to the allies the German scientists had already gotten uranium to sizzle in a lab in 1938 and Heisenberg would create another small neutron reaction in 1942.[10]

The Nazis took over the hydroelectric plant in Rjukan Norway where the innovative Norwegians had also built a heavy water plant in hopes of supplying a new industry—nuclear energy research. The heavily garrisoned facility was nestled in the fortified mountains and all allied attempts to bomb it had failed. In mid-1942, the allies parachuted in a group of brave Norwegian volunteers, dressed as factory workers, who were going to meet up with British saboteurs landing in a glider and destroy the factory. The glider crashed, the mission failed historians tell us, and they were all killed or captured—but not on the 2nd try. 9 Norwegian men trudged through rock and snow to the heavy water plant, knowing that if successful, the Germans would kill many Norwegian civilians in town. Nonetheless, at 1am, they planted little plastic explosives at the bottom of the 18, 4′ high boilers and blew holes in most of them. The heavy water gushed out and in the morning the Germans murdered civilians in the street, then repaired the plant.[11] After slowing down Heisenberg's supply of heavy water in 1943 the allies were finally able to bomb the factory out of commission.

Hitler and Heisenberg, unaware of the Manhattan project, had no more heavy water through which to test fire a high energy neutron into a critical mass of uranium. The power of Einstein's equation was finally proven by research from Columbia University in Britain and bottled in Los Alamos New Mexico by scientists working on the Manhattan Project.

CHAPTER 15

Only a Dream

The next 2 short chapters are about our very real magical and fictional dimensions, so you could say these next 2 chapters are fictional. You'd be almost right. After that I have a chapter on our dreams and then will tell the end of the story.

Edith's family happened to be living in Ankara Turkey, where east meets west, when one morning she had a dream. She never forgot one detail of this one. With lunches packed, and the kids on the school bus, Edith decided to tackle her self-portrait—she'd been putting off the scary task. She had a little cough, so she skipped breakfast, took 1 bite out of a granola bar and put the rest in her shirt pocket for later. She could not have known how crucial that was. She put a new white canvas on the easel and drew an oval for the face, like she always did. When the house was empty, she often painted in her birthday suit but luckily not this time.

Her mind wandered to the near human extinction she'd read about from that super eruption in Indonesia 75,000 years ago, wondering if it was true. In East Africa, only a small pocket of humans remained alive by a lake in what is now the country of Malawi. Edith drew a horizontal line through the exact middle of the oval where the eyes would go.

As she started filling in her facial features and hair, she was surprised that the brush was shaking a little. She kept glancing into the big mirror and back, then stepping away from the portrait and cocking her head to the right. So far, it didn't look like her. Something was off from the very start, but she had painted so many portraits she kept going. The painting started looking a little grotesque—she winced—as her face, some face, slowly came to life on the canvas. It was unrecognizable. Suddenly, she felt heavy-eyed in the middle of the morning, then oddly, got cold. Wondering if she was getting sick, she put a folded white blanket around her body, wrapped herself in it, and stretched herself across the couch. The corner of a throw pillow was poking her neck a little, so she tucked it under, like she always did when something was touching her neck. Instantly, she fell asleep.

"Holy shit," Edith said. She found herself standing at her easel in front of a small spaceship. The spaceship took up most of her painting studio and she couldn't make out how it got in there. She heard a little "click," and the outline of a door appeared from the seamless craft. Like a draw bridge, the door dropped open and settled silently on the Turkish rug. Terrified, she grabbed the little battery-powered record player from the coffee table and was ready to bounce it off the head of any pencil-necked alien who walked out. She hesitated. There was 1 little round room inside. It was empty and there was no skinny insect-eyed alien. Edith's legs walked her slowly into the craft. Her mind tried to stop her legs but to no avail, as if her legs were kidnapping her. You know how dreams are.

Looking around trembling, she figured it was a time machine because of the million-year clock in the middle of the little room. "Click," the door closed. Her hand involuntarily reached out to the clock, dialed it back 75,000 years and pressed go. "OK but *where* do you want to go?" asked a voice. "Lake Malawi Africa," her mouth said. There was no response. She looked down at her now steady hand still touching the dial, as if her arm belonged to someone else, when the computer finally suggested she sit down and buckle up because it would be a long ride.

The computer was a tad nervous. "Maybe Edith might know

something I don't," it thought, "most people like to go back to Victorian England or ancient Egypt." Those were shorter, less risky rides. "Why Malawi?" the computer pondered. Edith sat there bewildered as she looked at the many levers and dials making sure not to touch them again. She dozed there for God knows how long, unaware the ship was silently warping space and time, when she awoke to a small jolt. The spaceship was still. With a little "click," the door fell open again.

Edith slowly stepped out onto the ground into a haze of gray. It was very cold, but she still had the white blanket around her. There was no sound and she coughed again to make sure she'd not gone deaf. There was zero wind. The sky was whitish. The visibility was quite bad but she could make out some rocks, some thick green foliage, the occasional ghostly looking tree, and a large dark mass in a flat area. She was drawn to the silhouette of black as it had a kind of glow behind it. She walked slowly through the thick layer of ash toward the glow and the mass seemed to be moving a little. Wide-eyed, she couldn't believe what she saw. It was a few dozen little apes, a *shrewdness* of apes she thought, almost pushing 5 feet tall, as they huddled tightly together. And they were standing around a fire! Dumfounded, she watched as the snowflakes vanished above the flames. They stared at her towering 5' 4" frame moving toward them like a ghost and were more terrified than she but didn't move. Edith noticed they flinched in unison each time she coughed. There were about 40 of them.

She bravely tiptoed up to the edge of the group, accidentally kicking over what looked like a bowl under the ashes. They apes flinched again. There was a little female ape looking at Edith out of the corner of her eye, inching herself sideways into the huddle. Edith didn't know it was a female until she saw a breast and a little face. The ape was nursing a tiny baby with a head the size of a grapefruit. Edith wondered if she was dreaming, or had died. "Is this heaven.........or hell?" she said out loud, "or does it matter?" The mommy ape stared at her.

Edith was now standing inches away from the mom and saw the tiny baby's cheek, 2 tiny, closed eyes, big hairless ears, and a human looking hand, clinging to mom. The hand had almost no hair and her instinct told her it was a boy. The boy didn't know Edith was there and kept nursing, sheltered by the mom's shivering grip. As Edith's eyes adjusted to the light it hit her. "It *is* true," Edith whispered, "it's true, these aren't apes at all, they don't look like apes……these are humans." Lower jaw trembling, she stared at her ancestors realizing that they were as crucial to her existence as her own parents were. She started crying a little, the mom started crying too, and they bonded as only women can. Edith named the mom *Eve*, not knowing her real name.

Edith carefully stroked the mother's thick black hair and the mom turned bravely and looked directly into her eyes. She chattered something Edith could not understand which was followed by nervous chattering from the freezing humans, as if to say: "you're creeping us out here…what are you…and where the hell did you get those clothes?" Edith began picking tiny bugs and debris out of the back of mom's head and neck, and the little lady calmed down a little, after Edith had. The others followed suit. "Eve…Malawi…Lake," Edith said slowly so all could hear, and added, "an individual's gotta have 3 names." The humans cocked their heads and stared at her.

Edith then took the granola bar out of her shirt pocket, accidentally dropping one of the little bugs into it, and put the food in front of mom's face. Every human had already smelled it and knew how much food was there. Eve grabbed it with her free hand and woofed down half of it as the closest ones stole snippets from the other end and others snapped up crumbs from the thick ash. Shocked, Edith leaped away from the chaos, landing on that bowl again and almost fell. Two seconds later their little noses told them there was no more food. As for the bug in that kind of cold, the bug was as snug as a bug, in the bottom of Edith's painting shirt.

She had no idea what to do next, so she walked back to the

spaceship and grabbed that little record player and opened it up. Thankfully, there was a Beatles 45 still on the spindle, so she put the needle on the edge and started playing *Love Me Do*—maybe their worst song that McCartney wrote when he was 16. As she had taught them, her kids had the volume way up and the whole tribe leaped at once. Edith leaped too. "I should have flipped the record over," thought Edith, and played *P.S. I Love You* on the B side. It was too late. They tilted their heads and looked back at Edith then back at the magic box, listening to *Love Me Do*. Edith lucked out because the song is what musicians call a "shuffle" and those make people dance. They collectively started thinking the sounds were of magic, Edith was God, and they started moving together. The starving little humans were resigned to the fact that they were being delivered into the next life as Edith let the worst Beatles song ever play all the way to the end. They all kneeled in front of Edith, wanting to be taken. "My God they're religious," Edith said, covering her nervous laughter, "and they think I'm the rapture." "Shit," she said, "these *are* the last 40 humans on earth."

Edith didn't realize Eve Malawi Lake had little breast milk left and was close to starving to death. The new mom had been reluctantly eating bugs out of her own hair and felt happy for every crunch. "Time to go," broke the silence. Everybody nearly jumped out of their skin again. "Time to go!" the spaceship barked again and Edith knew it was time to stop playing God—her 15 minutes of fate were over. She bravely looked around at everybody. She walked up to frightened Eve, wrapped the white blanket around her, and said to her "you……Eve," pointing to her chest. Edith, patting her own chest said "me……"Edith." Eve stared at her and said "Edut."

Edith suddenly felt embarrassed in her painting outfit—her first clue maybe this was all a dream. She was freezing though, and that felt real. She grabbed the record player and the little bowl on the ground and walked back into the time machine. The computer in the time machine was relieved she brought back the record player—didn't know about the bug yet—and was worried about the bowl in the spaceship and the white blanket left behind around Eve's shoulders. Edith was changing pieces of both the past and the future. As if she read the mind of the computer, she reluctantly set the bowl back outside after thinking she could tell Jim she had bought it in Syria. "With no chipped edges it's probably priceless but they'll need it," she said and got back into the space ship. She dialed the clock back to present day, hit go, and buckled herself in. "Those were my ancestors," Edith choked, "maybe they won't make it......what if they don't make it?" Her heart skipped a beat, to make some room, as a ghost flew through her chest. "You better hope they make it," thought the computer.

The computer finally detected the bug in her shirt pocket and shot a little radiation at it, to kill it, before somebody discovered it in another spacetime. But it was too close to her left lung and heart so it shut the zapper down—Edith felt nothing—and the bug felt a little strange but lived. Edith began dreaming inside her own dream that she was a hero, as the spaceship rematerialized in her painting studio. She sleep-walked out of the time machine and went directly to her linen closet. The time machine was steering her, trying to cover up all the evidence, knowing when we play with fate and time, we are playing with Armageddon. She got another white blanket off the top of the stack and laid back down on the studio couch where all this had begun, exhausted.

Before she knew it, she was waking up on the couch and throwing off the white blanket. She didn't even notice the time machine was gone. It took her a while to come to her senses, and when she did, she stumbled over to the easel and couldn't believe her eyes. The *self-portrait* she had painted on the canvas, unmistakably, was Eve Malawi Lake. An electric jolt shot through her body like a lightning bolt and Edith passed out, for the first time in her life—draping herself across the carpet. After what seemed like hours, she woke up again—for real this time—but was in her own bed. She looked at the clock and it was 11:30am. "Holy shit," she said again, and wondered what day it was as she shuffled into the kitchen. The lunch she had packed for her son that morning was still sitting on the kitchen counter. "It's still today," Edith said, "and Miles forgot his lunch again."

As she prepared for her drive to school, visions of little hairy humans, white towels, and granola bars came rushing into her head. Slowly, she remembered the whole dream. Shaking, she ran over to the easel again and the canvas only had an oval painted on it with a horizontal line through the middle. "It was all a dream," she assured herself, "it was only a dream, but I know I was there."

"Or was I?" she wondered, fully awake now, and she walked slowly to her 1957 Ford Fairlane with the sack lunch and headed for the elementary school. She felt 3 pounds lighter (she was) and laughed aloud while sitting alone at the first stop light not noticing that Turkish passers-by laughed with her. She felt as if a weight had been lifted from her soul as *errand girl* parked crooked at the school, grabbed the sack lunch and did the fox trot down the street toward the elementary school. Edith suddenly realized she was singing: "I have often walked down this street before, but the pavement always stayed beneath my feet before." [1] She thought, "I'm on pitch and have better phrasing today; I never could really sing that song."

She hadn't noticed the little bug crawling around in her shirt pocket and didn't know……that she was 171 days younger than when she had woken up that morning. She could feel something though.

CHAPTER 16

The Aftermath of the Dream

It's 1967: 2 years after Edith's dream and 1 year before Jim's departure for Vietnam. Edith was contemplating getting her first dog since childhood, so she did just that. The kids knew she was puppy shopping but to their consternation she came home with a toy poodle. Edith told them how brilliant the dog was and her being right didn't change the fact that they wanted something more wolflike and you know who didn't like the dog from day one. The dog's tricks weren't ground-breaking but the poodle had such a tiny head and brain the kids started saying, "size doesn't matter," which made Miles, who never wet the bed after his 10th birthday, feel better.

As you know Edith had learned to speak Turkish and wanted to give the dog a Turkish name, so, she named him *Abi Beh Effendi*—Mister Mac Sir, is the loose English translation. "An animal," she reiterated to the kids, "should have 3 names because animals are individuals too." "There are thousands of dogs named Blackie," she continued with her sales pitch, "but only one named Abi Beh Effendi." Abi tore up expensive things, pissing off Jim to no end but Edith taught her kids those things can be replaced while Abi could not. Jim disagreed. Edith ignored him and started thinking about all her friends with 3 names.

Spotty Ann Feisty popped into her head, the kitten she had taken on that fateful train ride so long ago, and her mind went to Icki Buçuk. Icki was the very observant Turkish cat who had adopted Edith and Icki did not know she was Turkish so Edith would remind her every so often. "I hope Icki is still alive," she wished, "after I left that poor sharp-witted cat with those excruciatingly boring neighbors." Edith's mind flew all the way back to the day she bumped into Eve Malawi Lake who had hopefully passed on about 74,900 years ago. Suddenly she remembered the granola bar and was positive she had given it to those humans, maybe keeping some of them alive. Throughout time, entire species have hung by a thread until being rediscovered by one rain drop, one morsel of food, or one ray from the Sun God, after one of those damn super-eruptions.

"I'm sure it was only a dream", she laughed, "but I never found that granola bar or my 4rth white towel." "It's not every day a girl saves the human race from extinction and can't tell anybody for fear of getting sent to a padded room in some nervous house," Edith whispered, giving herself a pat on the back. Loudly she said, "if I told 'em, I'd have to"……well, you know. She didn't realize that was a true statement because she had naïvely toyed with fate. If her dream was not a dream and she did save us from extinction, it shrouds Edith's immortality with a mystique. This is not how Edith lives forever though—that comes later.

It was only Icki Buçuk who noticed something categorically different about Edith after she travelled through the labyrinth of spacetime. Edith was never sure of what Icki was sure of—something had happened in real life. Icki lay motionless on the living room divan, silent as a bat, staring at Edith. From Icki's vantage point, looking diagonally through the hall and into the kitchen, she felt safe. Icki couldn't take her eyes off her first doppelgänger and how beautiful Edith was. To see an animal who obviously got younger was a first and scared the bejesus out of the observant cat. Bedhead Edith's naturally curly hair had curls inside the curls and often looked like a bomb hit it but all the sudden it looked perfect.

Icki happened to be rolling all this around in her little head, blinding her for a sec, when Edith pranced into the living room with a smile. Icki, thinking she might attack, leaped from the top of the divan to the top of the curtain, turned her head 180°, and stared at Edith, wide-eyed. Edith had never seen Icki near the ceiling and got wide-eyed herself, thinking "is she in heat or turning back into Atatürk?" Equally confused, Icki thought Edith might suddenly morph into a werewolf and as Edith slowly backed out of the living room Icky silently disappeared as only a cat can.

To avoid a black hole, the time machine Edith had ridden in had slightly exceeded the speed of light for a few seconds, so time moved backwards and it had to slam on the brakes to keep Edith from returning only a little older than her own kids. When Edith got back to her apartment in Turkey, she was 171 days younger than when she had left. She enjoyed her fair share of compliments over the next few weeks from observant people—Edith being susceptible to flattery—but nobody saw what the horrified cat saw.

Having evolved on a machine planet the spaceship had an AI computer aboard that could crunch ungodly amounts of metadata instantly. It had also evolved a bit of emotion. As the spaceship cameras watched the skinny Africans, it calculated that with no help the cold and starvation would kill all of them in 24 hours. In the seconds before Edith handed the protein-packed granola bar to Eve the time machine knew that Edith and humanity were about to spontaneously combust, having never existed. "Maybe I won't have to fly her back to 1965," thought the mildly depressed computer. When Edith pulled out the granola bar and handed it to Eve the computer measured the protein and had to reverse the forecast. It then knew that a half dozen of them would live, and the future of humanity had to be left almost exactly as it had happened.

A day after their little snack our ancestors huddled around Eve and Edith's out-of-this-world new white blanket and the sun peaked through a void in the nuclear winter. Sadly, the computer was right and only 6 of the group survived the following week, including Eve and her son. That was enough. Armageddon lost at the buzzer and Cro-Magnons started anew.

The tribe worshipped *Edut*—as Eve always called her—for generations, passing down the story of their savior through their lineages until it was dispersed by mouth throughout Africa. The legend of Edut eventually got lost in translation and mistakenly became *Eve* for about half of the tribes, because Eve had been the original messenger. Each faction was sure they were right and religious wars erupted here and there from mistakes in pronunciation. Much later, for another irony, archeologists would discover the bones of one of Eve Lake Malawi's earlier ancestors and coincidentally name her Mitochondrial *Eve* too, because we are all related to her (Chapter 26).

The computer in the time machine still had 3 problems. Humanity was intact in 1965, and everything was the same except for 1 new bug, 1 missing blanket, and 1 less granola bar. This worried the computer because if one other person, or worse, God himself, noticed one thing out of place there would be hell to pay. The computer trusted that these scary details would remain a secret, they did, and thank God, God never bothered rummaging through her cabinets. And since insects have not evolved much, the bug fit right in. "He looks normal enough to me," the lady bugs noted.

Only the reader and I know about these things because this was really a dream your author had. I gave the dream to Edith for fun. Though I could have been God over 40 people, I was very scared during the whole dream thinking I'd never get back home, to present day, and my family. John Lennon wrote, "I was dreaming of the past…and my heart was beating fast." In my dream I felt as if something bad would happen and of course it did. After my encounter with the last 40 people on earth I turned to go and the time machine was gone! The lucid dream became the nightmare that I feared, and I woke up. I diagnosed the dream: I was spending too much time writing this book and neglecting my family.

CHAPTER 17

Our Dreams

"I got bats in my belfry, weevils in my barn," Mark Knopfler writes, and that's good because bats eat weevils. We can change the thoughts in our heads (the bats in our belfry) and teach them to eat the little lunatics (the weevils) in our bodies.

Eve, the first woman, means *snake* or *female snake* in Semitic language,[1] so a snake dream might be about a fear of a mother. The fear of venomous snakes (ophidiophobia) is worldwide, even where there are none, so we can know that our snake nightmares are not about snakes. Our subconscious pictorially exaggerates our repressed thoughts at 3am and the common female snake dream could possibly be about the penis, which they dream into a prehensile organ—pointing itself by itself—like the penis of an elephant, humpback whale, or octopus. She might be dreaming about sex, the devil, the garden of Eden, an evil mother, or a *copperhead*—which penetrates and injects its lifechanging liquid—so I won't oversimplify because the symbolic nature of dreams is unique to each person. There is no template.

Scientists are archiving dreams in mass and using this mega data to write algorithms for therapy, which is a perfect example of big tech writing a bias algorithm from a faulty premise. The books that categorize the meaning of dreams have also managed to go nowhere. Any two people may have an eerily similar dream yet the dreams have completely different meanings. Scientists are addicted to searching for patterns in hopes of finding some magical connectivity between all humans. They are attempting to further the work of Sigmund Freud, Frederick Pearls, and Carl Jung (who wrote down his dreams from age 4)[2] and assigning global meaning to them. The dreams these professionals interpreted—or any dream anyone ever had—are particular to one individual and these great counselors were only teaching method and giving examples.

We've been so indoctrinated into believing that people are identical computers that we can't think beyond that and scientists get huge grants to find patterns where none exist. We are Individuals with an "I," so unless we find an excellent counselor, we are left to figure out our own subconscious by ourselves.

Besides music, laughing, or experiencing visual art emotionally (simple unconscious association tests) or getting hypnotized, dreams are our window into the little-known world of our subconscious and each brain works differently which is why the fields of neuroscience and psychology labor along. "The variety of psychic constitutions is untold,"[3] Carl Jung adds.

Jung found that most of our dreams and delusions, up to the voices we hear in our heads, can be reverse engineered down to a specific psychological event from early in life. In other words, no one else went through exactly that, or repressed the memory in the same way, or turned it into that specific delusion. When we uncover one of our long-lost delusions it suddenly seems obvious to us because we've been writing plays about it in our dreams since we were toddlers.

Our dreamer talks affably, and sometimes not, to our asleep mind all night. Our subconscious is our seer, our messenger of personal insight, and whatever we dream is as good as IRL (in real life). As authentic as anything we experience, including daily irrational thoughts and emotions that we discard, dreams are chockfull of valuable information. Jung was his own shrink and he traded dreams with his patients to enhance a deeper interaction which he found was the secret key to get inside the crypt of the unconscious. He even cured a handful of patients with acute schizophrenia.[4]

Our dreamworld is a one-of-a-kind nightly lesson in what we repress when we're awake, and we just want it to go away, but this free information won't go away until we learn it. Since we are watching a movie that we are directing while we are directing it—the outcome isn't pre-planned—we can change the dream in process. By identifying and confronting what were afraid of, both while awake and asleep, we can fight back against the dream going nightmarish when it returns and wake up in a better mood.

Catch your bad, recurring dream and talk back to it throughout the day. Rehearse confronting it and your unconscious mind, who typically stays one step ahead of you, will get the email and upgrade your dream for you next time you have it. After you fight back in your dream, you'll realize it a fraction of a second later because the subconscious gets to go first. It knew about the monster under the bed before you did and showed it to. Then, while awake, you taught your sleep mind to fight the monster and with your 2 minds now on speaking terms—teammates—the monster will have second thoughts about coming back. The monster will eventually go away which will percolate your day and your 2 minds can get back to the business at hand—present day work life. You have to *get out of your dream and into your car*[5] anyway and begin hacking your way through the jungle. With one monster gone your conjuring dreamer will be dreaming up a new one for you as your head hits the pillow that night.

Planes occasionally crash simply because the pilot and copilot don't know each other and the same goes for our conscious and subconscious minds. Longevity increases when our cognitive and emotional intelligences converge.

Trillions of mental gears are formed in childhood by you, your genes, and your environment. All 3 realms, which keep changing, are shared by no other person. Your ego-societal mind (a real conceptual cloud), your personal mind, and your biological thinking machine (the wrinkled sponge) sometimes work as a team or as 3 competitors. Conscious debates subconscious, reality debates illusion, self debates society, extrovert argues with introvert, spirit argues with materialist, blue-collar debates white-collar, who you want to be argues with who your parents wanted you to be, and so on. It's a perfect mess with so many serendipitous options and evolution expects you to weigh each option after it went to all that trouble. You firmly see yourself as an individual but your brain is a committee of a dozen wise old owls and a dozen foolish chicks, vying for your attention. This makes us contradictory, hypocritical, confused, and sacrificially selfish. It's all normal, however, these are mostly internal debates yet we externalize all of them as if they are universal.

Leave the cellphone at home because it's yet another brain and an auxiliary one to boot. It's a good brain but we've assigned too much nervous importance to it and when you think about it, we don't really have emergencies anymore. The acceleration of useless information is already stressing out the wise old owls in our heads and keeping the young chicks in the 8th grade forever.

People can't confide anymore. Like the children's game of *Telephone*, conversations are repeated and spread out in ripples until there's little left of the original. The lies dilute the truth and this long existing brain disease now has a rocket attached to it—the cellphone. By injecting a trillion dollars into a handful of social media companies, the pyramid has created a new frenzy of 5 billion people whose only power is toying with the privacy of others. If only we had a thousand social media choices, at least this neurosis would be localized. Why are we crazy? We've deluded ourselves into thinking that the pyramid is solving all of our problems—it's the red-carpet mistake again—so our strange response is to turn the world into a drama class. Useless communication between non-thinking fragile egos is not only the psychological decline of any civilization but what has kept oppressive countries poor forever.

The human brain is about half cognitive and half emotional and these 2 spheres overlap or operate alone. The spheres work separately but simultaneously with unknown cross referencing.[6] I've said we do things "accidentally on purpose" so in a sense we half know what we're up to. For example, if you pick up a stick and throw it for your dog, your unconscious brain thought of that about a second before you realized you were going to do it.[7] Much of our computing is automatically performed without our consent or even awareness and a split second later we decide on an action, and suddenly know what we're doing.[8] That's why on *Wheel of Fortune* our deep brain already knows how to solve the partial puzzle but we can't say it unless we relax—reduce cognitive chaos—and simply allow the answer to leap from our subconscious to our conscious. It's the same with *Jeopardy*. By the way, Pat Sajak asked a contestant what he did for a living and he replied, "I'm an unregistered nurse." Pat paused and said, "you never seem to have one of those around when you need one." Here's another trick to get our 2 minds working together. When I reflexively, subconsciously, take a daily pill, I read the label and say it out loud. After that I always remember that I took it.

The Psychology of the Limbic System

Down inside the brain, the hypothalamus and hippocampus make up our emotional center. Nature imbedded this soulful part of us deep, maybe to protect it from blows to the head but more likely we inherited it from lower animals and then evolution built our larger, more cognitive brain around that. This limbic system is covered by a helmet called the corpus callosum, which is a protective dome and the main part of our firewall. It is slightly larger in females, proportionately, and is highly developed compared to almost all lower animals. This emotional chamber—housing our feelings, past present and future—makes us much more than walking computers and is an incredibly advanced emotional processor that cannot be programmed into AI.

The limbic system—the *under chamber* in Latin—includes the

amygdala, hippocampus, hypothalamus, basal ganglia, etc., and sits about 2 inches above the back roof of your mouth. It's a little subterranean mecca where our deepest dreams live with our deepest memories, as well as the art and music we love, or don't. When we suddenly start singing some old song, that's our under chamber chiming in without invite. The autonomous subconscious can be so irritating that it loops the same song over and over and we can't stop it. Like a recurring dream, it's telling us to listen to the words.

The hypothalamus attempts to keep us internally balanced. It controls circadian rhythms, body temperature, moderates or enhances our passion and sex drive, has a role in psychosomatic diseases, activates our smell-created emotions, tells the pituitary to tell the thyroid what to do, and triggers memories to help maintain a psychological wholeness.

Buddha says we aren't much more than the thoughts and memories we've had, so the busy limbic system is our selfness. Dreams provide us with a vivid exposé for free of our inner self. The whole brain dreams but as we slip into stage 4 sleep the more selfish, public, prefrontal cortex that protects our egos, goes silent, and the deep dreams slip down into the sacrificial, private, limbic system. The deeper the dream goes the harder it is for us to lie to ourselves because our deep dreamer tells it like it is and scientists have detected a treasure-trove of noncognitive activity emanating from this area.

The outer part of the brain operates on larger, slower brain waves (alpha waves) and the waves become faster and more intense (gamma waves) during the deepest dreams, for the highest state awareness.[9] Remembering daily events is a lazy brook while a recurring dream is white water rapids which is why we can retell an old recurring dream at the drop of a hat but have to think about what we had for dinner last night.

The hippocampus regulates memory and learning. As we age, we suffer from atrophy of the hippocampus which causes psychological disorders, but scientists haven't made a connection with these and childhood trauma. However, we experience a labyrinth of emotions that chemically work their way deep into the brain and cause observable bodily reactions. For example, noxious chemicals cause the hypothalamus to send signals to the exterior that make the pupils dilate (Hess and Polt 1960)[10] as they do when we lie. What happens in the hippocampus changes the other organs; bad news makes our stomachs hurt. Doctors are trained to separate the mind from the body while Dr Carl Jung says: "bodily traits are not merely physical, as mental traits merely psychic......the continuity of nature knows nothing of these antithetical distinctions." [11] We know little of how this *oneness* works, however, we can learn it for ourselves because each oneness is different.

The significant struggles, triumphs, and meaning in our lives are stored in the limbic system, which suffers significant volume loss as we age compared to the rest of the brain.[12] Keeping it healthy with diet and dream interpretation—our 2 main overlooked superpowers—is central to our wellbeing.

Surgeons operate on the hippocampus in severe cases of epilepsy or autism and if it's removed people can't remember their childhood, their own kids, or the people they worked with last week, making them robots—Lauren Aguirre intimates in her book *The Memory Thief*. I'd rather be blind, deaf, and in a wheelchair but have all my precious memories from life intact.

One problem can start when we ignore bad dreams or thoughts and unknowingly glom proteins onto a neuron which destroys the neuron but stops a recurring vision. This in turn stops some of the axons from communicating with other neurons and we end up with a tiny hole in the brain which can spread from there. Better it would be for us to keep attacking the nightmare while we're awake until we change it and keep those synapses firing.

The hippocampus houses those memories that make us human, including some things from childhood we decide to forget—to stay sane. When we don't remember large chunks of our lives it's because we muffled part of our limbic system. We need to revive the memories and process them because the hippocampus sometimes makes the self, attack the self, as Karl Deisseroth, the author of *Projections*, points out. Since Alzheimer's begins in the hippocampus,[13] or very near it, we could surmise that the bad memories and dreams we hesitate to process damage neurons and creates a wormhole toward disease. This is where our anger is unsafely harbored, and we need to do a psychological catch and release to prevent further damage. Harboring hate, honest but useless, takes up precious room in that tiny compartment that has so very much to do for its size. Tis better to process that anger loudly, start evicting it, and trip the imagination back to the colorful middle. Uncovering repressed thoughts will add synaptic connections to our brains and reconnect those precious essential reflections that keep us loving life. I don't know if this will reverse dementia but it will help because our deep dreams and our inevitable late in life Alzheimer's live in the same little place.

I believe Stockholm Syndrome is the underlying cause of mental disorder. SS injures the limbic system because when we try to disown something (violence, fear, hate, and adoring our perpetrators) we attack the system ourselves. Violence and psychological trauma shoot down through the basal ganglia, where "learned behavior is modified by its consequences,"[14] and inwardly tightens in the hippocampus, attacking our free thinking. When we don't psychologically process our Stockholm Syndrome, it balloons into depression which is the #1 cause of death no matter what the coroner says we died of.

Also in the limbic system, the ancient, unconscious amygdala (fear detector) is the sentry who alerts and saves us from predators, sometimes without us knowing. We can scan the vines around us in the jungle and not see a snake but the amygdala sees it and our hearts race. We don't know why. Our fear works opposite from how we believe it does because even when we do see the snake, the 2 following processes take fractions of a second: we see a snake, we automatically start running, and only then do we have full cognition of the danger. The running precedes the fear![15] When our amygdala alone sees the snake our unconscious guardian doesn't have time to explain, it just saves us first with epinephrine—suddenly were sprinting away—and we may never know why. This is akin to the famous Pavlov's Dog experiment.

A dog will react to an old fear all its life though a danger is long gone. Their subconscious can't learn that their environment changed while humans can because our better cognition keeps chiming in until our fearful subconscious understands. The band Genesis writes, "telling me the danger's past I may not feel the icy blast……again."[16] If a boy has a warm understanding mother, he experiences changes in the amygdala and prefrontal cortex which confers more self-control and less anxiety.[17]

Our ancient amygdala doesn't know we live in the modern world and no longer need to fear fierce animals—it's overactive and anxious for old reasons—and meditation will quiet this down. Cavemen had so many health risks, worrying was probably a benefit. Research confirms that our main survival methods remain automatic, [18] not conscious, and lie detectors record these unconscious stress signals when we're telling lies, while we feel rather calm (Chapter 22).

Medically, the brain remains a whodunnit and the science behind the mysterious limbic system no longer suffices for explaining all our emotions. [19] We are left with 1 option: psychologically repair our brains ourselves with dream therapy to postpone the onset of disease.

I believe too, that deep in the brain lie symbols, backgrounds, old themes, and primordial knowledge from our ancestors, that appear in our dreams. It's a million-year-old encrypted file cabinet containing experiences that were imprinted on our ancestors in the darker ages and shouldn't always be mistaken for here and now information. Carl Jung attributes many of these symbols to our million-year religious history (probably true) but I believe these themes are mixed with personal experiences. They are manifestations of the rote spiritual teachings we get in early childhood and of very young brains trying to fathom what death is or isn't. News of a plane crash gives us a creepy but safe feeling as we get to conceptualize real death in the abstract, unconsciously, while conscious.

Though they say our cognitive memory clicks in at age 3, long before that we process everything as feelings and our pre-ego brain doesn't add judgments to them—the feelings are just good or bad. Some dreams are nothing more than feelings that have no dimensional quality or intellection and they probably came from before our memory kicked in at age 3. Since I have very strange dreams of being born,[20] I believe our subconscious memories start before birth.

Even after age 3 we still can't make sense of many images we are shown so we sleep on them and morph them into wonderful forms and strange fears. Maybe children shouldn't be shown pictures of religious crimes and people burning in hell. Our unconscious dreamer paints them into incommensurable monuments, deities, dimly lit buildings, corridors, statues, spaceships, castles, cliffs, and under chambers! Carl Jung taught that these constructs are as real and pertinent as anything else we might perceive while conscious. But what do they mean? It's always different, however, occasionally we have a metaphysical dream. More than one person might dream of a statue they saw, knowing it represented what was going on in the minds of the people who lived at that time. That dream would be a rare, deeper understanding of the archetype of a distant time.

Having made the point of our infinite individual uniqueness, we *can* generalize about the skirmish betwixt the sexes to some extent. Men are emotionally simple compared to women and are more psychologically selfish, so let's talk about them behind their backs. Remember, a man is just a dick with ears so when social situations get tricky, they touch their crotch, giving the most vital organ, a little pet. "Good dog," they're thinking. Evolution brought men to this place without asking their opinion. Men always try to rush things to save time, and desperately want to do the driving. They won't ask for directions when lost so they make it to the Darwin Awards much more often than women do, because a *frivolous hero* is only an oxymoron to a woman. "If a man faked confidence or pretended to know what he didn't know, although he might be killed, he can die as a leader not a follower."[21]

Movies glorify this phenomenon: lead actors have the cig dangling, don't need sleep or food, and always get shot in the shoulder—males love to live dangerously and it's not conscious. One common scary male dream is you are a helpless passenger in a jumbo jet flying between tall buildings and steeply banking close to skyscrapers at 500 mph. Since you are the dream director, you are also the pilot. Evil Knievel and the innocent passenger need to meet each other and find the balanced man in the middle.

Women live longer because they mitigate risky living by living more in the here and now. Being from 2 different planets with different genetic and psychological penchants fosters misunderstandings between the sexes that are greater than that of people from different countries. Men are programmed to laugh at danger so women become alarmists and see a psychedelic mess where men see humor. Males see female signal amplification as turning a benign situation into a *Circus McGurkus*,[22] while women see men's callous disregard for what alarms them as unfathomable. In 1000 years when men and women live on the same planet, hysterical men will be screaming out ridiculous warnings and the women will be laughing their heads off.

Women, probably the first to use short sentences,[23] gossip more because they want to inform other women about who can be trusted. In the cave days calculating trust was about survival and since, there has been a dramatic decline in risk. Ancient women had to worry more and still do because it's in their blood and their worry is not directly because of men; that gift is courtesy of a bigger insufferable sexist—evolution. Men didn't get together and decide to take over, the old codger evolution did that for them. If evolution had picked women to be physically stronger, as it did with a few mammal species, women would have less depression and wouldn't be alarmists because they would be creating the situations. Individual female mistrust had little effect, so cave women teamed up to ensure group protection. Ignoring individual rights fosters groupthink.

Still common today, ancient women's estrus (menstrual) cycles would sync up as they sat around the campfire deliberating about the men. I think it was a show of cave woman solidarity—the first "labor union" so to speak. Those who had just given birth probably ignited this body-mind phenom of group-ology—a defense mechanism—and went further, explaining to the others, "the man went in this way and the baby came out the same way." Women knew first where babies came from and began strategizing about how to gain a modicum of control, more every generation, over this life-changing *mandate*.

The New Male Depression

When we're ecstatic we happily accept it so when we feel depressed, we can accept that too. I call depression "the Wabash Cannonball" because like a train it makes no sound until it's upon us. I used to do underground leak detection and I was working at this farm in west Georgia that had a water pipe leak between 2 of the buildings, but nobody knew where it was. I had the headphones on and the big stethoscope on the ground, which works just like how an elephant listens through its feet. I was eavesdropping around for the leak for a while, when I heard this screaming, piercing, high pitch sound. I ripped the headphones off and looked around, but everything was dead still. 2 minutes later, a freight train came charging by the farm. I had heard the disturbance underground but hadn't heard the train coming yet and our depression starts in a similar way. It begins down in an anxious limbic system and we have no clue it's there until it suddenly enters our outer brain. That's called a "daymare." ccc

We summon the Wabash Cannonball ourselves, and we do this for a reason—something happened in the past and we need to process it. German psychiatrists were the first to recognize depression as having nothing to do with demons, who don't exist, but rather from a deep loss long ago. There are few good pills for depression. Not only do placebos work better[24] but some studies show they outperform all antidepressants (Dr Irving Kirsch, PhD, 1998).

Male depression has long been attenuated by how males are trained and conditioned to respond to Stockholm Syndrome so historically female suicide was more common. This is because women held the shit end of the stick for a million years. The bigger your V-frame, as many men have, the less depression you will generally suffer from, but depression is converging for the 2 sexes, and then some. "*Red Rain* is coming down all over me," sings musician Peter Gabriel, and Bruce Hornsby tells us to "listen to the Mandolin Rain." Paul Simon, one of the pioneers, said, "hello darkness my old friend."

Those immune to depression (males who say they have no doom and gloom) are better at blocking it out, suppressing their dreams, or simply better at trying to transfer and project it to someone else—or taking it out on a dog. Identifying and dealing with depression can become a superpower for males if men start dealing with their nightmares while awake.

Since males have been less depressed in the past, and are not supposed to get depressed, families don't realize their sons are at risk. The statistics in *The Boy Crisis* [25] in my opinion lend themselves to an historical shift in raising children. Until 1969 we were raised by women trained to prefer male children—women rejected that training—and today I hear couples speaking glowingly of their daughters, muttering about their failure to launch sons, and have no idea what happened. By 1979-1981, 10 years later, male suicide surpassed female suicide. [26] Cultural pendulums always swing too far, especially in advanced countries, resulting in a current suicide rate which is now 3.5 times higher with males.[27]

A million years of programming has given males a license to

kill which naturally selects men to kill without specifying who. Nature's compulsory violent programming coupled with boys losing their historical standing, without explanation, creates a feeling of powerlessness. A son is an angry young man born into an unforgiving new world where anger is taboo and if he happens to be cast out by his peer group—that's a double squeeze. He's isolated now, not permitted to show anger, and becomes a ticking time bomb. Most boys, who unlike girls don't think they can't change the neurotic world, try to remedy their dilemma with marijuana and alcohol. A small minority of boys suppress that anger themselves until it erupts into random acts of violence. For a telling example, when your wife is flaming mad try shutting that down quickly. Realizing the double squeeze and finding creative, safe outlets for boys to express their anger is crucial. But "if you can't understand him and he don't die young, he'll probly just fade away,"[28] because his "prison is walking through this world all alone."[29] The suppression of anger, ironically is our auto reflex now, and this repression of anger is the start of our anxiety. The anger has to come out somehow, somewhere, or the shit hits the fan.

Evolved fathers who make the modern transition from combatant to fatherly money-maker can guide their sons through the storm but if a boy's father works all the time, or leaves or dies—that's the deep loss—the boy has no teacher and doesn't get clearance for takeoff. I was talking about this on the phone with my nephew David, who had leaped from cop to PhD in molecular biology, when his daughter came in from school. 10-year-old Danika told him her best friend's older brother had killed himself. The father had left the home 6 months prior. 2 years later another boy in her math class offed himself. About the same time, a guy we knew who went to the Naval Academy took his own life, and we could say they all died of natural but preventable causes.

How did a forager boy learn how to hunt and fight? From his father. Learning selection is hoarded within DNA connected families and when a dad didn't return from battle the boy saw his own future and cold needles shot up his spine. Every cell felt a deep loss. We could predict that if mothers left the house the daughters would biologically suffer too, because we identify most with our same sex parent. Those rare mothers who can't love probably compromise their daughters' health at the cellular level too.

With war and government sponsored violence waning,[30] boys who have not found a new purpose in life, one that replaces violence, are still finding ways to die early: "Today Billy Joe McAlister jumped off the Tallahatchie bridge."[31] Sinead O'Conner recorded the most haunting version of that song and died at 56 herself from psychological distress and a childhood of abuse from her mom. The band Creed sang, "I'm 6 feet from the edge and I'm thinkin', maybe 6 feet, ain't so far down."[32] The popular age for an unfocused male to commit suicide or shoot into a crowd is 20ish and getting younger. Suicide is a synonym of homicide, like an allele that got confused during a societal switchover, and furious boys who have lost their hope for the future want to destroy. When they started killing school kids—first high schoolers, then elementary schoolers—I told my nephew that birthing centers were next (it happened in Thailand) and this morbidly tells us that the psychological trauma the killers experience happens very early in life.

Military suicides are so off the charts that it led to a controversial statistic. The US lost about the same number of soldiers during Bill Clinton's eight years in office (1 UN war) as during George W Bush's eight years (2 US wars) but it illuminates how bad the suicide problem is in the military. "Suicide is painless, it brings on many changes, and I can take or leave it if I please."[33] This haunting song about the Korean War tells us soldiers get to a no-man's-land and living or dying becomes a Mexican Standoff. The lyrics about when we stop loving life were written in 5 minutes by man-boy when he was 15!

If you are a typical male with dyslexia, it helps hide your depression, Stockholm Syndrome, ADHD, sexism, and tendency for violence from you. These are not comorbidities or psychological diseases because we evolved that way—this is the world we live in—and manic depression, bi-polarity, or going from extremely angry to extremely nice, on the female side, are not diseases either. No pill will *fix* these things. Our conflicting tendencies were selected by nature for coping with our Stockholm Syndrome to make sure we each had many crazy options. Immanuel Kant saw this and called it "social unsociability," and Friedrich Nietzsche praised it as "wisdom full of pranks," telling us that our brains are not abnormal. They are rebellious for a reason and always will be. Nature decided long ago that everyone always agreeing would be a stagnant, psychological fizzling out of humanity because nothing would change.

The post-evolutionary pressure is on men to learn to love more and women to learn to love less. Women were sacrifice and men were selfish and as we painstakingly migrate to the colorful middle, everybody's cup may become half full. We are speeding this up because we can hear God muttering: "don't make me come down there—I didn't say goodbye to you, you said goodbye to me." What needs to evolve in the next millennia, and will, is less dyslexia-ADHD in men and less manic depression-bipolar in women. Once we exorcise a million years of Stockholm Syndrome from our DNA nature will have honed these so-called comorbidities into androgynous advantages—a healthier, more productive yet still competitive atmosphere—in about 1000 years.

"I used to rule the world but that was prior to my girls."[34]

As our now adult daughter Danielle explains, "men will get pregnant when the interior diameter of the nasty expands to 20 centimeters, and if that happens, there will be abortion clinics at every Quick Trip, not to mention it will be the end of the human race." During a family conversation she quipped, "if men could get pregnant, they'd learn the meaning of *no* and woman would learn the meaning of *yes*." My wife and daughter were laughing like men who ruled the world but they do put up with me at grocery stores when I put things in other people's carts and even on cruises when I introduce myself to people as Fassbender Kierkengärd. When Danielle's husband Steven was hesitant about getting a roach out of her bag of chips she said, "and you expect me to shoot a watermelon out of my vagina?" They had Sienna on May 30th, 2023, and we are now grandparents.

Raised in the south with her tongue in her cheek, Danielle says, "straight up, I'll tell ya straight, I shoot it straight every time." When I make fun of social media and call it "Spaceface" and "Instabored," she says, "I love it when people complain!" The only problem we have with her is, well, she doesn't like onions. Jeanne and Danielle talk in circles and sometimes it sounds like their goal is to use the greatest number of English words possible. As they're saying goodbye at the front door or on the phone, the same goal starts again. On a good day Danielle could win an argument with a Rubik's Cube, but I finally won on how she pronounced the word *booth*. When we'd go to restaurants her girlfriends would want to sit in a "beouth," which singed my ears. She was starting to copy them when I finally got her to enunciate it "booth."

Danielle introduced us to a new couple at a party and I referred to them as an *item*. "Dad," she said, "nobody says *item* anymore!" She even sticks it to the man: "I'm not going to lie to my kids about sex and Santa Clause," scrunching up her face. Danielle asked me why sexism only cuts one way so I explained, if there's a shooting and the only thing witnesses see is a green sedan speeding away, should the cops pull over females driving green sedans? They only target males because shooters are 99% male. When I told her to "fight sexism tooth and nail or you'll be screwed, glued, and tattooed," she said, "sounds like a typical Tuesday to me." When we have visitors from Europe there's always the discussion of how their clock is later, and Danielle says, "don't tell us what happens next, we'd rather be surprised."

Her wit began when she started getting my stupid jokes at age 5. I began talking blue-collar philosophy to her early, which is how she learned deception and the word *renovation*. She always wanted to stop at every ice cream shop but I always told her it was closed and under renovation, and the 3rd time I told her that she said "no daddy, I can see people eating ice cream inside." One fun night at a neighbor's house they had painted clouds all over their blue walls. Everybody was naming weird animals they imagined seeing in those white splotches. Every joke got a laugh, so I said, "that one looks like an ambidextrous amoeba." There was this pregnant pause, and 6-year-old Danielle moved close to me and whispered, "nobody laughed at your joke dad." She does laugh at my imitation of Cher's *If I Could Turn Back Time*, when I sing "if I could worship Yahweh, instead of Coors Latte!" If she broke something she used to say, "I did it on accident," almost saying *on purpose* and changing it at the last second. So much of life is accidentally on purpose.

Danielle was about 7 when we joined Jeanne, the night shopper, at Outback Steakhouse for dinner. I had 2, 16-ounce beers with dinner and Jeanne wanted to keep shopping so Danielle and I headed back home by ourselves. I was doing 75 in a 45, got pulled over, and told the cop I had no idea I was speeding. He must have smelled something, so he asked me where we'd been and I said, "we met mom for dinner at Souper Salads" (they don't serve beer) and Danielle said, "no we didn't dad remember we went to Outback Steakhouse?" Well, a breathalyzer test ensued which I barely passed, and he didn't even give me a ticket.

About a year later she said something funnier. Jeanne's sister Ingrid was visiting, and we all decided to go see the movie *Twister* on opening night. I said, "it's the sequel to *Gone with the Wind* (nobody laughed, foreigners!) and Danielle and I drove over there to buy the 4 tickets early. First, I stopped at an "ATM machine" (as I called them) and the guy in front of us was doing multiple transactions of course. After sitting there for 15 minutes I said, "Jesus, what is this guy doing, making love to the machine?" 8-year-old Danielle said, "if he did that dad, he would burn himself."

When she was 10 Danielle asked me why we've never had a female president, so I bypassed the question and told her about the major countries on earth who have had female presidents, including the first one in Sri Lanka followed by a female prime minister in India, where 30% of Danielle's genes started. With DNA from 12 countries, she tells people "I was born in a hospital that just happened to be built on an ancient Indian burial ground."

Danielle is a Christian and years after seeing the movie *The Matrix*, at age 16, she asked me "is it possible that we might live in a fake world constructed by powerful controllers who give us the illusion that our world is real?" "Maybe our lives are run by an advanced being and our daily activities are primarily illusions," she added. I explained to her how infinitesimally low the probability was, especially without any evidence, and added, "you already believe that's what is happening right now." She stared into space as I do often, because.........we are alone.

> *"Somewhere, somehow, somebody must'a kicked you around some......who knows, maybe you were kidnapped, tied up, taken away, and held for ransom."* —Tom Petty

Choosing to own our own Stockholm Syndrome will reveal the formidable, caged beast that still snarls inside our heads. People who don't realize they have SS develop schadenfreude by performing quite the magic trick on themselves. Their distraction is finding what they think is a flaw in somebody else and pointing it out, making themselves feel better, briefly. Those who are taken aback by a schadenfreude attack (who also don't understand their SS) only see what the insulter wants them to see: the top of his iceberg glistening in broad daylight, distracting us from his murky, bigger, bottom side.

When we don't respond to an insult, we keep thinking about what we should have said back, all day. The German's call this "treppenwitz" and what someone said becomes a pea under our mattress. Whenever we're emotionally shortchanged, casually with dismissiveness, we should instantly tell ourselves what's going on: the other person is using us to cover up something and they're pretty confident we won't find out what it is because they don't know what it is themselves.

When we get addicted to comparing ourselves to others, we give any neurotic insulter the power of attorney over ourselves. After growing up with abuse, we think we need it. "Nobody can make us feel inferior without our consent,"[35] because we are so heuristic that we always think our problem is bigger than the other person's problem. Schadenfreuders know this and exploit it so when we stop feeling someone's jab and look at them calmly, we become the scientist and *they* become the mouse in the maze. The insulter must swallow their sword but might take schadenfreude out of their toolbox, leave the maze, and go get a soft mannequin who looks like their dad, older sibling, or mom, and beat it up. It works. "You gotta get in to get out," Peter Gabriel knows.[36]

For millenniums the all-male religions throttled women by accusing them of "heresy" whenever they strayed beyond the umbrella of control. Hauntingly, the word "heresy" comes from the Greek word *hairesis*, which means "choice." Historically, women have had less choice and more SS than men, however, the pendulum has swung.

I break Stockholm Syndrome families into Type 1, (the healthiest), Type 2, and Type 3. As simplistic as this is, we can usually observe a family and place it into one of these categories. Spouses with Type 1 SS don't marry an abuser like their father or mother was and neither spouse talks down to the other. Type 2 men are abusive rulers and marry passive Type 2 women because it's what both have always know. Type 2 misogyny is the historical template. On the good side, Type 1 relationships are increasing in number while Type 2 relationships are decreasing.

In the typical heavy SS family, Type 2 men tend to become the next generation of abusers because with 6 times more testosterone, according to researcher Pranjal Mehta, they project their own histories of abuse and take it out on anybody who wasn't involved. There is little progress because the kids get the same treatment, Type 2, and the cycle repeats. After that imprinting, everybody wants their fair share of abuse.

Last, and this shouldn't surprise anybody, there is a modern phenomenon of SS families that I call "Type 3." This family type is increasing the fastest. Type 3 women marry very nice but overly passive Type 3 guys—not a son-of-a-bitch like their dad—but Type 3 women remain locked inside their slave DNA, and not knowing that, try to take over the relationship and the family 100%. Their confusion about this epigenetically inherited feeling makes them feel trapped forever, even if the husband tries to make 5% of the decisions. Type 3 wives feel this 5% grab as if they're being kidnapped and held for ransom, because their mothers never got that 5%.

As the man caves disappear from Americana, Type 3 women don't know why a little compromise makes them feel as though they have lost all control. Heavy SS will make us feel as if the roof could collapse any minute, until we understand the phenomenon. Type 3 families prefer daughters and the wives avenge their bad fathers by taking it out on their own sons. Type 3 husbands may pretend they are still in charge, or, concentrate on their vocation where they still have some control—smoke pot when they get home—and are careful not to express opinions lest those conflict with you know who. Type 3 women tend to marry a stud so their children will get those genes then get rid of him and marry a slave husband for 2nd part of her life.

The unwritten rule of the 21st century is that female psychology is off limits, which again, throws out half the needed information. I am breaking that rule here to illustrate that the sex war is in full swing globally and like all wars it has a revenge element, which is far from a cure. Women will say they're not angry though they are spitting mad and have every right to be, but they don't attack the source. They hate to go back, back so long ago, to the memories of their mean dad, therefore, women often follow their own unwritten rule—female psychology is off limits. Such is the comradery of

Stockholm Syndrome.

In Type 3 families the daughters happily soak up the mother's misandry and the angered sons become passive aggressive which manifests later in a failure to launch or worse. For 40,000 generations that's what men did to daughters, keeping them weak and unactualized, and all could plainly see that boys were favored. Now the pendulum is mirrored in these Type 3 families. Easier said than done, let's let the revenge of the pendulum swing back to the colorful middle.

Most of us harbor anger toward a parent or 2 long after we've left the insane asylum but we go on to take revenge on the innocent. We are simply juxtaposing our own real story onto a new family who wasn't around when the old imprinting occurred. Type 3 mothers need to get mad, then get even with the real Steven—probably their father but I have no idea who. Instead of fighting certain kinds of sexism we need to fight sexism itself and after that breakthrough we are freer to assess situations objectively. The block is that Stockholm Syndrome leaves us worshipping our abusers making it so easy to subconsciously protect them and transfer the abuse to someone else.

Gen X parents tell me their sons are weird—usually not—because the modern metric is measuring their sons against the new ideal: the female child. These 2 very different brains need dissimilar attention and we can learn how to do both after recognizing the sexist programming from our previous family.

We suppress anger because expressing it seems selfish and injurious. Anger *is* injurious when transferred to innocent bystanders and when we don't focus on where our anger began, we injure ourselves too, deep down in the limbic system (Chapter 17). Again, beat up a soft mannequin until your voice changes and you start yelling a certain person's name. Scream it out like you were in a black church—repeat. Write angry letters. Don't send them as a rule, write them and feel your power returning. After hitting the jackpot, revenge subsides, and abusive people aren't attractive anymore. I get these cricks in my neck, like calf cramps, so I hit the punching bag a few times and they go away.

We are so unique that each sibling reacts differently to the same crumby parents. We are all mad at a select few: father, older brother, uncle, who knows. It could even be a mother or a sister who didn't stand up for us but don't let me put words into your mouth. Whether these people are alive, missing, or dead, no matter, we now own what they put into us. The problem is all ours to fix because we own our own bodies and knowing that is step 1 for aborting those old invaders. I'll repeat a sentence from the introduction: this is not a self-help book because *I* don't know *you* so I can't help you. I can only tell you what I have learned. Our greatest power is our imagination.

CHAPTER 18

The House on Cielo Vista

After 3 years in Turkey, Edith's family got their marching orders for El Paso Texas. Both spouses said, "too good to be true," at the same time, and smiled at each other. Edith was especially happy to get back south; her uptown downsouth nostalgic spirit was comfy anywhere in the broad swath of Dixieland, where you get a kind of traditional wisdom found nowhere else. The kids had loved Turkey but couldn't wait to see R-Rated drive-in movies, pizza places and Del Taco, the idiot box, lots of grass, and way too many traffic lights. After living on Biggs Airfield (now Fort Biggs) for a couple years, "Gemini" as Edith would say, meaning "Jim and I," decided to venture off base.

They bought their first house in the suburbs, with 4 bedrooms and no steps, for $25,000—the price of a small backyard deck today. It looked like the house Edith had grown up in and for the first time, Mary and Miles got their own bedroom. Electra and Rachel still had to share one as they had since birth. Before, during, and after Jim went to Vietnam the family lived in that brick ranch in El Paso Texas within a mile of the Burgess High School Mustangs where all 4 kids attended.

Edith's father, Jesse, drove down for a visit. Abi, her miniature poodle, would snap at his hand when he reached down to pet him. "I'm fixin' to knock the far (*fire* in Missourian) outa Orbi," Jesse would say. Jesse had recently put his dog Snapsy, whom the kids loved from the Missouri visits, to sleep. Everybody but Jim was upset. Edith told the kids, "he just didn't want to take care of him anymore, or, he did it so he could drive down here to El Paso."

That afternoon it just so happened that the whole family was looking for Abi Beh Effendi, who had gotten out again. He heard them yelling his name and happily came running toward them from across the 4-lane. They watched horrified as a big Plymouth bat mobile with those ridiculous fins, drove directly over him at 40mph. Abi rolled out from under the rear bumper, black from soot, and almost unhurt! But the accident changed him and he lost control of his bowels. Trauma overcharges the brain like an electric shock and like our panic attacks with their all-too-real physical symptoms, Abi kept reliving the incident in his head. He didn't know what had happened, not knowing what a car or a road was, and proved Pavlov's Dog experiment. For every psychological reaction there's a biological one. Jesse, having gone through a similar accident, didn't connect with Edith's family very well and a few days later drove back to Missouri while Edith found Abi a rescue home.

Money was tight with Jim sweating over 3 girls headed for college so Edith and her neighbor Esther went out Christmas shopping anyway. They had to get something. Edith and her 3 girls already had the closets looking like Imelda Marcos's shoe room and she had no idea what to get them. "Why don't you get them each a lava lamp?" Esther suggested. Edith said, "nobody buys those anymore, they're too popular." "Who are you now, Yogi Berra?" Esther quipped in that fresh Boston accent. Esther was a Boston Red Sox fan and didn't like the funny Yogi Berra you see, since he played for her archrival, the New York Yankees. Edith didn't get it and looked puzzled. Esther helped, "Yogi is the baseball player who said, *nobody goes to the games anymore—it's too crowded*!" Edith tried but still didn't get the jokes and could only recall Yogi the Bear. This led Esther to explain the last joke again and Edith laughed, pretending like she got it. "90% of baseball is half mental," Esther continued, "get it?" "Oh," said Edith, politely laughing a little, "maybe I'm getting my first baseball lesson." Esther would not give up and said, "pretend like I'm Yogi Berra." "Ok," Edith said smiling. In a man's voice Esther said, "if I had known I was going to live this long I wouldn't a drank so much." "Oh!" Edith said cracking up, "now I get it!" Edith never knew that people other than her made Yogi Berra jokes so she usually didn't get them. It was one of her entertaining blind spots. Esther was suddenly Edith's epiphany so Esther, being ahead, decided to stop there and not to go into the Bob Uecker jokes.

Edith's family would try her on for size and mock her, rarely missing a laugh at her expense, whereas when one of their stories was going downhill Edith would encourage them along and appreciated the rare chap who did the same. The kids never picked up on that. Esther didn't put up with crap from anybody and chose the times wisely when she dished it out. She'd seen a few lonely *dugouts* in her days in Boston—with 1 sister, 12 years older—growing up an only child as Edith had.

Not only did Esther and Edith become fast friends, they each had 4 kids plus Esther's husband was a Border Patrol agent and Jim was an army man. Both husbands had the war gene and neither wife had a money job except for the hardest one—kids. On the weekends they rarely knew where their 8 kids were and both husbands would've preferred to be at work anyway. After a couple beers Jim would join in the fun: "I always wanted to be a engineer and now I are one!" That was probably the 1 time in his life he made fun of himself and 3 people politely laughing was enough for him.

The husbands, Bob and Jim, passed the time by watching football, making sure to avoid eye contact or anything queer in nature. Neither had any buddies. Bob would always say, "if you wanna see a touchdown just wait 'till I have to pee." They didn't have instant replay yet so leaving the room was a risk. Bob came back from the throne and said, "what'd I miss?" "Nothin', Jim said, "he was stopped for no gain, if any." Missoura Jim had heard an announcer say that and Bob laughed, not knowing if he should or not, while the wives laughed the afternoon away with an uncounted string of highballs and an ashtray full of red lipstick butts—lighting the new one from the old one—with the familiar white noise of 50,000 football fans softly chorusing in the background.

On weekends Edith and Jim played Bridge, attended parties or went to the officer's club, and drove home drunk. The bumpers were so big and thick back then if you dinged one you just drove away. Back at home and the kids asleep, the partiers would typically make a strong pot of caffeine and drink it in the living room. The conversations were generally peaceful, not always, and the kids listened, holding their breath at every word. One night the argument got heated, fast, and the sleep pretenders heard what sounded like a cup and saucer hit the living room wall. On Sunday morning everything was as normal as it ever got.

In 1970 Fort Bliss Jim worked at the Institute of Nuclear Studies simulating the damage from nuclear blasts at various distances from the epicenter by throwing sheep from army trucks going 60, 80, and 100 mph. Then they would inspect the wounds of the silent lambs to estimate human casualties at different distance from the center of the hurricane. His studies were of course secret and he kept tight-lipped except for telling Edith and Miles about the sheep. "That's baaaaad," Miles said. "Heaven forfend," Edith said, "why don't you use lawyers instead?" Jim wrinkled his mouth.

The 3 girls had gone to an R-rated drive-in movie so at dinner, over some flank steak, sugar peas, and 3 of Edith's outrageous baked potatoes, Miles asked Jim how to make a nuclear bomb. Jim mashed up his potato with tons of butter and salt, stuffed it back into the crispy shell, and took at huge bite from the ice cream cone. He thought while he chewed.

Maybe it was the mouth-watering spud that loosened his tongue: "Well, you spin some uranium 238 in a centrifuge until it is separated from the impurities, and enriched, then you take this critical mass of weapons grade uranium and shoot a high energy electron through some heavy water—D_3O, a good neutron modulator—into one uranium atom, split it, and create a sudden chain-reaction across the other high energy neutrons, which releases enough heat, pressure, and radiation in less than a billionth of a second to destroy a city." He continued making love to his spud while Miles and Edith were speechless, hoping there were no microphones in the house. "Heavens to Murgatroyd, Jim, nobody needs to know all that," Edith said wide-eyed. Miles and Edith started putting together all those away trips he took to Izmir and Northern Turkey, on the Russian border. Edith quelled her secret guilt by wondering where else he had gone, pretending to concentrate on a small bite of skinless potato.

"Life Goes On, Long After the Thrill of Livin' is Gone"
—John Cougar Mellencamp

It was now 1971 everywhere, including inside that brick ranch house on Cielo Vista Drive. 1971 seemed to last as long as 1969, with *bad news on the doorstep.*[1] Edith happened to read that they'd put Charles Manson away for good and in her unexplored mind, as it were, her thoughts jumped to her dad Jesse, whom she hadn't heard from in 2 years. She didn't feel like calling him. Jim, who had always devoured the morning newspaper, started going right to the comics section, and he had stopped watching the dismal Vietnam news on the idiot box. He retired from the army there in Texas and the nuclear scientist took a job as a pool inspector, of all things, for the El Paso Water Department. Always cleanshaven, he wore a 5 O'clock shadow all weekend. It seemed to Edith that America itself was getting depressed, or was it her?

The clock on the kitchen wall slowed to a crawl and Edith would glance at it like a bored office worker. Edith felt the frailty of too much alone time—the time she used to cherish the most. As with all of us, it felt like the pain was coming from an external source, but it wasn't—causing more confusion—then acrimony set in at the young age of 44. "What happened," she said to herself, "why am I bitter?"

She started singing Bob Dylan's, "the times they are a changing." She was on target because America was still afloat but sitting lower in the water. "Everybody knows the boat is leaking, everybody knows the captain lied," Leonard Cohen sang. Edith wanted to "go back where love wasn't jumbled so"[2] and so did America but their eleutheromania froze them in place. "There's a crack in everything, that's how the light gets in," Cohen sang; however, these were not cracks—these were labyrinths. She woke up to another beautiful December morning in that empty house in Alton Missoura. She was 8 years old, just looking out the window and the little town was dead still. A tumbleweed suddenly blew down Cielo Vista Drive, it jolted her, and she realized that she was still in El Paso, as 1971 and the US, faded from glory. She craned her neck to look up and down the street—no children were outside playing.

1971 was finally over and that spring, Rachel, Electra, and Mary, squeezed into their little stick-shift Renault and took off for the University of Texas together. They blended right in because every student was white at the time except for half the football players. The opaque quarterback James Street (a terrible passer) had thrown a bomb to beat Arkansas by 1 point for the national championship. Richard Nixon was at the game. The Longhorns won several championships and every post season touchdown sent a tremor shuddering through the campus and beyond. Tiny animals, primordially fearing another apocalypse, scurried into burrows as the windows at Texas Tower lit up to spell #1 on all 4 sides of the monolith.

Except for Miles, who wasn't exactly an emotional support dog, Edith was alone. The bitter optimist was gone but so were Mary and Rachel. Miles didn't mind the privacy and Jim enjoyed the quiet right off the bat—the quiet worry of how to put 3 daughters through 6 years of college—and Edith had all the freedom a slave could want and she didn't know what to do with it.

During her marriage she constantly complained about the Army doctors and that might be what saved her. If she had let them, they would have medicated her with happy pills—all her friends had a handy bottle of valium in their purses. Edith medicated herself and talked on the phone with her friends about nothing. Her life was an unexpected retirement she hadn't made plans for, and like the sign shop that she'd mistaken for a laundromat, she didn't know she was standing at another fork in the road, so she didn't take it. Her next 4 years crept by with no change of scenery.

Edith's daughters got married in faraway states and the parents flew to each wedding. All 3 married a tall Austro-German-Englisc archetype, complementing their SS from Jim, and as each couple got into their mid-70s honeymoon limos (Impala, Bug, Mustang) Edith always shouted, "have fun!" Blushing, like she didn't mean it *that* way, she covered her mouth as if she'd said something naughty. In one church, with the minister in earshot, she told this joke: "a Rabbi, a Priest, and a Baptist preacher walked into this bar and the bar tender looked up and said, *OK what is this, some sort of a joke*?" There were a couple of laughs. Jim looked at the carpet.

Back home after the last wedding Jim felt 3 missions had been accomplished while Edith stood at the schism separating X-mom from X-painter. "I can't leap that far," she whispered, "both of me are gone." Nobody needed her anymore, hadn't for a while—it happens—and she couldn't cut that cord that her kids had rather casually cut not so long ago. In a trance she stared down the hall where, at the very end, her painting studio sat faithfully gathering dust. Suddenly, she got tunnel vision—a minor nervous breakdown, unless it's you—and she saw a serene light coming from the long corridor. "Come," she heard a voice say, "come into the Kingdom of Heaven" and she froze with verklempt—a daunting fear that left her speechless.

Edith moved her mouth, nothing came out, and she took the deepest breath she'd taken since right before her wedding. "Heaven can wait," she finally said, yet the weight pressing down on her chest remained unexplained. She dreamed too many times she was someplace she didn't want to be and kept trying to get someplace else but kept ending up in the same place. She needed to get a job, not for the money, but to get outside of herself and away from the dead end that life had presented her, as it does.

CHAPTER 19

The House on Tomwood

Miles had left for the University of Texas, 4 years behind his sisters, so Edith and Jim built a new house to give their marriage a shiny look for 1975. The Army had moved them so many times, moving was imprinted in their psyche and they moved themselves this time but didn't know why they were moving.

They built the house high on a hill overlooking southwest El Paso and stood abreast in the backyard looking down on the shallow Rio Grande—a faint silty line in the sand between Juarez and El Paso. They'd go to bullfights in Mexico and watch bulls and even horses get bludgeoned as the bull's horn went under the padding and through the stomach, pinning horse and rider to the wall. They'd stand up in horror at the occasional goring of a bullfighter, as the cheers turned into shrieks, and Edith liked it more than Jim did, watching her macabre fantasies play out in real life from the safe seats above the intimate, circular arena.

Jim met his new neighbor who owned a lucrative McDonalds on the outskirts of El Paso and they small talked about the suburb. Jim told him: "when the little Mrs and I first started driving around here we both really liked the area!" He was sincere. Edith sincerely started over with a new garden, a new painting studio, and new curtains. In a quick month they were all hung and at 1730 they still couldn't summon up those pretty good conversations they had in the 50s and 60s. Awkward kissers at the best of times, Jim would get home at 1730 and find Edith sitting by herself in the formal living room, crying on the divan, and he had no idea what to do.

Jim had a dream one morning. The dream felt like it was 1948, a few months after their wedding. He and Edith were driving around Washington DC doing nothing, just having Saturday fun and there was one little lonely cloud in the vast, blue, perfect sky. Jim was trying to think of a clean joke to tell when lucky Edith noticed a magnificent church in a valley, all white, with several out-buildings, also pure white. All the sudden they were strolling around the nameless place.

For some reason Jim had a black suit on—he didn't own one—and Edith a long, white, billowing dress that danced across the ground without ever touching it. He's never seen the dress either, or her shoulders bare. They were holding hands and marveling at the beautiful sculptures on the outside walls and the modern unchurch like architecture when they suddenly again found themselves in a wide hallway where priceless rare art littered the walls. It looked like J. Paul Getty's mansion and art collection, or a modern European castle. Jim wondered what kind of church it was and how they'd come up with the countless millions it must have taken to build it. Ghostly statues appeared to be walking toward them, floating halfway through the interior walls, as their footsteps echoed into infinity. They were in love, the honeymoon was in full swing, and artless Jim's dreamer was painting the mural for him that he had repressed since childhood.

Jim was now up and making his morning coffee, enthralled with his dream. It seemed 100% real, like it really happened, and in a way, it had—long ago. He felt warm, like he was still in the dream. Edith was asleep. He was perplexed thinking about the train tracks running right through the middle of the church yard, and the old-timey locomotive sitting motionless on the edge of the property, followed by several cartoonish, yellow and red train cars. The black locomotive had a way too tall black smokestack that made his heart skip a beat as it loomed against the all-white background. He wondered why the train was in the dream although he never thought dreams meant anything, or remember one until now. "Every part of your dream is part of yourself, they say, and I haven't taken the kids to church in years," he muttered. Jim made a good guess *he* was the black locomotive charging crudely through the middle of the church yard and the cartoonish cars were laughing at him.

Jim picked up the dream from there and recalled glancing up again at that little lone cloud in the sky. It looked like a child asleep in a womb but Edith hadn't mentioned anything about being pregnant. Neither knew that it was Rachel who had just taken form, inside Edith. He and Edith stood there staring at the train without speaking when something beamed them instantly into the main cathedral. A small group seemed to be practicing a play as there was no audience, just endless rows of empty white pews blending into forever. They listened to the singing and joking—it seemed to be a musical comedy they were putting together. The newlyweds laughed at the jokes and loved the music while the performers paid them no attention. The songs were unfamiliar but uncommonly lovely. (You know how dreams can be heavenly on occasion. Jim was composing songs in his sleep, as his suppressed dopamine was escaping.)

The lead actor was unmistakably the Missourian Harry Truman and there was a mixed set of actors getting direction from a messy-haired man. Edith politely whispered to Jim that the guy with all the Phyllis Diller hair was the director. Jim had a tiny piece of broken glass in his dry mouth that he was trying to spit out without getting noticed. (You know how occasional good dreams are, there's always a catch.)

The last 2 songs went by in just a couple seconds in Jim's dream. The stage people took a break and the straggly haired director smiled and walked over to them. "You guys are in love," he said and Jim smiled sideways and told him how good the music sounded. "Thank you," said the director and a new thought hit Jim. Uncharacteristically, he just blurted it out: "I can sing and my wife can play the piano real well, and occasionally we can turn a joke, do you guys need any help?" The director looked at Harry Truman, listening from a distance, and saw the twinkle in his eyes. The director looked back at the couple. "We could use some talent," he said, "it's going be quite a time investment." In a nanosecond Edith said, "that's okay, we have all the time in the world." "Great," said the director, "we meet here every Saturday at 2pm," we'll see you next Saturday! In unison, Edith and Jim both said, "break a leg, we'll be here." Jim had never felt this happy in his life except for the damn little piece of glass in his mouth.

Jim took another sip of coffee and realized Edith hadn't had a cigarette in the whole dream then was startled by a single tear hitting the black pool. "I haven't cried in 4 decades." he said, staring at the ripples. Edith was still sleeping so in the safety of the kitchen he started practicing telling her the dream. He couldn't finish a sentence without crying. He wanted to wake her up but he was late for work for the first time in his life. He collected himself and got into his 1969 Ford LTD and headed for work. He tried again to practice telling her the dream but got to the point he couldn't see the road in front of him. He reflexively turned on the windshield wipers like an idiot. He felt so stupid but made it to his parking place, put on his game face, and headed in.

His workday flew by like Christmas morning and his cohorts stole tacit glances at him, wondering who he was. He thanked everybody who laid a piece of paper in his inbox and almost told his favorite secretary, harmlessly, that he loved her. When he got home at 1730, he was re-summoning up the courage to tell her the dream when Edith ran up to him with some bad news. A crack had appeared floor to ceiling in the main hall of the new Tomwood house. Low and behold, the house had been built on some sinking ground and was splitting down the middle. Jim called his friend the builder and told him the custom house was coming in two. A few days later the brick exterior separated into a 1-inch crack—front and back of the house. The builder had to jack up one whole side of the house and pump in concrete to shore it up.

When they had built the Tomwood house, Jim said, "my next move will be to the cemetery," but fate saved him again and Jim got transferred to Atlanta. They sold the fixed house in El Paso and bought a 1-story brick ranch house in fashionable Dunwoody as it was earning the name: the *golden ghetto* of Atlanta. He got a much better plain clothes job as an engineer for MARTA—the rapid transit system forming a chromosomal X through the city. The long arm in the northwest was missing, having been voted down by Marietta. After a 27-year Army career, Jim was only 51 years old. He took the MARTA bus to work and back, from Dunwoody to downtown Atlanta, and for lunch he packed a banana, some nuts, and a thing of yogurt. He ate at his desk and hated to go out go to lunch with the "spenders." They dreaded it too because he would talk about work and teach them how to get ketchup out of a bottle Missoura style.

MARTA sent Jim to London for a mass transportation conference and while there he visited the WWII memorial wall for the American dead. As he read through the names, recognizing some of them, he got down to where his brother Craig's name should have been. Craig's name was not on the list. When he got back home, he gathered up the letters his parents had sent him, mailed them to the British government, and Craig's name was added to the wall. Jim once lit it slip that he had applied to engineering school all those years ago to get out of the draft, although he denied saying it for the rest of his life.

Back in Atlanta, Jim was bulldozing an eminent domain trail for the public rail system and grew a dislike for the lawyers who fought for their building owners. The MARTA lawyers themselves loved him for his ability to cut through red tape and knock down entire neighborhoods, strip malls, and oversee buying the French railway cars that still operate today. He bitterly complained about lawyers when he came home—he was distracting himself from seeing Edith who was a couple of vodka tonics ahead. He sang to himself, "Scotch and soda, jigger of gin, oh what a spell you've got me in."[1]

They say, "if you don't like the weather in Atlanta just wait a few minutes," but in November 1976 it rained for 4 weeks and they started hating the hub of the south. A tiny constant stream developed, running between their house and the neighbor's house, and that Saturday the guy next door tried to build a little dam to stop the water. Jim the civil engineer said to Edith, "that idiot next door thinks he can dam up water." "You can't do that?" Edith protested, "I thought people did that all the time." Jim frowned. Out of the blue that horrible feeling hit him that he was supposed to be somewhere else. The Germans call it "fernweh." He glanced at his watch as he often did and it was exactly 2pm on Saturday afternoon. He gathered himself, then chuckled. "Why are you laughing," Edith said. "Nothing," Jim said turning away. There went his last chance to tell her the dream, and he forgot it was their anniversary.

CHAPTER 20

The House at Marsh Glen Point

Never needing one of those male menopause mobiles, Jim had found that green Ford LTD at an AVIS rent-a-car closeout sale and after his promotion to Head Engineer of MARTA he still wouldn't replace the old clunker with duck-tape holding the driver's seat together. In 1982 Jim and Edith drove it from Dunwoody where the neighbor was still trying to dam up that little stream to the posh estates of Riverside where they had designed and built their grandest house. On a wooded lot, with diagonal brick facing up the front, it had a 4-car garage round back for 2 cars and their new ski boat. Their neighbors, 2 being Atlanta Braves baseball players, didn't have to look at his slimy Ford or the tape holding it together. Edith bought a fast, gold Buick and shopped from Little 5 Points to Sandy Springs because her life's work of instilling a wonderous sense of life into her kids, with varying degrees of success, was over. Her dad Jesse's peculiar existence was finally over too and after his stroke, 50 years after that major concussion from his car accident, Edith drove him, with a bored look on her face, to an old folks home far from Atlanta where he died shortly thereafter at age 69. "That halfwit asshole never got lonely," she grumbled on the way back to Atlanta, "ain't that a kick in the head."[1] Laurinda, Jim's mom, who lived 34 years longer than her husband Walter, visited the house at Marsh Glen Point a few times in her 90s.

Laurinda's mother had drowned herself in a pond when Laurinda was a teenager. Snarky Miles was visiting and true to his schadenfreude he joked: "they tied rocks to her, threw her in the lake, and when she didn't float like a witch is supposed to......that's when they realized they'd made a mistake." He and Edith had a good laugh but Jim and Laurinda thank God never heard the joke.

Like so many millions who never went to WWII Laurinda was numb because she would have died to save her son Craig. Her spirit died on June 12th, 1944, when his P-47 went down and her heart kept beating for 54 more years.

Laurinda the avid knitter was sharp as a tack in her 90s and when anybody made a sandwich for lunch, Laurinda would not take her eyes off the process. She would stare at each knife spread of mayonnaise, watch where they put the jars back, and watch them eat it without saying a word. Laurinda wasn't a meddler though, so she and Edith got along without really connecting. With Jim at work, they had the house to themselves, and Edith had the awkward feeling Laurinda didn't understand her only living son's choice of a wife. Those were the gamma rays but Laurinda simply never talked about people, including herself. You worked all the time and were quietly admired, or you didn't and were stared at. Edith, who enjoyed the company of women, had never met one like Laurinda and wasn't particularly enamored her.

There was no evidence Laurinda had ever had a selfish thought in her life and Edith suddenly saw Laurinda for what her life had been. It hit Edith like a bag of doorknobs. She whispered, "this is the female role model Jim grew up with, maybe we got our wires crossed." Other than the occasional wry smile that you had to stare at to make sure because the smile was mostly in her eyes, Laurinda never showed emotion. After the last visit, Jim and Edith drover her back to her old folk's home in Florida where she died at 101.

The Wabash Cannonball

Edith put a mirror on her easel, stared at herself, then put a blank canvas over the mirror. She painted an oval on it with a horizontal line going through it and noticed that her hands were shaking, just a little. It wasn't a shake like her last attempt at a self-portrait, before her dream in Turkey, that was a different shake; this one was a new tremor that no one else could have noticed. She didn't really care, something else was bothering her, and she removed the canvas for another look in the mirror. "I could paint myself fuzzy or even with an ear missing," she said, "and tell people I've gotten into impressionism, but nobody will see the painting for what it is anyway. What was bothering her was a coming-and-going feeling of dread. "My blind family will only see a self-portrait painted by a narcissist," she added.

The weight of her thoughts pushed her anger down into her under chamber and left here with oscillating between boredom and dread. She laid the brush down, shooting her free will in the foot. She was losing that power that all true artists have, lose, and must get back again; the great power of not caring what anyone thought, and Edith settled back into the afternoon cocktail routine while the chaotic orchestra of the kids echoed in the halls of her memory.

"Was Jim born without depression and addiction or did his free will defeat them?" she wondered, "is it his impenetrable fire-wall?" Edith knew she had never finished building her firewall between her conscious and subconscious because she had accepted her subconscious mind but it didn't seem to fit into this world. She stabbed an olive with a toothpick, dropped it into her martini, and took a sip, thinking, "is being a free spirit a curse?" She could poison Jim, she thought, and laughed. She wanted to leave him but the alcohol took the edge off of her courage. Jim was the only person she had in the world now; without him she would be all alone, and broke. She was wrong.

Depression starts with suppressed anger and Edith thought hers was that Jim was a bad communicator. Surprisingly, Jim was always a person who didn't mind being told what to do. He did what his dad told him to do on the farm for 20 years, did what the Army told him to do for 30 years, and was in the top 1% for following instructions to the letter. Men hate the long political process but he had the genetic patience for these things. If Edith had figured this out, she would have taught him how to communicate *her* way and he would have learned it, but she only taught by example. She repeatedly repressed her anger—mistake #1—and, as it will, life turned blasé with the Wabash Cannonball screaming toward her without a sound.

Edith had been at the tip of the evolutionary sword for so long and started feeling as if she was on display and people were laughing at her. "Send in the clowns," she sang, and like a ton of bricks a thought hit her—she had not married her soulmate. Jim could not fill her silent world, in fact, he had no idea people had those but maybe it wasn't his job anyway. *Edith finally realized she had made the great sacrifice so many women make; she had married for the longevity of her children, not for her own happiness.*

"Evolution won," she thought. "Evolution used me," she said softly, "and I have no soulmate." She started looking for her spare pack of Kent menthol 100s. She thought of the John Lennon song, *I'm so Tired*, and sang, "and I curse Sir Walter Raleigh, he was such a stupid get." The Kents and the drinks were her only soulmate now. "Those damn cigarettes" she said to no one there, and her mind went back to her high school boyfriend Miles. Neither had dared contact each other. "*He* was my soulmate," she said, "I thought there would be more of those…

Gestalt Therapy

As Edith's grandchildren started elementary school, she decided to start therapy—Gestalt Therapy. Germany's Fritz Pearls pioneered this innovative method in the 70s (the therapy decade) which uncovers the reluctantly discarded pieces of yourself strewn about your unconscious mind during childhood. These are the unknowns we leave behind in dreamland and they represent all the unfinished traumas we blindly repeat in adulthood.

Pearls was probably the best dream interpreter of them all. He made patients retell their dreams in the present tense—relive them in the here and now—and when they tried to transfer and project a dream, he would roll his eyes at the hogwash and put them back on that old forgotten road behind the firewall. As Buddha taught, Frederick Pearls wouldn't ask what got broken, he would ask "how do you feel broken?" Edith started down this scary road and though it appeared travelable there were layers of her childhood to pull back, a pensive undertow to decipher, and a Wabash Cannonball to derail.

"Things get damaged, things get broken." [2] Thousands of comments, like straws on a camel's back, had gone unchallenged by Edith. 1001 tiny cuts—like a bull in a ring—had exhausted her. Although those around her did it casually with dismissiveness Edith felt fleeced, she never got a pick-me-up bouquet, and was still waiting for her congratulations dinner that never came. She needed very little but the *dreams of the everyday housewife*[3] weren't on the 20th century menu.

It happened so fast. Edith Virginia's kids were having more babies as she chain-smoked her way through Gestalt Therapy. She had a very good counselor, Ann, who smoked right along with her. First, she tried to get Ann to fix Jim who wasn't even there—an old trick psychotherapy patients always try—but Ann told her "you want me to fight him while you watch." Going to therapy and talking about other people is like going to the emergency room and telling the doctor about your cousin's injury. After a year Edith went from individual counseling to group therapy, a major step up. Ann got her to talk about her father and Edith realized he was a man who couldn't love, which damaged her chromosomes, and she got angry, then cried, and felt lighter.

She jumped up a tier and started painting again. Forever a stay-at-home mom, she started teaching oil-painting classes—her first money job at age 55. She was starting to feel immortal enough for a 4rth attempt at a self-portrait, when Edith's family had a reunion at Mary and Lloyd's dairy farm in -40° New Glarus. On most visits Lloyd would say, in his Fargo accent, "there's sno on the bern and the coze are sleeping" but this time the cows were miserable. It was Wisconsin's wolverine August and God had dialed the heat up.

Everything started out well, with Miles and Rachel's husband John making a real-looking cow out of a sheet of plywood to see if farmer Lloyd would spot it way out in the field. They jig sawed out what looked like one of Lloyd's standard cows, having measured one from asshole to elbow, then painted it white with black markings and stood it out in the pasture with dozens of its comrades. They waited an hour for Lloyd to walk by and glance into the pasture. When he did, he froze in his steps. The only reason he recognized the fake cow was because he didn't have a cow with those markings. Everybody had a good laugh and he eventually nailed it high over the entrance to his barn.

That night the smoking police were in rare form as Edith and Miles puffed away inside the farmhouse. The "one part per million" crowd was faking pulmonary embolisms and quarantined the 2 smokers to the outside. They went out and lit another one up by moonlight when Edith, already upset from the argument, noticed she was having trouble breathing. She felt something pushing on the left side of her windpipe and when she got home, she went directly to the hospital. It happened so fast. It wasn't long before her 4 kids were taking turns driving her to chemotherapy and radiation and hoping against hope that it would work. She had just turned 57 that August. Her colorful middle was gone; everything was black and white now.

When her suppressed anger caused boredom, which descended into depression, the weakest link in her immune system snapped? We'll never know for sure. One cell gave up the ghost at the same age her non-smoking mother was when she got cancer so it could have been a gene with a clock, or a good gene that both of their depressions deactivated. Edith might have had weak TP53 genes too—genes that keep our cells from dividing too fast—while Jim's were strong. Barely knowing what cancer was, she smelled Jim's protective genes for her future kids.

Edith was diagnosed with adenocarcinoma, a very aggressive lung cancer, in October 1984. This most common lung cancer is the deadliest and afflicts smokers and nonsmokers 50/50. Intertwined with her windpipe and heart, the tumor was inoperable. I believe cancer was the symptom, and depression, the #1 killer, was the cause. The whole family was dumb with shock, and Edith needed some of that magic she had discarded when she was 6 years old. The kids were magicless too and just stood there trying to grasp their own mother's gloomy future, "like desperados waiting for a train."[4]

While still young, Edith stared death in the face, having never gotten much credit for her unfinished life—but her life wasn't over. Miles was only 30, and an atheist, and didn't know then that her essence would long outlive her. That's not bad when you think about it: the parts of your parents you inherited cannot be uninherited; our genes will survive inside our lineage for eternity.

In that last month with her 4 kids beside her—last call for alcohol—she smoked pot for the first time and laughed like a school girl. She wasn't in any pain and told her kids "I'm going to beat this thing." Things went downhill fast. On oxygen for the final week, the minutes became more valuable than the hours. Through her oxygen mask she said, "I know there's a place in heaven for me," not knowing Miles was standing there. Edith saw herself watching over her flock from heaven—there are no apatheists in ICU.

Edith's friend Dot was sitting beside her at 4am Friday, and still talking to herself, the body of the girl who lives forever, peacefully slipped away. The bass guitar player of the band, the glue that stitched the family together, was gone. The 2nd part of her life had just begun.

Edith's family scattered her ashes at Lake Lanier. It was a windy day on her vacant lot, near where she had water skied so often, even that summer. It would have been her last house and her favorite home, and where her self-portrait would have hung. Now Edith has great grandchildren running everywhere and sometimes the little girls show shades of crazy grandma, though that variety is not encouraged. Most if not all her *still living genes* push on inside her lineage and will glow for millenniums, if not forever—we can hope—it may be our only hope. "You can check out anytime you like but you can never leave."[5]

"This is all the heaven we got, right here right now, in our……Shangri-la," as Mark Knopfler sings, reminding us to enjoy our half full cup, and adds, "your beauty burns into……my memory……the wheel of heaven turns……above us endlessly." Maybe the Buddhists are right—we are nothing but an infinitesimal part of everything. Her last breath was January 25th, 1985, which took the life out of the family for she was the only glue it ever had, and she left knowing that she married Jim for his genes to save her kids from the known and the unknown. She lived her sacrifice accepting who she was, who each of her kids were, and accepting strangers—an accomplishment few can claim.

I asked [Edith Virginia] how lonely does it get,
[Edith] hasn't answered me yet,
But I can still hear [her] coughing, all night long,
Oh, a hundred floors above me, in the Tower of Song

—Leonard Cohen

I had but one bout with vanity later in life when I had a couple of moles removed, which I now regret. The plastic surgeon was finishing up a quick surgery when I asked him if he'd noticed how many Scottish people have a mole under their left eyebrow. He didn't say anything, he was like that, but the Scottish American nurse leaned right in and showed me her mole under her left eyebrow—right where mine was. Mary had both her moles removed too and they were in the same places mine were. Your author, Keith Fraser, is the same person as Edith's son Miles in this book, as you may have guessed. Fraser is our family name,

Edith's maiden name was Sipe, and her mother's maiden name was Highfill.

When I wrote that I went into the attic of that old house in Missouri and stumbled upon a trunk full of letters, it was an elaborate lie. I'm sorry. Edith didn't even write letters. I left in the small clues while removing the big ones—hopefully maintaining a floating anonymity throughout the book—which makes me a chicken-shit but it freed me up to write. Being born last, I heard about the years I missed, and remembered things people said since I was 3. After writing through everything, I no longer considered myself low in the family pecking order. I still cringe when I think back to those times I made fun of my mother. Although I brought Edith past Jim to her rightful place in the pecking order, "I just wish I could have told her in the living years."[6] I also thought Edith was the funniest and after writing the book I must give that trophy to Jim, though he might not have been trying to be funny.

I made up names for my sisters too. Many thanks go to Rachel and Mary for helping me with this book. Rachel edited the entire book and Mary and her husband Lloyd caught a few historical errors in the story. Electra is still Electra and still despises me for getting the Y chromosome. She never did get that bee out of her bonnet. That was her lament from before I was born and though would still eat glass to be a male, she expertly gaslights it to all as something altogether different.

Decades ago, she would call me and ask, "how's your brown wife?" *After* finally confessing to me that she was a "verbal terrorist" she spread heinous lies about me—heavy Stockholm Syndrome is a mindbender—and she has had her subordinate Rachel trapped under her wing since 1954. They watched me grow up through my toddler years and to their shock, I was hardly abused. They couldn't take their anger out on Jim, their abuser, because they worshipped him like a god so they transferred it down to the next male. A book written by a woman that included some details of her evil older brother would be readily palatable, and Rachel too was a victim having gotten a double dose of Stockholm Syndrome.

Jim's philosophy was damn near mandatory, Edith's was optional, and…merely a suggestion. I discovered and corrected or deleted much of my own revisionist history while writing; the main discovery was Edith was my hero and role model in life, not Jim. I was torn. I never realized I had subconsciously adopted her free spirit, her humor, and her sense of life……until my 60s.

Maybe the purpose in life is to propagate our genes and leave behind a better world, by making smarter, more responsible, healthier kids. That's not so bad considering the mystical explanations are dubious—I won't be flying around in the clouds with my grandparents. I replaced that void with the knowledge that those 4 souls, and everything they went through, would live forever. The pensive sadness that followed Edith and follows the rest of us around is simply knowing that one day we will have to say goodbye. Maybe dying isn't as lonely when our genes are still running around.

Life, space and time, the only known perpetual motion machines, keep expanding. We do constantly eat and breathe, obeying the law of conservation of energy, and perpetually become better people by infinitely expanding coincidental happiness. It never crossed mother evolution's mind that one of her animals would find her, come to know her, and replace her. From 2, chosen, encoded molecules, joining into a singularity, we grew into a math-defying universe of souls. Restrained only by self-doubt we briefly steal our way toward evolutionary perfection and when the body our genes built is spent, we can know we've left the best genes behind. What looks like chaos is northern growth and the chaos of Edith and Jim is now the hope of 24 souls. Matter cannot be created or destroyed but over endless time it can be reassembled into a magical consciousness that wants everything from life, infinitely fears its own death, and knows to do no harm. That's the illimitable passion of evolution. We are made of something unfound and one day we will find it. It is just beyond the mind's eye. Keep your cup half full.

The End of the Story

CHAPTER 21

"I Don't Always Use the Internet"

That is an apocryphal quote from the Dos Equis man, the most interesting man in the world.
In the final chapters I will combine evolution, science, economics, psychology, art, and philosophy.

Subatomic particles exchange information and atoms upbuild into complex molecules that go on to work like machines. Whether these microscopic particles are conscious or not is a debate in the physics world because, in a way, they "talk" to each other. Each atom has its own energy signature[1] and in turn each electron, whether in wave or solid state, is a different piece of information in this universal internet of exchange. Electrons are traded around like baseball cards so each must have infinitesimal differences in mass-spin-speed and momentum. The sun's photons knock electrons from atoms, they're single for a while, and other atoms marry them. The nearly endless but static supply of electrons is nature's money. Some are sloughed off; some are snatched up—one girl's ugly is another girl's lovely—and the players are hoping to build *better* molecules. We can't witness the nano activity yet but know that atoms of the same element decay (half-life) at different rates, many of them live for quadrillions of years, and we know that their rogue electrons go on strange, physics defying trajectories. Many books touch on the phenomenon of a primordial, self-motivated quality at the subatomic level, and if true, this nano brain, the crudest consciousness, simply needs proteins, water, and heat.

It wasn't long after earth cooled down, for carbon (the top-of-the-chart electron hunter) to form long chains. Carbon eagerly attached to so many other elements and created complex molecules who wanted eternal life, so they encoded blueprints for their own reconstruction (DNA). Eventually, ambitious RNA molecules who are shockingly good at their jobs, and patient, created enclosures (cell walls) to protect the information inside. The cells formed orchestras who composed their way up to the promised land: the human double helix. Where, during all that building, did life begin?? "Stay thirsty my friends."

They say humans are mostly made of water but since electrons are so far away from their nucleuses—like planets from suns—we are mostly empty space. We don't know much about what's in that empty space. It is probably dark energy. We are 99.99% dark energy and we don't know what it is.

The 1st *human* internet started 3 billion years after the first bacteria cell had built itself. One beautiful Sunday morning 1 million years ago two young guys from distant clans happened to be hunting in the same jungle. From opposite directions they came around a wall of dense foliage and froze like 2 alien statues, staring each other down. The rest of the world disappeared. Standing 20 feet apart and wrapped in muscle as if they had a steady supply of steroids, both hearts skipped a beat together. "A man.........alone?" each thought, "where are the others?"

There were no others. As adrenaline filled their bodies, they watched each other carefully through the eyes of wisdom, knowing one would probably die before brunch. The short one looked like a badass and the tall one didn't really......"but what if he is?" thought Shorty. They were both thinking the same thing at the exact same time and also knew that pride came before a fall, so they could always run. The taller one had a long, sharp, glistening spear and he noticed that the other guy, whose back was luckily to the sun, had a club with spikes on it...and something strange around his feet. Simultaneously they both saw what neither had ever seen before—a spear and a pair of shoes. Well, the shoes weren't quite what we think of them today. The short guy wasn't exactly "gonna be dancin' around in the moonlight with a cane and a top hat."[2] Still, everything seemed roughly even......except for the strange new items.

The brave men advanced slowly for closer inspection, making sure to make no threatening gestures. This is when an incredible event unfolded and I'd pay 10-grand to be able to watch it instead of imagining it. Certainly, they had each figured out what the new contraptions were for and wondered why they'd never thought of them. Standing a few feet apart now the short guy slowly pulled off his shoes......held them at eye level and offered them......for the spear. The tall guy was drooling so for those shoes that he reached for them, and ever so slowly, boldly, traded in the spear for the pair of shoes, with their eyes still affixed to each other.

As the barefoot shorter guy spent a precious second inspecting his new spear the now defenseless taller man came to his senses—after his impulse purchase—and motioned for the club too. Sometimes a bit of insurance goes a long way. Their eyes met again and the shorter guy gave up the club. Notice that the insurance wasn't a future promise, to be borrowed or created later, it was a real, here and now possession. He had bartered for the first financial instrument and the trade was complete, keeping the playing field level with profit on both sides. They could still fight or flee but both had a 3rd feeling: it was a new level of morality they could see in each other's eyes. The guys didn't quite create individual rights but were the first to risk the game of fair-play resulting in the discovery of mutual profit between strangers. Born, a million years ago, was trust in a stranger.

The first human internet had travelled at the speed of sight from 1 mind to another. After tossing aside racism and violence they gave birth to quadruplets: coincident interest, tempered risk, the free division of labor, and capitalism. It didn't matter which item took longer to make because both men benefitted enormously along with everybody in the 2 tribes soon afterward. Imagine the industrial activity that followed: collecting obsidian for the spear tip, hardwood soaked in pondwater for the shaft, and gathering strong grass, leather, and vine for tightening the shoes made from ungulates. More people were doing intelligent work.

This first trade launched the world-wide internet and the continent of Africa changed at the speed of light from one pair of eyes, to the next, to the next. Suddenly people had less interest in killing each other or sacrificing a virgin to the sun God; they instead created wealth by using thoughts that no 2 people had had before, and built on them. The 2 men didn't realize until much later, when they saw more smiles, that they had created culture and civilization by putting trade on line for all.

After foraging gave way to farming, and farming led to cities, what made some places wealthier? I think we learned in the above section what creates wealth though some evolutionists emphasize geography, weather, and disease. Water *did* protect Britain and the US with great moats and the cold water does protect Britain from hurricanes. And Britain *did* have the right trees and hemp for building large ships but why didn't the vast majority of the other large islands prosper? And why didn't most landlocked countries prosper while Switzerland, the bass guitar player of Europe, did?

I might have convinced you chapters ago that it was brain genes, evolving differently, that created many stripes of wealth. Even with the old foragers, it was a smattering of savvy individuals chipping away at tribal monopolies who set us all on this slow path to wealth for non-elites. The monopoly gene is still formidable and always requires exterminators because it is the dark-green mold of humankind.

Hunter-gatherers tried to get everyone to give according to their ability and consume according to their need—it was the first semblance of communism. But as we learned from Chapter 2, like communism, the society was far from egalitarian because the elites took the lion's share and if anyone's consumption surpassed their ability to help, or they couldn't keep up, the tribe couldn't afford them. Weak genes died. Smart, bold genes died too, fighting for and against monopolies, but nature has a way of rooting for the good guys. Evolution kills off 49% of the smart genes and 51% of the greedy genes, every generation, until the monopolies decay. That is when individualism can triumph, unless the pyramid goes to great pains to maintain the monopolies. After a million years we're not free of them.

As the first human internet spread, an infinity of new thoughts germinated in the minds of the smarter individuals who wanted more options for food, weapons, clothing, and sex. I think murder was common in hunter-gatherer society, often the only choice, and justifiable in an evolutionary sense. If the alpha male will kill a man who messes with his harem, he is stopping the genes of that man forever. Each man is helplessly programmed to pass on his own genes, so when the alpha male killed a rival or a child who looked like a rival, he was essentially killing that man's entire future lineage. Young males unconsciously considered this genocide because of the DNA propagating software ruling from their brains, or maybe from 2.5 feet below that.

Sometimes, a sneaky boulder to the alpha male's head was a justifiable move, and a dangerous but irresistible one, because getting your genes to the next generation is more important than life itself. Evolution made sure some men would take this all or nothing gamble. "It's still the same old story, a fight for love and glory, a case of do or die, the fundamental rules apply, *As Time Goes By*."[3]

Back then nobody said, "I'm a lover not a fighter," because you had to be both, and to this day the ephemeral sex act—the animal part—lasts a few minutes because that's about how long it would take for another man to go find a boulder and plant it on the back of a rival's head. 2 men probably teamed up with the moral boulder for mutual sex benefits. As the alpha male lay bleeding, the women instinctively knew they were not in danger because they knew what the men wanted. They watched and wondered if the new guys were going to be better or worse.

Competition for sex inevitably led to a more equal distribution of sex, which is progress, and the guys who killed the alpha male knew it could happen to them too, so they shared the women more. Ironically, pre-meditated murder led to more cooperation (our contradictions, like war and trade) and a larger percentage of the tribe was happier or at least somewhat satisfied. Intelligent work grew, wealth grew, and few longed for the steep pyramid of the old tribal communism. As the pyramid flattened, people exchanged more reciprocal favors[4] (you help me, I'll help you) and hoarding decreased—not only to stave off the next boulder but because the social and economic benefits to the tribe were noticeable. "We've been trying to tell you guys about that for a while," offered the women, "and have you noticed kids live longer with 2 parents?" Individual families slowly evolved because.........we went to a fight and a hockey game broke out.

CHAPTER 22

The Lying Gene

I will start with human lying although we will soon learn that animal lying started at least ½ billion years ago—even a single gene can molecularly deceive another for gain.[1] Animals lie all the time which means on some level they know they are conscious and know the deceived animal is conscious too. These were the first hints of free will in living things. With the exception of lying for gain (manipulating others for unfair advantage) our lying was blameless, cunning, necessary, and the beginning of our rich, illusory thinking. Several authors have observed that lying came in a bundle including story tellers, jokesters, myth spreaders, saboteurs, etc., and we adored these yarns because they made us think, "what would I do if that happened to me or one of my kids?" Initially these strange, creative people were slow to evolve because tribes would often kill the village idiot (free spirits are too risky) and sometimes eat them. Example: these 2 cannibals were eating this clown and 1 said, "does this taste funny to you?"

Everybody lies but because of the taboo that lying has been branded with, lying has gone subconscious so the typical liar doesn't know when a snow-white lie leaves their lips. This keeps us more comfortable with ourselves and everybody else, and the most successful people, as we view success in the pyramid today, are often the best liars. On the more palatable side, our deflector shield—lying for protection—gained such utility it became a moral necessity. Long ago we learned how to thwart Stockholm Syndrome by disrupting the designs of would-be predators or brutal investigators. We skillfully constructed diversions and dead ends for them. Fiction gained such a vital role in our lives that our lying imaginations have gone to genetic fixation and permanently armed us with a *3rd option*: we can fight, flee, or *lie*.

We have evolved the lie into a sophisticated, intricate mechanism, which includes the half-innocent practices of misrepresenting the truth through exaggeration and omitting facts. It has been said for a lie to be a lie one must *know* they are lying but I'm skeptical because it is a volitional act for an adult to bury information so deep that they sabotage the retrieval of it, or, repeat only the gossip that makes them personally feel better. This fosters an apophenic life, which, along with lying for gain, is the downside of fictional thinking.

The best way to get away with a good lie (to distract an overzealous investigator) is to first comfort your stress by telling yourself that the lie is justified. Squint, lower your voice, don't blink and look directly at who you're talking to. Add superfluous details at the end of the lie as I did when I told you I found a trunk of letters in that attic in Missouri.

The eyes tell lies, especially with humans because the sclera (white around the eyes) is pronounced more in humans, showing off the shifty eyeball too much.[2] We evolved wanting to be trusted, no matter what we said but our fast-evolving eyes came with a drawback: they showed visible signs of nervous energy. In the center of the retina is a little black dot—an aperture, a hole that allows light in—called the "pupil," which changes size with the stress of lying and it was Charles Darwin who first suspected this.[3] We might unconsciously know this, so we look away to avert the detection of our falsehoods, though it's very difficult for another to detect these miniscule changes.

Our normal pupil is 3-4 mm in diameter and when we lie it gets

.1 mm to 1 mm bigger in a fraction of a second but can grow as big as 8-9 mm with the heavy stress and work of lying. Because a doubling of the diameter makes the little pupil 4 times bigger in area (Bernoulli's equation) some people can see this. By measuring *slight* changes in pupil size, scientists can now detect lies with more accuracy than with Dr David Raskin's old analog lie detection machine. Even the old analog test was accurate and Dr John Kircher proved this to me in the 90s. He's my brother-in-law and the only guy I know who doesn't laugh when somebody falls down. He hooked me up to the machine after I secretly wrote down a number from 1 to 10 and stuck the piece of paper in my pocket. After I'd said "no" to each number, a minute later he told me that I'd picked the number 4.

After a century of research by many a scientist the team that came up with the pupil measuring machine (Eye Detect) was Dr Kircher's team and they thought of it while sitting on top of a mountain. You can read about it in chapters 3 and 6 of his book *Credibility Assessment* and in his University of Utah paper, the Ocular-motor Deception Test. "Each person is different" rears its head as usual during these tests—brown eyes make lie detection more difficult for instance—and they can't discern between lying to derail overzealous investigators and lying for personal, unfair gain. However, lies in general are now detectable and Eye Detect will soon be available on cellphones. You'll be free to film someone's eyes while they are talking and determine with 75-90% accuracy if they are lying, at least until everybody catches on. But if we woke up tomorrow into a world without lies, we would feel more and more uncomfortable as the strange day stretched on. On second thought, we seem to be entering a strange period where the truth doesn't matter anymore.

The First White People

Humans lived outdoors and we could all take a page from that book. 2 mya, back in our watering hole—Lake Malawi Africa—

we started losing our hair and our pink skin had to darken to deflect an overdose of the sun's UV rays and vitamin D. Humans turned dark so slowly that no generation noticed and some lineages that darkened too slowly died young. Nobody knew why. Africans, as all of us ultimately are, have had many hues of skin from black to brown to hazel to copper to beige—as they got further from the equator—but unlike animals who change skin color to lie, human color changes were for health and longevity.

The diseases that are encouraged by vitamin D deficiencies are as long as your arm; when you get to tennis elbow, you're only half way there. Hospital workers know that critical patients don't live as long with too little or too much vitamin D. Since Vitamin D is a master of all that ails us, including depression, mutations that lighten or darken skin spread faster than most genetic changes. The first *Europeans* were the first people to evolve slightly lighter skin because it was so cloudy that nature mutated toward lighter skin to absorb more sunrays. Those in snowy Asia employed different skin color genes to lighten up and absorb more vitamin D. [4] I have it on the best authority vitamin D in a bottle is a good as what we get from the sun but it can't be true—no 2 things are the same.

Gene studies by Lain Mathieson and David Reich found evidence that Europeans began turning white only 8000 years ago—only the last 400 generations of parents. Maybe that's why Southern Baptists estimate that the human race is 6000 years old, because that's when we started turning white! Baptists won't have sex while standing either—they're afraid people will think they're dancing. The Europeans acquired tall genes, blue-eyed genes, lactose tolerant genes, and lack of pigmentation genes from the constant migrations of various groups who happened to carry some fortuitous genes for that environment. Archeologists found the remains of the first blonde, that we know of anyway, and she was a Siberian girl who lived 18,000 years ago. Her clan may not have walked east to Alaska, as the North American Mandan tribe is the only blondish tribe we've found, and it is speculated those genes came from the Vikings. Females evolved slightly lighter skin than males to steal more vitamin C, as if evolution knew their daughters would need it to live through many pregnancies.

It is likely the Kings from biblical times were not close to being white. Many icons throughout history (Atatürk, Constantine, Genghis Khan) were selected in part because of those rare, blonde highlights.

One of my favorite historical figures is Jesus of Nazareth because he was so genetically different. I think Jesus was born with a man's body and a woman's brain—a Chimera Child—which afforded to him a new charisma that drew people to him. He was an odd altruistic man, who lived his own life for sure, while he could very well have buddied up to the Pharisees and their monopolies. He held steadfast with his uncommon empathy and singular awareness of the human condition. I was struck by Carl Jung's take on these paucities: "…in this unlikely soil there flower rare blossoms of the psyche which we would never have thought to find in the flatlands of society." Jung warned of the fine line between genius and insanity. [5] I believe that Jesus and Mohammed were guys like me, who walked the earth like me, and unlike me, had charisma.

Jesus had a newfangled set of genes no doubt and must have been attractive to women, being unlike any man they had encountered. He saved strangers from hypocrites, including Mary Magdalen, who loved him but didn't know how to love him.[6] I can imagine Mary singing: "there was a boy…………a very strange enchanted boy……and while we spoke of many things, fools and Kings, this he said to me……………the greatest thing you'll ever learn is just to love and be loved in return."[7] That's probably what they were both trying to learn, along with the rest of us, so he didn't know how to love her either and somehow knew he wouldn't live to grow old with her.

Semites started getting lighter skin about 3000 years before Christ so Jesus very well may have had lighter hair and lighter eyes. Still, I'd give those blue-eyed, blonde hair paintings of him in West Georgia a C- because Semites today are rarely blonde. Blonde alleles spawned many a Messiah throughout history who tried to pull the rug out from under the pyramid's monopoly, and like Jesus, they all fell short.

Long before Christ there were many isolated stories of Adam and Eve, a virgin birth, and a Messiah. Many shamans told their best guess story of how we got here and they told those stories at about the same time in our evolution. None of them stumbled upon the rights and sovereignty of the individual which is the only mass defense against naked power and groupthink because it includes everybody.

How Animals Lie

"I told my dentist my teeth were getting yellow, he told me to get a brown necktie." —*Rodney Dangerfield*

Before the industrial revolution, the buildings in Europe were plaster white, and most of the moths happened to be white. Hungry birds had trouble seeing these snacks until the industrial revolution turned the plaster buildings black with coal soot and the birds pigged out on the white moths contrasted against the new black buildings. The occasional black moth, in its relative safety, did what its genes told it to do and in a very short time almost all of the moths were black. Evolution doesn't play favorites and will lie for any animal who hasn't learned how.

The seahorse is a great liar. Seahorses *become* the color of their surroundings over many lifetimes and eventually look like the weeds they live in or the coral they hide in. Nature provides each new generation with fresh skin mutations—random changes of appearance—and some little seahorses are lucky with these while some have parents who can't kiss up to the camouflage. Those couples who can't marry out of their league can marry sideways and hope for greener pastures. The luckier children are coral-colored and some of them happen to have orange spots.

Everybody's favorite liar, the octopus, evolved about 500 mya along with squid, cuttlefish, and other cephalopods. A cousin, the thaumoctopus (T. mimic octopus) was only discovered in 1998 for reasons that will become apparent. This animal from 300 mya took prevarication to a new level. Not only can this shapeshifter instantly look like rocks, seaweed, or coral but can take the shape of poisonous (aposematic) animals and deadly plants. If a certain fish fears a plant or animal the T. mimic can identify that fear and assume the shape, ostensibly making its rare talent not random but willful. That's a sentient lying technique performed in an instant while humans spend hours in the make-up room making themselves look like somebody else. The most common defenses for the T. mimic are to instantly become a sea snake, a lion fish, a crab, or a jelly fish. It could be a beautiful genetic accident—an instinct that lengthens the life of their young—but their talents are so sophisticated that I can't convince myself they are not sentient. The tool making Octopi are very smart compared to fish but they have no verbal communication that we know of so they lie with a mind-body interconnectivity. Now that we're studying their muscle flexibility and the light receptors covering their bodies, we may come to understand the magic within. Sadly, octopi only live for a couple of years because after they reproduce, they suffer from *senescence* (fast aging) and cellular function breaks down.

Octopi have 6 arms and 2 legs—1 leg of the male is a prehensile penis—and they have copper based blue blood. With too many hearts, the wrong color of blood, 9 brains and no bones, and too well-endowed, the mimic octopus is an alien. In an infinite universe an infinite number of things will happen and in our infinite dreams we get to see some these creatures too.

Great white sharks are grey on top and white on the bottom and the octopi know this, so, it shouldn't be surprising if one day a scuba diver startles a mimic octopus and it suddenly turns into a great white shark. If you could see it from every angle it wouldn't look like a great white but from your angle it would—the octopus knows what you see. Imagine wolves are attacking *you* in the forest and you could instantly convert into a grizzly bear.

Since there is no group name for octopi because they are solitary, let's call it a *secrecy* of octopi. How does a secrecy of octopi play hide and seek? That's the whole joke.

We might be green now, if not for inventing weapons early on. If we had to hide in the shrubs and bushes to escape other predators, like the reptiles and amphibians *lying* in the tropical flora, our skin would be green too. We would consider our green skin beautiful and seek to mate with people who adapted faster to this camouflage. Grey is another powerful color in nature but we only get grey hair from weak stem cells or a deep loss. Most of us turn grey later in life anyway but our skin might well have turned grey too if we were left in the wild. The most successful mammals of their species are grey: wolves, squirrels, elephants, silverback gorillas, whales, and old people.

CHAPTER 23

Empathy Capitalism

Evolution made us competitive if nothing else (the understatement of this book) and we are adding empathy but trying to eliminate the struggle of competition, as academic elites suggest, would eventually stop the main gear. Elon Musk said if his electric car company Tesla fails, he will win anyway because he forced other electric car makers, through stiff competition, to think harder and *everybody* will win from that. He was resonating this philosophy: empathy capitalism + creative destruction = general wealth. He also received hundreds of billions of dollars in loans from Uncle Sam which caused us a bit of inflation.

Elon talked about how violent his greatest generation father was ("a terrible human being") and Elon and his siblings didn't follow in those footsteps. The brainiest step in moving a lineage north is to get violence out of the home and replace it with healthy competition.

I finally found a dentist who understood empathy capitalism, and I call him "Reza," because that's the ancient name his Iranian parents gave him. He went to dentition school in France, set up a practice here in West Georgia, and patiently explained what was going on in my mouth—in detail. Several other dentists have been interested in one of my teeth because it represented $4000 but Reza seemed interested in my teeth, plural. I've been to my share of dentists and they all told me *once* to wear a mouthguard at night because our dream machine is always grinding out those nightmares. We're angry. Reza listened to all my excuses regarding the mouthguard but wouldn't take no for an answer, as if he knew he was talking to an idiot genius who didn't pay attention in school. I started wearing the mouthguard.

He would make more money by letting us keep grinding away but I realized his spiritual goal was to improve the lives of his patients. People see this subconsciously and keep coming back to him without realizing that much of what empathy capitalism gives us is free of charge. When we individually try to make everybody around us a little better off there is almost no way to stop the colorful rewards coming back.

Empathy capitalism evolved from sacrificial selfishness. It's our economic yin yang, our elevated valley, and the lower animals gave it to us in spades—that's why we feel so bad when they die. Empathy capitalism is realizing that the product or service you are selling is not as valuable as the person you're selling it to. As Stockholm Syndrome fades, the vertical structure of our hierarchical institutions (government-religion-mega cartels) should flatten out into a gentler pyramid. Monopolies will fade, anxiousness will too, and we'll concentrate more on preventative maintenance.

Reza got me thinking about why we grind our teeth (bruxism) after he suggested a gene caused it, so I researched it. Scientists haven't finished pinpointing the genes that cause this stress but the MECP2 gene in the long arm of one of the X-Chromosomes keeps popping up as the culprit. This gene is highly heritable because both parents likely have one. In common cases the overexpression of this gene can be inhibited by exercise, yoga, laughing, yawning on purpose, expression of anger, and meditation. Strife, unfocused anger, comparing ourselves to others, and caffeine will increase our bruxism. If you live a stress-free life but still grind your teeth, you have repressed anger, and MECP2 is trying to push the anger out while you are trying to push it in. *Tears for Fears* might tell you to, "shout,

shout, shout it all out, these are the things you can do without, come on, I'm talking to you, come on."

I don't wear the mouth guard anymore because in 2016 I learned how to stop grinding my teeth. Every time I woke up, I held my jaws wide open for a few minutes as if I was laughing hard. I kept saying "no" to my dreamer, knowing he was close by and listening, and kept saying "no" to bruxism. Holding my mouth open twice as wide increased my airflow by a factor of 4 too (Bernoulli's equation). It was uncomfortable but I kept pushing back against that clenching gene and…it gave up. I don't grind my teeth anymore and haven't lost a crown since. We *can* change the mandates of some of our genes.

Even more interesting, decades ago my dad Jim was talking down to me again—rather smugly—right in front of my wife and his new grinning wife. I exploded. I chewed him out for 2 minutes. Mr Perfect had no idea what was happening or why I finally let him have it. Anyway, a couple weeks later I was checking out a little cut on my hand and I noticed that my fingernails were really long—I had stopped chewing them.

Right after Edith had passed, Jim remarried a devout Christian lady and unbelievably he turned right into a tempura husband (lightly battered.) Jim's 2nd wife and her youngest daughter stole his estate—bit by bit, lawyer by lawyer—for themselves, as the years went by. They sat at our dinner table dozens of times, enjoying the company, the food, everything, while they were stealing $2 million from my siblings and I. Jim finally died a month before his 93rd birthday.

Jim's 2nd wife already had millions from her previous dead husband and I told her she was a narcissist parading as a Christian. All she could do was stare at me so I added, "some people can see it you know." When Edith was so sick so many years ago, she told me that this theft is exactly what would happen but no one could have foreseen what lie in wait for Jim's widow's family as their karma made its way into the world.

Inventing Fire, Laughter, Religion, Burial, and Agriculture

Einstein said, "imagination is more important than knowledge." Imaginative speculation is an essential, human only tool (we think it is anyway) and we can learn about the deep past using a non-scientific method. In this section I simply imagine being a caveman, a hunter-gatherer, and then an ancient farmer.

Fire may have been a gracious gift of lightning rods from the great beyond, or, cavemen all over Africa created sparks by accident, while accidently knapping away at a flintstone to make a spear. No matter, it's more fun to think about how our sarcasm and laughter evolved around the campfire because for the first time we were cozy enough to contemplate beyond survival. The best explanation was in a Johnny Hart cartoon from the 1960s: a shrewdness of apes was sitting around a fire when one of them said, "hey, why don't we become cavemen?" "We'll need a leader," another caveman said, as he tossed a couple more sticks in the fire, "a person who is capable of making intelligent decisions." Yet another caveman said, "that disqualifies *you*," and the whole circle burst out laughing. Johnny Hart condensed 4 million years into one cartoon.

Like a cellphone to an 8th grader, a fire was coveted by each member of the tribe. It was such a personal moment to see a fire—"I'm home, I'm safe, I'm warm"—because it was the leading cause of life and kept those selfish, personal genes at play. We can know that the caveman who could start a fire was quite the ladies' man and this was a major inflexion point of that era. Individual invention began infringing on brute force, which exposed the frailty of violence, and unveiled to all that the ideas coming from empathy capitalism benefitted individuals, but extended *more* benefits to everybody in the tribe.

We still covet fires. Watch how each person plays with a fire and gets a warm fuzzy with how they place every stick. That's no accident. Fire is sexy because without it, humans would have, well...you know. Fire quiets us and evokes ethereal memories of kindred spirits, hiding deep in our DNA—we can't help but stir the fire and contemplate.

When Jeanne and I were dating she asked "why are all the Super Bowl parties on the same day?" (She grew up in India.) After I answered her Super Bowl question, we picked a Super Bowl party and during the game I put a new split log in the host's barely flickering fireplace. I noticed he noticed—eyeing the ritual jealously—and I asked him if he would have preferred the log to go in backwards from how I put it. We both laughed. Fire remains an obsession, illuminating how our brains retain the activities of our ancestors—even if it's only an emotion. I wrote this book by an outdoor fire—I hope you can still smell it. It's snowing now in West Georgia.

When we started losing our body hair about 2 mya (evolution made a booboo?) we found ourselves in a long-drawn-out dilemma. This kept prompting the only animal who can invent, to invent, and scientists found evidence of campfires from 1 mya.[1] Soon after, the forager men and women always agreed that "there's no such thing as too much firewood." Sitting by the fire we breathed smoke and smoked plants and got a bit high—the trillion-dollar industry of smoking began—and those brave enough to make eye contact would look at each other and smile with their eyes, like Tyra Banks does. Those two peep holes to the soul were a good start and the foragers yearned for more free information, like facial clues. Frowning and teeth clenching was getting old after a million years anyway.

I've always wondered what it was like when the first human smiled, or laughed, and then made a sarcastic remark and nobody knew what to think. Smiling came first, around the fire, and laughter likely evolved alongside humans burying our dead—a seemingly ridiculous conclusion I know. But I sez to myself I sez: the evolution of symbolic thinking (abstract conceptual thought) suggests humans were capable of being grave so they could feel joy too. And each had watched the birth of a baby and knew something really big was up.

The joy and solemnity, which took many forms—mostly religious—filled the spirit of most all the ancient groups scientists have unearthed, and probably every single tribe got religion. It gave them hope for the future. For an appalling analogy, I love basketball and especially Duke basketball. I still love it when they win and hate it when they lose, although I don't know any of the players anymore. The Pontiff Coach K is gone too and I don't even know who the new coach is. But I still believe in Duke, and they, whoever *they* are, spark my hope for the future when they win. The team symbolically got into my subconscious fairly early and since then has had nothing to do with my cognition. My belief in Duke offers me nothing tangible to touch or point to except a symbol. It's as if I worship a huge, far-off building on Chapel Hill that I've never been to—the steel and concrete basketball arena—no matter who's inside.

Getting back to smiling, smiling was the tangible expression for a whole bunch of intangible stuff. It was a whole new way of communicating and had a long evolution. Parents opened their mouths to get their baby to open theirs—eating was akin to smiling—and other humans imitated that, opening their faces and baring their teeth, as many animals do. Smiling was important because as our sense of smell weakened our sight improved. The first smiles weren't so good having arisen from instinct, imitation, and competition and blind people have a slightly different smile because they've never seen one. For generations most foragers didn't know what to make of all this so they dutifully bared their brown teeth. It scared some while others enjoyed it (it's that eleutheromania again) and eventually humor would evolve into little brain twisters delivered by jokesters.

Maybe one forager walked right through the middle of the campfire in front of the tribe and though it hurt a little he laughed. The others stared. Gradually like chainmail the concepts of risk, frivolity, and deception dawned on the rest. There was plenty of meat that night, so a celebratory mood filled the night air, and he said "look," pointing out into the darkness. When everybody looked, he stole a piece of someone else's mammoth meat, ate it, and got a couple laughs. That was the first joke and we still do it today. Everybody suddenly realized that him grabbing the piece of meat during a rare abundancy didn't matter so they bared their teeth and accidentally on purpose released a sound. It felt like evil spirits were leaving their bodies, not knowing they were pushing back on their clenching bruxism, and they all laughed a different way—each evil spirit is different. They discovered their own risibility, learned that each laugh had a little verbal info inside, and a sharp forager girl could tell if a laugher liked her or not by the way he laughed. There had to be that guy there too who waited for others to laugh then laughed himself, and one cave girl did laugh so hard she peed in her animal skin and accidentally taught others how to belly laugh by example.

Laughing, something scientists still don't understand, was born. To this day no laughter science exists that I know of because it's another example of that mysterious, undiscovered mind-body emotional oneness that makes us human.

An educated guess would be that laughing started about 500,000 years ago. This smart forager didn't know he was bolstering his immune system and reducing bad hormones but it caught on because others intuitively felt he was onto something—longevity. This guy might have been showing everybody the first throwing spear, selling his javelin with a smile and moving his body as if he were going to toss it into the darkness. The tribe's collective brain stared blankly. He had a modicum of free will or maybe he had accidently dropped a sharp stick and it stuck in a piece of meat. He stared at it for a few seconds, something clicked, and his aha moment made him laugh.

The slow tribe knew what a spear was for—just didn't get the "throw" part—but they couldn't help but dream on it and in the morning a few of them tried to make throwing spear #2. Imagine the inventor's popularity growing as his comrades finally realized he was the guy who thought of how to kill a dangerous animal without getting near it.

There is evidence throwing spears go back 500,000 years. [2] Remember, Chris Stringer found DNA evidence that some Cro-Magnons were here 500,000 years ago which might explain the leap to a projectile weapon...and laughing. Humans slowly became funny and a tich more philosophical, bringing a new charisma which turned the definition of sexy from big and powerful to smart and entertaining.

With no shovels, burial was grueling work, so they probably weren't burying their dead because they stank. And they could count too so at the burial everybody saw their own future, especially the lucky who had gotten to the auspicious but seasoned age of 30. The scarce 40 somethings were already out on the edge of the bell curve, and terrified. As the scattered forager clans gnashed their molars and came to grips with inevitability, the unconnected tribes each adopted religion and buried important people with beads, carved bone and ivory, and pretty colored pebbles that archaeologists found hanging on their skeletons. How imperative religion was to our psychological evolution and still is!

Both humor and burial involved abstract thinking but death and beyond remained an unsolved mystery. I'm sure there was a preachy guy who noticed the solemn faces and it hit him that he could profit from that. He told everybody exactly how to perform the burial—making it up as he went—while he watched with a piece of choice animal skin covering his mouth and nose. He had found a little loadstone earlier you see, hid it in his hand, and became self-ordained by moved little pieces of iron bits around magically, as people stared in disbelief. Preachers do more than lay people and those moving particles landed him the cushiest position—the missionary one. Much later the church doors would open automatically as the pontiff slowly walked up the marble stairs. Quasimodo was in the basement you see, frantically cranking the wooden gears.

Religion evolved from cave people wishing for miracles during a sustained evolutionary shortage. Cave parents wanted more for their children than they had had and pleaded for some supernatural strength because they were already overstressed when the new stork arrived. Then, a lookout told them another tribe was coming. When we get that dread feeling and another emergency hits, we look up to the sky for "someone to watch over me."[3] Today we've figured out that priests can't save us and the next step is to include politicians. Then, we can stop looking for gurus, stop trading seats on the Lusitania, and get off the ship.

We can see into the future better than our gurus can because we want a future for ourselves and our families and they want something else. Our brains are time machines too whereas most animals have trouble thinking a day ahead so we can go anywhere in the future or past and learn![4] This ability enabled us to start farming. Rare is the animal who can think a year ahead for food, and when it appears that a lower animal has, that farming happened by mechanical trial and error, not cognition. Our time machines are 3 times better now because it wasn't that long ago when our lives were 1/3rd as long.

Let's make another bold assumption, using imagine learning and intuition: women invented agriculture. They stayed near camp and saw the same plants day in and day out—saw them as living things, not just objects to push aside—while the predator men were out killing animals……and grunting. In synchrony, farming sprouted all over the world, so it could have happened by trial and error too. The agrarians out populated the foragers, so the genocide gene, and the programming for men to kill and hunt, only took its first hit 12,000 years ago. Agriculture changed us much, some good (organization and tool revolution), some bad (diet and exercise). James Suzman says in his book *Work* that global warming in the Middle East started 12,000 years ago, prompting wheat, barley, and rye to grow right under our feet in the fertile crescent.[5] Things change and now the badland is a dust bowl, but the first amber waves of grain were in Syria. There had to be one person, probably a female, who sifted a handful of wheat, ground it up with a rock in a clay bowl, and mixed it with water. She kneaded it into a leaven, somehow knew to keep part of it, and thought to put it over a fire. Even if you haven't read *Clan of the Cave Bear*, can you picture a man making bread?

When my wife, mom, and grandmother (Jeanne, Edith, Helen) saw a nice plant that "volunteered" itself, they all softly said, "it's pritty," and they all said it with a distinct 'i' in the middle as they smiled at it for too long. Long ago, wheat "volunteered" itself to women and this observation would eventually reduce food scarcity worldwide. Women are built closer to the ground and are assiduous with flora while paying no mind to time going by or how much work is involved. My wife cuts up food slowly and precisely while I do it fast to get it over with. Women live longer by living in the here and now. It seems to us that our anxiety is in the here and now but it lives in the past and the future.

Most accounts of Native American tribes say the women did the planting. Women love plants and gardening, are more earthy, and have evolved more patience and impatiens than men. Since hunting and gathering was still a fairly perfect way to live 12,000 years ago after the last Glacial Maximum began receded,[6] and earth warmed again, I think women stumbled upon farming accidentally on purpose. I carried a bag of grass seed through a forest on our property, not knowing there was a hole in the bag, and noticed a month later there was a long, slender line of grass growing through the forest. When we stopped walking Eurasia and started farming wheat, we built little houses because we realized we weren't going anywhere. Women loved the houses, more than their husbands sometimes, while husbands loved the yard more, and in this time-honored way we became domesticated. In his book *Sapiens*, Dr Yuval Harari says "we didn't domesticate wheat, wheat domesticated us."

May I speculate, *women* domesticated us? It wasn't perfection, the wheat domesticated the bacteria in our stomachs too and it takes a long time to nurture them back to their wild origins. The gamechanger, if I'm right, was that women didn't always have to rely on men for food anymore. It was in their blood to start empathy capitalism, whether growing grain, propagating the species, holding babies for years, or taking care of the sick in their spare time.

The power of empathy capitalism is hard to explain because so many unknown individuals notice tiny changes in demand and supply, and respond quickly. We can't explain it, but when a baby is born a farmer who doesn't know that that happened, tills a new row. Much later modern megafarms evolved. Those are about export and were created by moving obscene amounts of money. They are run by men because refined poison is profitable, and this probably isn't how women would have evolved farming. We do need to chew a lot to get more surface area, but we don't want food so refined that it leaks through our stomach lining.

The mostly female silent economy (nonmonetary) operates under the radar and is so massive the GDP numbers we get for each country are ludicrous. We define work by how much one is paid—as bad as judging someone solely by IQ—and intelligent work doesn't have that much to do with money, especially in what we'd call "poorer" countries where the silent economy is bigger than GDP. Better yet, imagine there was no such thing as money—each country would still have a vibrant, trade economy! Economics is not digital, it's about people.

Ignoring these economic truisms that haunt the western world makes it impossible to accurately measure economic growth, debt, or inflation. Those hired to create fictional inflation numbers know that the silent economy brings down prices while the pyramid is raising them. Restaurants, for example, could charge a lot more if men cooked, so, if most of what you eat is cooked by the silent economy (women) than you are eating better and cheaper. Pilsbury Inc doesn't hold a candle to the silent female economy. The point is, people take care of themselves no matter what the pyramid does and if we added up all the intelligent work women do for no pay, we could write another book called *The Forgotten Woman.*[7]

Charity

In school we are taught to think as a group in a play for equality of outcome (egalitarianism) while nature has more than engrained the opposite philosophy inside each of us. I couldn't find the quote in *The Selfish Gene,* but Richard Dawkins wrote something like this: "if we're trying to create a cooperative society we're not going to get any help from nature." He is also the author who taught me that genes are so selfish they can live for hundreds of millions of years.

We live for the happiness of ourselves and our families, some relatives, a few close friends, and *maybe* 100 acquaintances. The close relationships are not short on brevity, sustainability, or similar values, so right or wrong they fortify our belief systems, and to be blunt we don't care what other people think. We already picked them after lots of thought, thank you, and strangers cannot analyze our personal decisions with objectivity. "We all want the same thing," is caveman talk. The group values we have in common are tenuous, fleeting, and ultimately for personal gain. We work in groups when the pay is good, spend it all on our families, and when another group offers us more, we change groups.

There are nature shows on PBS reporting that lower animals practice conservation by eating less to save other species. This is beyond the thinking of the lower animals—people see what they want to see—and almost beyond the thinking of humans. Jonathan Haidt writes, "these claims [animals practicing altruism] were naïve because the individuals who followed this selfless strategy would leave fewer surviving offspring and would soon be replaced."[8] 3 pages later he said human altruists are so rare "we send film crews out to record them for the evening news."

Charity is humanmade and is a product of affluence, the free market, and free will. We give value away, even to strangers, and our genes say "no." We simply override them. Charity is also an individual act and telling others about our charity or pressuring them to sacrifice value for our charity muddies the singular act of selflessness.

I fancied Jonathan Haidt's book *The Righteous Mind*. He said we are 90% chimp (work as individuals) and 10% bee (work in a collective or hive) which is about right. This is why 90% of us copy our own genes. Our 10% cooperation is for mutual but ultimately individual benefit as we are aware of coincident interest more than any other mammal. Michael Tomasello said, "it is inconceivable that you would ever see 2 chimps carrying a log together."[9]

In a search for dolphin intelligence, I finally found a picture on the internet showing 2 dolphins launching a boy into the air by simultaneously pushing up on the bottom of his feet with their 2 heads.[10] The dolphins did this for playful reasons—it wasn't exactly work—making it a more sophisticated feat of empathy capitalism. Dolphins understand coincident interest better than chimps do and I can't understand how that happened. Cold brains make the world go 'round?

CHAPTER 24

India

Our genocide gene shrank or precariously civilized itself using the contradictory ingredients of naked imperialism, widespread affluence created by free trade, and the rule of law. Less obvious is how these institutions have spread brain genes to many places while not so much in others, causing separate groups to evolve differently. We'll spend time in Australia, the Middle East, Israel, the Americas, and Vietnam, and a longer stay in India, 11 pages from here.

50,000 years ago, swollen glaciers lowered the sea levels, and created a southern land bridge from Thailand to Malaysia to volcanic Indonesia. From there, Aborigines followed little islands southward through the *ring of fire* and kept boating all the way to Australia. It's now called "Straya" by the locals. Thrice my family went *Down Under,* braving the 14-hour plane ride from hell. My wife and I took a touring motorbike down Great Ocean Road—probably the most beautiful and expensive road on earth—from Torquay to Great Otway National Park. There were hang gliders dotting the sky and sheer cliffs dropping away along the hairpin turns as we drove past the towering 11-1/4 apostles (one of the natural pillars in the ocean was falling apart).

Australia's civilization is built up around the edges like Japan and Florida, but the people are funnier Down Under. When you're in Straya and stay too long in the loo (the bathroom) they yell, "are you dropping the kids off at the pool?" It doesn't matter if you're a Bloke or a Sheila, they'll *take the piss* outa ya—no worries—unless you're too 'ot to 'andle. The country doesn't take prisoners: "we want the best, chuck out the rest." They also say they're "hyping for a victory" but we know what they mean. If you're drunk you are *năked*—if you talk about yourself, you're a *wanker* or a *tosser*, then they'll say, "how ya goin' love?" "Yanks are wanks," and if you've let your Yankee arse go, you've gone *pear shaped*. If a local surfs all day, he's *bunking* school or on the *dole*. Don't say "rooted" or "stuffed" unless you really mean it or a Sheila might tell you to *gor horme* [go home], and the androgynous Australian blokes call their buddies "mates," which may have come from their grandparents who were inmates. Fair dinkum! I can't say "no" the way they do because they somehow get 4 syllables and 5 vowels into that 2-letter word, and sometimes Y.

When the Aborigines go on walkabout (a traditional sabbatical inherited from foragers) they say their going on "bushtaka in Nunawading," and they "walk down to the shores of *billabong* (meaning *lake*, or *drink* as the Aussies call it)." It frees the mind to get away from the everyday, and in Straya, as in Europe, everybody takes 2 months off a year. When Straya gets up to 95° in the "shide," all outside workers can go home but as they say, "it's just Celsius."

They have the best zoos I've ever petted, by far, but you can't smoke or use your cellphone in your own car and for the biggest beer consumers on earth their alcohol breath limit is draconian. Australian police are far from catching up with the Canadian police who apologize for inconveniencing you, or catching up with the Indian police who just want a US 20. Now, back to how the island, I mean *continent*, got settled.

Some of the pre-ancient ice ages sustained thriving life underneath a world covered in ice. The last ice earth was 600 mya and the temperature gradually warmed into a semi-predicable warm-cool cycle. 50,000 years ago, the earth was a bit further from the sun than it is now, and the glaciers soaked up so much water that islands were exposed like steppingstones all the way to Australia. Over many generations, Cro-Magnons rowed their way there. To this day, we don't fully understand the erratic, sporadic, yet emphatic ice ages.

Scientists Milutin Milankovitch and later Michael Wysession found that the earth's orbit gets a little more oblong every 100,000 years (we are further from the sun) and exacerbates these periodic ice ages. 50,000 years ago, earth was at this furthest orbit (apogee) and today the earth is orbiting closest to the sun (perigee). 50,000 years from now we'll again have many more islands and lots of new coastal property.

There's a 3-4% difference in the 2 extreme earth orbits and according to BBC science focus if we were just 1% closer earth would be uninhabitable. The late Milutin Milankovitch painstakingly calculated that the procession of ice ages is influenced by this time cycle and more researchers are coming around to this piece of the climate picture.

The next ice age, if it isn't small, will grind up Paris and pulverize New York City into gravel and sand, pushing both into the same ocean in about 50,000 years. Glaciers will cover half of the US, Europe, and the bottom half of South America. With that kind of ice, the nice Canadians will have to move in with us. But the real nightmare is that everybody will be squeezed near the equator where there isn't near enough land except in Africa. Imagine the price of land in mid-Africa way surpassing Manhattan and billions of African migrants watching icebergs circling the continent like shark fins.

Even so, our descendants have lots of time. Our Goldilocks orbit, with the sun's heat, radiation, gravity, and solar wind, is preposterous fortune. With space weather, we won the lottery dozens of times in a row. Somebody had to.

The Aborigines got their name from the Latin word *ab original,* which speaks for itself, and these Pacific rim peoples populated islands all over the bottom half of the Pacific. They rowed to Australia and found kangaroos as tall as basketball hoops with talons like raptors that could casually rip their guts out. About 12,000 years ago, the glaciers began retreating and thousands of islands vanished back into Davy Jones' locker, stranding every rock and organism in Australia. It was a good time to make better boats but coastlines rarely have enough straight hardwood and as luck would have it there were tasty, supersized animals everywhere. Australia became its own petri dish for evolution and a mecca for dozens of animal species endemic only to that continent, because they evolved in isolation. The giant mammals were eaten by the aborigines and finished by the British, leaving only the smaller animals.

The first Brits landed in 1770 and nearly starved to death not knowing that reinforcements were on the way to Botany Bay. Captain James Cook landed in 1788 and as settlements rapidly expanded, he flooded the coasts with rifles, livestock, and new diseases.[1] The Aborigines population declined rapidly. "By the 1880s Australia had the fastest-growing economy and the highest per capita income in the world,"[2] and the Aboriginal population is now less than a million.

Clades

74,000 years ago, the Africans who went to Spain and the Africans who went to the Middle East eventually clashed. This was the first meeting of the east and west and the beginning of the long Neanderthal/Cro-Magnon war. We won but Europe remained sparsely populated and Cro-Magnons gradually clustered into 3 clades: African, East Asian, and West Asian, roughly 40,000 years ago.[3] A 4rth rogue clade coalesced inside the West Asian clade (India), went northwest, eventually populated Europe, and learned to live with snow. These 4 clades of very dark people were fairly set by about 41,000 years ago and they rarely intermarried. Although all 4 clades had very similar Cro-Magnon DNA, they each looked a little different and still do.

Some people from the Asian clades (China and India) migrated southeast, half the journey over water, and a few made it all the way over to Papua New Guinee and down to Australia. Another group went to Alaska and became what we might call the 5th clade. The very first Native Americans walked from what is now Russia and China to North America, probably 15,000 years ago, when the oceans were 300 feet lower and the Bering Strait was 600 miles wide.[4] The Indians still retain the Asian epicanthic fold over the inner parts of the eyes, cementing their Chinese origins.

They migrated east guided by the stars through generations of ice, snow, ceaseless freezing wind, and little food, which begs a question. Why didn't they turn back? Was wanderlust that powerful or maybe the giant elk (7-foot-long antlers 12 feet across) migrating right along with them, gave them hope. There were giant camels, bears, saber tooth cats, wooly mammoths, and if they could survive, why not humans? With starvation thinning out the tribe, they put their brains together, plus 10 spears, and learned to bring down almost anything. The comparably small price of losing a man or two to a tusk meant that these star trekkers would eat for months and be the first to see North America though they couldn't have known what was ahead.

Though many tribes of these short, fat people unbelievably stayed in Alaska because they'd perfected the tools to hunt in the sea, it took the moving tribes only 5,000 years to spread south from Alaska, following the left coast, all the way down to Patagonia. Their similar DNA was found and microscopically mapped from Alaska down to the southern tip of Chile, 600 miles from Antarctica, but it turns out they had conquered the Americas at a snail's pace. The 15,000-mile slow walk—over halfway around the globe—was just 50 miles per generation.

Another group, the Clovis Indians with flatter faces and better arrow tips, split away from the tribe that went south from California to Mexico and on down. The Clovis traversed southeast to Colorado, then just under Missouri because the Laurentide Glacier covered most of state, and made it all the way to the Atlantic Ocean. Little did these first Native Americans know that they would be caught in the crosshairs of history again when in 1492 the east would meet west for the 2nd time but going the opposite direction. Both assimilations—from Malta to Gibraltar, the short and long way—were violent, but those long, icy journeys through Alaska's frozen badland were more painful. After those millenniums of travel, they slowly realized there was yet another problem: they weren't immune to the diseases of the tribes they met, peaceful or not. As for the fierce tribes who stubbornly stayed in Alaska and learned from the wolves and lived like the wolves, they never knew that it would be their future lineages, who would help keep the Russians (crumby ship builders with bad reputations) from settling the northwest of America.

If you *Don't Know Much About History* (by Kenneth C. Davis) he says there were once tens of millions of Indians living in the Americas. After smallpox, war, and much propagating by the survivors, there are now about 4 million in the US so we can consider this one of the larger genocides per capita.

Christopher Columbus had no idea Florida was just to his starboard side when he first landed on a populated Caribbean Island now called "Samana Cay,"—part of the Bahamas. He guessed he was in Indonesia, so he named the natives there "Indios."[5] After visiting Haiti and Cuba, Columbus called the entire area the "West Indies" because there was no written evidence of another continent in between Europe and Asia.

Columbus brazenly renamed the indigenous population "savages"—a name that later left the lips of Thomas Jefferson and Charles Darwin himself. Darwin would come to suspect that all "races" were the same species because they could all reproduce with each other, though this was not completely proved during his lifetime.[6] Some isolated groups were simply starved for information and thus starved of new inventions so fell behind in the arms race. They weren't savages—the colonialists were—and after the systematic carnage began, they became savages too because there is only one way to win a war: be more ruthless than your enemy.

We still call those hundreds of Caribbean islands the "West Indies," from Cuba down to the old Danish West Indies, almost to Venezuela—collectively, the Greater and Lesser Antilles. For early sailors the thick chain of islands was like a Maginot line barricade so if they missed the eastern seaboard altogether, they hit a Caribbean so crowded they couldn't help but bump into one. It became a real estate race for the Europeans, a smorgasbord of beachfront property, and when a nation-state overextended or lost a war, they would have a fire sale and sell other people's land to richer nation-states for gold. For land, nations want real money.

It was thought of as progress in hegemonic Washington DC to not recognize Indian hunting grounds because they didn't have a fence around them but competing Indian tribes did recognize these boundaries. The Indian version of property rights was a system never to be seen again as the noose shrunk around the Iroquois coalition of 5-6 quasi-democratic nations who had formed the first Unites States in the 16th and 17th century. There was still plenty of land when the Europeans got there but we instinctively followed the Us vs Them software from evolution, and the ambitious settlers were undeterred by true rumors of the Iroquois art of extended torture.[7]

In the song *Sailing to Philadelphia* Mark Knopfler wrote poetically about the 2 boys, Charlie Mason and Jeramiah Dixon, who joined the royal society, surveying and charting out the border between Maryland and Pennsylvania and beyond. In 1776, while the French were defeating coalitions of Native American tribes for the colonists, Mason and Dixon drew a line through the middle of the Iroquois nation. Knopfler sang:

You're a good surveyor Dixon but I swear you'll make me mad,
the west will kill us both you gullible Jordy lad,
you talk of liberty, how can America be free,
the Jordy and the baker's boy, in the forest of the Iroquois...

Mason was not altogether wrong (only about 12,000 colonists were killed by the Indians[8]) but with sailing ships bringing more protestors (protestants) from Europe the Indians were outnumbered, fenced out, then banked into gambling casinos. It was agriculture, according to Dr Harari, that finished off the American Indians but America wasn't special. Killing people and stealing land was so common throughout the world it had been considered normal since Adam had house cats.

To set the map straight today, how many hundreds of invasions do we reverse, and how many thousands of years do we go back? Most countries change hands or alter their borders every century. We can't go back; all we can do is not repeat.

After wiping out the North American Indians, the US went down to Central America in 1900 and *annexed* part of Columbia because the Columbians weren't building a canal to connect the Atlantic and Pacific Ocean.

Between the great oceans, Panama is a narrow earthen damn once claimed by England, Spain, France, even Scotland, and finally America. The Panama Canal is 48 miles long, took 500 years to build, cost thousands of lives, and the US made it appear annexing Panama was a wonderful thing. For most it was. The Panama Canal cuts 27,000 klicks out of the trip from the Atlantic to the Pacific Ocean and shippers saved countless dollars, not to mention they avoided the treacherous 900-kilometer-wide Drake Passage around Cape Horn, between Antarctica and South America.

Teddy Roosevelt eventually dug the canal in 3 years, with machines, after ditching those hand-held shovels as well as somebody's idea to "dig it with spoons" to hire more people (quote accredited to Milton Freidman). The US was so magnanimous with annexation we sewed Panama a flag and wrote them a constitution while Teddy Roosevelt paid the Columbian soldiers $50 each to not fight, historians tell us. Everybody who was anybody went along with Teddy, even his wife Edith, and Panama *had* declared its independence from Columbia.

It wasn't a typical Brit-style takeover—more like stealing a gift for the world—and dominion became utility. Don Henley, the songwriter who kept the Eagles going through their stretches of mediocrity, wrote: "the road to empire is a bloody stupid waste," but it's great for speeding up world trade.

Ho Chi Minh

The US decided to *improve* Asia next and the seeds of their worst US war, Vietnam, were sewn just after they created Panama. My least favorite Scot, President Woodrow Wilson—2nd wife named Edith too—was groomed by religion and a PhD in the History of Government but failed to comprehend the 1st Amendment. In 1918 he revived the Sedition Act from 1798. He arrested, convicted, and jailed thousands of people for years for what they wrote or for protesting the WWI military draft while the constitution forbade involuntary servitude or tampering with free speech. A complicit supreme court justice Oliver Wendel Holmes distracted us with "you can't *falsely* yell fire in a crowded theatre," using a bad analogy to shut up so many Americans.[9]

It was Wilson who was falsely yelling fire in a crowded theatre. WWI didn't have to be our war—we barely helped anyway—and his jailing of antiwar speakers by the thousands sparked the creation of the ACLU, as the armies in Europe were giving up and going home. But, after 150 years, Wilson had finally paid the US war debt to France.

Woodrow Wilson would have hated to be mistaken for a Black, a Jew, or an Oriental. This president ended up meeting Ho Chi Minh in 1919 Paris where Minh asked Wilson for help in getting the French imperialists out of his country. Minh had already written to Woodrow, pleading for reason, and explaining the right of Vietnam to decide its own future. Woodrow shunned Minh though the US president was preaching self-determination as the new policy for the entire west, and Woodrow's racism inched the US toward the Vietnam disaster. Minh had studied socialism and communism as FDR had but Minh was just another nationalist going it alone to get the French out of his panties, which got him the label *communist revolutionary*.

Many US politicians, groomed by hegemony, translated *foreign nationalist* to *communist* automatically while purchasing a stock from an anonymous tip. Geography, capitalism, banking, foreign policy, and history weren't strong suits for the golf cart politicians, even back then. And they forgot what *our own* Revolutionary War was about—getting European imperialists out—which was all Minh wanted.

Minh admired the US and had lived there for a spell. As he rocketed to power back home, he declared Vietnam's independence in 1945, directly quoting the best parts of Thomas Jefferson's Declaration of Independence.[10] He petitioned Harry Truman in 1946 for help towards independence but Truman ignored him too. 8 years later Vietnam defeated the US-backed French army decisively in the battles at Dien Bien Phu, and Vice President Nixon wanted to send in American troops to replace the defeated French.[11] Eisenhower said "no" initially which is when Britain, of course, suggested the US divide Vietnam into the north and the south.[12] The first US soldiers went in in 1956.

After shocking the world in 1975 by defeating the US, *communist* Vietnam became an arguably prosperous country, meaning, there was a whole lot of capitalism going on there. Full of small and medium size free market-based businesses, Price Waterhouse forecast Vietnam to be the 10th largest economy in the world by 2050. Being directly south of the communist Chinese border, Ho Chi Minh—code name Agent 18—could not exactly announce he was going to start a democratic capitalism in Vietnam. He died a hero in 1969, never knowing his tiny *Buddhist* country would be the first to defeat the US in war, and prosper. The Vietnamese people felt as the American people did after defeating imperialist Britain—another largest and best trained Army on earth. The stunned world, including the radical Muslims, looked at the ghost of Minh as David defeating Goliath. The terrorists around the globe were excited, realizing they could goad the US and keep them broke as a joke without ever losing a war in the Middle East, teaching us something we've forgotten: money isn't what wins wars. That's why Israel inflicts so much damage when they are attacked—they *can't* lose 1 war—and the only way to keep the peace is to make your enemy pay double as the Middle East does to the US.

Reshaping the World from Foggy Bottom

In 1916, the Brit Mark Sykes and the Franc Georges Picot separated Palestine from Jordan and Lebanon from Syria.[13] In 1917 Woodrow Wilson signed off on another British Parliamentary document called the "Balfour Agreement," initiated by Lionel Walter Rothschild and Arthur James Balfour—a former British Prime minister. This document initiated the new state of Israel, which had been a Zionist dream in the European works since the US Civil War. In 19th century Switzerland people collected donations to buy up Palestinian land sold by powerful Arabs who owned large swaths of the nomadic area.

As colonialism was thankfully falling out of favor there were a couple final orders of business: Woodrow Wilson signed off on Balfour, Harry Truman signed off on the new country of Israel, and the Middle East heated up. Thankfully too, foreign policy didn't seem to be guided by those 2 little black books—the Torah, the Bible—but this oddity slipped right by the people. Each year since Balfour or the 1947-48 establishment of Israel any old person like me can tell you what the headlines were: US Holding Peace Talks in Middle East.

Britain has no separation of church and state or a constitution for that matter, or a supreme court until recently, while the US has long held all 3, however, the God of Abraham dictated some western foreign policy during and after the world wars and beyond. Envision how they view America's *separation of church and state* in the Middle East. As my dad would say, "there's *a rat* in the word separation. Do we think the biblical apocalypse is predetermined? Are we going to follow it over the cliff as if we have no free will? Are we going to slap the Middle East in the face until they let one fly? Palestine, Pakistan, and Iran are not strangers to suicidal war and are now the most likely places for a nuclear war to start. Israel will have no options left.

With the contradiction of hegemony, Israel has so far prevented the unthinkable. The Israeli Air Force took out the nuclear power plants in Syria and Iraq, for all of us, and they did it right before either country could upgrade these engines into breeder reactions to purify weapons grade uranium. Israel didn't bother with the cooling towers, they bombed until they saw the little domes—the reactors—collapse. Israel, who beats the US in dogfights using US planes, is the only country systematically reducing the threat of a nuclear launch or an accidental one. They cleverly messed up the centrifuge computers in Iran, "Stuxnet" the spies called it, ruining their enrichment process along with all that expensive uranium. Iran, who has sworn to eliminate the Jewish state and New York City, so far doesn't have the super-tool to commit suicide and Israel has yet to destroy Iran's nuclear reactor.

Conquest is always a double-headed ax, and we must ask ourselves again, over and over, what would the world look like if the FCDO in Britain and the US Department of State hadn't reorganized the world from foggy bottom?

Roughly half of the Jews in the early 1900s Europe didn't want a homeland and were not all that religious either having read in the Torah what evolution had already told them: "life on earth is the only gift." The Old Testament contains no commitment to an afterlife with your body intact,[14] too late for the 1.3 million mortals in Vietnam. It was 1973 before Christians promised eternal life with your body intact, in the New Testament, 500 years after Islam promised it.[15] Instead of invoking the Bible, the west could have justly given the Jewish people half of West Germany to rebuild New Jerusalem there.

Or, we could go back thousands of years and support Abraham's homeland but how many thousands of indigenous groups have been scattered, wiped out, or forever lost their homeland? Nearly every country on earth is now occupied by non-originals. Rarely do the diaspora gain their territory back or get help to do so without the rarest of commodities: divine providence, manifest destiny, and a big army.

The Mystery of India

After defeating the Pashtun in Afghanistan and dividing that country down the middle in 1893, Britain partitioned India in 1947 and told the US to divide Vietnam in half in 1954. In 1947, Indian Hindus and Muslims murdering each other was cresting but I believe that giving the Muslims a new state was a trade to minimize the psychological impact from the creation of Israel—the 4[rth] partition. Although these 4 partitions created 4 new war zones, the west believed they would have been continuous war zones anyway. However, the west almost insured the last thing anybody wanted: a nuclear arms race in the 3rd world.

The UK dreamed up 2 more countries, each called Pakistan (*Land of the Pure*) within India's borders and stuck them to the left and right of India. Most Muslims stayed in India but millions moved to their new homelands. The US, or Nixon, threw support to Pakistan even after Pakistan had attacked India in 1971, bombing almost a dozen airports. Border battles erupted and Russia quickly supported India. The tiny part to the east of India (East Pakistan) disappeared in 1972 and became Bangladesh, during a Muslim vs Muslim genocide, followed by an Indian invasion. But whether we called East Pakistan "Myanmar, Burma, Dhaka, or Bangladesh," no matter, the Brits made a mess and left.

Christopher Hitchens, who called the partition "an amputation," asked, "how could it be worse if we shifted our alliance and instead embraced India, our only rival in scale as a multi-religious and multi-ethnic democracy, and a nation that contains nearly as many Muslims as Pakistan?"[16] The US and Britain are looking over their shoulders at all their mistakes, which ultimately pushed Israel and Iran to have nukes. Pakistan and India have nukes, and India has an aircraft carrier from which F-16s *and* Russian MiG-21s (flying coffins) takeoff and land.

After the partition, Pakistan and India were not only genetically isolated but prevented from communicating. Families were cut in half and forbidden to cross the border, so people would send letters from Pakistan to friends in Kuwait, where the friends would mail the letters to the people's relatives in India. Britain had literally quarantined people who used to live next door to each other, ate the same food, and spoke English. The mess got bigger. What followed was the serial killing of political leaders in India and Pakistan, which I will describe 10 pages from now.

Bengaluru

After I met my wife Jeanne in 1987, I got the rare opportunity to visit India in 1991. She's an Anglo Indian (more correct is "Indo Anglian," says Christopher Hitchens) and this minority picks who they marry and are partial to the British. Even the early British occupiers like Rudyard Kipling who grew up mostly in India, called themselves "Anglo Indians." Though he hated imperialism he saw an England bringing order to a godless universe.[17] The Anglo Indians are imperceptivity looked down on by the Hindus and Muslims and if you visit, you'll probably never see it, because that's how the Indian people are.

Two notes of equal warning: Indian bread is out-of-this-universe and the beer is terrible. People will sell you great bread, or make it for you and give it to you—it hardly matters to them—in the poorest (or maybe richest) democracy on earth. Their major beer brands, King Fischer and United Breweries, have historically been protected from imported beer by Parliament blocking the imported beer (except to the rich). With no competition they don't have to make their beer better, but protectionist India is slowly opening up markets. Their desserts are not unhealthy because they don't have much sugar inside—there's just enough sugar in a dessert to make Americans wonder what the hell it is and why anyone would eat it.

Author Arundhati Roy says, "with 700 languages India is a continent masquerading as a country," and for its size is probably the most efficient economy on earth. The government has little choice but to leave the everyday markets to the people. India enjoys the small side of capitalism—countless tiny businesses—

and tourists can't turn the vendors down because they speak English so well. There are too many small businesses for the socialist government to attempt to manage, or tax, so the ingredients to pass China as a *real* capitalist nation are all in place. What I mean is that the Chinese government tries to run every Chinese business, which is not capitalism but socialism on steroids. Managing a vast market from the top down is impossible because that will constantly create too much of some things and too little of others. It's as bad as a government official in Beijing sending everybody their shopping lists for the day. India, with nothing to steal but "how to get along with others" (except China), teaches by example and cannot be successfully invaded. With 1.5 billion people and being so decentralized, taking possession of it would be a fool's errand.

The war gene is weak in India, and we can see this by talking to people. Competition and confrontation have been replaced with friendliness and acceptance—as if the west was half a world away. A thousand years of meditation became a new form of learning selection, largely unknown in western countries until the 1930s. In the Buddhist *vissudhimagga* they teach how to meditate away the monopoly mentality that we harbor in the west and replace it with kindness. Philosophe Robert Pirsig might say the west is stuck in the static (only wants to consummate monopoly) and the east meditates on the dynamic (the whole changing picture that monopolies blot out.) On the B-side, steeped in culture and tradition, the eastern avoidance of confrontation happily leaves many of their differences unresolved in perpetuity which is fine with them.

With eastern philosophical thinking we also hear polar logic—Yogi Berra/Bob Uecker type sentences—and seemingly contradictory concepts. I was talking to a guru on a street in Mumbai (Bombay) about this very thing and asked him about this ambiguity. "We hear opposite logic," I said, "like non-self, the problem is the solution, you are meaningless but you are infinite, in the beginning there was neither something nor nothing," and his poignant response was.............."exactly my friend, exactly."

I didn't tell him the joke of the guru teaching the Beatles about Buddhism and how nothing really exists. "Reality is a construct you create," he told the Fab 4 as they strolled through a narrow residential alley, when suddenly a truck came barreling toward them. Everybody dove through the nearest window into somebody's living room. Paul brushed himself off and looked around, hoping to find a beautiful girl inside. Everybody collected themselves back in the alley and George asked the guru, "if the truck didn't exist, why did you jump out of the way?" "It only appeared that I jumped out of the way," said the guru.

Parties in warm India are often outside. Let's say a party is slated to start at 7pm. People show up between 4pm and midnight, and nobody says anything. They are just happy to see them. I jokingly offered that on Indian clocks, maybe the big hand and the little hand are the same length, which got some laughs instead of getting beat up like I would in some countries. The people who show up to party at 7pm are laughingly said to be using *Indian Standard Time*, as there are no time zones, or they ignore them as we do in Arizona and Hawaii. It isn't odd for 11 people to pile out of a mid-size car and happily join the fun at 10am. They will bring the food out again, for 1 person, and enjoy watching you eat it, wondering what could have happened to a person to sit there and pig out alone. To this day, the Asian lower jaw for eating vegetables, fruit, and some fish and chicken, is noticeably smaller than the western beef-eating lower jaw.

Indians invented door-dash and rideshare before anybody knew what a gig economy was. If you need a motorcycle, people will trip over each other to give you one. I got lost on these bikes often and people would always stop what they were doing and try to give me directions. They helped, or not, and after I drove away, I could see them in my side mirror still talking with each other about where I was going. Casual friends in the expansive Indian social networks will bring sick people a curry dinner, or take them to the doctor, wait there, and bring them home.

Hairdressers spend Sunday at convalescent homes and cut everybody's hair for free. Personal time is not coveted in India, and Amity Shlaes, in her book *The Forgotten Man*, tells us how America used to be that way.

Homeopathic medicines are common in India: turmeric, herbal teas, barley water, and fenugreek seeds (for high blood pressure) to name a few. They call it "auyervada" (holistic medicine) which means: *the mind-body is 1 inseparable thing*. Most homeopathic medicines have no side effects but can take a while to heal our bodies because it took us so long to screw them up. My intuitive wife can diagnose people by listening to a sick person and recommend they take large doses of one of these homeopathic medicines. Sometimes it works fast and I've seen her erase symptoms without Rx drugs, surprising both patients and doctors in the US.

India doesn't have the money the west has but they have the medicine they need—capitalism always adjusts to the existing customer base, when allowed. In the US, medicine has become a monopoly so the prices of these services will always rise faster than inflation, while the small businesses in India raise prices slower because they are in perfect competition. That's the economic harmony that keeps prices low in India. The conundrum of monopoly-based economies, as the US has, is that monopolies grow fast. Eventually these private and public institutions, like the Medical Industrial Complex, will become so expensive that the government will not be able to provide them for free.

The vast majority of the active ingredients for US medications come from India and China and my wife buys them in India for 3¢ on the dollar. If a bottle of Rx pills has a 33,000% markup some clever Indian will buy them wholesale from the west, or copy the active ingredient, and mark them up 300%, and you don't need a prescription to buy them in India. Yankees overlook the free market of medicine and one Indian doctor told me, "America has too many pills and not enough diseases." There are Yogi Berras all over India.

There is growing evidence that we can die from simply believing we're sick and cure diseases by the reverse method. Like religion can cure some addictions, we don't know exactly how this mind over matter works. Author Dr Joe Dispenza explains how optimists live longer and how cultivating the mind-body oneness will actually create the medicines we need, naturally, inside of our bodies.

In Mumbai we ate Gujarati vegetarian food—scary good—and chicken or fish never crossed our minds. Next stop was Jeanne's hometown of Bengaluru, and we ate some equally good food, if that's possible, at the Indian/Chinese hybrid restaurants. A few days later, against our better judgement, we stopped for lunch at a hole in the wall. We asked the man if the food was clean and he rocked his head from side to side a few times, which I found out means *yes* in India, but my first impression of his answer was closer. It tasted great but a week in bed (not the good kind) will remind you to wash everything and eat at home, or eat at high-end restaurants. The food wasn't dirty, it had bacteria in it that my domesticated immune system had never met and Jeanne's immune system had happily forgotten about. A relative of Jeanne's, a doctor named Paddi, stopped by to check us out but there wasn't much he could do.

Paddi, who died of leukemia in 2023 at age 82, often traveled house to house and after we recovered, we bought him a nice tie for his free house call. Later I was talking to him about the unpaid house calls he made daily, and he said something profound, "most people just need somebody to talk to." Imagine an American doctor saying that. For every little psychological boost, there will be a nice biological boost and Paddi had that innate knowledge. In the US we spend trillions on medical, while loneliness and depression are the real purveyors of disease, and these cannot be cured by throwing money at them. Oddly, India has one the highest male heart attack rates in the world and few show any hint of stress so it could be nudged along by the high carb diet and those arranged marriages.

In 1996-97 we stayed a month in Jeanne's hometown again, Bengaluru, where her parents brought her up in a middle-class section called Fraser Town(!) named that for the heavy Scottish influence. Middle class is a relative term. Jeanne's brother Lew says that for Christmas the kids got a new toothbrush, a new pair of socks, and extra pieces of chicken in the curry.

At 7 years old, from halfway across the world, Jeanne dreamt that John F. Kennedy had been shot. Since she was 10.5 hours ahead, if she had the dream at about 2am, she dreamed it as it was happening at noon in Dallas. Imagine, our unconscious minds might be gathering information that our conscious minds cannot decipher, or block out, and Carl Jung found evidence of these premonitions in his own dreams. We dream of so many things though that some are bound to come true.

The sought-after city of Bengaluru (Bangalore) has tripled in population since the 90s, and now you can spend hours getting to a nearby restaurant and back. Even then, the bustling streets were a sight to behold. I rode around the town of Bengaluru daily on Mel's motorcycle—Jeanne's father—and as you can deduce, lived through it. At one crowded intersection including 2 cows ("4-legged constables" as Mel called them), bicycles, cars, trucks, hand-pulled carts, rickshaws, and a family of 6 on 1 motorcycle, a large bus ran over my foot. I learned to not stop at crowded intersections; it was safer to weave nonstop through the city. No rules create a natural flow.

Jeanne's nephew Sameer took me on his racing motorcycle for a death ride through the busy streets, dodging traffic and various animals, while I filmed it. Luckily, we didn't "meet with an accident" as they say in India or "turn turtle." He told me if I get pulled over in India, just hand them a 10-dollar bill, which works in so many countries and most of Latin America, but inflation has tripled that.

I shopped for chess sets along Brigade Road, walking the sidewalk with the occasional cow, and I asked around but nobody knew who owned it or cared. I came back to the US way too soon and with hideous jetlag but packing an incredible collection of hand-carved chess sets. It hardly mattered I paid too much for them. Jeanne's uncle called it the "skin tax" but they were ridiculously inexpensive. Sarcasm is muted in India but I found a nice big chunk of sandalwood to bring back too and told Sameer I'd like more pieces. He told me to just cut that one up into sections.

Aryabhata of India coined the number zero, super-evolving mathematics. Some say the number zero started in Iran, some say Egypt, and the Sumerians stake a claim too. Maybe math needed an eastern, existential philosophe to imagine a *nothingness*, and Aryabhata is the most likely to have invented the number zero, and did,[18] because that's what Indians try to bargain the price of everything down to.[19]

On that second trip to India, Jeanne's niece won Miss India, then got married in the biggest church I've ever been in. I haven't been in that many. The next night, the bachelor party crashed the bachelorette party and I got home at 5am again, riding in an earlier version of the smart car with 8 other people and had to climb a 10-foot iron fence to get to Pam's (Jeanne's mom) front door. She got up, unlocked the door and of course asked me if I wanted something to eat. There were parties every night—I was still trying to get over the 80s—and was beginning to think that Indians didn't sleep. We laughed until 5am and often at 11am I had to fast walk to Paddi's house for a game of chess. I was often late and he didn't care.

Pam told me a joke about an Indian worker whose supervisor was going on vacation, so the worker was put in charge for that week. The worker excitedly told his wife he was "off shitting for the manager," meaning *officiating* for him. Pam cracked me up again when she referred to somebody passing gas as, "calling from down below," and added he had "all the perfumes of Arabia." The biggest laugh I got out of Pam, whose kids had moved west, was when I said, "we all came from abroad."

The Last 200 Years of Occupation

Prior to the British occupation, India was itself. Shashi Tharoor writes about this India as rich and one of the first large major export countries. His take on the British impact is the harshest.

In my reading, the takeover was gradual. The crown chartered the East India Trading Company in 1600 and Britain's relationship with India was more about trade for the first 150 years. Britain, seeing nothing to stop them—and with no Paul Revere to warn the Indians—gradually increased pressure on the subcontinent. During the last 200 years of occupation Britain ran the show, bleeding India of resources in exchange for paper money, and the bleeding was administered by fascist twins: the East India Company and the Royal Navy. The British invasion also westernized the Indians—those they didn't shoot or starve.

The first major rebellion, called the "black hole of Calcutta," occurred in 1756 at Fort William. 50,000 Newab soldiers killed 50-100 British occupiers, took the fort back, and locked the remaining soldiers in a small hot dungeon. Only about 23 British soldiers of the 146 survived the gruesome night. Later in the same month Britain retook the fort with only 3000 men—their superior rifles routed the 50,000 Newab soldiers.[20] These killings were miniscule compared to the famines some historians say Britain helped cause.

The British kicked the French out of India—1756 to 1763—winning naval battles off the east coast during the French and Indian War (called the "7 Years War, by the Brits) and they put a hurting on the French in the New World too. Britain was everywhere.

The French losses inspired them to help the American colonists against the British, whom they hated anyway,[21] but in an irony for the ages, it was *India* who won the American Revolution for us....by proxy. Britain had military resources protecting their homeland, protecting colonies in Africa, fighting France, and had about 1000 ships and 200,000 soldiers dedicated to India.[22] From this scattered position, the Brits started the American

Revolutionary War with a scant 250+ warships in 1776[23] and could only muster a 50-66 ship attack on New Orleans in 1815. Britain lost both wars. Losing America turned out to be the most expensive mistake by any empire in history and only Britain was in position to make it. They also hated the snow. Without the warmth of India as the spoiler the US would have a prime minister and we'd be rolling those perfectly placed British adjectives effortlessly off our tongues.

In 1850, the British shot about 400 Indian protestors dead in Delhi square while protesting was legal in Britain. Next there was a 2-year mutiny 1857-58 involving the entire subcontinent and after England tamed it, the Scottish officers tried to turn the *philanthropy* of the occupation into an almost civilized one, with a few orders of business. They outlawed the 3 practices: meriah, suttee, thugee, (Hindu sanctioned murder and human sacrifice, mostly females) and India got an odd, sanctimonious upgrade in human rights. [24] Prior to these changes, daughters were occasionally sold or murdered and when a deceased husband was cremated, the wife threw herself on the funeral pyre because her financial support had been reincarnated elsewhere. The more the Indians negated self and sacrificed for others, the nobler and more sanctimonious you would be in the Hindu pecking order, although for males, pathnee ko maro (wife beating, or worse) remained common in India.

The new era (1858-1947) was called the "British Raj" which began a new reign of terror in Britain's crown jewel. As more died of heat, drought, and famines, Queen Victoria proudly became empress of India in 1876. There were no more major uprisings until the British massacred more protestors ("celebrators" as the Indians called them) in the city of Amritsar, as late as 1919. The death toll was 300-1000, nobody knows (Churchill buffs say 400-600 dead) and Churchill called the dead, "terrorists." The Indians *may* have been disguising an uprising with a celebration but that's not likely, as the jack-booted thugs (*thugee,* an Indian word) suffered no casualties and didn't count the spent shells, which was protocol—there were too many. That last slaughter paralleled another disaster when 5% of the Indian population died from the Spanish flu. After Amritsar, India's iconic spiritual leader Mahatma Gandhi, downgraded Britain to a "dark, satanic force," and ordered a boycott of anything British. Winston Churchill—a racist like most everybody of his day—told the Indians to "tighten their belts" while people were starving in Calcutta and the British soldiers were at the officer's club eating eggs and bacon.[25] WWII would change everything.

By 1942, the British army had folded in Ceylon (Singapore) and folded at the port of Tobruk (Benghazi, Libya). The Atlantic and the Mediterranean were swimming with beetles (U-Boats) and Churchill, who suffered from lifelong depression, felt that his soldiers had lost their fight. Even the British war gene was waning. The Indian Army was fighting side by side with the retreating British as the Japanese pushed their way from Vietnam to Malaya (now Malaysia) to Burma (now Myanmar), to the eastern door of India. FDR wanted Churchill to forget India and leave altogether but Churchill thought it too risky at the time. It might spur a Muslim/Hindu war during a global war, [26] or worse, leave Delhi for the Japanese.

My wife's father, Melville, an Indo Anglian, was a British Medic trying to put allied soldiers back together in Burma in 1942. Before he died in 2005, he told me about one soldier whose guts were spilled out on the wooden table, and with the morphine long spent, they sewed up every shrapnel hole they could find. It took all night to stop the bleeding and carefully put his entrails back where it seemed they had been. The soldier died a few hours later but it didn't matter because the field hospitals became murder wards as the bayonet Japanese, with more blitzkrieg (lightning war) than the Germans, easily swept through the Indian/British forces protecting Burma. The Burmese people were little help. The Japanese onslaught from Malaya to Burma was the most grotesque massacre of British and Indian soldiers ever, shot as they fled and the wounded bayonetted in hospital tents. They raped the nuns so we know they raped everybody and congressman Nehru was never more disgusted with his British occupiers after their string of defeats across Asia.[27]

Pushed back into India the soldiers regrouped and in 1944 annihilated 85,000 Japanese invaders in the city of Imphal.[28] The Japanese fought to the last man. The allies pushed the rest east of Burma which spelled the end of the Japanese expansion westward. Melville, wearing a British/Indian military uniform, lived to tell the tale but was never recognized as a veteran or paid by the British for his military service in WWII.

The generation after Mel went to the National Defense Academy in Puna, where the members of all military branches still train to become officers. Ironically Mel's son-in-law was named *Surinder* at birth and graduated #1 in his 1969 military class with the highest marks in English—the official language for the Indian armed forces. Mel's only son Lew graduated the same year with the highest marks in math. They both went on to be pilots and I know them well but had to pry this information out of them. They did offer that the mess halls (army cafeterias) were so bad they were always leery of a pea rolling off the table and injuring somebody. Lew would joke that Surender bought 2 pairs of the same military slacks so if he got a hole in one of them, he could patch it with the other.[29]

The British occupation was comparable to the length of the Spanish Inquisition but with many, many more needless deaths, according to historian Jacob Mchangama and others. In spite of Spain's imperialism and its long fondness for Russia, it gets a bad rap because we read history books in English. France was a better actor than Britain too and even the Ottoman Empire, minus the late genocides, simply exported religion without many economic strings.

A lawyer by trade, Gandhi didn't believe in an armed uprising thinking it would be "worse than a disease" so he chose "passive resistance." In and out of prison all his life, Gandhi threw a psychological spanner into the British trade machine which the

Russian and Eastern Bloc people would later use against communism: *they pretend to pay us, so we pretend to work.* Mohandas Karamchand (Gandhi's real name, Mahatma means *Saint*) was a book reader, learned civil disobedience from Henry David Thoreau, and stalled the British engine peacefully. The Indians working for the British sabotaged ship inventories, orchestrated work slow-downs in mass, and under Gandhi's post-WWII leadership India slow walked their way to independence in 1947. As the daylight shrunk around the last empire, I can't help but think of Mark Knopfler's words: "the sun's droppin' down in the bay and fallin' off the world."

Mahatma Gandhi was emaciated from fasting after a 6-year prison sentence—for speaking his own mind in his own country—when he was assassinated in 1948 by a group of Hindu nationals for *allowing* the partition.

The British had imprisoned the radical socialist Jawaharlal Nehru many a time before he first became Prime minister in 1945. He was from a long line of leaders. His original last name was Patel, very common, and there are countless families with the surnames Nehru, Patel, and Gandhi. Nehru was the father of Indira Gandhi and the grandfather of Sanjay Gandhi (no relation to Mahatma Gandhi) and Sanjay died in a single seat airplane in 1980 under suspicious circumstances. His mother Indira was assassinated in 1984 and Sanjay's brother Rajiv—the youngest prime minister from 1984-1989—was assassinated in 1991. It was a natural royalty like the Kennedys, with half the luck. This doesn't seem like the peace-loving India we know, but the turmoil had been simmering for a hundred years because the people were no longer free to work out their own differences. That talent was India's forte and Britain killed it.

There is hammer and sickle graffiti here and there in India. India is Marxist and Karl is remembered and admired there for his humanistic passions. Christopher Hitchens in his own books reveals the admirable side of Marx better than most. Marx rightfully hated the oppression and imperialism he saw, and though Nehru (the father of India) hated oppression too, he didn't eliminate it because imperialism begets Marxism. Though this is always unintended, the transition from imperialism to Marxism is a lateral shift and simply switches the oppressor from a foreign one to a domestic one.

India can't control or tax the millions of tiny businesses but when companies start growing, the government levies new taxes on them. We know a diamond broker in India and one day the Indian IRS burst into his office, took all of his computers, and left. He never saw the computers again and got a huge tax bill in the mail, based on how much money they thought he had, after he'd already paid his taxes. The only real tax revenue India can get is from strongarming rich people with arbitrary taxes, often made up on the spot.

In contrast, the larger a company is in the US the more money the US government lends them. Socialism isn't left or right anymore, it can mean almost any direction in which an economy is overdisciplined for the benefit of the controllers, and that's when socialism loses its luster, left or right. With this in mind, and with millions of small unregulated businesses in both India and America, each has about the same percentage of real, grassroots capitalism. It never crossed Marx's mind, or Nehru's, or most US president's minds for that matter, to leave the economy alone and let the middle class slowly reach affluence on their own.

I read *Hitch 22*, Christopher Hitchen's life story which ended way too soon, in 2011, when he died of esophageal cancer. He was a smoker-drinker and checked out at the apex of his intense writing and speaking career. Even with our philosophical differences, I admired him as a passionate, cussing, sarcastic wit, and honesty. Hitch's mother had an affair with a poet when she was about 50, flew off to Greece with this man, and they both committed suicide together in a hotel—that night. She had vanished for a few days and everybody was looking for her. Christopher learned about her death in the morning newspaper, and informed his retired, Navy Commander Dad—who was still married to her—that his wife Yvonne and her new boyfriend had both taken a bunch of sleeping pills. She had told Christopher when he was a teenager, "the one unforgivable sin is to be boring," and she lived by that as he did but maybe she was referencing her husband. There's a formal dress-up picture of baby Hitch with his parents in the book, and underneath he wrote, "with no previous qualifications, I became a member of the Church of England."

Arguably, the *people* of Britain didn't make a brass farthing from the trade with India. The products were for the clerisy and invited guests to enjoy exquisite linens, cardamom, coriander, the Kohinoor diamond, and a conversational cup of spiced tea while discussing a few orders of business on the docket. The killings required to manage Britain's vast enterprises were a bit dear but only a trifle unappetizing. Paid for with paper money, the Indians footed the bill for the royal indulgence by shouldering the inflation Britain exported to India. The population was so large, nobody noticed the inflation.

Paper money imperialism was a fascism the British employed almost worldwide which illuminates the philosophic solecisms of Karl Marx and Christopher Hitchens, referring to the British economic system as "capitalism." When the capital and trade is hoarded and managed by the government, that's fascism. It should have been managed by the people and the free market in both Britain and India, which brings us up to present day. India is copying what they learned from Britian and Karl Marx—ironically twins— and this monopolization of money causes high inflation in India which the people cannot afford.

The modern Prime Minister, Narendra Modi, suddenly got rid of 85% of India's cash, ostensibly to curb corruption and tax evasion, and the economy collapsed. He put it back into recirculation and defaulted back to deficit spending. With about 10-12% inflation yearly (they are usually told it is 6%) businesses must raise prices every year so the people hoard gold and are as suspicious now of government manipulation of money as

Americans were in the 19th century. If India still used silver, instead of what they call "stamped silver" (the paper rupee) the government couldn't manipulate money at all.

Liberty is preserved in India with 2 big caveats: insults are illegal and all the newspapers know not to get too far out of line. I was shocked to never read of a murder during the month I was there but their newspapers put a positive spin on everything. Two decades after my visits the Hindu Narendra Modi, who hates the 1/3rd Muslim minority, effectively ended democracy in India. He won't tolerate free speech so nobody really knows what the rules are. They trade quietly in small networks as the Russian people do, and like Putin, nobody likes Modi but he keeps getting re-elected. To protect himself, he is reverting all the way back to British rule, arresting journalists, jailing activists, controlling the internet, and changing what is written in books.[30] Modi's political opponent, Rahul Gandhi, was sentenced to 2 years in prison in 2019 for making fun of Modi's name. "He's a little Hitler," people we know say, "and he has people killed." Better than learning from TV, newspapers, or even books...listen to people. India is long overdue for a revolution in political theory, and marriage.

Arranged Marriage

Arranged marriages are the norm in India. Volitional gene mixing spreads smart genes faster and creates wealth too because everything evolves from the ground up, starting with mutual attraction, sexual trait selection, and ending with open, dynamic, free trade societies. In this section we will find out that these double oversights are holding back 2/3rds of the world.

Arrange marriage in India is so common that it is described by several researchers as *normal* to *up to 95%*. The 4 parents (the knot makers) have no idea how to match up the phenotypes of their teenagers, but the daughters know. Even the sons have a better intuition about marriage, so ignoring volitional genetic trait selection, i.e., not allowing sacrificial selfishness to work its wonders, is the unused philosophical vehicle slowing down India. Not only do they often shy away from economic free markets which would elevate the general wealth, but they avoid the free market of sex. As I laughingly told our daughter, "you have to test drive the car before you buy it." Visitors from India are now optimistically telling me prearranged marriages are down to about 50%.

China banned arranged marriage in 1950 but absurd laws and attempting to regulate family interfaces are even beyond the ambitions of communists. Any state could outlaw everything from unprotected sex to psychological blackmail and nothing would change. There is a shortage of young people in China (government birthing policies *can* be policed) and young women are rebelling against the pitfalls of sexism, arranged marriages, and stupid laws. If it doesn't lead to revolution, it's going to be an interesting mess but arranged marriages and fewer young people create 2 more problems: China will have to ship in labor for decades and keep stealing western technology. Love Children simply have better ideas and if that population rises in China, one of their new ideas will be revolution. The Chinese government knows this.

Arranged marriage in Korea is diminishing but still exceedingly common and some researchers estimate that 85% of the Koreans don't marry out of mutual attraction. This historical momentum is compounded with a genetic twist. Most East Asians have a variation of the gene ABCC11 which prevents them from having body odor (Ian Day, *et al*, 2013) whereas in western countries and Africa everybody has the odor—the smelly variation of the gene. You can't find deodorant in Korea and John H. McDonald found that the no smell gene goes back 2000 generations. Women must evaluate a man's phenotype by sight, if given the chance.

Another study concludes western countries have "love" marriages while Africa has "arranged" marriages.[31] Western marriages, with the liberty to choose partners promotes healthy competition and since *Love is a Battlefield*[32] Asians and North

Africans are less competitive people. Southern Africans (more westernized) are more competitive while the Ottoman North African women grow up sheltered from the stress of dating. In the west, we all know the trials and tribulations of dating and that necessary struggle, which we discuss with friends more than any other topic, is an education many miss.

The Quran doesn't say arranged marriage is required, however, Islamic females are given so few rights in the holy book, their conscription is assumed. North African women surely smell the immune system of a man and naturally know how to match it up with her own but must practice it on the sly to produce the occasional Love Child.

Latin American/Caribbean marriages are described as "child, early, and forced."[33] From socialist Mexico down to the southern tip of Simone Bolivar's poor South America, 30-40% of girls are children when they get married or get pregnant from an Hombre. "Watch your mouth," they are told when they talk like their husbands do. Notice something odd about this huge continent? Most everybody is poor. Inadvertently, to keep it poor they deny the invisible hand of personal choice in both marriage and economics. Akin to Stockholm Syndrome, this control must be ingrained early in life for it to work. As toddlers, females in South America learn that they don't own their own bodies and someone else is going to be planning their future, which lulls them into accepting a controlled economy too.

Many EU countries are now half socialist and still rich but every single area on the globe that has a history of arranged marriage plus a dictator is very poor. Arranged marriage may be as big a drag on economics as socialism is. After I noticed this, I found out Frederick Hayek came up with this theory in the 1940s. I was staggered by how arranged marriage hindered wealth as much or more as socialism did, and a little surprised that western countries going half socialist after WWII only slowed the growth of wealth. This is probably because capitalism and choice, so deeply rooted in Europe for so long, created a solid base for wealth.

The solution is simple: Asia, South America, North Africa, and the Stans of the Middle East, need more Romeos and Juliets, fewer people giving advice, and freer markets. We can see what makes a country rich with a glance: a history of capitalism and equal treatment under the law combined with a history of mutual consent marriages. This psychological and economic wealth will extend longevity too, regardless of geography, natural resources, or weather.

I asked people in Indian why China and India avoid each other and got no answers, as if it was something they'd accepted as a given long ago, as they are wont to do. Both countries have long practiced arranged marriage and have the least body hair on the planet but even with a few similarities the Indochina split goes back 40 thousand years, evidenced by the fact that the Chinese epicanthic fold never made it across the 2000-mile border into India. The languages don't intersect either—Hindi and Mandarin—however, the benign power of Buddhism broke through that barrier and almost took over China.

The biggest and longest invisible wall stopping intermarriage runs between China and India—1.5 billion people don't like 1.5 billion of their neighbors. Maybe the Chinese were too violent for the Indians, at least in the old days, but I don't think it was about Indians having darker skin and neither are the prejudices in the white orient. The Japanese feel superior to the Koreans who feel superior to the Chinese who feel superior to the Vietnamese.

When avoidances *are* about skin color it is a neurotic, apophenic reaction (making connections in our heads that have no counterpart in reality). Skin colors represent miniscule genetic differences but our prejudice eyes choose appearance over the other 99.99% of a person so we subliminally see "races" where there are none. With nature's priority on brain genes an artistic white man has more genetically in common with an artistic black man than he does with an unartistic white man, which is kind of what the fun Chapter 27 is about. My wife and I know many children who are half Indian/half American, including our own, and Indians say they look more American and vice versa. Neither are true because we evolved to notice differences. Nature didn't make races, we did.

Kind of on the same subject, my wife Jeanne is the best cook this side of the international dateline and she prepares food standing at the counter with one foot on top the other. Early in Jeanne's career at IBM she hosted an exotic dinner at our house with several big wigs and their wives. It was a formal 7-course Indian feast with white tablecloth and ironed, cloth napkins. As people were oohing and awing, one of the highly paid executives asked Jeanne "where did you learn to cook like this." She said, "my mom taught me when I was growing up in India." "India?" I said, "I thought you were from Indiana!" There wasn't a sound in the room. It was the politically correct 90s.

The Happy Gene

It's been about 1000 years since India invaded another country. Peaceful India does have 1 violent blemish on their record: 1000 years ago, they took the southern island of Ceylon, now called "Shri-Lanka." This was a Naval invasion by the Tamil's of India historians tell us and they were kicked out after a few decades but repeated the invasion in the 12th century, only to be repelled again, and Ceylon became a chiefly Buddhist country.

Coupled with the lack of violence, I can't stop thinking about a different happiness I saw in India. Like the American farm kids back in the 1920s, Indians have a charming shyness, having never become jaded, so they don't make the crucial, modern, American mistake of assuming their problems came from society. It perplexes me the poor people smile easily and have a happiness that is beyond materialism.

They coexist with the digital world while a cellphone problem makes westerners act as if their food supply has been cut off. The day-to-day Indians don't know the anxiety of always trying to live in the tech created future, they simply export kindness and humbleness as a good banana republic, and to them, it raises their GDP. They are happy with what they have instead of being unhappy with what they don't have, and they love who they have instead of loving somebody they don't have. When you visit a poor family, they aren't hurried or worried—transferring that feeling to you—and they always offer you food. They may sometimes put on a good face, but I saw happier poor people in India than I see in the much richer lower middle class in the US.

Instead of holding out their hand and saying "give it to me," the Indians say "show?" Instead of pointing, they extend an open hand and if you challenge them, they smile and say "touché," mocking you for pulling out your sword. With psychological tests Americans respond with how a situation will impact themselves and Indians respond with how a situation will affect their family and co-workers. I'm not judging either one, but I did make a strange observation: when 3 Asian people are hugging and celebrating they jump up and down in unison but when 3 westerners do it, they jump out of sync. Somehow Indians have gotten rid of their specialness and the more we in the US lose our own neurotic identity without replacing it with anything, the happier we'll get. I'm not advocating getting rid of our material possessions, I'm just suggesting we move then into 2nd place and put happiness first. I was a happy tourist, and interestingly different to them, so maybe it seemed a nicer place to me but that doesn't seem to work in many countries.

Total strangers in India who thought I was rich would give me nice pieces of art, offer me food and *beer*, and take me golfing. I'm a terrible golfer as they were but the difference is they didn't care. Salmon Rushdie says, "the reason Indians are taught sports is so they can learn how to lose." Buddhist meditation seems to have a snowball calming effect on India and those who go there.

They loved my American jokes and busted a gut as my Indian accent improved: "I cannot get a date, because I am roughly the size of a small church," I would say, making fun of myself and their accent. I got pretty good at their accent, and some would say, "who talks like that?" It turns out I wasn't so good. "Aiyo" or "Podar daiI," some would laughingly tell me in Tamil, meaning *get lost.* "Aiyo"—a proper English word now—is more polite and means *somebody screwed up a little bit* and if they think you're fibbing they'll say "you're telling stories out of school." I'm such an irksome jokester that after being introduced to one Indian lady I said, "I am pleased to meet your acquaintance." She didn't know I was an armchair comedian, so she skipped over my sarcasm and said, "hopefully it will be the beginning of a long friendship."

You don't need much money in low-cost India so during little negotiations you might hear, "cash or kind?" Some respond, "the cash kind," and some move their head side to side meaning *it doesn't matter. Kissing*, they refer to as "uptown shopping for downtown business," so some *are* shopping for those brain genes. If I hadn't known arranged marriage was prevalent in India I never would have guessed. Their forte is harmonious contradiction and taking everything at face value, or with a grain of salt, including evolution. Always staying cautiously neutral in the colorful middle, India is the Switzerland of the east and the paradox that is Buddha is the enigma that is India.

It's time to talk about how an ape became a human, so "I must be wenting" as they say in India.

CHAPTER 25

Well, I'll Be a Monkey's Uncle

Imagine the cocktail of gasses that make up our air happened to push the oxygen in our atmosphere down to only 3 feet above the ground. We would need to start crawling to breathe which would reverse the 10-million-year process of all our bones changing shape for vertical motion. Crawling for us would be as exhausting as it was for the first primate lineages to learn to walk upright. 8 billion people would go through hell, as the stand-up crocs did 66 mya, until we learned to comfortably crawl and run like a deer. This is how arduous it was to go from crawling to walking too, and illustrates how much walking meant to those enduring tribes who stood up and walked out of Africa to every corner of earth. After 6 million years, the upright walking knee still isn't strong enough.

In sports, Howard Cosell said, "it's the knee, always the knee." Walking and running are more difficult for women with wider pelvises because their thighs go in like a V down to the knee, which strains the medial (interior) part of the knee much more than the lateral (outer). Walking made all of our organs change too. With gravity at a new 90° angle, we evolved spongier spinal discs and millenniums of hearts had to learn how to pump blood at a different angle.

After evolving up from our knuckle-dragging pre-human cousins, we walked with our knees bent, butts sticking out, and still had a long prehensile tail for balance and grabbing branches. To this day we occasionally have to cut a human tail off. Research by Olivia Judson at the Imperial College of London tells us that grass only came along 80 mya, as mammals were getting bigger—convenient for hiding—and grass took over the planet as ape evolved into man. It was 10 mya when grass became tall and abundant. The first upright humans became periscopes for better hunting, defending, and reproducing. We hid behind it, ate it, slept in it, hafted weapons together with it, and smoked it. Smoking actually prevented some colds and some infections, kicking off the trillion-dollar smoking industry.

Scientists Whitcome, Lieberman, Shapiro, and others found that about 3 mya our spines had to make a Darwinian adjustment due to bigger brained babies. Our spines, especially female spines, went from straight to curvy. Guys like a *gal's* (as Jim would say) 3rd vertebrae from the bottom (L3) to be at a 45°angle, making her lower back dip in and her butt go out. Because the S shaped spine allowed more room for birthing, cave girls could often take care of the baby immediately.

Given the choice, a caveman would have chosen to fight another man with a club over giving birth and, still true, would rather have gone hunting than take care of a baby. How to give birth and raise a baby was at first driven by instinct. As cave people became foragers, the first human internet formed and woman learned how to help each other with birth and campfire living. No different than the silent economy is now, instead of trading weapons and shoes, they traded services. This required a more sophisticated communication because services are more abstract and conceptual than *things* are. To this day, women talk about people and men talk about stuff.

Male mental progress was restricted to making a stone-tipped spear, herding, and surrounding an animal, which didn't involve emotional complexity. Slaves struggle and hence evolve faster than slave masters so the *bass guitar players*, the women, were slowly setting the stage to take over the band. A million years later, brute force was maligned, intellectual parity became apparent, and now one teleological animal *can* see into the future, whereas evolution, in spite of my musings, can't.

Giving birth is still scary and if you were a barefoot cave girl fortunate to reach age 11 you were perhaps already pregnant. I use the word *girls* here because puberty came earlier, often induced by stress, and twins were more common too. Infant mortality might have been as sad as 50% and if 2 mothers died trying to give birth, 3 of the 4 deaths were female. Evolution didn't mind making females the sacrificial multipliers of males and making males die in war—it never found a way around either, until humans got smarter.

Our unique brains, pelvises, and spines set us a breed apart from the tree dwelling, color seeing, swimming chimpanzees but unlike most mammals, chimps have the exact same hemoglobin in their blood as humans do.[1] This makes both species vulnerable to malaria but removes hemophilia (non-stop bleeding) from both gene pools. The blood clotting chemistry was simply one of nature's random experiments which *happened* to extend the life of 51% or more of the chimps and humans. Chimps also have the same body temperature and blood pressure that humans do (most mammals do though). Most any land animal evolved a pressure at the skin surface to exactly counteract earth's atmospheric pressure, which we conveniently call "1 atmosphere." If you're healthy, your resting blood pressure added to the greater mechanical strength of your blood vessels = 1 atmosphere (14.7 psi).

Humans are 99% genetically the same as Chimpanzees (a great ape) but these same genes are in a different order, plus, they're not the same genes anymore. The way Robert Wright explains it, "the great apes are not, of course, our ancestors; all have evolved since their path diverged from ours."[2] Going back 6-million-years down the primate tree of evolution, we came from the ape branch but apes have a significantly smaller prefrontal cortex so the CEO part of their brain is much weaker.[3] Knowing we're not 3-year-olds, as chimps are, and knowing our neocortex is 3 times bigger tells us our brain genes have been slightly ramping up their game every generation for 6 million years. Astonishingly, scientists attribute it to 1 gene, ARGAP 11B, that expanded the human brain. This mutation is so unlikely they think 1 hominin got this missing link(?), made some Love Children, and the rest is history.[4] If that 1 gene had not survived, we might still be chimpanzees.

Researchers have found that the human brain is pound for pound far superior to any other primate brain. Homo erectus could process protein into energy more efficiently than monkeys could,[5] so the bigger pre-human brain, and the chemicals to make that energy available to the brain, far surpassed the power and efficiency of a monkey's brain about 1.9 mya.[6] It might be how Homo erectus thought its way through the massive damage from the Yellowstone super eruption. Apparently, cooking meat has great mental bonuses and Homo erectus, with a brain that evolved to twice the size of a chimpanzee's, cooked. Pre-humans were vegetarians, then scavengers, and 1 mya archeologists found evidence of campfires. Cooking meat evolved the bigger brains and the more efficient, smaller stomachs we have today.

Ragini Verma from the University of Pennsylvania made a deep dive into the differences in male and female brains. Men's left brains are denser while women's right brains are denser and this might be weird but I've noticed men tend to cock their heads to the left and women tend to cock their heads to the right. We know that female brains have more connections (the corpus callosum) between the 2 brain hemispheres than males. These connections allow women to change their mind easier as they shoot questions back and forth from left to right, equally weighing emotion and cognition to get a more balanced answer between the competing halves.

Because of this left-right thinking and the recent deselection of violence, females became better arguers than men. Now when there's a rare tie in an argument the *woman* is the tie breaker. It's hard to win an argument anyway without left to right thinking and straightforward thinking men see sideways thinking as a maddening distraction. When men feel their oats and *do* argue well for short periods, women will keep changing the subject—we all know they do—and that's to throw a wrench into the man's brain. The man gets dyslexic, then angry—he's not allowed to get angry anymore—and the women wins again. The next day, not completely satisfied, like Lucy she pulls the football away from Charlie Brown right before he kicks it, and that puts the cherry on top. The red flag is when there's no arguing at all, because that smells like Stockholm Syndrome to me, unless you're one of those 621 couples on earth who make a perfect fit.

Men's brains work better front to back, which is associated with sports, math, and measuring. This has another advantage: it allows men to disengage their minds when they sense that new information is clutter, or sleep better, while women cannot disengage as well. Women have more wrinkles in their gray matter, so have accumulated more knowledge, suggesting that having a 10% smaller brain than a man is not a disadvantage because women have made more neural connections per cubic millimeter. Still, this information tells us next to nothing about any individual we might meet.

The female sense of direction and perception of spacial relationships is not as ingrained in their DNA because they didn't hunt across vast landscapes. Today women have trouble using mirrors to back into a parking space (though it's easier than backing out of one) and this is because women can't reverse the mirrored picture in their minds as well as men, who think front to back. Ancient hunters had lots of practice, having to reverse the landscape in their minds to find their way back to the campfire.

Men are more predictable because evolution optimized them for fighting and sex. Other than being good big picture thinkers, that's the entirety of the male mystique—*have gun will travel*. The penis, for example, according to Dr Gordon Gallup and many others, is perfectly fashioned to scrape another man's sperm out before getting his in. This mushroom plunger, or *scooper*—

common in animals too—decreases the genetic choices of a female and increases the choices of a male. Scientists don't know when that big rim evolved but mutations usually start with 1 family. Nature came up with the perfect cockblock—evolution doesn't miss much—and the rim of the penis spread throughout the population because form follows function. It is still shaped that way, telling us monogamy is so new that evolution hasn't gotten around to changing it. Evolution has a "wait n see" preference.

Scientists Laura Tobias Gruss and Daniel Schmitt researched the evolution of the human pelvis. To cope with larger human brains and a new locomotion, the female pelvis had to suffer through more naturally selected changes than the male pelvis. Natural selection came up with a stronger narrower pelvis, and a bigger hole in the middle for birthing, similar to auto ads that claim their new car is smaller on the outside but bigger on the inside. Narrower hips helped dissipate heat too. Apes didn't need these pelvic changes because their method of locomotion and brains remained the same but as the human brain started gaining mass the pelvis had to adapt fast to deliver evolution's highest achievement—the new human brain.

Since no pelvis changes in one lifetime, there was a time when it was dangerous to have sex with a smart, big-brained man. Although a baby brain is ¼ the size of the adult brain, some female pelvic bone changes were do or die adaptations as many unlucky cave girls suffered horribly trying to give birth to a big brained baby through a smaller hole in the pelvis. The horrors of creative destruction were good for the tribe because they got rid of old genes. If evolution could talk, it would say, "it's been no bed of roses, no pleasure cruise.........but I ain't gonna lose."[7] The lucky females born with the bigger rounder hole in the pelvis, and their lucky daughters, jumped the human race to the next level of brain growth. The wide-faced, bigger brained Neanderthals had bigger pelvises with even bigger holes for birthing and may have had 12-month pregnancies.[8] Now that we have so many C-sections—yet another human invention that further widens the gap between us and the next smartest animal—will that sexy pelvis change again? It will but don't hold your breath because women born with pelvises not conducive to childbirth will not be deselected, because of caesarian sections.

In the book *Big Brain* by Lynch and Granger, they teach us about 2 other genes that changed the size of our brain over many millenniums: the FOXP2 gene expands brains, the ASPM gene shrinks them. [9] They write about the Boskop humans—killed off only 10 thousand years ago in South Africa—who had a brain 25% larger than ours and surmise they had 15-25% higher IQs. Unlike Neanderthals, Boskops were a little taller than us, skinnier, and bigger brained (protruding back skull) but the hole in the female pelvis may not have grown as fast as the brain did. C-sections might have saved them. A Cro-Magnon female, after one look, surely wouldn't want to mate with a Boskop. Imagine our female ancestors from only 500 generations ago seeing men in the distance through the foliage with a head some say was 50% larger than theirs. They instantly did the math as the blood in their veins turned to ice water. They probably held up their thumb and forefinger and whispered, "I am crushing your head,"[10] as they quietly slunk away. Conversely, a Cro-Magnon would occasionally run into a fairly reasonable person who was 2.5′ tall with a head the size of a cantaloupe.

A Chihuahua can weigh 1 pound and the largest dog can weigh 200 pounds. I always wondered, if say, a man is going to be 6′ 6″ tall when he grows up, how does his DNA know to elongate all of his body parts? Well, nature has an *app* for that—the Hox gene. We have a little assistant CEO called a "body plan gene"[11] and it lengthens all the organs commensurately as well as fitting the skull to the size of the brain, like a peanut shell fits a peanut. Conversely, as our jaws shrunk so did our teeth. The Hox gene "talks" to all the genes—it has all their cellphone numbers—exchanging more crucial information than the entire internet to build a person.

When a species is highly evolved, it has a bone structure that's suitable for its environment; every bone has near perfect tensile strength, compression strength, and shear strength for however fast that animal needs to move, without breaking. This trial-and-error *design* is eons better than if the most brilliant engineers burnt the midnight oil to design your frame. The engineers might have greatly thickened the knee joint after we came down from that tree though, while evolution didn't. But alas, those engineers would have killed off the human race by making all bones the same. We need as much variation as possible so that some will always survive nature's peculiarities. Darwin's axiom of adaptation tells us why we are still walking around: if our brains were all created equal, no one would have created fire or spears and we'd have all gone down in the same ship.

Anti-Darwinian scientists call the phenomenon of all body parts working well together "irreducible complexity" meaning that all of our organs—or even the parts of a living cell—work so well together they must have been intelligently designed. How *did* animals evolve with all the parts perfectly synchronizing? Well, they didn't. Over evolutionary time many of our body parts did not work well together leading to countless extinctions and since we stood upright, we've had numerous problems with our backs, knees, and muscles. This intelligent designer made a good 4-legged walker and a bad 2-legged walker? Not really, species slowly improved their own lineages as fast as evolution would permit and most of them did not survive. There were so many species of crocodiles and humans and only one of each made it.

A better argument for irreducible complexity is this: how did opposite sexual organs evolve *simultaneously and separately* in 2 different tiny creatures in the first place and end up working so well? At first glance it appears that evolution built the penis first and designed a man around that but it was a long process involving random mutations because the living genome is ultra-flexible and creative. Some animals grow genitals in different places, some have both sets of genitals, some species are all the same sex, and some have genes that turn limbs into penises (octopus).

Martin Cohn of the Howard Hughes Medical Institute found that nature makes random tubercles—experiments that *stick out*, or do the opposite—and a few microscopic organisms were able to mate. Brains and genitals evolve fast, are unendingly varied, i.e., divergent (go off on tangents) and over vast periods of time some fortuitously become convergent (happen to fit each other). We don't see all those mutations that were unsuitable because they're not walking around anymore, creating the illusion of intelligent design.

CHAPTER 26

Lamarck, Scerri & Quammen

Jean-Baptist Lamarck

I'm going to take another long walk off a short pier and talk about the deist Lamarck and his pre-Darwinian attempts to understand evolution. He isn't out of the picture yet; he might have missed something about our free will: volitional trait selection. Evolutionary scientists who've been questioning Lamarck's conclusions for 200 years are cringing right now because Lamarck's theory, using giraffes, is that a giraffe can acquire new physical characteristics during his lifetime. Let's say it's a male giraffe, and he can somehow pass on these acquired traits to his children too. With rare exceptions, we now know that after his birth, the genes he may pass on are already set in his stones.[1] Lamarck's theory might just need a cherry on top if my theory of learning selection is right, which is part and parcel to Darwin's natural selection with an emphasis on will.

Lamarck contended that if a papa giraffe stands on his hind legs and stretches his neck to eat a tasty clump of tree leaves way up there, he acquires a longer neck and a better reach during his own lifetime. And, he could pass that trait on. As science marched on, Darwin somehow thought (knew), long before the discovery of the double helix, that the giraffe couldn't pass on that acquired characteristic because his biological traits were fixed at birth inside his unchanging sperm cells. But there's another step that doesn't involve genes. The gentle giant cannot pass down his *acquired characteristics* but his daughter can! Let's call her "Whiplash."

Whiplash *saw* her father reaching high into the trees and eating the thicker leaves way up there. After that observation, she *raised* her sights a notch, and looked horizontally across the tower of giraffes, for a young, tall, male giraffe who smelled good. Most female giraffes didn't have the freedom to accomplish this, however, evolution can't stop the mind and Whiplash showed her new boyfriend how to stretch his neck, knowing he could reach further than she could. She saw her dad's acquired characteristic, taught them to him, and created a new potential. She schemed to pass that trait **through her mind**—using learning selection and teaching selection—into some unsuspecting young male giraffe's mind, and hopefully into her calves. Whiplash seduced him right there. "And if you've learned your lesson well, there's little more for her to tell.......one last caress, it's time to dress, for fall."[2] Consciously she passed on an acquired trait. We have to learn one or steal one before we can teach it.

With the dirty deed done dirt cheap and the big job just starting, her kids have a great chance of getting the characteristic of height and the acquired characteristic of stretch. This *teleological* female giraffe took quite a circuitous route, and the only one available, knowing it would keep her teenagers fed.

In 2018, scientists from Oxford (Britain again) led by Eleanor Scerri, tell us that Mitochondrial Eve from 200,000 years ago is everybody's mom—only 13,000 generations ago—because we are all specifically related to her. Eve was a combination of populations from every corner of Africa but Eve did have reliable sequences of Cro-Magnon DNA.[3] Scientists mark a place in the what is now the Kalahari Desert where Mitochondrial Eve lived, when it was lush and green. I believe when Eve acquired complex speech (delicate manipulations of the tongue) and spread that gene, the melting pot of Africa simmered down into a genetic goldmine. One and the same, great genes equals sexy to humans, so her DNA would have made Mitochondrial Eve smart and beautiful in the eyes of men. Keats said, "beauty is truth, truth is beauty," and natural selection is *that* beautiful, decisive accident.

Chromosome

Let's go back much further. What came first, the chicken or the egg? Well, it all started with this single celled character—a lowly bacteria cell—who to this day, reflexes to avoid what we call pain. It's like poking the Pillsbury Dough Boy.

Humans are made of trillions of 1-celled organisms but over billions of years, 33 trillion cells have joined forces. As with a beehive full of bees our cells became altruistic[4] and cooperated to form a contiguous orchestral miracle of unimaginable potential. We also know our mitochondria DNA—all from mom—comes from 1-celled creatures because they are still circular shaped with double helixes wrapped around each one having been born engulfed by a membrane in an eukaryota cell. This was our humble beginning.

When we say "DNA" we are talking about 2 separate areas inside a cell. Mitochondrial DNA (an energy factory made of only 37 genes) is in a different part of the cell than the linear shaped X and Y chromosomes in the nucleus. Of course, men too can transfer their DNA but our other DNA, the mitochondrial genes, are almost always transferred by females, hence the name of our ancient mom. That said, scientists discovered a family in Germany and the sons have passed on a whopping 76% of their mitochondrial genes. There was probably a Chimera Child back in their lineage and evolution allows every random experiment to proceed until there proves no adaptive advantage.

When the mitochondrial genes in a cell (the oval shapes)

express proteins (RNA, enzymes) these permeate into the nucleus or double helix area (the X and Y genes) and the gene enabled proteins in the nucleus also permeate into the mitochondria area. At that point the mitochondria and the nucleus are "talking" to each other. Many genes are unused bits of genetic information that nature, or you, might use later.

Think of an embryo as the builder of a sprawling mansion and it employs 2 communicating management teams to build this structure. Each team, the mitochondria and the nucleus, is responsible for millions of decisions delegated to thousands of separate contractors (genes) and the vast majority of the genes do exactly what they are told. Information is exchanged, orders are carried out, and the disobeying rogue genes mutate and change you beyond your parents. Maybe your mansion will have more windows than planned (a *variant* few get) or almost no windows (a disadvantageous mutation?). If violent storms erupt then having no windows will become the variant and too many windows will become a disadvantage.

For a 2nd analogy, imagine a gene is a car. You have 40,000 cars in your garage, 20,000 from each parent, and the matching alleles are slightly different. For instance, 2 matching genes are blue Toyota Camrys, 1 from each parent, but one of them has better cameras and the other has better brakes. Nature usually picks the best one for us to use depending on the environment it thinks we'll be born into. However, nature lets us use all the cars at different times throughout our lives as things change or when we see fit. Epigenetics is the vast, new study of how, if, when, and why, we use any particular gene and these include the automatic genes, the mutations, and the genes we volitionally call to duty.

Free will and transgenerational epigenetic inheritance is how humans have become continuously smarter for a million years. The main catalyst is the individual and the 2nd catalyst is that most of us are not marrying a 3rd cousin, but maybe a 33,000th cousin.

Before conception occurs, the egg and sperm cells have a lot of work to do inside. The DNA is originally a mess of unraveling tangled string and the little elves working inside do the worst last-minute work—snipping, moving helixes, mending—to organize the mess (exactly what we do with our lives later). The elves make a pretty good human most every time. To astronomically illustrate the big picture, you can look at your tiny set of genes as if a swirl of gas and dust created an entire galaxy around itself.

For a 3rd and final analogy imagine you were born into a peaceful village and just happened to be very resilient to stress. You didn't overreact and your fun-loving tribe thought you were a little strange, detached, cold. After 10 years of peaceful living, suddenly things get stressful—war, financial collapse, infighting—and most villagers can't wrap their minds around it and are having emotional heart attacks. Your cooler tolerance for stress and the few who have your same gene—the bass guitar players—can assess the situation and fix it. This is why we like the live and let live dreamers in the good times and the nickel-backed heroes in the hard times. As author Ruchir Sharma says, "when things are going great, we vote left and when things are not, we vote right,"[5] or something close to that.

Fantastic Voyage into The Chromosome

According to Dr Sharon Moalem, females were always genetically stronger though because they have an extra full chromosome (46 as opposed to a man's 45½) to fight back against most diseases or even wounds.[6] We can guess nature selected this slight advantage because giving birth is so wounding. Let's get up close and personal with those ultra-microscopic chromosomes that is preparing to build us.

Think of getting into a nano-sized submarine—you are a sailor in the sub and even more microscopic than it is—and travelling through the blood stream of a human like in the old movie *Fantastic Voyage*. Pretend you are going back in time and inspecting your own fertilized egg inside your mother where so many life choices have already been made for you. The die has been cast but you will have opportunities outside of that predestination and the more you exercise them the more choices you'll get.

You move in closer to your fertilized egg and see a bunch of little X and O shapes inside, each much bigger than your submarine. You have 23 pairs of chromosomes—46 Xs, or 45 Xs and 1 Y, if you're a boy, and that Y has less than half the DNA the extra X contains, that a girl gets. Girls get about 2% more DNA than a boy (1/46th more approx.) which has been multiplying with compound interest for millions of years and this is how women finally surpassed men. With the silent economy (women) being almost as large as GDP and women permeating the money economy from every angle too, women are going to be running the world sooner than later.

Anyway, imagine that your tiny submarine permeates into a cell and floats up to 1 of the giant X chromosomes. Imagine twisting 2 fishing lines around each other and wrapping that twist many times around a tire wrench, which is shaped like a big X. That's what a chromosome looks like. As you get closer you see that the twisted strings of double helixes contain cross sections. These are the genes, or the rungs, holding the twisted ladder together.

Your submarine inches nearer. To you, your chromosome is an overwhelming complex built by microscopic super-intelligent aliens over eons and you might be right. You can now see single genes connecting those now thick, twisted cables—thousands of rungs inside a spiral ladder—each rung about the size of your body. Each rung has 4 genes in a row AT CG; a Tootsie Roll with 4 sections. The A and T bond together best, as do the C and G, so when the strand splits lengthwise to make you, it breaks easily down the middle between T and C.

At the 4 ends of an entire twisted strand of your double helix there are caps called "telomeres." This protective cap—like the metal clasp on the end of a rope—can weaken or become shorter due to stress, violence, or a bad diet. Bad things happen to good people and this will eventually transfer to other chromosomes and maybe every cell in your body. After telomeres are damaged the genes fray like a scissored rope which can speed up cancer.[7] You can run your hands over the frayed, damaged chromosome and wonder if one of your parents was abused or had lost a parent early in life.

Most of the gene pairs (competing alleles) are healthy but nature sometimes gives you the weaker of the newly paired-up genes. Think of having 2 copies of the same key, one better than the other, and nature puts the bad one in the lock first, can't get it out, and the good key never has a chance to go in and unlock the door. Nature isn't perfect and often falters into negative selection but it picks the better of 2 genes more often, making each generation better. Unconsciously we know nature does this so we speed it up by acquiring good traits from our parents.

That lonely Y chromosome delineates men from women. The Y is coded for sperm, greater height, more strength, bigger feet and hands, deeper set eyes, more selfishness, and an anti-depression gene. With no matching genes connected to the Y, a male may have to live with a few weak genes. He won't be able to listen to 2 conversations at once and will probably be a spastic at emotionally rescuing people, whereas a female can do both because her matching genes usually contain these skills. With all the other chromosomes, males do have choices. An inherited tendency to be mentally robust or too sensitive depend on which gene of each pair nature picked for you, or, which one you picked later. You might get lucky with your 100 mutations so those glitches in the matrix give you unique perspectives that strangers will see and learn, and by doing so, you might change *their* genes a bit. And if they are young, they might even get those options into their children's DNA.

Getting back to your submarine voyage, as you look at 1 side of an X double helix—half of a railroad track twisting into infinity—you probably got those 3000 genes in 1 shipment from 1 parent. You might be using your entire limbic system from your mom genes and your leg genes from your father. As you grow you can occasionally default to the other side of the X strand and change which genes you use. Scientist are just beginning to understand this field called "epigenetics."

Can you imagine floating up to this magnificent, sprawling structure for the first time—a factory full of inner working parts—and not knowing it was there? Your first thought might be, "take me to your leader," but this well-oiled manufacturing plant, that never makes 2 of anything, has no supervisor. Now we know a little about how Watson and Crick felt when they discovered the double-helix that day in 1953, 2 years before Albert Einstein died. Mileva Marić, his wife, lived 35 years past him.

We are but 92% Human

My hair stood on end when I read David Quammen's book, *The Tangled Tree,* as he explained how foreign 1-celled organisms and viruses create new human traits. Our symbiotic relationship with bacteria in and out of our bodies changes us but a tiny living thing that intrudes our sperm or egg cells (gametes) can change our children and change the future of human DNA.

All life, so similar, came from a single 1-celled bacteria that formed 3.5 billion years ago. They say "a" bacterium because molecular biologists (Starvin' Darwins) think it only happened once! I find that hard to believe but it's twice as hard to believe that it happened twice. I named this first cell *Adam* and Adam had to eat but there weren't any other living things to eat—only amino acids, lipids, sugars, and simple nonorganic molecules, free-floating in the primordial soup. Adam was bound to happen with an infinite mix of chemicals but a better explanation for Adam is that we don't have the foggiest idea how he got here. We'll find bacteria creation wide, strewn about by icy comets. These stowaways probably evolved shortly after the big bang 14 billion years ago and now populate the Goldilocks Zones throughout the universe, mostly on the *rare earths.*

It wasn't 6000 years ago when time started, it was 14 billion years ago when all atomic clocks started. Universes come and go, and everything is "just a *matter* of time," the Einsteins might say. On earth, it would be 11 eons after the big bang when Adam crashed or formed here, and evolved into a plant or an animal. The first 1-celled bacteria were creatures called "protists" (not good enough to be plant, animal, fungi, or even male or female) and these creatures would next spawn archaea, and 3rd, evolve into eukaryota, from which all plants/animals originated. Only then did earth get male and female plants and animals.

David Quammen in *The Tangled Tree* tells us that only in 1977 did Dr Carl Woese discover the billions year old but previously unknown 1-celled lifeform he named "archaea." Archaea was the 2nd step in all of evolution and a crucial find because we are more related to archaea than bacteria. Not only did humans get our original genetic material from bacteria, archaea, and eukaryote but we acquired more DNA from viruses via Horizontal Gene Transfer (HGT). The egg is usually more prone to infection than the sperm is but some infections will invade any gamete. If that gamete happens to get fertilized, the baby will be born with some virus DNA. This is the shocker that made my hair stand on end: we are more than just our parent's genes.

Every selfish living thing wants to join with a healthy host to help its genes live forever—find the Holy Grail—and living pathogens are no different. Good or bad, some viral and bacterial lifeforms have lived through the attack from our immune systems and changed the entire human race. Over evolutionary time, 7-8% of our collective gene pool came from the invasion of the body snatchers! Was this the start of Chimera Children? After we killed off all of our human cousins, bacteria and viruses are our only source for new DNA so if the earth gets too hot or too cold, for example, we need these foreign invaders to help some humans adapt quickly.

The body plan gene must be a nice master planner because a baby isn't born resembling a virus but the virus does add sneaky attributes to a new human, because it's alive. Envelope viruses rarely occur naturally and have a spike protein that sticks out from the surface which is the key that allows it to invade a gamete cell.

As they do now, reptiles laid eggs 200 mya, leaving caviar laying around everywhere. Much of that got eaten, so evolution—accidentally on purpose—used one of these very rare envelope viruses to biologically change reptiles and keep the eggs inside protected from predators. To illuminate how great these body snatching viruses are, the invading envelope virus that created the uterine incubation sack in one female reptile turned her lineage into the first animals born alive. This transformation, reptile to mammal, was the most spectacular turn in evolutionary history.

CHAPTER 27

I Got 50¢ More than I'm Gonna Keep

The Miracle of Rock and Roll

When I was 13 Jim and Edith bought me a clock radio from Radio Shack and showed me how to wake up at 7:30am—a gene I never got and haven't acquired since. I dialed it to the radio station that sounded best. From this tiny $5 box leaped Marvin Gaye, Carl Perkins, Chuck Berry, Diana Ross and the Supremes, *Gonna Be a Showdown* by Archie Bell and the Dregs, and *Stand!* by Sly and the Family Stone—I found my radio station. I heard Smoky Robinson's *My Guy,* sung by Mary Wells, which he later turned into another hit for himself, *My Girl,* and I slowly started realizing where the Beatles got their inspiration.

The evolution of art directly reflects, or sometimes leads, our psychological evolution north and the unlikely blend of 2 different music styles, classical and African American, did both. And this new music species evolved to be greater than the sum of its parts. When we find a better culture, we adopt it but American music wasn't exactly what black Americans had in mind. They thirsted for their own individual identity and headed for *higher ground*. It didn't take long: they dubiously listened to western music and each decided to evolve it without having a meeting about it.

Creating art—creating great music that people love—is one of the most advanced and difficult endeavors of the human brain. I think the African American musicians outdid the British musicians who had thousands of years of classical music and literature in their DNA. Even more startling is that black musicians came up with a genre that didn't exist and something consumers didn't know they wanted. This time, it was young white people who heard a new culture and in spite of their parents they slowly adopted it, one emotional art lover at a time.

It's much more common for black Americans to make millions in business or athletics than with music but it's not as fun to write about. Plus, I love music as much as philosophy and as we have seen, the 2 are inseparable. Until the 2nd half of the 20th century, African Americans weren't allowed to do anything except entry level labor anyway so only after 300 years were they in position to grasp the capitalist economy. Besides doing the menial work needed in the white neighborhoods (no whistling!) they were kept out of sight and afterhours black people dove into music behind closed doors—for fun. *White America*[1] didn't mind what a man did inside his own castle.

In the roaring 20s the only economy they *could* create was music and they got swing and jazz right on their first try without being told how to do it. They ripped past the whole industry with no help and set in place an unmovable, invisible historical marker. No one could have predicted this percussive, sexy, anti-melodic, even bloody revolution that erupted from an unnoticed slow country boil in the Mississippi delta and swept the US, then the planet. Musicians like Robert Johnson, W.C. Handy, and Muddy Waters, innovators of this strange music, changed the whole world from the banks of those Huck Fin muddy waters. The delta region of Mississippi was a zeitgeist with a capital Z and almost every single early blues musician was born there.

We didn't try to wipe each other out as the US and the Native Americans had, we voluntarily segregated, and black music then integrated the US more than the military did. Black people got tired of bowing, smiling, and dropping grapes in people's mouths. They had loftier plans, and thank God they couldn't afford music lessons—that would have slowed the revolution down. The black music revolution exemplifies Einstein's best idea, "imagination is more important than knowledge."

Unlike the trained classical composers, who were taught that some notes were *wrong*, black musicians played by ear which can't be taught and thankfully they never learned about the wrong notes. Charlie *Yardbird* Parker ignored written music and his enviably intricate melodies, which surpassed the learned composers, were based simply around chord structure. "Don't play the sax, let the sax play you," he said, giving his music an unconscious polarity.

The renaissance sprang from emotion and the subconscious, not the calculating mind. The cognitive part fell neatly into place after the emotional brain had done the composing. It began with blues music which simply had a more high-minded, frivolous nature, and survival value because it reduced stress. That's what art is for anyway and they improved on happiness by greatly enhancing the aesthetic side of life. Frivolity is a top prerequisite for identifying high intelligence and it led these underdogs to write not only better music and better lyrics but write the most heartwarming rags to riches story of America the beautiful.

Nobody can pinpoint the origin of the blues but Gerhard Kubik's research places it in Africa. It sounds like the rhythms and emotions of Africa blended with the over-disciplined melodic western scale and a new sound popped out. From what I've read about the foragers in Africa it would be safe to say they loved rituals, dancing, drums, and sometimes the religious celebration went on all night. They invented the concept of the *show must go on* around the campfire, and everybody had a blast. I can almost hear them singing, "celebrate good times, come on,"[2]—a song born from religion too. They had an appetite for fun—cloaked guiltlessly inside religion—and they used their free time quite creatively which is a frivolity that has always attracted females.

In the New World, Africans sang peculiar songs in their own languages while working in the fields and intermarried with Native American neophytes. East met west for the 3rd time. At night they would toy with their owner's old, out of tune guitars. Not knowing they were inventing string theory, they slapped at it, drummed on it, and turned "this here guitar," as George Benson sings, into a different instrument. Without changing the instruments themselves, they changed the sound of every musical instrument they got their hands on. We can go to New Orleans, the birth of jazz, and still hear this stuff live, with the string bass slappin' behind the clarinets—the best sound I've ever heard sitting in a joint.

Wikipedia and other reliable sites tell the 1955 story of Elle Fitzgerald's arrest in her Texas dressing room along with Dizzy Gillespie for singing to an integrated audience. Ella was always drug free and the cops didn't know what to do so they changed the charge to gambling or "shooting dice." The confused cops were grasping at straws and asking for her autograph at the same time. They had acquired Lima Syndrome (guilt from giving the musicians Stockholm Syndrome) and after Ella and Dizzy posted a $10 bail, they let them out to go back and do the 2nd set. Ella's mistreatment was minor compared to what they did to Billie Holiday and by the late 50s the whole world was watching on TV.

After the blues, African Americans were the main inventors of swing, ragtime, jazz, rock and roll, soul, funk, rhythm and blues, hip-hop and rap (everything but classical, gospel, pop, folk, and country music). Christian America fought "race music," didn't understand it, jailed it, murdered it, and still failed miserably to even slow it down because when we ban something, we promote it. The canary (Blues and Rock) flew out of the coal mine and spread around the world at the speed of sound. Some of my 1960s white friends would give blood then take the $3 to K-Mart and buy the new Motown album.

Has there ever been another time when the poorest of the poor changed the richest country in the world? Imagine, if you will, that most of the great American paintings of the 20th century were painted by Oriental people who migrated here from China, or were brought here for railroad labor. What if we kidnapped Orientals, worked them like slaves, and they later became the best painters in the world? It would be unexplainable—a shocking statistic—and as shocking as the blues revolution was in real life.

100 years *after* the "Emancipation Procrastination" (as musician Christian Scott calls it) America recognized in the early 1960s that black people had all the basic individual rights, on paper at least. That was a long wait—4 generations—for their voting rights to be enforced by the federal government and in 1964 many southern blacks cast their first ballot. 100 years after the 13th Amendment had banned involuntary servitude and the 14th made those born in the US, citizens, black people were starting to feel free to move about the cabin. At that historical point, there occurred an odd twist: the government began thinking of black people's rights as *group rights*, as if they all thought the same way.

Since all individual freedoms had already been granted, the Civil Rights Act of 1964 was largely for show and as historian Eric Foner put it: "The new movement did not need a constitution; it needed the existing one enforced." [3] The federal government skipped over the individual rights of African Americans and replaced them with group rights because those were easier to manage. What's wrong with group rights? It holds the black community and the white community hostage and thinking of themselves as opposing groups instead of individuals who each think differently. It was a crime to stop an individual citizen from voting and the federal government didn't want to prosecute and sentence officials in certain states for the crimes, which would have solved the problem quickly.

Another dilemma in our thinking and in our laws is the conundrum that we can make discrimination illegal. The well-intentioned 1875 Civil Rights Law outlawed certain forms of discrimination and was struck down by the supreme court. This is a tricky point. The court realized that a law must apply equally to all people and not just to certain groups, so a law must either outlaw all of our dislikes or none of them. There are so many forms of bias they cannot be legislated without indicting everybody. The 1964 Civil Rights Act however was *not* struck down when it outlawed discrimination on the grounds of race, color, creed, sex, age, and national origin. After the act was passed, I asked myself, "would it still be OK to discriminate against short people, fat people, and stupid people?" Those and countless other groups weren't included in any of the protections. In hiring we discriminate by age all the time and simply make sure never to enunciate it. When I'm in a hurry at the grocery store, I pick the youngest cashier. With the hiring quotas that followed from the 1964 act, companies were forced to hire people *because of* color which was ostensibly illegal *because of* the very wording of the 1964 act. It had specifically outlawed discrimination by color in hiring. This is quite a dilemma for a well-intentioned law to be in.

As ugly as this sounds, we can't outlaw likes and dislikes without removing free speech and other freedoms from the millions of ways in which we interact. Instead, the government should start by cleaning up the justice system. 1st, they should empty the prisons of everyone who was arrested for possessing small amounts of drugs, if there was no violence involved. 2nd, they should dig into the records of judges on the bench and if the judges give black offenders more jailtime than white offenders for the same crime, the judges should be prosecuted for not upholding equal rights under the law.

Just as we made the unphilosophical switch from individual rights to group rights, the wheels started coming off again with LBJ's war on poverty, the unintended displacement of black fathers, and drugs. The last wheel fell off when a disproportionate number of black soldiers got their 2nd and last plane ride from Vietnam to Arlington, and in 1971 the sensitive Marvin Gaye asked "*What's Goin On*?" None of this slowed down black music, in fact, it kept getting better, even in the 70s. They kept pushing the envelope and today are still trying to resurrect their individual rights with help from the best comedians who say everything they're not supposed to say. They might save us all, including themselves, by bombarding Uncle Sam with reminders that in no way does he govern our sarcasm, our speech, or our individual likes and dislikes.

They Took the Classical Scale and Put Sup'm on It

All musicians have the advantage of standing atop a history of music and Pythagoras from 500 BC Greece was no exception having been a decent piano player himself. But he tackled a different task—the science of music. He finetuned the classical scale (often called the "natural" scale) by defining the frequencies of each note, and, by figuring out the physics of sound Pythagoras standardized it to our ears. Every note in do, re, mi, fa, and *so* on, has a different frequency (wavelength). These are in mathematical ratios of 2 or 3 from each other and it doesn't matter if the instrument is not tuned exactly to the note A (440 vibrations per second) because most of us don't know if a piano is a little flat or a little sharp. As long as the vibrations are separated into perfect ratios it sounds good, unless you are one of those rare people with perfect pitch, like the iconic bass guitar player James Jamerson Jr. With A 440 stored in his brain, he was the musician's musician who took us from the old stand-up bass days (no frets) to the electric bass guitar era (with frets). Rare is the person who can hum perfect pitch without hearing the tuning fork first and rarer yet is the person who can hum A 440 just after hearing a song in the key of A♭. They don't get that from nature and nurture, they learn it.

The blues introduced *wrong notes* (notes not often used in the classical scale) that were noticed by composers and listeners alike. The founders of the blues didn't go for the sadness of the minor scale as we might think, instead, they transformed the classical major scale into an *edgier* major scale with the 7th note flatted. This was their first wrong note on their way to inventing rock and roll.

The tonic chord (the resolving chord) rarely included the 7th note (B♭ in the key of C for example) until the blues sprouted, giving the old 3-chord progression a tense edge. Historically, flatting the 7th was only used in the 5th chord, for resolving, but black writers started songs and ended songs with the tonic chord and the 7th thrown in—like ending a song with a question mark. It worked so well live that the Beatles and Stones copied it.

Who else but non-conformists would create new harmonies knowing our ears would accept it just because they liked it? Next, in the key of C for example, blues composers routinely flatted the 3rd note which became E♭. A telling example is the song *Runaround Sue* by Dion. In the break, this white band sings: "she goes…*out* with other guys now," and when he sings the word "out" you'd think he'd sing the note E because the song is in the key of C, however, Dion sings E♭! 25 years earlier he would have sung E natural but the blues influence showed him how to emotionally spice up the words with a new half step.

Black composers played around frivolously with the 3rd note of the scale, slurred it back and forth a half step, and made the guitar cry, knowing to stay a spec flat instead of a bit sharp. Black guitarists brought back the previously unpopular pentatonic scale too, with no half steps at all, and considering how well it fits the guitar and how rarely it was used prior, they brought it back to life. Jimmy Page would know.

The old classical scale now had 2 wrong notes zinging from our radios while the radical pianist Thelonious Monk was saying "wrong notes don't exist," and proving it. Taking the que, black jazz musicians made 3 other wrong notes popular by flatting the 5th, the 6th, and the 9th, of the major scale. With 5 wrong notes and no notes left to flatten, the millennials old classical scale no longer resembled itself and white America couldn't get enough of it.

Those "wrong notes" were always used sparingly throughout history as transitions but rarely used as the melodic motive. The old classical scale had 2 beautiful half step transitions already inside and black composers added 5 more half steps which were sexier than the original 2. They even shied away from the original 2 half steps. The late jazz great Wayne Shorter went much further and became the king of the wrong note.

You can't lose your concentration for a second when playing jazz, on any instrument, and with so many men having attention deficit disorder, jazz is a miracle. More likely, attention deficit disorder is another mass misdiagnosis by academia and men just aren't interested in half the crap they try to teach us.

The Psychology of Blues Lyrics

Coincidentally, when black musicians were coming up with the blues because they had the blues, this was long *before* German psychologists diagnosed depression, as a loss of something precious. Depression was considered demonic prior to the Germans. Many hear the blues as depressing because it doesn't have fake happiness in it, so at first, the blues was misunderstood. The blues was more of a *release* from tension and depression, like a little nightmare relived while awake, which was crucial for health because of the generationally passed down stress imposed upon slave lineages. Black musicians sang blatantly about the day of the breakup, drugs, and how they were treated at work. The words were so moving it woke up white America's own Stockholm Syndrome, exposing the cultural blind spot: emotions and anxieties were the same everywhere.

This united victims of sexism and racism and the white girls found therapy in the blues—finally songs were *about* their real lives instead of glorifying their fake, pedestalled lives. This infuriated white parents who then blamed the blues for the *downfall* of many a white girl. Rock and roll unzipped many a girl's "party dress," as Elvis Costello sings, and Eminem wrote: "*White America,* I could be one of your kids." As one of my black friends told me, "don't tell your daughter not to date black guys because when you make her mad, that's what she'll do next." By the way, he hadn't told me that yet when we were at a neighbor's house and 13-year-old Danielle asked: "is it okay if I date a black guy." I said "yes" and the neighbor said "no" at the exact same time.

After 100 years of integrated music, one strange factor still looms: Darwin's sexual selection. The most pejorative statistic is that sexual selection by skin color is almost unanimous. The US leads in multicolor marriage (up to 15-20% of marriages!) and the world lags behind but there is much more opportunity for mixing in America the beautiful. We're on track to become the least color-sensitive country, however, the 80% decision to marry a person of the same skin color tells us about *most everybody's* ultimate bias, which means the fascinating trend to marry for the health and longevity of the kids is far from genetic fixation. We've got 1000 years perhaps before everybody has deep, olive-colored skin.

When Ella Fitzgerald sang, "god bless the child who's got his own" (my most referenced song) I knew what she meant—from the singer *and* from the songwriter—because Holiday wrote the song it with Arthur Herzog. The child who's got his own—probably a Love Child—is headed out into the world to own it in his or her own fashion. The late Tina Turner convinced us with her *Legs*. You can't lose when you sing the blues because you "ain't got nothing' to lose" and as Benjamin Franklin did, Carmen McRae reminded us "it 'taint nobody's business but my own."[4]

In the jump blues song *Let the Good times Roll*, Louis Jordan and Sam Theard provide us with a gambling brain-twister: "I got 50¢ more than I'm gonna keep." Back then 2 silver quarters was a cart full of groceries and Theard lived off his performing and music royalties, including the song *New Rubbin' on that Damned Ol' Thing*. There are many blues songs saying, "you can't beat the house" and the "house always wins," but when Jordan and Theard are down to their last 50¢, they're goin' home. It's the spirit of the words in the brain twister that say "I'm all in, I just need enough cash for dinner," cuz these tinhorns had "a fire in their soul and little or nothin' to forget."[5] "I wish I'd thought of that," musicians say, when they hear stark, beautiful lyrics. Though simplicity is easier to write, it's harder to do!

Authenticity is defined by Buddy Guy from Mississippi who sang "after 2 long years, my mama had the nerve to kick me out." He saw her in a limousine later but that's the whole story—he's always in the here and now and doesn't cloud the lyrics with a history. Little Buddy would wait till his dad's gallon of wine put him to sleep with the guitar in his lap. He then snuck off with it and learned to play it by himself but the years would leave him a starving adult in Chicago when Muddy Waters discovered him. Buddy, who didn't act because he played himself onstage, had a *Back Up Mama*, way cross town and he called it "love insurance." Buddy Guy says "everybody in a hurry and ain't nobody goin' nowhere," but he was, and he made Eric Clapton hurry out and buy his first Stratocaster in 1965. Buddy got hooked on the blues from John Lee Hooker and we can't forget Freddie King, Albert King, and B B King who helped Chuck Berry morph the blues into Rock and Roll. Without these singer-songwriters there would be no story.

One loss somewhere late in the rock revolution was clearly understanding the lyrics, and Heavy Metal, which I call "I hate my parents" music, made it obvious. The worse the lyrics are the more they turn up the band. We must give Karen Carpenter, Ella Fitzgerald, and the Big O, Roy Orbison, the trophies on elocution. Roy sang about real dreams he had and with that unpretentious, effortless, silky-smooth voice and those haunting, pretty words he had us rooting for him from the first sentence. Black lyricists wrote in the present tense too, teaching songwriters long ago to tell us how they were experiencing life at the moment, instead of the long-winded explanations that give us dyslexia.

I lived through the latter part of this surprise volcano, leaving me dumbstruck when I think about what music would sound like if the renaissance hadn't happened. What if we were still listening to "happy together, how is the weather?" or "life is funny, bees make honey," or "*Danke Shane*, baby, Danke Shane?" I have about 20 RAP CDs and these musicians (the richest young people in the world) brought lyrics back in the 1970s when the lyrics were putting us into a diabetic coma. Besides the lyrics, the only thing I didn't like about the 70s was the music. I survived on Berry Gordy's Motown, Chess Records, The X-Beatles, Genesis, and early Pink Floyd. What if we were still listening to, "*Crimson and Clover*, over and over?" Without a great songwriter, a great singer has little.

Duke and Ella

I learned to love jazz accidentally on purpose. Remember my friend Kevin who said, "a man is just a dick with ears?" He gave me a couple jazz CDs and later, when I was vacuuming, I couldn't hear the music so I accidently turned it up too loud, and kept vacuuming. It was Duke Ellington—the piano player, band leader, and songwriter—and after getting the house "man clean," as my wife says, I put on Kevin's other CD—Thelonious Monk. Monk reinvented jazz and the piano before he was a teenager (I would find out later) and he simply told us, "I learned to play piano on my own." Years later Kevin asked me what my favorite kind of jazz was and I said, "the older and the blacker, the more I like it." "What's that noise?" Jeanne says when I turn on the vacuum.

Today we have hundreds of thousands of songs to listen to—far more songs than there are English words—but in the 1940s there were only a few hundred standards and most every band played them. A reporter asked Duke Ellington "who is going to write the new standards?" "*I* am," he replied, and he did. In 1931 he wrote *It Don't Mean a Thing*—in 1940 he wrote *Don't Get Around Much Anymore,* and true to his word he kept going with *I Got it Bad and that ain't Good* in 1941 and *I'm Just a Lucky So and So* in 1945. Before Duke Ellington plays *Take the A Train,* written by Billy Strayhorn, Duke announces, "this one features the piano player." I've always thought the opening for *A Train* and Duke's big band openings as well as the writing of Johnny Hodges spawned the

James Bond Themes, not to mention Henry Mancini's *Peter Gunn*. (Dave Grusin's version is fantastic.)

Duke's best album might be *Duke Ellington, Live at Newport, 1956* but I had some *smoke from a distant fire*. In fact, I was *one toke over the line*. If you can't find the album, I can make you a copy when you come over. You can turn the volume up on the Ellington band because Duke—the conductor too—already did the mixing, so there was no need for that guy in the back to run the mixing board.

At the intermission of Duke's 1956 extravaganza, the mayor of Newport New Jersey said a few words, including: "it's great to have...you people (gesturing to the band)...here." The audience was "ladies and gents," the band was "you people" and the mayor was Horace J. Poinier. In the 50s he probably thought it a compliment and so did "I'm all ears" Ross Perot in the 90s. He was the last to learn what *you people* meant.

Duke Ellington, tinkling the ivory, had the best horn players and took them from copy band to writing band. They all had PhDs in music courtesy of the sidewalks of New York. Ellington said, "I contend that the negro is the creative voice of America, *is* creative America, and it was a happy day when the first slave landed on its shores." It was a different time.

During this jazz revolution Louis Armstrong was asked by a reporter after a great concert, "what is jazz?" and he said, "if you gotta ask, you'll never know." Winton Marsalis said, "Armstrong was a genius of such magnitude that you could lie about him and you still wouldn't be saying enough," and added "white people tried to stop the jazz movement altogether."[6] Speaking of *trumpet playin' bands*, Wynton Marsalis and his Quintet, in their album *La Vie En Rose*, have the best horn sounds I've ever heard. Horn players climb up through the scales like no solo guitar player can; the guitar seems more suited for descending through the scales.

As much as I admire Billie Holiday, by any measure Ella Fitzgerald stole the show for 50 years. She wrote many hit songs including *Muffin Man, You Showed Me the Way, A-Tisket A-Tasket*, and my favorite, *Dream a Little Dream of Me*. Now that's a great song. And her unparalleled interpretation of other writers' music/lyrics made her a composer in a whole new sense. Never getting out of the chord structure, she would insert pieces of other songs inside the song she was singing and was so smooth that many didn't catch her tiskets. Performing from the famous Apollo Club to the Savoy, to Minton's, she had street cred too—something most black musicians had and still do. This netted Ella the blue-collar dollar which was a cash of paying customers that many white-collar musicians missed because they never sang about "payin' the rent."

Ella Fitzgerald made lyrics come alive by stealing every song she sang from the songwriter: "those things that you're liable, to read in the bible, they ain't necessarily so," written by the Gershwin brothers. Somehow Ella was the tip of the sword even with competition from Billie Holiday, Aretha Franklin, Dion Warwick, Carmen McRae and many other legendary leading ladies. They sang to each of us as if we were alone in a room with them.

Ella was hardly a controversial figure (she cried when she got arrested) but Glenn Miller's band made more money than all of her bands combined, though inferior, and she finally let us know how she felt about racism in music. She made up new words to *Mack the Knife*: "I forgot the words dear," instead of "oh the shark bites, with his teeth dear." In the last line of the song, she took a shot at my dad's cousin, that *so and so* Glenn Miller, "and oh that Miller, still spinnin' that trash."

The American Enlightenment: Rags to Riches

As the blues chopped its way into rock and roll, under the ax of Chuck Berry and many others, it spawned the free love generation and shot the divorce rate up in the 1960s. Most black men adapted to marriage but the Missourian Chuck Berry never jumped the broom, and may have had sex with more women than Wilt Chamberlain. Berry is the unapologetic black alpha male and his lifestyle helped him invent rock and roll which changed the culture as much as the inventors of birth control would. He probably sped up the research on birth control and Berry "never did any [drugs]" either he said in an interview with Robbie Robertson.

White people were keeping the soft porn out of music (underusing the 1st Amendment); black people wouldn't have it and routinely wrote risqué lyrics. Since life was rated R anyway, they gave America its first R-Rated music and everybody loved it. Barry White sang "my hands just won't keep still" and Muddy Waters says he gives his women, "steak, potatoes, and cheese." In the song *Porch Light,* Robert Cray who put notches in his guitar, sings about how his girlfriend would flip the porch light on at midnight if her husband was gone. Sugar Blue sang, "one man's last is another man's first." Ferdinand LaMothe, the great African/European pianist who claims to have invented jazz—he helped—named himself *Jelly Roll* Morton. In street talk that means, "the perfect pressure at the perfect time for the perfect orgasm."

Black musicians sang about things they stashed in their shoes, gettin' up in the mornin,' *Makin' Whoopie,* masturbating, and cheating. Blues lyrics made the end of monogamy, the in between part, and the beginning of a new infidelity, aesthetic, because everybody goes through it. "My key doesn't fit my lock anymore" (a fantastic pun) and "when I open the front door, I hear the back door shut."

The theme of "all night long" is echoed throughout black music and was copied by everybody and their brother. Black people were saying to white people: "have sex all night long." "Oh shit, we've never thought of that!" said the whites, "how do you do that?" "Well," the blacks said, "how do I put this…you have to start singing about sex first, something all y'all don't do." Whites were slow to adapt, still thinking of sex provincially, as reproduction. On cue though, AC/DC sang, "you shook me all night long," and vanilla musicians wrote hundreds more with the same lyrics. Lionel went from *All Night Long* to *Running with the Night* and ironically took over the *Night Shift* as the sentry of the lost love ballad.

Through black music whites learned to stop lamenting lost love too and quit letting 1 x-lover depress them until their friends couldn't stand us anymore. "Now I know you're not the only starfish in the sea," was Paul Simon's version and Brian Wilson pleaded: "Help me Rhonda yeah git her outa my heart."[7]

It's almost impossible to make up a blues song if you haven't lived it and singing the truth as you lived it started another revolution: the birth of the singer-songwriter. Early on in American music there was usually a white singer and a white songwriter who didn't know each other and a record popped out. Combining 2 people into 1, however, gave music purity, truth, individualism, and affordability—only 1 artist had to be paid. After that economic innovation, singer-songwriters came out of the woodwork.

Rock and Roll

Some say Billy Ward invented the phrase "rock and roll" in his song *60 Minute Man*. Next, Alan Freed claimed to have invented the iconic phrase in the 50s, but the phrase *rock and roll* goes back to the slave days. Rockin' and rollin' was their description of the horizontal cha-cha. Chuck Berry's original guitar rift sounded like sex, giving the slave phrase a rebirth in the 1950s. His rock and roll driving rhythm, bouncing between the 5th, 6th, and $\flat 7^{th}$ notes of the key, forced many a guitar player to finally develop their baby finger. He had borrowed that rift from the boogie-woogie black piano players who had borrowed it from upright string bass players and it translated sexily to guitar. Complimented by bass and drums, Berry evolved a guitar rhythm that was copied more than any other meme in music. Carl Hogan's lead guitar style inspired Chuck Berry to reinvent those first unforgettable, trailblazing guitar solos and Berry got yet another lesson from Nat King Cole: sing your lyrics very clearly. By then, the inventor of rock and roll, singer-songwriter Chuck Berry, was the whole package.

Jerry Lee Lewis, who said all his #1 hits were "first take" in the studio, claimed he invented rock and roll which prompted a show down, throw down. On tour in the mid-50s Chuck Berry got into a fist fight with Jerry Lee Lewis over who was the king of rock and roll and Berry won the fight and Lewis gave him the title. Do we need any more evidence of who invented rock and roll?

Lefthanded Jimmy Hendrix played his Fender Stratocaster as nobody ever had or would, not even Chuck Berry. Joe Satriani picked up a guitar for the same reason so many did—Hendrix. The Stones, Beatles, and Clapton too tried to sound like Hendrix but they didn't have the intangibles or those long fingers like he and Robert Johnson did.

The next generation after Hendrix introduced us to the gifted white Stevie Ray Vaughn (SRV) who did have the intangibles and lifted some licks straight from Buddy Guy's Stratocaster, not to mention his style of singing. Eric Clapton heard SRV while driving through England and had to stop at a phone booth to find out who this Vaughn guy was and how a dude from Texas could do the blues better than the British copiers. After Hendrix died in 1970, Stevie Ray Vaughn took up the Hendrix style too until his fatal helicopter crash in 1990. Stevie Ray Vaughn ripped into *The Sky Is Crying* (written by Hendrix) and did an edgy version of *Tin Pan Alley* that raised eyebrows because Vaughn, like McCartney, had learned to pour his heart into every note. Bonnie Raitt said, "nobody tears into a song like SRV." Now the virtuoso Joe Bonamassa is surgically tearing into the blues in Stevie's slumber and Joe's keyboard player, Reese Wynans, plays so possessed that his mom might have been a sorceress. They all stand on the back of a century of black risktakers.

Stealing Music

White artists jumped on the blues scale the moment they heard it. White musicians stole rock and roll too and for Freddie

Freeloaders they stole it pretty well. They probably didn't know it but John Lee Hooker taught ZZ Top how to write *Lagrange* and they added some great black lyrics. Copying a style is fine but copying a song is not and the music industry finally decided that copying 4 measures in a row, music or lyrics, is stealing. *Surfin' USA*, by the Beach Boys had already been written by Chuck Berry in the song *Sweet Little Sixteen* and Chuck sued them and won. Only the lyrics were different. The Beach Boys wrote songs that sounded too much like *You Can't Catch Me*—another song by Chuck—and Chuck's publisher even sued John Lennon for *Come Together*, settling out of court. George Harrison lost in court over *My Sweet Lord* because it was the same song as Ronald Mack's, *He's So Fine*. The Beatles incorporated Berry's songwriting and lyrical style into countless songs, from Berry's *Roll Over Beethoven* all the way to *Get Back* and *Revolution*. *Satisfaction*, the #1 song of all time according to Rolling Stone Magazine, is a compact compilation of the entire blues music movement. Imagine a black man, not Mick, singing those lyrics, and it's even better. Otis Redding recorded original versions of *Satisfaction* and *Day Tripper* but he never got to hear his *Sittin' by the Dock of the Bay*, on the radio. It was a rainy night in Georgia. Whatever you do don't miss Oscar Peterson's solo masterpiece recording of *Georgia* by Ray Charles.

Even if Andrew Lloyd Webber did steal the *Phantom of the Opera* theme song from Roger Waters of Pink Floyd, one of the biggest *natural* monopolies besides African American music is British music. Occasionally monopolies are good. Incredibly, all the super bands are from England and it was no small feat for that tiny country to sell more records than all other European countries combined. It was an invasion we loved, from the Beatles to Pink Floyd—they got half their new ideas from you know who—and try to imagine the Stones or Cream without the black influence. The UK had that British aestheticism and deep history of literature but history should give the credit to the American inventors, who made scant money, while the super bands made trillions. Now we know who invaded who and with the top tier income tax in the UK at 90% usually, we could say the black music movement helped bail out the governments of John Majors and Maggie Thatcher. Whether it's the Bee Gees or Elton John, the UK bombards the music market from every angle—they always throw the best white curve balls—and are still competing worldwide with Coldplay and U2.

America's Renaissance

"In sum," James A. Cosby wrote in his fun book, *Devil's Music, Holy Rollers, and Hillbillies,* "rock and roll music helps fans get in touch with that place deep within themselves that no one else can touch, repress or manipulate—thus allowing them to feel more alive," and added, "rock and roll is, at its best, an inclusive, pure expression of an irrepressible spirit set to music."

I believe struggle is imprinted inside of us and without it, people stagnate. Struggling black musicians simply evolved faster, without hating, and they told their own stories. They taught us more than we taught them, if you people were listening.

The music renaissance of 20th century America received no public money. It sprang spontaneously from ground level without government loans, and Motown for example, grew past all the 1960s record labels with no backing. Berry Gordy built it from scratch. An endowment renaissance wouldn't have been a renaissance because the banks would have bribed away their edge, anxiety, and creativity, which are the key ingredients for any personal, national, or cultural renaissance.

CHAPTER 28

The Best Kept Secret in the World

"Human nature dictates we don't spend other people's money as wisely as we do our own money and rare is the chap who can be saved, with money." —unknown author

There was no conspiracy surrounding the creation of the US central bank. In the 1700s central banks popped up across mother Europe and this paper tiger, finally, after 200 years, spread to the US in 1913.

By WWI, the old, private ultrarich banking families, most of them with non-Jewish last names, had happily vanished into the woodwork. Banking was too lucrative for any nation to pass up. And the typical ultra-wealthy banking family was rather macroeconomically benign, compared to the typical national bank, who paid back its foreign debts but not its inhouse debts. This switch came to be called "deficit spending," and later became what I call "deficit lending."

The US Congress acted to create what they knew would be the largest central bank—the Federal Reserve System—called the "FED". It was any other Tuesday, 2 days before Christmas. The first cross-word puzzle had come out in the New York Times 2 days prior and the first answer was rule, *from the clue,* to govern. *On Christmas Eve, 20,000 people gathered at the capital for a Christmas celebration, historians tell us. The weather wasn't bad and the crisp sound of President Woodrow Wilson's voice snapped in the cold air, as the man who signed the banking* act *spoke about the naked aggression from Germany. "The world must be made safe for democracy," he said. WWI officially started 7 months later. The US didn't start it but knew our friends in Europe would need some help fast. The new money would hasten the economic transition from butter to guns and help free Europe, which was a good use for a central bank.*

The congressional banking "act," or any act, isn't exactly part of the constitution but congress is part of the constitution, so whatever they create is subject to the will of the people. And an act, for all intents and purposes, is a contrary loophole that must ultimately harmonize with the constitution. Since the federal government could only "coin money," they created an autonomous agency that lived down the road a piece from the constitution. The Bill of Rights and later constitutional amendments weren't about money, they were about principle, so the central bank is a platypus. Is it a mammal or a bird? I believe that this platypus, that so many have come to love, should only be used for military defense or to blow up earthbound meteors. In fact, until Vietnam, so very long ago, the western central banks were fantastic at winning the wars that had to be won, and then quieting down.

The electronic revolution of the 20th century was overshadowed by the western transition from 1:1 value to the undertow of special interest groups, paper money, and inflation. It created the 2 Americas we see today and I didn't want the research to lead me to that answer.

The Federal Reserve System—the central bank in Washington DC—steers the economy of the United States. In many important ways the "FED," as the bank is called, steers the country more than the federal government does. The bank creates new money out of nothing, doles it out to certain groups, and this constant creation of money causes all the inflation. I will show you that this consumer tax, this inflation tax, has become the biggest tax of all.

Washington DC and their TV outlets have tried to sell us on other causes of inflation including weather and the price of oil or diapers—don't be bamboozled. Something borrowed, something green, causes all the inflation which everybody pays for, but through a tricky process that you will understand shortly, the top half of society ends up with much more equity.

The top half represents 2 demographics: they earn above median income and usually have college degrees. Low-interest home loans and business loans are the reward for those who pass the pyramid's educational litmus test. In a nut shell, if you make it through 16 years of the academic pyramid you get a coupon for a desk job with air conditioning, a nice house, plus equity. The bottom half gets some new car loans, few housing loans, almost no business loans, and represent the low-ownership society. Christopher Hitchens says central banks are, "socialism for the rich, and free enterprise for everyone else." Other than the welfare going to the bottom half of the workforce, which is rather small in comparison to the money the pyramid sends upstairs, truer words are scarce. I have much evidence to back him up in the following pages, plus a solution.

First, let's define words. Communism and fascism are systems where the people have no individual rights so anything goes. Under socialism and capitalism people do have various individual rights and with real capitalism the economy is not helped or hindered while with socialism the economy is controlled by the government. But what is socialism? For starters, it doesn't mean left or right anymore. Because of TV we are sure that the welfare goes to the poor but with western neo-socialism it's the exact opposite—the central bank sends more welfare to the top half of society. Qualified home buyers get the cake and the top

5%, the billionaires, the trillionaires, and the investment bankers get the icing. The cheap home loans are little bribes so the top half of the economic stratum, the more involved people, won't complain about the FED's broader ambitions.

The same size economies of the US and the EU are 50-50 blends of capitalism and socialism. The governments tax, create, or redirect about half the money and I will lay this out for you in numbers. The US and the EU have the same inflations at the same times so that tax (the inflation tax) doesn't fall out of the sky, it is carefully planned. Strangely, the unelected EU commission and officials in Germany and Brussels make most of the decisions for the 27 member countries,[1] so the EU is even less democratic than the US is. Both are half capitalist places, to generate real wealth, but the planned overspending, the overborrowing, the trillions going to mega cartels and to social welfare, plus control of the money supply, make them half socialist and half capitalist.

My conservative accountant said "Washington DC only spends 35% of the economy so the US is 65% capitalist." I then reminded him that that 35% number doesn't include state, local, and city spending which is about half of federal spending. Government spending, in what we happily think of as the freest economy on earth, is about 50%. Spending that is also not included are the yearly federal deficits and the yearly deficits of each of the 50 states, or the trillions sent to investment bankers yearly. I will detail for you these seemingly unconnected piles of laundered debris—much of it never paid back—that cause all the inflation.

Inflation is the most misunderstood word on earth, by design. When you finish this chapter, you will know what that simple word means and how far it reaches into your life. You'll be angry too, wondering why the pyramid lied to you about it all your life. A stick of butter, insurance bills, and vacations could remain about the same price all our lives. If the money supply stayed constant, an increase in the price of gas would force us to spend less on other things, pushing down those prices, and overall inflation would stay around zero.

Except for DC protecting us from enemies foreign and domestic, the allocation of money should be left to market forces. Yes, some people have ergophobia while some work harder, smarter, or longer, and those people will have more money. But the income spread is further out of balance than ever—Eastern European dictators are jealous—and this did not come from a free-market capitalist economy. The central bank is creating massive economies of scale with ungodly loans to obese mega corporations who then buy up their competition. If a company wants to buy another company they should use their own money—this is common sense 101—and these transactions that should not occur are rarely reported as having been funded by the central bank.

James Madison and Thomas Jefferson repeatedly warned of the government favoring certain economic players over others and their 10th Amendment, they thought, would make damn sure that would not happen. After confining the federal government so succinctly, they never dreamed DC could end up running the economy. Today, tranches of new federal dollars go to foreign governments, billionaires, developers, homeowners, Facebook, movie producers, the CIA, and to blow up sand dunes. Sometimes they simply drop $25 billion dollars on a pallet into a country they want, and let it disappear into circulation, because whoever they subsidize, they might end up owning.

Central banks introduce 4 new economic factors to what used to be a free marketplace: perpetual monopolies, perpetual debt, perpetual bailouts, and perpetual inflation which is twice what they tell us it is. The bottom half rarely gets bailed out but must pay the beguiling inflation tax—a theft by deception—every year, which negates their yearly raises. The top income earners do pay *more* in inflation taxes and income taxes but at the same time, banking is designed to trap trillions in long-term wealth in the top half of the population which more than covers their other taxes. The elite know that the cheap business loans and mansion loans they get add up to an equity that more than trumps what inflation costs them because the central bank loans are much cheaper than inflation itself. That seems mathematically impossible, doesn't it?

I realize most people reading this book are in the top half of America, as I am, so it's going to be a little painful to learn what the FED is doing *for* us and what they're doing *to* the bottom half of America.

To understand the math of equity transfer, consider loaning $400,000 of your money to a friend of a friend to buy a house. If you charged what the banks typically charge (4-6% compounded monthly) you would be making a bad investment because your $400,000, that you earned, would be devalued by 4-6% inflation in each of the *good* years. During these periods, you are breaking even because the interest your buyer pays you equals the losses from inflation. In the bad years, when the FED is *seizing assets* (called "purchasing debt," their own debt by the way) sometimes you'd see debilitating inflation taxes of 10%, turning your 4% profit into a 6% loss per year. At best, you would lose some of your $400,000 over 30 years unless you charged your friend of a friend 20% interest or so. If everything went well and you got paid back $600,000 after 30 years it would be the worst investment you every made because you would have made much more in the stock market.

The reason the central bank can charge such low interest rates (4%) for home loans is because they create the money out of nothing. Before they approve a mortgage there is no *real* $400,000 that exists so they don't care what inflation is and are simply making a 4% profit yearly on top of whatever inflation happens to be. The bank profit from each house may be small, but keep in mind they created a huge asset with no work. After someone in the top half gets one of these charitable, cheap bank loans, created by a computer keystroke, it immediately turns into $400,000 in equity that never existed before. The money wasn't earned or worked for but now someone owns it. The bottom half rarely gets these windfall profits and the solution is to stop giving the top half windfall profits. They'll survive! It's rather simple why we have 2 Americas: some get to make $400,000 magically appear and some don't. And all these home loans added up, cause inflation, so the general population pays part of the interest for the proud new homeowners.

There exist, I swear, PhD economists who do not want you to understand how money is created. Hyman P. Minsky actually wrote "anyone can create money" and that if you lend $5 to a friend, you have increased the money supply by $5!![2] This is intuitively and materially impossible, even by the laws of physics. This is what we are up against folks—Harvard scholars who obfuscate reality to protect the 4rth branch of government—and rare is the PhD candidate whose thesis gets rejected.

More millionaires become billionaires every month by getting this funny money. The funny money instantly becomes *fungible* (mutually exchangeable) by tricky substitution, meaning that it instantly assumes the same value as the already circulating money. *Fungible* is easy to understand. An hour of your time is about equal to an hour of your neighbor's time so both of you will help each other bring a piece of furniture inside. This is fungible trade and the unseen beauty of capitalism is that most trades add up to more than the sum of their parts because neither of you could have gotten the furniture into your house alone. Smart trading of this significance has a snowballing effect but when the pyramid changes the definition of "*making* money" it is hoarded in unearned assets."

Another dirty trick with the brand-new fungible money is that it happens to be more valuable than the old! This is because the quack capitalists in the private sector or the autocrats in DC get to spend their new money *before* it pushes up prices. Later, we all pay higher prices as their sneaky pseudo-fungible money devalues our existing money. By the time we are age 70 our net worth will be more commensurate to how much money we were able to borrow from the central bank and not so much about how much intelligent work we did.

Many want to divert the new FED money down to the lower stratums but they are making the same age-old Marxian mistake that made Russia even poorer. In fact, running an economy with new money is the biggest mistake possible. Sending the new money to the top half and creating the widest income spread in history is ridiculous enough, so trying to make everybody rich is doubly ludicrous. Wealth only occurs after intelligent work has been performed and moving money is not intelligent work. A little more socialism up or down equals a little less capitalism (where we get all the stuff we want) and this is a truism economists cannot legislate around. Nobody should get new money.

Lots of people don't want you to know anything about evolution and there is another clique who is hellbent on you knowing nothing about banking, or how expensive central banks are, or how much damage they do to families. That's why you can't understand what bankers say on TV. It befits central bankers to speak in jargon—now called "Greenspeak"—because of Alan Greenspan. This longtime FED Chairman spaketh Greek to us while he was creating the housing crisis and destroying earth's economy. We did comprehend it when he spoke English and blamed the crash on our "irrational exuberance" which was like Bernie Madoff accusing somebody of shoplifting.

Like idiots we believed we did something wrong when in reality Greenspan had told the senate to deregulate the banks and that he would create tens of trillions of new dollars to ramp up housing. With the noblest of intentions, the senate told the banks that if they didn't deregulate and didn't expand their customer base quickly, they could lose their charter. Senator Chris Dodd told the big banks, in so many, many words (the 1999 Bank Bill that Clinton signed without reading) to give home loans to people who probably couldn't pay them back. And I'll give the new class of Federal Reserve Chiefs a veiled compliment: they've got us talking about inflation as if there has been a stranger in our house for donkey's years and we've finally come around to liking him.

Cheap federal loans for cars and houses are one of the major causes of inflation in America. There are people working in DC right now who think we wouldn't have houses if the government didn't have them built and these policymakers have never held a cordless drill in their lives. My wife and I practiced a little *Civil Disobedience* and built 2 small houses by ourselves with saved money though it would have been cheaper to get a low-interest loan and let society pay half the interest. That's the irony of housing economics today. The algorithm the FED wrote to extract equity from the economy and put it in the laps of the top half is a little complicated so I will take you through their 3-upsidedown cups trick, piece by piece.

You might remind me there are about twice as many homeowners as renters, but this true statistic is misleading because it tells us more about housing than it tells us about people. A rental house is owned by a corporation or a quasi-rich person who lives somewhere else and there are *more humans* in each rental dwelling. These people represent the bottom half of Americans who pay inflation taxes for their landlord's loans which transfers some equity yearly from the have nots to the haves. Making landlords use their own money to buy rental property would, over a generation, level out the playing field because the bottom half could, in the absence of equity transfer, use what equity they have to build their own small houses, like they used to. Certainly, we would soon see a thousand small houses go up for every mansion, in a real capitalism where the capital (the blue-collar labor) had to be paid for in total, without subsidy. The top half doesn't know how to do this work anyway and they're terrified of poison ivy.

The more expensive the house the better it sells because the top 1/3rd has 95% of the stock and many can pay cash. The middle class can't move up from a paid for house because a slightly nicer house is much more expensive—they've been reverse gentrified. The government's addiction to inflation pushes housing prices up faster than inflation simply because that market is so subsidized, creating the opposite of intentions: the American dream is losing ground.

With all those trillions in freshly printed equity going to the top half yearly (most to the top 5%) it will become clear that a free-market economy would make for a richer middle and lower middle class. Though blue-collar workers get much of the $2.5 trillion a year in benefits (Medicare, Medicaid, social security, welfare), I will talk soon about how they are overcharged and underserviced by these so-called benefits. But *tens* of trillions go to the rich each year and they get most of those aforementioned medical and retirement benefits too. These wheels within wheels are difficult to wrap our minds around because the economy is layered with masks—many hands giveth, many taketh away—and we can no longer see what capitalism used to be or how much better it would be now, because it suffered from a thousand cuts over the last century.

It takes decades of social engineering from the deep federal state to create an elite class of people who then believe that they became elite on their own merit. This kind of apophenia (believing whatever makes them feel better) is easy to keep shielded inside the mind. The corruption at many levels in the US is now obvious to those living just outside the monetary machine because nothing adds up anymore. And history shows that these elites shapeshift into a form of life that sees itself as independently wealthy. "I earned every penny," they say, "and I want more."

If we need new money for a defensive war congress can create it, and the economy will suffer but after the win and a 1-year clean up, they can stop creating money. This may come as a shock to those in DC but the economy will repair itself quickly on its own after a war. The reason this didn't happen after the crash of 1929, is that the FED had created so much new money in the roaring 20s—as if the US was in another world war—that they destroyed the economy of the world. Economist Murray Rothbard explains this as well as anyone in his book, *America's Great Depression*. What followed the 62% increase in the money supply in just 8 years during the roaring 1920s,[3] was the meowing 1930s, and Franklin Roosevelt came to power. Since most of that new money had vanished in the crash of 1929, he took control of whatever capital remained, small businesses struggled, and high unemployment dragged along until WWII.

When the trillions stop flowing from Mulberry Lane to 1 Hacker Way and the Wall Street Wankers, the bottom half will get a little richer by default. The economy will naturally downshift toward them and away from the subsidized rich. Zero deficit spending and lending, in turn, will end the inflation tax which the bottom half cannot afford, and they can put that money into building a small house or business, or both. With no further government support the monopolies won't have the money to buy up their competition and will slowly wither on the vine.

The blue-collar middle-class, the collateral damage of neo economics, can once again become the gravitational center of the economy, by getting their free market back. We forget "it's a small world after all" and most of us wanted it to stay that way because small businesses were competitive, income spread was naturally more compressed, people were freer, value was 1:1, exchange was fairer, and we had 1 America.

I saw a movie in the 60s where a mom occasionally gave her 2 sons a Snickers Bar to split. She'd give it to the older boy who would break it roughly in half, hold the 2 halves up to his eye, and bite off the end of the longer piece. At that point both pieces were about the same size and the two brothers would each get one. Imagine, after a decade of Snickers Bars, how much more *equity* the older brother would have. The older boy is the top half of America, the younger brother is the bottom half, and that big bite is how the FED makes ends *not* meet.

There are no graphs in this chapter because I can make a graph say anything I want it to. Don't be duped by the CNN graphs that show inflation holding steady for 35 years (1984-2019). Inflation always goes up—each year it is additive like a staircase—and to calculate how much inflation has cost us we would need an accurate staircase graph, then integrate the area under the stairway. My estimate is 100 trillion dollars. With propaganda like

CNN's inflation graphs, they could show us that our children stayed the same height as they grew up.

Government economists who enjoy this channel will excitedly remind us that vehicles and electronics did not increase in price at 7% per year. In fact, the price of electronics—flatscreens, laptops, DVD players—went down. That's true. These are gifts to us from Japan's capitalism that economists use to insinuate the price of *many* things go down. Ask them "what else fell in price?" Economists also won't remind us that without inflation these products would have gotten even cheaper each year—including the price of a congressmen. Before printed money, Gutenberg's printing press reduced the cost of a book from the price of a farm down to the price of a loaf of bread, in 100 years.[4] This is how capitalism creates deflation, or value. Music, forever unsubsidized by the pyramid, is a perfect 100-year example. You could buy a song on a 78 record for a dollar in 1919, then a 45 record was 99¢ in the 1960s, and it's still a dollar to download a song today.

The word *economy* comes from home economics; it is simply running a household, managing a budget, and carefully studying price and *scarcity*. We all know economics—it's simple—but we've been duped with the new economics because what the FED does, doesn't even involve economics. They embody the disestablishment of economics by removing math from the equation and practicing abundancy for the few. Scarcity keeps all ledgers balanced but you could read 100 books on economics and never know that, or learn that creating new money is the only cause of inflation. In fact, the only definitive and measurable thing the FED *does* do, is cause prices to continually rise.

Political Science became a new study in the 1930s, meaning DC was getting into so many aspects of American society that congress needed advisors to help them manage their own intrusions. Poli-Sci is the newthink that promoted university professors (90% of them employed by the government) into a new layer of bureaucracy. We call them "policymakers" (policy, from the word *police*) and any unelected "expert" from any field—

economist, sociologist, doctor, lawyer—can tweak how DC runs society. These policemen who don't wear guns aren't managing minor law breakers; they are managing the peaceful conduct of the adult citizenry.

Today the FED gives money to economics departments, loans students tuition money, then forgives the loans, then hires these students to further their education in forged economics.[5] These twenty somethings are taught to be conservative with their inflation estimates and minimize the visible impact of the FED. These rookies never consider that the system might be rigged which is why the headhunters at the FED like those straight A students. They're the nicest, most educated people you'd ever want to meet and have never had an independent thought since childhood. They can't learn by looking around because they've always been told what to think, see, and do. That's how they make perfect grades. In what used to be the freest thinking country on earth, these new "economists" minimize the equity choices for half the country.

We struggle to make ends meet each month while the pyramid throws trillions around, making the US economy change so rapidly that experts in the various agencies make our rules now—with no pushback rules become laws—because the big-ticket legislature is too busy managing the booty. One perk of running an economy from the seat of power used to be insider trading and now it is consignment trading (getting friends and relatives to buy stock for you). Honesty in government is great if you can get it but since it doesn't naturally arise from public service anymore the only way to get it back is to close the floodgate of new money. After that they can go back to grappling with issues as statesmen again, and return to their sole purpose of protecting citizens from enemies foreign and domestic. The constitution never said a word about reallocating wealth, up or down.

The central bank creates new money, the Treasury creates new money, and the little bank on the corner does too—that's a mechanism called the "multiplier effect." Each corner bank generates more new money as loans are paid back and reloaned over and over (the same $400,000 ends up buying dozens of houses) until the bank profits dwindle down to zero. Then, the little banks—sadly out of money—call the FED for another *injection* and start the abundancy process all over again.

Fractional reserve banking would be better described as "zero reserve banking" because most depositors spend their entire paycheck every month or invest it elsewhere so there's no deposit money to loan. Old, earned money is too valuable to loan at these low interest rates so all the money banks loan is *just out of the oven* money. The 4% *deposit to loan ratio* is a public relations stunt to make us believe loaning has something to do with deposit money.

The stark difference between old money and new money goes over the head of Harvard trained economists, low-paid workers at corner banks, and even people working inside the main FED building right now. If existing money or earned money was loaned and paid back over and over as the decades flew by, inflation would never get a toehold. They create trillions, which doesn't create wealth, rather, it simply moves wealth from one place to another. Aristotle and Adam Smith, thousands of years apart, both said that the amount of money circulating has nothing to do with a country's wealth.

We have 1 bank in the US, the FED, and the tens of trillions of loan money for cars, houses, businesses, investment bankers, and foreign governments is new money that originates from that 1 bank. The 5 major competing banks (reported on TV as such) don't exist and even the import/export bank is just another arm of the FED. On top of that, every single new idea or expenditure the government comes up with requires new money to be created at the central bank because the US government has been spending more than it took in since 1900 and probably since the civil war. Even in peacetime they ran deficits in the booming 1920s.

Half of the Washington DC budget is medical and retirement, the other half is military—both insurance policies—and the *other half* of the budget is central bank financing. That's the big slice of the pie chart we never get to see, making my strange math add up. I will start laying out hard numbers in 2 pages to show you that the US central bank often spends more money than the entire governmental apparatus.

Don't relax with a romance novel waiting for the democrats to fix anything. The banking bills are the most bipartisan bills coming out of congress because nothing obliterates political barriers faster than free money. And if you're looking for a fiscal conservative in DC, you're going to need a microscope or a shovel.

Most cling to 1 party but would never have voted for congress to raise the debt limit every year or to spend more every year than they took in for a century. We wouldn't have voted for the last 5 wars (or 7, many say) or for the military draft—involuntary servitude being unconstitutional. We would not have voted for the last 10 bailouts either, or for congress and millions of state employees to get a special exemption from social security taxes. We wouldn't have elected anybody who thought all of this was too complicated for us to understand, or voted for anybody who would lie to us for our own good...or to secretly collect and archive every text, email, and voicemail we send. Edward Snowden is an American hero for exposing the NSA. Some of our heroes have to defect now instead of getting a parade and the federal government is still casing each of us without a warrant.

And the Feds *knew* we wouldn't have voted for them to empty the Social Security Trust Fund so they didn't ask us. If we lived in a democracy we would have voted "no" on most all of the above but the elites didn't need us to get involved or alarmed. Their favorite line is "things are not that simple." We can wake up from the dream they have us in. We got mutual consent in marriage in 1900 only to gradually lose mutual consent in government over the next 100 years.

The old line between the right and left is a construct of the collective western imagination, as well as the apophenic illusion that we live in a democracy. At least those who don't live in the west—those in the east—know they don't live in a democracy. Epistemologically, they are ahead of us because they know what we don't. If we're yearning for a free market of products and ideas, and a democracy that tells Washington DC what to do, we are going to have to restart one.

The Best Kept Secret

He who wins 2 world wars makes the rules, so the US plays hard ball with their artificially over-valued dollar. For starters, this makes the balance of trade appear perpetually lopsided. It is impossible for the US to buy more from every country than those countries buy from them, for generations. After years of 1-way trade the other nations would be all monied-up and start buying more from the US but it doesn't happen. This is proof that the US dollar is artificially **over-valued**. We in the US love it. What devalues other currencies is printing too much new money and the FED xeroxes more money than any central bank yet works in reverse: financial markets rise during heavy US printing and fall during monetary tightening. This is why so many economic graphs we see are misrepresentations; the 45° graphs mean that the FED is inflating the *financial sector* and the rest of us are flatlining along the x axis.

The US gets away with it by being a decent international actor (of late anyway) and we don't want the rules reversed because China and Russia are prone to bad acting but we should be teaching the rest of the world about free market forces instead teaching how to manipulate them.

The overvalued dollar creates the illusion of a trade imbalance so we camouflage that by doing something even more intriguing: we export ungodly amounts of money. In fact, **money is the biggest US export** by a furlong, which surprisingly still surprises most people. The FED exports much more money yearly than the sum total of the 3-4 trillion dollars-worth of *real* goods and services the free market ships out each year. The #1 export, money, is sometimes more than all recorded federal spending plus state spending, combined.

One bill we don't know we paid was the $10 trillion the FED created in 2009, which was a hefty 6 times more than what they told us our total exports were that year, not to mention it was 3 times more than all government expenditures. Why doesn't anybody report who the biggest spender in the US is or what our biggest export is?? Bloomberg Surveillance, where are you?

The quirky 10 trillion-dollar *swap*—the US sent that much to the EU and vice versa—in that fateful year of 2009 is telling because it was all new money yet they called it a "trade." Fox News reported that this $20 trillion historical first occurred all in 1 day but Ben Bernanke, in his book *The Courage to Act,* said the exchange was in smaller amounts over a period of months. Ben also understood that the FED caused the Great Depression, and countless economists, left and right, are finally, 100 years later, acknowledging the disaster that is the FED.

They didn't even add that $10 trillion to the debt. They raised the national debt the next year by a mere $1.5 trillion. How is that possible? We will soon find that much of the deficit spending across the US is not added to the national debt, or even paid back.

These 3 comorbidities—artificial value of the dollar, total FED spending, total FED export—are only 3 of the best kept secrets in the world. That's why they always remind us that consumer spending is 2/3rds of the economy. It is *far* less.

The 4rth secret is that the inflation tax plus the federal consumption tax (spending taxes) is America's largest tax. Everybody pays these taxes too and the inflation tax was never levied by congress. Since no one knows exactly what inflation has added up to we can skip past the government's fictional numbers and simply look at the yearly national deficit.

The yearly government deficit is the aggregate inflation tax added up for us because what they borrow each year equals what they tax us through inflation. (Inflation is higher than what I will calculate here because they conceal some debt.) In the 2020 and 2021 budgets, deficit spending totaled $6.5 trillion so that was the aggregate inflation tax in those 2 years. In the same 2 years income taxes brought in $7 trillion and social insurance taxes brought in $4.2 trillion. Now, the pyramid tells us that federal excise taxes brought in $1.5 trillion (value *added* consumption tax) in those 2 years and when we add the $6.5 trillion inflation tax to that consumption tax—both being consumption taxes—the total is $8 trillion. **This tax was larger than Medicare, Medicaid, and Social Security added up** and **larger than the entire federal income tax too**.

To strengthen what I've been saying about inflation being twice what they tell us it is, US deficit divided by GDP in each of those 2 years was $3.25 trillion/$22 trillion = 15% inflation in both 2021 and 2022. They have our collective credit card and the bill comes a year later. The media happily reported that shopping was up 30% in 2023. The clueless media thought we bought more stuff but they were accidentally telling us what our 2-year inflation tax was, not including off the books spending. Off the books deficit spending shows up in the construction industry—a large basket of goods and services—and building something, anything, increased 50% in those same 2 years, so yearly inflation was somewhere between 15% and 25% in reality.

When prices on many necessities double, we know it and with a straight face they tell us inflation is 8%. They don't even flinch and they certainly weren't looking at the things I bought. The bailouts from 2020 to 2022, when Google almost doubled their income, also made 4 out of the big 5 mega-monsters worth over a trillion dollars each.[6]

In the dismal science (economics), dividing deficit spending by GDP is a good start for getting a correct although conservative number on inflation. The big story is of course we want to know what the total money supply is in the US, and since Milton Freidman's heyday, nobody will tell us. If we knew that we could take the total money supply at a given time and ask how much they added to it the previous year. The formula: all the new money created in 1 year divided by total money supply = inflation, would be right if they would simply tell us the numbers.

Another wrinkle the FED doesn't mention is immigration. More immigrants coming in lowers inflation a little because the new money is being used by more people. Imagine a village with 1000 people and a total of 1 million dollars getting traded around. If that population doubled, prices would naturally have to deflate to about half of what they used to be, for everybody to eventually be able to buy what they needed. However, if a central bank doubled the money supply while the population was doubling, prices would stay about the same and nobody would know anything changed.

It's no coincidence that the recent heavy immigration into the US (2021-2024) paralleled the heaviest inflation which lowered the already embarrassing inflation numbers. Still, home insurance prices went up 20% across the board from 2021 to 2022, while labor pay stayed flat, and our insurers immediately invest our insurance payments into the market and start making more money. They love the cheap labor immigration supplies them and the only workers I've seen hammering houses together came from south of Texas. The IMF and the World Bank keep the most accurate statistics on populations for a very good reason but what we all want the most (no inflation) is what central banks fear the most. I'll explain why.

Ludwig von Mises

Ludwig von Mises of the Austrian School of Economics wrote a famous book called *The Theory of Money and Credit*, showing us that an honest economy would have deflation—most prices slowly dropping. Real capitalism (pure competition) always puts downward pressure on prices and upward pressure on quality. True economic gains only come from real capitalism and if you make anything better and cheaper the world will send container ships to a port near you.

Mises taught us that a free enterprise economy with no increase in money supply will create a natural 2% deflation,[7] and with computers and cellphones, we could imagine more deflation. The FED operated on a designed-in 2% inflation which is a low number we'll never see again because they must accelerate money creation. A slight deceleration slows the financial growth at the top and screws up the elite, who can't ever lose a penny. A natural economy operates on a 2% *deflation* so the FED is designed, at the best of times, to skim 4% yearly off the economy yearly. To get from negative 2% inflation to positive 2% inflation equals a 4% increase.

I call falling prices "deflation," which is the benefit of a static money supply, while Mises reminds us that in a free-market economy it is economic innovation that brings down prices. This reminds me too that the blue-collar wages, even without raises, will gain buying power each year as prices go down. White-collar workers will gain even more buying power but they won't be getting free equity which will slowly compress the wealth spread. The economic wonders of deflation bring us back to my original question: "why do central banks hate deflation?"

Deflation makes all saved money get more valuable over time which turns every person who saves into a tiny little bank. This is how legitimate little banks sprang up literally 7000 years ago lending real, earned, deposit money, loaned out with permission because the depositor got part of the interest. 50 million savers in the US would make for a massive bank and the FED "no like" as Tonto would say. Fearing competition from solid capital, the FED destroyed the concept of frugality (a cornerstone of economics) by making us lose money when we saved it in a bank.

Worse, when we save money now the pyramid will tax it with inflation into nothing and replace that lost value into someone else's account, using the 3-up-side-down cups trick. In a normal deflationary economy, without deficit spending and deficit lending, the money under your mattress would grow in buying power by 2-4% a year. The FED knows this and this is why they fear the approach of deflation as witches do sunlight.

Boldly, Japan attempted a sustained deflation. As their yen

increased in value, it forced the 1985 Plaza Accord decision and the US had to greatly devalue their overvalued currency. Try not to burst out laughing, but this is when the US *pledged* to reduce the federal deficit.

In the 1990s, Japan decided to *reduce* their pyramid and see what real-world economics was like. What were they thinking? Well, they were thinking *value* and for a moment the house of the rising sun was a brief and shining Camelot. After a housing bubble, Japan cut way back on creating new money, resulting in a deflationary economy for about a decade (the yen got more valuable) and the central banks around the world were pressuring Japan to stop this economic sanity. Japan's unprecedented deflation was increasing the value of their citizen's buying power. During this "horrible deflation," as int'l bankers called it, Japan took over the electronics market and almost took over the US car market. Japan destroyed the popular economic myth that manufacturing suffers during deflation because, as deflation haters say, "the price of the end product will have dropped by the time it goes to market." They forget that this lower price has a higher value, and will buy more stuff than it would before. It's pretty amazing for an export country to see economics in the old, Milton Freidman way, and pull off an industrial deflationary win while simultaneously creating value for all their citizens. They were exposing the cheaters of the banking world and the yen was acting like Bitcoin(!) before the Japanese invented Blockchain.

The tricky Japanese though, following the tricky American manufacturers, began using screws nobody'd seen before and soldering the main parts of appliances together so the replacement of one little broken part wasn't possible. That's why appliances have short lives and by 1994 America and Japan had killed the Maytag repairman. He was a blue-collar guy. And he had a more fulfilling job than those after him, working those assembly lines.

Nevertheless, 1990s Japan was modern proof that a deflationary export economy is no hinder, already proved in the 19th century when the US outproduced England just after the Civil War, allowing the US buy Alaska from Russia. England had a central bank; Russia had a central bank; the US didn't. Japan's experiment with sanity couldn't last forever inside the insane asylum of int'l banking but "once there was a spot, a brief and shining spot, for happy-ever-aftering, there in Camelot.........in case you forgot."[8]

The Solution

When we stop creating new money, deflation will set in and the dollar will become more valuable than the artificially high value it has now. When the bailout money for mega corporations, nowhere wars, and foreign governments ends—thinning down the dollar's clout and hurting the US—the static supply of dollars will increase in value (deflation) faster than all other currencies and bring investors right back. Investors with real ideas that go beyond mirroring the FED and flipping assets around will be happier with more gains during a natural deflation. We could use gold, silver, crypto, copper—anything of value could be money, anything that's 1:1—and even keep the existing US dollars in circulation, just not create more of them.

But what will the central bankers and their *standing army* of pencil pushers do? Since they don't produce *anything* that we could buy and use, getting a real J.O.B. comes to mind. When we produce real goods and services that other people voluntarily buy, it has an inherent integrity. Free trade is good for the soul which is a truism we gradually lost over the last 3 generations, because it appeared we were still the richest country in the world. When DC got rich quick, they quickly forgot about what made us all rich.

No more newly created dollars going to Washington DC would solve so many problems. The government could live like they used to, on what they can tax, which returns some power to the people and brings the US closer to the economic democracy we lost in 1913. The supreme court ruled that you and I *speak and vote with our dollars*—it's the same thing— so we can mail 20 bucks to a candidate who says stuff we like, or a lot more. However, DC, the FED, and their mega corporations spend our money on veiled political opinion all the time (sold as financial *public* information that we don't understand) so these entities get more political opinion votes than we do. Example: they use the public airwaves to tell us the economy has been repaired because the key sectors got bailed out. Translation: you didn't get bailed out, the multibillionaires did, because you *aren't* the economy, they are. The FED itself creates these billionaires at a clip of about 5 per month and these plutocrats can make unlimited campaign contributions too!

The free market was created by the people, 1 dollar at a time, and the old public servants, now extinct, simply protected our individual rights. They were about principle, not money, and we are waking up 100 years later to find them *Living in Our Material World.*[9] How could our parents and grandparents let all these mistakes pile up? They were raising us, the politicians knew that, and as the decades went by, they had fewer and fewer candidates to vote for who didn't come with invisible strings attached.

It's not too late to have a mini-revolution and go back but the people must select learning, reject their eleutheromania, and re-educate themselves at 2 schools: common sense and hard knocks. We have to resist this financial oligarchy with every fiber and vote out the cash congress by only electing those who refuse to borrow or lend, period. That's not in the congressional or presidential job description anyway.

As of now, the congress created FED fills the glass to the brim, the FED knocks the whole thing over, then they fill the glass to the brim again—it's insane. Instead of the monetary nepotism we get served, *our* economy can become predictable and prices can stabilize for generations. This is what our government was able to do throughout most of the 1800s and they can do it again.

Congress, who created the FED, tells us that what this bank does is lending and spending. That's misleading because those activities include risk. What they do is *splending*, if I can make up another word here, because the new money is splendid for the people who have access to it. If the FED can't splend, "boom" as

John Madden used to say, prices begin falling in the US and the equity stops flowing uphill. But the overweight stock market will shrink down to a solid foundation—a deflation that keeps trying to happen—and start growing real value. A sane economy doesn't look at all like a boom economy to the elite, because it's a gradual, splendid thickening of the middle and lower middle classes.

With blue-collar workers putting small amounts of money into the stock *system*, and social security being so "bankrupt" that FDR is taking up smoking again, the FED is forced to nurture the stock market into the new Social Security System. They're still printing for both but the FED won't tell us why they sometimes buy more stock than we do—up to $100 billion a month(!)—and they call it "Quantitative Easing." QE is, of course, to prop up their paper fortress for the top half who own 96% of the stock, and the other private reason is that know they've caused every economic crash. The FED itself caused most financial panics when many lost their life savings while others got windfall profits, so my tough love cure for the US economy will not sit well with the powerful, who've been livin' large in their *Gangster Paradise*.[10] Each year we postpone the cure—getting their hands off our monies—the now unrecognizable US economy will get even more grotesque.

Watching the boring senate banking meetings can be entertaining. It's fun to see how they twist sentences into pretzels so the layman won't know exactly what they are saying. At one meeting though, they were quite frank: according to Van Hollen, senator from Maryland, banks are even loaning money to us without telling us. We can overdraft our debit cards multiple times—the lenders design this into the system—and by August 2021, banks had made, just in profits, $31 billion, using unsuspecting Walmart shoppers. "Attention Walmart shoppers: you are missing $31 billion." This is not monetary policy folks; this is full-on predatory lending. During these banking hearings on C-SPAN, senator Bob Menendez was concerned only that these predatory lenders—who only cry when they're slicing onions—were not hiring enough Hispanics.

The War on Wages

Since 10% of Americans own 90% of the stock and 40 families in Germany have as much wealth as half of the German population, we know the central banks have been singing, "First we take Manhattan, then we take Berlin." [11] This isn't natural economics, this is public money levitating to the top of society.

We know real wages were rising in Europe/US through the 19th and most of the 20th century during low inflation but the US reversed those gains with way too much post WWII borrowing, too much debt during Vietnam, high taxes with low benefits, and cheap money for billionaires. This chronic inflammation resulted in a sick economy by 1969 called the "Great Decoupling" which created the 2 artificial Americas. Additive inflation piled up, real wages fell, large corporations grew fast, competition slowed, and the middle class slid down into the lower middle class.

Using the government's own conservative inflation numbers, I will show that workers in America are in worse trouble than we think. In the book *Work*, James Suzman has a graph that shows the real US economy (private productivity) doubled between 1980 and 2015. [12] He used the government's own graphs and during this same period, real earnings for workers flatlined—the Great Decoupling. 1980 is when the 2 America's became so apparent that we could prove it on paper. Prices tripled during those 35 years (Ian Webster's easy to read inflation graphs) and worker pay tripled too, adding up to a zero net gain in buying power.

We know it was slightly worse because inflation was higher than the government reported but the picture gets darker. During that same period, government spending grew 6 times and government borrowing grew 7 times. Could it get even worse? Well, CEO pay increased during these 35 years 300 times more than worker pay did. [13] The big money is in the CEO cozying up to the FED, getting hundred-billion-dollar loans, and buying up his competition to get in position to raise prices faster than inflation. At that point the board of directors applaud the CEO by giving him a sizeable chunk of that loan. They BORROW to pay him 300 times more than they pay their workers and we pay part of his salary with the inflation tax. If companies had to use their own profits to expand the US could not have become a money oligarchy run by bankers and corporate czars.

Let's look at Adam Smith's concept of supply and demand—an economic offshoot of nature and nurture—which simply means that we make things and we consume things. Everybody does both so these seemingly competing concepts are inextricably woven together inside each of us.

After WWII, DC adopted "supply side" economics and began fattening up the Fortunate 500, megafarms, universities, builders, investment bankers, and eventually fintech (financial technology). That money, they said, would trickle-down to the demand side (consumers). Instead, it created a surplus on top and a deficit on the bottom that would have made any European King jealous.

Median family income in the US is approaching $100,000 a year but 2/3rds of the people live below that because these parents have about 16% *more* children, making my joke on the word *median*, true. A minority of US children grow up with free equity and a majority of them do not. After freezing blue-collar buying power in place in 1970 the pyramid attempted another nonmarket based remedy by giving the bottom half a real increase in benefits,[14] mainly retirement and medical. Government subsidies have soared to $50,000 per person per year (most of those FICA benefits are after age 62) but it's the Snickers Bar trick all over again. If employees weren't taxed 7% and their employers weren't taxed 7% again, and employees weren't always paying the 7% inflation tax, employees could live 21% better. That WROI (worst return om investment) is the blue-collar worker's money anyway and they are triple taxed for these *freebees* on top of dozens of other taxes they pay. The system is designed so workers can't save money or build equity but is sold as the opposite—as we say in the south "kill 'em with kindness." Blue-collar workers could put that money into whatever businesses they want, or build their own houses like they used to, which would be reversing what the pyramid has done with it—they spent it long ago and have been printing since.

You might remind me that there are people in the US who will make bad decisions, or no decisions, and end up old, broke, and helpless. True, fewer than we might think, but true. Without all these tripled-edged taxes we are paying, the private sector would be so rich, including a robust middle class, there would be free, dentists, motels, cafeterias, and hospitals in every town. If we got our $100 trillion back from 100 years of deficit spending and lending, we'd again be the envy of the west and the example to the world. The message would be simple: If you get rid of your central bank your people will get rich—blue collar too—and tough love private charities would run circles around the slipshod, detached, uninvolved, corrupt administration of it by the state.

The pyramid could have millions more small, blue-collar corporations that didn't need subsidizing or regulating and the senators wouldn't have to do squat but watch tax revenue go up. They could keep doing what they've been doing: vote themselves 20% raises, pay no social security taxes, golf all day, and do minimum damage. Those trillions they send to mega cartels could be in the hands of middle-class families. Instead, we get customer-*no*-service (Clark Howard's obvyism) from their monopoly mega corporations that are indistinguishable from government agencies.

For example, if we had 10 thousand baby food companies shortages would be impossible. When we have 4 mega corporations—Nestle (Gerber), Damone, RBMJ, Abbott, controlling 90% of the market[15]—any one of them can say they are retooling and shut down a factory. Suddenly, wouldn't you know it, demand is greater than supply and all 4 companies raise prices, then restart that factory. New mothers take note: if we had thousands of small baby food companies a few might go under without causing so much as a blip on your economic radar screen. You could be getting all the formula you want and have choices you've never seen—including foods that are good for your baby. These monster monopolies are brought to us by the US central bank and their already rich friends for the sole purpose of circumventing competition. The only path to big money is to get in bed with the FED then raise prices faster than inflation.

Centralizing power in the public sector and centralizing money in the private sector is a mega-sized global mistake made in every country. And centralization of the computer systems and utility networks make innocent populations sitting ducks for a team of computer hacks in Moldova to hobble entire sections of a country. Imagine, 100 hackers can cut off the power to 50 million people which means that extortion will always pay more than work. *Bigger is always better* ensures that we will one day fall into the WTF dilemma when our ultra-centralized supply lines of Water, Toast, and Fuel…stop. The financial *health* of the US, and the world, now teeters on the financial health of a handful of companies.

Free Speech and Money

"Saying that you don't care about your privacy because you have nothing to hide is no different from saying you don't care about free speech because you have nothing to say."

—Edward Snowden[16]

We might ask, "what does free speech have to do with commerce?" Every transaction (and *everything* is a transaction) begins with a conversation and both parties want personal gain. When neither party has the upper hand (neither has political power) they are bargaining on a level playing field. Both parties can freely walk away and neither need accept or believe a lie. The absence of force minimizes false information automatically and both parties can go on to negotiate toward coincident interest, which pushes transactions toward a 1:1 value. To ensure this equal force for prosperity (in a letter to Madison) Thomas Jefferson wrote that "libel, falsehood, defamation, heresy, and false religion, are withheld from the cognizance of federal tribunals...and acts of congress, for punishing these crimes against the US, is not law but altogether void and of no force."[17]

Jumping forward 200 years, the pyramid is using fake money to amplify public speech, by giving 2 or 3 social media companies massive loans that their competitors don't get. After DC had built these special trillion-dollar corporations, the mega cartels could control free speech for the government. In "meetings," DC policymakers instruct them on what to censor and what not to, as if they don't understand the 1st amendment. This is just another version of the 3 upside-down cups trick because the government has maneuvered itself into making some of the decisions on what a lie is, in direct violation of the 1st amendment. Free speech is turning into a different law by moving around obscene amounts of money, and the details are hammered out by the cabal—CEO's and senators.

If big tech can shut millions of people up then any small business can refuse service to anyone for any reason, as the sign on the front door reads. Only congress could conclude that a small cakeshop is in the public domain and Facebook is not. Neither are. A cakeshop is a private business built from scratch and is closer to a private house than a public business. Conversely, communication companies get so much steering and money from the government that they end up acting *on the behalf of the government*. At this point, the cartels are quasigovernment agencies but nobody acknowledges that. The easiest way for a pyramid lawyer to bypass the 1st Amendment is to explain that the government didn't censor anybody, a private company did! The quasi-private company censors somebody (perfectly legal) then the government decides whether it was censorship or not (exactly illegal) and at that point the government is deciding who has free speech and who doesn't. They win, we lose. What you can read has already been decided. I've watched the free internet go from wildly interesting to boringly mainstream right in front of my eyes.

The initial launching of Al Gore's internet in the 90s created a free speech haven unheard of even in the US, run by the audience—the only impartial mediator possible. Now over half of the content is filtered by the favorite sons of the central bank: Google, Netflix, Facebook, Microsoft, Apple, and Amazon.[18] DC made sure that the internet was about big money, not culture or intelligent work, which is something the free market wouldn't have, and couldn't have done. Without your money mysteriously flying to the genuine imitation capitalists we'd have thousands more choices for providers, websites, and information. "Big brother" now includes quasi-private cartels which have become the domestic enemies that Uncle Sam is supposed to protect us against. They inundate us with fake money and fake speech until we can't figure out what's true and what's not. A free internet would let untruths die from lack of interest.

This irascible oil-water mix of the public and private sector controls how we communicate with each other more than any free nation ever has or could.[19] This observation is from the author Jacob Mchangama who said, "free speech, in fact, may be the most powerful engine of equality that humans have ever stumbled upon." I don't think James Madison stumbled upon it, he passionately singled it out and fought for it to encourage a "commerce of ideas" that created the richest nation in history. He did not know, as we will soon find out, that the US would become the richest nation in 1899, without a central bank.

Now that the government runs the information networks, books are coming out telling us that there are circumstances when there's a "compelling government reason" to silence someone. Since the pyramid can now indict a ham sandwich does DC need more power to shut people up? RFK Jr said on 7/20/23, "the people tell the government what to think, not the other way around." Prominent authors say that false election information "poisons our politics" but fail to mention that major media outlets reported Hillary Clinton and Joe Biden both had stultifying leads over

Trump, often reporting a mind-numbing 8%-12% advantage, days and hours before both elections were decided by 1%. If that wasn't coast-to-coast election manipulation without a 501(C)(3)—a special license to politically campaign—what was it? I defend their right to lie though or freedom of speech is gone.

Those who hate free speech but never say it also don't mention Louis Lerner, the head of the IRS, who shut down the Tea Party's legal campaign to help Obama win the 2008 election. Obama had called the Tea Partiers "terrorists," knowing his backroom deal would surface, and Louis Lerner retired with full honors and benefits. This high-ranking government official defiled the first sentence of the 1st Amendment, retired, and walked away wealthy, while the same charge—using powerful government agencies to go after political enemies—worked wonders getting rid of Richard Nixon.

For my best but strangest free speech argument, put your seatbelt on! We've all said "I'd like to kill that person" but if we don't start planning to do it, is it a crime? If it is we could turn the US into a jail. A spoken sentence isn't a crime unless an individual's rights have been violated and we must be diligent about delineating between emotional talking and planning.

The US government is also forbidden by the 4rth Amendment from illegal searches and seizures of persons, houses, papers, and effects, without a judicial warrant. The founders were so skilled at protecting us, that the word *effects* meant *all your stuff*, including any gizmo the someone may invent in the future that you might use to write on, communicate with, or convey your ideas.

The Bill of Rights had teeth, in fact it had sharp fangs, because the founders knew that the haters of freedom had never rested and never would. The founders simply considered debt something to be paid back, which should have been interpreted on its own merit. Instead, it turned into their biggest oversight because they never dreamed that congress would become engorged with itself and quietly begin borrowing more and more during peacetime, and never paying it back.

Understanding the Debt: Think Backwards

When politicians talk about the national debt, they somehow say with a straight face, "we owe that money to ourselves." Translation: "John Doe was dead broke so he borrowed money from himself and is now rich." This is not only impossible but backwards from reality. US senators get on TV and report that our biggest debtors are Japan and China who lent the US a mere 10% of the miss-totaled $35-trillion debt. Unbelievably, most politicians aren't exactly sure where DC is getting all these free trillions and are content with Bloomberg News telling them that agencies or entities are "acquiring money," or, when a country is borrowing (issuing bonds) the channel reports that they are "selling bonds." If you were borrowing money to buy a car, would you tell everybody you were selling a car? No wonder so many politicians are financially braindead—Bloomberg's newspeak reverses the meaning of words—and to pay people back after their bonds have matured the politicians have to borrow more money. The 5th part of best kept secret in the world is that wherever the FED throws these trillions of new dollars, we pay that exact amount in higher prices because they never pay the debt back. The equation does balance when we see it as pilfering.

The $35-trillion national debt is closer to $150 trillion. The trick is to show us most financial numbers with inflation already added in, like what your portfolio is worth now, however, they show us the national debt in nominal dollars! They never say what that borrowed $35 trillion over 100 years would be worth now. For example, the money they borrowed and never paid back 50 years ago would be worth 5 times more today. This is a difficult concept to grasp so here's a better explanation: what if a college friend borrowed $35 from you when you were 20 and paid you back the $35 when you were 70?? You'd know you were cheated by many orders of magnitude. Families are missing $150 trillion dollars and the US could have a very rich, robust middle class right now, but has the opposite.

After WWII all European currencies were collapsing, the Marshal Plan saved them, and all this debt was wiped off the books. Gradually since then, the west has quietly accelerated the use of this invisible money. Mathematically, western debt is *so much* higher than reported. Let's just look at the $10 trillion that the FED created in 1 year, 2009, and the additional $20 trillion they created for all the bailouts in and around the housing crisis. That one crisis that they manufactured for us almost adds up to the national debt of $35 trillion right there! Their invisible ink is coming to life in front of our eyes under the stark light of investigators who do simple math.

They had to invent a new language to hide all these separate piles of debt and to make it impossible for outsiders to add it up or calculate the total. That's why they call these countless piles of debt "assets" instead of debt but the more depressing part is that the national debt doesn't exist! We pay it off every year through inflation taxes.

Not to be outdone, debt has become a *common good* for each of the states, followed by the coast-to-coast domino effect of county, local, and city debt. DC dangled a carrot to all the states and many cities and called them "matching funds." Translation: "if you do what we say" (like screw up all your freeways) "you can borrow more from us every year and never pay us back." All these "operating losses" which should be renamed "operating gains" raise the cost of living and we can't forget to add in the floating debt that every institute of higher learning has, or the coming high school, grade school, and daycare debt. They call the public debt, "the common good," which is sophistry at its best because it's not common at all—there are losers and winners.

Per capita, Texas has less debt than any state and California has the most, perpetually, but every state's debt is rising with no ceiling in site. To understand state debt, imagine if California told Texas that the west doesn't have enough water, has too many natural disasters, needs a new power grid (electricity bills rising 10% a year), has too many mental health problems, and can't maintain its ports, mass transportation, or skyscrapers, so all Texans must work 15 more minutes a day to pay for Californians to live in California. Next year it will be 18 minutes.

How Millionaires Become Billionaires and Thousandaires Stay Thousandaires

Have you ever heard the joke about the 2 girls coming out of a bar late one night and an armed robber pops up from behind a bush and says, "give me all your money?" The first girl thinks fast and quickly pulls $100 out of her purse, gives it to her friend, and says, "oh, here's that hundred I owe you." The girl who paid off her debt for free is now basically in cahoots with the robber and we the people are the other girl. The robber is the central bank, the girl who paid off her debt for free is an investment banker, and the money we lost is used by the investment banker to buy a free asset (a corporation). The actual process is more complicated, at least compared to the 3-person joke, and here's how it works:

In 2002 I knew an investment banker whose group had just bought Burger King for 3.5 billion dollars and I asked him if they got a loan to do that. He said "no." He had talked about how investment banking was "creating wealth out of nothing." "It's like manufacturing money," he added, and his investment banking group got the money to buy Burger King (drumroll)—from the FED.[20] That investment group waited in the doldrums through Bill Clinton's underreported recession until George W. Bush and Greenspan had finessed the new bailouts. Alas, the financial sectors were booming again. They then resold BK in 2006 to another investment group and quadrupled their money using our emergency money.[21] I just happened to be at lunch with this guy at Burger King with our kids. Maybe this is why Hillary Clinton said "I can't be responsible for every undercapitalized business."

Investment bankers love to call their free cash "liquidity" because it's the only liquid that flows uphill and the only way it can do that is by making our cash flow downhill. Bloomberg News often reports that a private investment group is "leading" a corporate takeover. Translation: the investment group is *not* leading the financing, the FED is. And since Burger King is such a small example, we can now add 3 zeros to all that jargon.

The FED uses these shell corporations, (investment bankers) to increase the money supply, with untold benefits for the chosen, and this unnamed young financial guy knew at age 25 not to talk turkey with me about the FED. He had even asked his group at a previous meeting where there were going to get this money to buy Burger King and everybody else in the room burst out laughing. They train them fast to talk *Greenspeak* to us (a great color pun). The FED even gives investment bankers a Reverse-Repo option for the *hard times*. They let them take their free money back out of money market funds and reinvest it into the FED's *balance sheet*, at a nicer percentage rate, while we keep buying stock during a declining market. In Europe and Japan, sometimes the borrowing rate is below zero(!) and companies are *paid* to borrow. When I say "free money" I'm not being dramatic because the inflation paying public pays part of the interest on these loans, all of it, or even more than that.

We will never see the FED's dossier on how many trillions in cheap money Jeff Bezos, Bill Gates, Mark Zuckerberg, Elon Musk and that My Pillow guy borrowed—nobody adds those secrets up for us. Musk was in the process of borrowing $25 billion in inflationary money from Chairman Powell to buy Twitter, more than half of the total purchase, when the deal fell through in early 2022 because the US was on the edge of hyperinflation. He ended up borrowing $12 billion and may have to choose bankruptcy protection, which puts his loan under a shield. You can't make this stuff up but I'm not singling him out—I'll include Carl Icahn and Warren Buffet in this club too. Family and friends gave Buffet $100,000 to invest in 1956 and he grew that into over $100 billion?? Please...that's impossible—he got investment money from the FED which is why on TV he always emphasizes his *shareholders* and never mentions his sugar daddy. Today this *private* citizen issues bonds! There's an addiction within the FED to pierce the corporate veil with trucks full of money and turn all these aforementioned guys into remora fish, sucking on a big shark's back. We think those armored cars are always driving deposit money to the bank for these large caps but often they are delivering money to them.

To have a $trillion US you must get $3000 from every man, woman, and child—that's impossible too. The FED gives the rich swimming pools full of money, we make the interest payments, and the band Switchfoot might say "they want more than this world's got to offer."

If we stop manufacturing billionaires, the invisible had will create 1000 x 1000, thousandaires instead. These new thousandaires would help considering the average family can cover one $750 emergency. Families would have more appliances, vacations, and savings instead of the ridiculous skyscrapers and stadiums we see everywhere.

We used to live in a galaxy where businesspeople and sports team owners—only millionaires back then—paid for their own structures. The central bank started a precedent where these rich guys get their skyscrapers and stadiums at a discount—it's called the FED's "discount window," and for once they named something for exactly what it is. The local taxpayers, most of whom don't care about sports, foot part of the bill and the rich guys borrow the rest from us. If the pyramid can tax us to pay gazillionaires, why are we surprised when they tell congress what the minimum wage should be, or how much *we* should make?

I like to call the FED Chief "Chairman Powell," because it sounds like *Chairman Mao*. Powell has a name for controlling what everybody makes: "nominal income targeting." May I translate? "We don't know exactly what each *ability or need* is but we are fixing the haphazard allocation of money by the free market." Marx is verklempt, unable to speak; tears of joy gush from his dead eyes as he gives his #1 student an A+ in Marxian philosophy.

Let us imagine...50 kids playing on a playground where of course the whole point for each kid is to have the most fun, however each define that. Now imagine a *fun regulator* showing up to manage the situation and setting up mandatory drills designed to maximize the fun of those who appear to be having the least fun and minimize the fun for those having the most. Most kids will trust the regulator even as they get more and more uneasy as the hours drag by.

A few of them will discuss it over dinner with their surprised parents and conclude the regulator missed the entire point of the playground. These are the kids with the least amount of Stockholm Syndrome and everybody at the table might realize the regulator doesn't even have a playground inside his mind. Ringo sings, "we could be so happy, you and me, no one to tell us what to do." Most socialists don't want to know what socialism is; they want to see the top 1/3rd of the iceberg glistening in the sun, and not see the murky bottom 2/3rds lurking under the sea. We are well practiced at this iceberg concept—it's the same way we look at ourselves.

The Leaky City

Imagine an un-centralized America built from the ground up. Imagine a hundred thousand more small businesses slowly eating away at the market share of illegal monopolies. We could be trading more with people we personally know as our grandparents did. Imagine many more small towns, small private airports everywhere, and an airplane or helicopter in every 5th garage. Speedy flying machines are *still* threatening to replace land vehicles for all manner of deliveries. There's more space up there and we don't need Uncle Sam to pave it.

Imagine a country not run by a bank—things would look rather quaint to us unless we lived out in the country or in a small to medium sized city. These efficient little nerve centers (small debt Salt Lake City is a good example) would grow into dynamic pockets of solid trade because the big cities wouldn't be draining the system. Big cities even pay rent for people to get them to stay and they can't raise taxes anymore, or taxpayers will keep leaving, so most of the large cities stay afloat by borrowing from the federal government and never paying it back.

This very question was hotly debated in a clash of opinions with James Madison and Thomas Jefferson on one side, and Alexander Hamilton on the other. Historian Jay Cost writes: "To Madison, Hamilton's system was too heavily biased in favor of the commercial interests of the large cities, whereas in a republic the benefits and burdens of policy should be evenly distributed across the populace." Madison's passion was to install a full stop to the tendency of governments to pick winners and losers, saying "landed interest, manufacturing interest, mercantile interest, a monied interest, or many lessor interests should not be able to use government for their own ends at the expense of others.[22]

Small business as usual, only 3 generations behind us now, would come back fast if the US central bank would stop subsidizing insurance conglomerates, skyscrapers, tech giants, medical manufacturers, mass transportation, and city dwellers. The FED way overshot the optimal size for a corporation and way overshot the optimal size for a city. Skyscrapers are selling for half price if they can sell them at all, and as the corporations cut bait and leave the worst cities will become ghost towns.

Small private companies with tight knit groups of dedicated employees are magnitudes more efficient than an army of clock-watchers working in mega cartels surviving off FED money spent on advertising. Eminem said, "let's get down to business is there a new circus in town what is this."

Sociology researchers inform us that people are happier in cities than in small towns because of more group interaction—I see the opposite. After building too many skyscrapers, the cities spare no expense to squeeze natural parks into the area so residents can get away for some mental health. Cal Thomas jokes, "crime is so bad they feel unsafe to leave" (it's not nearly that bad) but oddly, the coddled finance industry is gradually leaving New York. And, the campuses where the sociologists work don't look anything like the cities these professors defend.

What draws young people to cities are plenty of simple, readymade, cookie-cutter jobs with air-conditioning and anonymity. They can get laid more often. Are they trying to forget something that happened in a small town? Jimmy Buffet sang, "I spent 4 lonely days in a brown LA haze and I just want you back by my side." There's nothing wrong in itself with liking cities, however, the vast majority of families jet to the suburbs and we are taught by academia that they do this to be unhappier.

From the city that scrapes the sky, New York, the female philosopher most of us could name is Ayn Rand. She was a C Child—a chimera of nature—having been born with a women's body and a man's brain. Being born right at the turn of the century was perfect timing to employ her rare genome. She spoke as a possessed man, and, as some men do, married a trophy spouse, the chiseled but weak Frank O'Connor. Objectively speaking, Ayn Rand is the undisputed Queen of emotional capitalism, nose to nose with the cognitive King of Econ, Adam Smith, or a little ahead because the left hates her far more. Ayn's rather high ranking comes from moving the world with a longer lever, fiction. Maybe only a woman would think of turning the abstract concept of laissez-faire capitalism into a beautiful story, something no one else had thought of. I literally stole that brilliant idea from her because I saw how she had found her way into the subconscious minds of her readers. Coming at capitalism from the demonstrative side caused her to think the New York City skyline was a monument to capitalism while the infrastructure and the tallest buildings shot up using new, unearned money from the central bank. More money *was* in private hands but too much of it got there on public legs. The proof of the massive FED subsidies going to NYC is in the high prices there, so it follows that the city that never sleeps is the planet's most expensive.

The first publicized bailout of NYC in 1975 was a furious debate and the routine city bailouts are changes of underwear now. The borrows never mention that the money isn't paid back. The monetary affection from DC to NYC is long and storied: the funding of Grand Central Station, putting all overhead utilities underground, financing LaGuardia Airport. The point is that other cities had to fund their own projects with local tax money, and NYC, already a financial powerhouse, didn't. The iconic example of inflating the big apple was in 1933 NYC when bankers built what was the tallest building in the world—the Empire State Building. It was more of a statement of an *empire state* than an office building because they couldn't rent out the office space for years. It was poorly planned because it was almost free for the owners and it started a domino effect for massive loans in the northeast and around the coasts of America.

It wasn't long before the rich cliff dwellers were gazing out over their empires in New York, Philadelphia, Baltimore, Chicago, and Los Angeles. It was "free real estate in the sky" they smiled, as they helicoptered from castle keep, to the airport, and back to the crow's nest. The great unwashed were thrilled to be a part of the snazzy infrastructure while the cliff dwellers neglected to tell them that they were paying for it.

Contrast those Empire societies with San Francisco's Golden Gate Bridge, which sprang up in 1933 too, and was funded by selling local bonds, collecting local tolls, and the residents who needed it. The Empire State Building symbolized the beginning of a new, surreptitious way to leapfrog that old American ingenuity. In that sense the piercing of the New York skyline was perfect, and the new *Lords of Finance*[23] were now building castles in the sky instead of church steeples, as the west made the transition from religion to statism—a lateral move. The skyscrapers were vertical, phallic symbols of empire, without the cross on top.

Although Ayn Rand loved New York City, her books were fictional, idealistic, and about reviving a *spirit* America the beautiful had as it was making a left turn onto the state route. As we went there reflexively, as aging societies tend to do, Rand's novels struck a hard-to-find chord in a different key, and many unjaded readers saw that the path to cradle to grave protection came with the loss of financial freedom. She, perhaps more than any author, sounded the siren for the exponential increase in state power, in a fiction tale.

If you happen to pick up one of Ayn Rand's early books, you'll never say "I've read a book like this before" or "I know people like Ayn Rand." Rand the atheist was so powerful that she created a split between the believers and the nonbelievers, a little too early, while the leftwingers, faithful or not, followed McCartney and just *Let it Be*.

Rand's fictional James Taggart was a railroad tycoon who murdered a senator for trying to block the expansion of his railroad. His daughter Dagny Taggart completely skirted the government controls too, but finally went on strike to speed up the economic deterioration begun by the pyramid. In real life these captains of industry cozied up to the senators and were a murky blend of ambition, idiot genius, and monopoly money. Atlas didn't shrug, the powerful industrialists joined the pyramid for gain. John D Rockefeller, the railroad and oil tycoon, lived James Taggart's life but the Rockefeller family later got so deep into pyramid banking that it became difficult to see their industrial side.

For example, John D Rockefeller's brother William bought Anaconda Copper Co in 1899 without spending a penny of his own money. He wrote a banker friend a $39 million check and told him not to cash it. He then created paper instruments and loans that had zero value, stalled the payments of each one to cover with the next one, and offered up what we now call an "IPO." Then he sold the stock as the proud new "owner," on paper anyway, told the banker to cash the $39 million dollar check, and pocketed $36 million.[24] I do a card trick that works the same way. The trick is so smooth that you'll believe my 1st lie, I cover that with the 2nd lie, and cover that 2nd lie with a 3rd card I do know. The lie is the distraction, the prestige is showing you I got all 3 cards right, and Rockefeller did this with fake piles of money.

Ayn Rand alluded to this Rockefeller sting operation in her fiction books, so I researched the world output on copper over the last 200 years. Wouldn't you know it, world copper production was rising and Chilean copper production was declining in 1899. Right when the graphs crossed is when William Rockefeller shorted the stock and swung the deal.[25] As lazy speculators borrowed willy-nilly from the central bank to buy his paper tiger, Rockefeller cashed out right in time with $36 million in 1929 and some say that was the flap of the butterfly's wings that crashed the market. Every domino was teetering though as the FED threw money at investors, speculators, and friends, and a good question is, how did Rockefeller, who had owned Anaconda Copper for so long, know to sell it right before the crash of 1929? Paper money, inside information, and divine providence became more lucrative than work itself as the Rockefellers led America's descension into power and corruption.

Ayn Rand was a character herself. If you believed in God, she would brand you a "mystic" and throw a copy of *Atlas Shrugged* at you, as she did at Murray Rothbard.[26] She didn't sugar-coat anything; being blunt was more than commonplace in her day. At parties, she prophetically called Alan Greenspan "the Undertaker" because he looked like one, and because he said he couldn't prove he existed.[27] She later nicknamed him "the Sleeping Giant," and in 2009 both names for him came true—he crashed earth's economy—which brings us back to the dreaded subject of banking, where disasters begin.

The fateful transition of the US becoming a paper money pyramid paralleled Ayn Rand's life in the US (1926-1982) as the central bank gradually superimposed itself into economic position for most any event. Orchestrated behind closed doors, nobody, not even John Locke, Adam Smith, David Hume, or Ayn Rand—saw how high the pyramid was growing. Rand *was* the last of these 4 bank whistleblowers who offered an ounce of prevention for the growing bank algorithm but it wasn't the pound of cure the US constitution needed. What was brewing in those remote, smoke-filled rooms—reporters not allowed—we now know because we've seen the macroeconomic fire, but these above philosophes didn't see the road to vassalage[28] taking a circuitous route.

Britain had perfected the international paper money bait and switch in the 17th century and I'm convinced they lied about it to the greatest economic thinkers including Adam Smith himself. This was the very *first* best kept secret in the world. In the late 19th century, they passed the Peel Banking Act for international public relations purposes and they established a *ratio* of gold to paper. Translation: "We will raise the ratio of paper to gold whenever we want and you won't know." Across the pond, John Maynard Keynes followed up in the 1920s by "allowing" a standard of less than 100% gold backing to paper,[29] as if this was a new thing.

Britain invaded 9 out of 10 of earth's countries according to historian Stuart Laycock, and if true, that would have been impossible to fund with only taxes in a small country. Britain's paper currency was understood worldwide—the understanding was called the "Royal Navy"—so when a country pronounces their gold standard "dead" we can now know it happened long ago, and the body has been lying in state ever since.

Imagine you could print as much money as you wanted, down there in your windowless basement. You could print up $1 million in cash and go on a spending spree, which would push prices up in your little town by about a penny. Because of you, everybody else would pay an extra penny or so for stuff they needed. All those lost pennies would add up to the million dollars you scarfed(!) and this is why money creation is the naked transfer of wealth. Maybe Jim was right when he said, "it doesn't matter if you steal a penny or a million dollars.

Getting back to the city problem, in his book *The Evolution of Everything*, Matt Ridley writes, "like cities, bodies get more efficient in their energy consumption the larger they grow."[30] He might have forgotten about the fly in the ointment though: the

FED. When cities overextend—New York City, Baltimore, Detroit, Chicago, Los Angeles, Sacramento, etc.—they always get bailed out. They never change their paradigms because they get forever loans and only pay back a little interest while the total debts grow. In James Suzman's book *Work*, he seems to contradict Matt Ridley and writes, "entropies eternal diktat is that the more complex a structure, the more work must be done to build and maintain it applies as much to our societies as it does to our bodies." I think James Suzman is right. We can look at the poorly managed cities for what they are—national shrinkage. Now we don't even hear about the dozens of cities that are on continuous intravenous drip from DC.

Citi Bank—now called "Citi" because the word *bank* has negative connotations—had a commercial on the air in about 2013 which inadvertently let the cat out of the bag on the bailouts of cities. Citi bragged about lighting up dimly lit, rundown cities and they thought it would be good PR but it exposed something the FED never talks about: the price of bailing out cities. Citi even shows the Golden Gate Bridge in the background of one *public service* ad and they didn't help build or exist at the time. The FED isn't going to tell us that their research indicates that too many cities are sick and their debts are rising faster than inflation.

Since prices are always higher in the cities than in the counties do we need any more proof where central bank money goes? And all too often, the northside is richer than the southside. Municipalities invented malls on the higher ground to appeal to "civic leaders, bankers, and real estate people" historian Alexandra Lange tells us. Density increases costs too which is why the self-sufficient, self-correcting rural counties never need bailing out but the people in those towns must pay for the cities anyway. Everybody kind of knows this because the city dwellers still vote for Alexander Hamiltons and the rural folk still vote for Thomas Jeffersons.

The news is saturated with city problems without offering real solutions, which is the loud *distraction*, and the quiet bailouts with your money is the *prestige*. Behind closed doors, the cities and the FED play a shell game by switching around piles of paper instruments. We know them as municipal bonds, negotiable securities, matching funds, sludge funds, and God knows what, which amount to the perpetual forgiveness of debt. When they get 3 commas behind, they get another loan, but they can't buy time; time is not for sale. When a city can't make the small interest payment, they issue *more* bonds which is explained as *debt restructuring* or *drawing from surplus funds*. You'd have to be 140 years old to remember a surplus fund or a balanced budget. What cities and states do to all of us is no different than me borrowing a penny from everybody in my county to triple the size of my house and never paying them back.

The World Karl Marx Didn't Want

What is ultimately scrambling world economics is a 19th century oversight by a great economist named Karl Marx and the western economists who took up his ideas without telling us. Marx could be vague, like Frederick Hegel, and spoke in lofty, esoteric language that the masses couldn't understand which opened doors for despots to control their populations. The west adopted Marxism too (top-down command and control) and simply gave it another name: capitalism.

Young Marx, the evidence suggests, pragmatically believed in many individual rights and freedoms, while intent on shifting wealth from business owners to the working class by force. "Why not?" he thought. To wrest the capital from the upper classes Marx had to make the individual public enemy #1 by condemning the concepts of private property, individualism, family, and any *belief*. Even with ideology, nothing could compete with the state. One could not make a country poorer faster than with these 4 bullets. It never crossed Marx's mind to simply not monopolize anything and watch the farms and small manufacturers grow and a country slowly get rich.

Marx knew that labor was the capital but didn't realize it would organize itself. Labor is the work, ideas, imaginations, contemplations, and risks of all the people combined, and people work together when it increases production and income. That's the capital and Marx knew it yet he didn't realize that the infinite free division of labor would reorganize itself spontaneously as consumer demand changed. In an angry emotional response to imperialism, he theorized a top-down command and control government which bypassed all the natural drivers of wealth.

Posthumously, Karl Marx loves that modern western governments practice his economic top-down command and control, but he doesn't like them buttering the bread of the rich first. When Marx was alive, he didn't realize that supremacy corrupts and the appointed elite, whether proletariat or bourgeoise, will always put too much butter on their own bread. Marx was saying "let Gollum put his magic ring on another finger and he won't become corrupt!" This is the collectivist's dilemma because the only way to minimize corruption is NOT to amass power and money. After "Lennon read a book on Marx," Don McClean and I might add, if you give them all that, "no angel born in hell, can break *that* Satan's spell."

Mass corruption doesn't happen spontaneously. It is the inevitable symptom of something previous and Marx missed that, thinking that corruption was caused by itself. The more power at the top, the more corrupt the system will be, all the way down to the KGB. An unregulated free market is, in certainty, heavily regulated by countless shrewd purchasers who inadvertently minimize corruption. We can't see this phenomenon as it's happening—Marx couldn't either—but we can conceive it with help from Adam Smith who named it "the invisible hand."

Here's an example of how the invisible hand minimizes corruption and maximizes labor: One forager finally builds his family a house and another forager doesn't, so the house builder isn't hoarding all the capital—there are building materials laying around everywhere—he is simply capitalizing his project with his own ideas and labor to makes his family happier. The other foragers see this house and copy it, improve on it, and so on. Pretty soon there's a team of home builders who build multiple houses in exchange for food. Few would steal because they might be cast out, and why do something stupid to risk everything anyway when the economy is working for all participants?

Karl E. Marx wrote *The Communist Manifesto* with coauthor Frederick F. Engels and they defined a government that would control every major socioeconomic sector. Their 5th bullet point was "centralization of credit in the hands of the state [federal] by means of a national bank with a state capital and an exclusive monopoly." [31] That idea was about as new as imperialism, however, run *everything* from the capitol building wasn't explicitly written anywhere except in Marx's *Communist Manifesto,* though most countries were doing just that. Marx simply inspired dictators the world over by copying olde Britain(!), as Alexander Hamilton had wanted in the US too. Jefferson and Madison knew about the historical addiction to grab all of a nation's potential and did all they could to prevent Alexander Hamilton from coming back out of the woodwork years later.

Like John Baptist Lamarck missing 1 answer about evolution, Marx and Engels missed the answer of how to accidentally maximize wealth—individual freedom and happiness. As John Adams mistakenly thought, they were thinking of *public* happiness! That concept doesn't exist. Individual freedom IS happiness and this is more than obvious because it's what everybody strives for. A wealthy economy accidentally on purpose occurs next, and given the choice all individuals will negotiate this agreement with their government.

Historically, Russia has been so oppressive that small businesses have *never* flourished, and this is why the most educated people on earth are still poor after 1000 years. After manufacturing too many PhDs, Russia has 1 item for sale online—those wooden nesting dolls that fit inside each other. A Russian-Ukrainian friend of mine said "bananas are curved so they can go around Russia," and "to study Ukrainian history you need a backhoe." He told me about the toilet paper czar in Moscow who was selling rolls out of his mansion because for some reason you couldn't find them in stores.

Nevertheless, pure Marxism has been exported to China, India, the Middle East, Africa, and Simone Bolivar's Latin America. The corruption starts at the top, then trickles down to the governors, the inspectors, the police, and anyone who has a modicum of power. The people are watched when they trade freely among themselves and a price must be paid for every trade. These stolen profits go to government bureaucrats or tyrant loving Swiss banks, free trade grinds down to a sputter, and the people are left looking at yet another poor country with a rich government.

Marx was watching after the Civil War when the US surpassed Britain as the world's #1 economy. What Marx didn't get to see was that by 1899, the private US economy was bigger than Britain, France, and Germany combined—without a central bank. Those 3 competing countries did have central banks, and inflation, and there was almost no inflation in America in the 1800s! No inflation = middle class wealth yet America integrated Europe's Achilles heel into the US economy in the next century. Marx is now rightfully convulsing in his 1883 grave watching the new capital flowing to the rich, artificially creating the 2 Americas with a gaping hole in the middle—exactly what he spent his life trying to prevent. In the irony of ironies, Marx was reincarnated in 1883 into John Maynard Keynes, the famous British economist who crossed the pond and supercharged the US central bank in the 1930s.

After winning WWII, it wasn't the legacy of Keynes or FDR who empowered the blue-collar worker, it was capitalism. When America made the transition from guns back to butter and the US began hitting full employment in the 1940s and beyond, supply equaled demand in the job market. With short unemployment lines, workers finally had parity and this didn't arise from policymakers or labor unions. Ironically, it was capitalism that fulfilled the Marxian dream by empowering the wage earner, until monetary manipulation, equity transfer, and asset hoarding assumed greater value than work. You might remind me that the US already has the economy I'm advocating because the private sector in the US is rich. Yes, the top 10%, with 90% of the stock, are way too rich and the bottom 50% never gain much equity.

Isaac Newton's Principia: 1687

Isaac Newton and Gottfried Leibniz both came up with *calculus* in the late 17th century, introducing Europeans to a brilliant new way of quickly calculating accelerating change over time. Prior to paper, lending was calculated with simple interest or no interest (1:1) and created no inflation. Both mathematicians inadvertently taught the elite how to accurately compute continuous compound interest without spending all month adding up the tedious progressions. Newton did not intend for his new math to spawn the covert expansion of the world money supply, ad nauseum.

Newton's distrust in paper money provoked him to help create new gold and silver coins for the government that were more difficult to shave or copy. In spite of Newton's efforts, the headwinds of history were upon him and European banks made the fateful move to paper. The historical coincidence of Newton's book *Principia* in 1687, telling them how to do it, and the first paper money bank in England in 1694,[32] cannot be overlooked. The new bankers were acutely aware of their long-term impact on society and used his calculus to make sure inflation didn't become obvious to all. Central banking was already booming rich Holland, and next bled over to Italy, France, and Scotland, and expanded throughout Europe. Switzerland, ahead of the game, had started their central bank in 1668 and may have gotten math help from the well-traveled German Gottfried Leibniz who came up with calculus prior to Newton.

Historians write that these banks increased the general wealth—not true. It is impossible to create wealth by making money disappear from one place and appear in another. The banks did increase the income *spread* and economies *appeared* to be thriving because the peaks of the economies (the cities where foreigners were supposed to be awestruck) were so visible.

At the start paper money creation was slow—inflation was tiny—but bankers knew that for their profits to grow and to enable people to pay most of their loans back, the country's supply of money had to increase forever. The misuse of Newton's idea brought endless inflation to Europe for the first time in the 18th century. As with any Ponzi scheme the British banks knew they could only exist long term by paying off the Kings and Queens but they skipped telling them that the process would continually decrease the value of money and the value missing from families would equal the spoils. After the bankers included the Kings in the secret feast—replete with a magic war chest—the Kings looked the other way. The Kings and Queens, with all those recessive genes, weren't smart enough to see that all this new money would devalue everybody else's money.

1760, it turns out, is noted as the start of the *age of imperialism*, and it was free money which enabled the great powers of Europe to cheaply colonize the globe 3 generations after the inception of paper. This was the 2nd scary coincidence of fiat money banking and in 1762 the French signed the treaty of Paris, handing over India to Britain and signing away all France's territorial designs on North America. British banks outperformed French banks in global conquest.

The people are always building their own horizontal economies on strong foundations with no debt but some clever people figured out how to make much more money without working—the same job the King and Pope had. Born was socialism for the rich. Oliver Twist picked pockets and got arrested but if you pick *everybody's* pocket you get vested. "A British Bank is run with precision; a British home should be nothing less." [33] The propaganda that Britain was maintaining a gold standard was still echoing through western culture with movies like *Mary Poppins*, in that quixotic year, 1969.

Banks Pierce the Corporate Veil with Counterfeit Capital

Uncle Sam and Uncle FED work hand-in-hand to create *too big to fail* entities that become too big to jail. Corporations become monstrosities by using FED money to buy up their competition—they politely call it "acquisitions"—so it's not a brain twister that large cartels can raise prices faster than small businesses.

The book *The Economics of Industrial Organization* lists 21 ways the US *system* keeps small companies small and helps large companies grow. The biggest of these market interferences is corporate welfare from the Federal Reserve System which has created systematic cancerous growth.

DC has been so invasive that the 5 biggest companies in every major category—communications, pharma, insurance, food distribution, even retail and publishing—each have 70-80% of the market share! 4 companies dominate the sterile publishing industry too. DC feeds the publishers money and they in turn publish books written by people who work for the government—professors. If we know anything from history it is that we don't want the government to be the #1 book publisher.

When the boomers were wee lads the top 5 had 10-25% market share and a plethora of small companies competed beautifully together. It is literally impossible for 5 mega corporations to have cornered every market; it could not have just *happened*. Imagine if the central bank of America the beautiful gave 5 universities most of the sports recruitment money and they won every athletic championship, over and over and over. We would know the fix was on, we'd stop watching sports, and we'd see America the ugly......the corrupt.

The meteoric rise of the big 3 automakers (why don't we have 30?) was and is because the FED finances all 3 as well as providing their entire customer base with cheap loans. Even so, 2 of them crashed. When we bailed out General Motors and Chrysler in 2009 Sweden didn't bailout Saab and Volvo. Sweden said "if you can't run a business, we can't help you" so China bought both companies at a discount and Sweden is doing rather well for a no bailout, free-enterprise, oxymoronic welfare state.

Every monopoly is a product of government interference in the marketplace. The growth starts with government contracts, exclusive rights, tax incentives, or eminent domain and the favors are followed up with large loans. What if struggling families had that inflationary money back and could enrich their own children's lives? Why do they keep stealing our time, our life, and why do we keep letting them?

Who paved the way for big oil, the railroads, big aluminum, big pharma, and the big 3 automakers? The government, or rather, the taxpayers did. We would still have all these products; they would simply be provided at a lower price by hundreds of thousands of small companies instead of by 4 or 5.

Henry Ford was suspicious of central banks to say the least and tried in vain to use the assembly line and innovation to W.I.N. (Whip Inflation Now). Ford kept decreasing the price of his cars in the 1920s, the FED kept increasing them, and this is how value vanished from the economy. Henry Ford was going to run for president (probably would have won) when Calvin Coolidge talked him out of running during a secret meeting.[34] Coolidge said, "what's good for big business is good for America." What silent Cal, the lawyer-banker meant was, "the *central bank* is good for America," and like Alan Greenspan he left public service just before his economics crashed America in 1929.

The railroad, telegraph, and oil magnates (Teapot Dome Scandal) were put on steroids by DC and the banks. We can see what the quickest way to get rich is: ask DC to pierce your corporate veil with a potent syringe and give you a monopoly. This practice never changed. When a modern company buys up its competition, they call it a "leverage buyout," and they use Uncle Sam for leverage and us for the fulcrum.

For example, the CEO of T-Mobile gets in front of congress and with a straight face tells them he needs our money to buy Sprint so he can reduce prices! After a *feasibility study*, probably done my interns, congress then approves the money, and the CEO swallows up his competition, raises prices, and blames that on inflation.

It's the same story of the little monkey who screamed for his mother, faking a crisis. I wish I could remember which evolution book I read this in, but after the commotion, the mother ran over and shoed away this close by bully monkey, thinking he was the problem. After that distraction, the little monkey ran over and grabbed the bananas from behind a bush that the bully monkey had been guarding.

Today we think economically backwards because the 5th best secret in the world is: Debt Forever = Equity Forever. When we started businesses in the 19th century, we would *capitalize* the enterprise with our long labors—truly borrowing labor-ideas from ourselves—and cause no debt or inflation. Now after a business shows profits for years the bank is happy to corrupt and help it overpower competitors. Unseen, central banks destroy more businesses than they create, and the small businesses—decimated and counting down—employ the most people. These are the face-to-face businesses that confer trust, provide us with real customer service—no passwords, no confirmation numbers—and still struggle as the forgotten backbone of a free economy.

Conclusion—No Clapping Please

Milton Freidman said, "whatever you tax you'll get less of and whatever you subsidize you'll get more of," so DC simply began subsidizing whatever they wanted by replacing real taxes with unseen taxes. If we do go back to the monetarist theory of Milton Freidman or Steve Forbes (print less money and the same amount per year) it won't be long before somebody yells "crisis" and heats up the printing presses again. As Brandon Flowers sings, "the devil's water it ain't so sweet, you don't have to drink right now, but you can dip your feet every once in a little while."

Robert Wright said in his book *NONZERO* that the way humanity is trending, a 1-world government and a 1-world central bank is inevitable. Einstein encouraged this too, even while saying, "blind faith in authority is the greatest enemy of truth." Albert saw the horrors of fascism and thought that it came from 1 country while Europe was drenched in *fascism*. Einstein also advocated for *socialism* and like his fellow German, Karl Marx, arrived at no comparison between the 2 *isms*. Robert Wright wrote casually about a 1-world government but he forgot about something—there will be no competition among nations or banks. Evolution's mandate of competition is the only force that pushes the various nations and banks toward honesty.

The best kept secret in the world is out. Thomas Jefferson, James Madison, and Ludwig von Mises were right and Alexander Hamilton, Karl Marx, and John Maynard Keynes were wrong. The first 3 guys laid down constraints against a history of tyranny—drew lines in the sand—and the last 3 said, "well, we could do this, or we could do that." Like Dr Mengele they began experimenting on society using loopholes instead of scalpels. If the pyramid doesn't want to understand its own malignancy and we stay sheepish, we are more than in trouble; the people have eleutheromania and the pyramid won. If we throw off those chains, and are brave enough "to say the things we truly feel,"[35] we can get back what we lost: a hope for the future where our free will lives.

Thomas Jefferson knew that the *people* were the 3rd rail of politics, which is definitive, and we gradually forgot we had 1/3rd of the power. His legacy was to leave our future to a triopoly of competition: the federal government, the states, and the people. It's time to re-envision what he gave us and get out of the red and back into the black before the elite own everything. If Jefferson was here today, he would be heartbroken and inform us that Washington DC has to cut up its rolodex of overdrawn credit cards. Reverse mortgages don't end well. As you read this, we are saying goodbye to the middle-class and the American dream. The biggest bills are yet to come. It's time for us to find that old charm that only America has and again become the fountainhead of humanity. The whole world is waiting for us.

The End

ENDNOTES

Introduction, About the Book

[1] Music, Sweet Georgia Brown, Bernie/Pinkard/Casey, 1925

[2] Fetch the Devil, Clint Richmond, 2014, p. 9, 17% of Americans are full-blooded German

[3] Music, Our Shangri La, Mark Knopfler, 2004

[4] Hitch-22, Christopher Hitchens, 2010, p. 13-14

[5] Music, Mickey Newbury, San Francisco Mabel Joy, 1969

[6] Music, Don McLean, Bye Bye Miss American Pie, 1971

[7] Inherit the Wind, a play by Lawrence/Lee, about a teacher tried for teaching evolution, 1955

[8] quoteinvestigator.com attributes this quote to Rosyfelt, in his book, The Foolish Almanak for Anuther Year

[9] Music, Undertow, Phil Collins and Tony Banks, 1978

Chapter 1: A Long Walk off a Short Pier

[1] Research by Lars Schmitz

[2] The Evolution of Everything, Matt Ridley, 2016

[3] Discovered by Walter Georg Kühne in 1949, reclassified by William A. Clemens in 1979, confirmed in 2011 by researchers Butler, Sigogneau-Russell, and Ensom

[4] A Series of Fortunate Events, Sean B. Carroll, 2020, p. 23

[5] Sensory Perception in Cetaceans: Part I, Fron. Ecol. Evol., 11 May 2016

[6] Mass and Supin, 2009

[7] Research: Louise Roth (Duke University) and Rachel Roston (Washington School of Dentistry), published in the Journal of Anatomy

[8] Philip D. Gingerich, *et al*, (Univ. of Michigan, Ann Arbor) calls whale evolution the "Rosetta Stone" and traced whale origins back to hippos and a marine animal called artiodactyl, who had unique, intact ankle bones.

[9] pbs.org, Extreme Diver Community Evolved Spleens Similar to Seals, Tiffany Dill, 4/24/2018, and, science.org, Tibetans inherited high-altitude gene from ancient humans (Denisovans), Ann Gibbons, 7/2/14

Chapter 2: Sacrificial Selfishness

[1] Origin of Australopithecus is disputed, I always err on the earlier side of evolution

[2] Music, Folsom Prison Blues, Johnny Cash, 1955

[3] In 1990 many scientists changed their minds and now include apes as hominins too

[4] 51% improvement per generation is a nonscientific concept that I have gleaned, and roughly estimated, from studying genetics

[5] Brian Greene, Until the end of time, 2020, p. 161

[6] A Troublesome Inheritance, Nicholas Wade, 2015, p. 45

[7] Guns, Germs, and Steel, Jared Diamond, 1997, p. 89

[8] Haidt said this in a TV interview on RT, Russia Today, a channel which was taken off the US airwaves after Russia invaded Ukraine

[9] Sapiens, Yuval Harari, 2015, p. 14

[10] Oxford Handbook of Anthropology

[11] Music, Another One Bites the Dust, John Deacon, bass player, 1980

[12] Music, Wait, Lennon/McCartney, 1965

[13] Music, Modern Love, David Bowie, 1983

[14] John Adams, David McCullough, 2001, p. 134

[15] Music, Separate Ways, Journey, 1983

[16] Human brain growth seems to have stopped however this is probably just a blip on the radar screen because of diet

[17] Music, The Great Gig in the Sky, Pink Floyd, Richard Wright, 1973

[18] Projections, Karl Deisseroth, bookTV

[19] Music, Devil Baby, Mark Knopfler, 2002

[20] Music, Across the Universe, John Lennon, 1969

[21] Memories, Dreams, Reflections, C. G. Jung, translated by Aniela Jaffé, 1963, p. 95

[22] The Recorded Sayings of Linji lu, Translated by J. C. Cleary, 1985, p. 6,16

[23] I'm skipping over Alfred Wallace, Galileo, Aristotle, Epicures, and others that helped Darwin eventually win the trophy for explaining the subject of evolution so thoroughly

[24] Music, Then You May Take Me to the Fair, Lerner and Loewe, 1960
[25] The Moral Animal, Robert Wright, 1994, p. 29
[26] Lila, Robert Pirsig, 1991, *dynamic quality* was his theme
[27] Baddest is another one of my obvyisms
[28] The Moral Animal, Robert Wright, 1994, p. 10
[29] Why It's OK to Speak Your Mind, Hrishikesh Joshi, 2021
[30] Music, Carry on My Wayward Son, Kerry Livgren, 1976
[31] Friedrich Hayek, The Fatal Conceit, 1998
[32] Music, Crossroads, Don McLean, 1971
[33] Gestalt Therapy Verbatim, Frederick Pearls, 1969
[34] Memories, Dreams, Reflections, C. G. Jung, translated by Aniela Jaffé, 1963, p. 147
[35] Modern Man in Search of a Soul, 1933, translated by Dell and Baynes, Carl Jung, p. 116-117
[36] The Folly of Fools, Robert Trivers, 2011, p. 67-68
[37] The Evolution of Everything, Matt Ridley, 2016, I'm directly quoting him
[38] Music, Hello World, Lady Antebellum, Douglas-Lane-Lee, 2010
[39] Time Magazine article published in 2017 by Jeffrey Kluger
[40] Lesion Studies, parts of brain removed to determine function
[41] Winans and Scalia 1970; Scalia and Winans 1975, Scientific research from Italy
[42] Study by Plomin and Deary, 2015
[43] Cochran, Hardy, and Harpending, University of Utah gene study
[44] A Troublesome Inheritance, Nicholas Wade, 2015, p. 201, 205, 208
[45] A Troublesome Inheritance, Nicholas Wade, 2015, p. 197
[46] My 51% guess is not scientific, information is scarce, but we all see the improving generations
[47] Music, Dancing in the Dark, Bruce Springsteen, 1984
[48] The Better Angels of our Nature, 2011, Steven Pinker documents how war deaths have declined per capita throughout history
[49] Origin of Richard Dawkin's word *meme*, The Selfish Gene
[50] Dr C M Kinloch Nelson and Dr Raymond Bunge, 1974, from the 1950s to the 1970s, sperm counts dropped by half
[51] Music, The Summer of 42, Michael Legrand, 1971
[52] Music, A Day in the Life, Lennon/McCartney, 1967
[53] Music, Mercy Street, Peter Gabriel, 1992
[54] Music, Neptune City, Nicole Atkins, 2006

[55] Leonardo da Vinci, Walter Isaacson, 2017, p. 12-14
[56] Music, God Bless the Child, Billie Holiday and Arthur Herzog Jr, 1941
[57] Socioaffective Neuroscience & Psychology, Oct. 25, 2016, King, Dempsey, and Valentine
[58] 2020, John L. Fitzpatrick, et al., Royal Society of London, Biological Sciences 287, 1928
[59] Research from University College Cork, 2016, published in Socioaffective Neuroscience & Psy.
[60] David Kircher PhD, Molecular Biology, University of Utah
[61] Immanuel Kant originated the term *enlightenment*, The Illimitable Freedom, p. 202
[62] John Adams, David McCullough, 2001, p. 81
[63] The Liberation Trilogy, Rick Atkinson, bookTV
[64] Michael Meyer, Benjamin Franklin's Last Bet, bookTV
[65] John Adams, David McCullough, 2001, p. 256
[66] Eric Jay Dolin, Rebels at Sea, bookTV
[67] John Adams, David McCullough, 2001, p. 271, 284
[68] Thomas Jefferson: Author of America, Christopher Hitchens, 2005, p. 118
[69] Free Speech, Jacob Mchangama, 2022, p. 129
[70] Thomas Jefferson: Author of America, Christopher Hitchens, 2005, p. 10
[71] Thomas Jefferson: Author of America, Christopher Hitchens, 2005, p. 90
[72] Modern Man in Search of a Soul, 1933, translated by Dell and Baynes, Carl Jung, p. 209
[73] Nicholas Wade alerted me to this observation in his book, A Troublesome Inheritance, 2015, p. 224-234
[74] Arguably, Christopher Hitchens, 2011, p. 554, 558
[75] Music, Richard Thompson, Guns are the Tongues, 2007
[76] Music, Nobody Home, Pink Floyd, Roger Waters, 1979
[77] The Folly of Fools, Robert Trivers, 2011, p. 122-123

Chapter 3: Stockholm Syndrome Detected, Violence Rejected, Learning Selected

[1] Research by David Frayer, University of Kansas, published in livescience and Laterality
[2] Rationality, Stephen Pinker, 2021, p. 113
[3] Music, Guns are the Tongues, Richard Thompson, 2007

[4] James Madison, Jay Cost, 2021, p. 17
[5] Music, Jefferson Airplane, White Rabbit, Grace Slick, 1967
[6] Rationality, Stephen Pinker, 2021, p. 253
[7] The Moral Animal, Robert Wright, 1994, p. 49
[8] Until the End of Time, Brian Greene, 2020, p. 166
[9] The Third Chimpanzee, Jared Diamond, 1992, p. 50
[10] Until the End of Time, Brian Greene, 2020, p. 166
[11] The Link, Chinese News CGTN, 8/11/21
[12] I will attempt to prove the existence of free will in Chapter 9
[13] Neanderthal, 10/24/18, WPBA
[14] Free Speech, Jacob Mchangama, 2022, p. 50
[15] Memories, Dreams, Reflections, C. G. Jung, translated by Aniela Jaffé, 1963, p. 154
[16] Human: The World Within, Public Broadcasting, 6/2/21
[17] Music, All the Way, Sammy Cahn, 1957
[18] John Adams, David McCullough, 2001, p. 256
[19] Music, Popsicle Toes, Michael Franks, 1976
[20] PBS History Special, Ella Fitzgerald

Chapter 4: Epistemology

[1] Published in *Nature*, 8/24/22, study by Guy, Mackaye, Likius, Boisserie, Moussa, Pallas, Vignaud, and Clarisse
[2] Music, Colors of the Wind, Menken and Schwartz, 1995
[3] Music, Old Devil Moon, Lane and Harburg, 1947
[4] The Extended Selfish Gene, Richard Dawkins, p. 1, 1989, first published 1976
[5] Music, Against the Wind, Bob Seeger, 1980
[6] It wasn't *quite* that far back. Round numbers are easier to remember.
[7] wikipedia.org/wiki/Toba_catastrophe_theory
[8] Memories, Dreams, Reflections, C. G. Jung, translated by Aniela Jaffé, 1963, p. 15
[9] The Edge of Evolution, Michael J. Behe, 2007, p. 11
[10] Wikipedia, Lake Mungo remains, last revised 12/27/22 and First Peoples, Kerry Shale, first aired 7/1/15
[11] PLOS Biology, published online, Nov. 30, 2004
[12] Why Nothing Can Travel Faster Than the Speed of Light, Zimmerman, 1996, p. 87
[13] Work, James Suzman, 2020, p. 64

[14] Loannidis, Blanco-Portillo, and Morena-Estrada DNA research
[15] NOVA, Ancient Worlds, article by Sukee Bennett, June 7, 2022, David Bustos, Kathleen Springer, *et al*
[16] A Troublesome Inheritance, Nicholas Wade, 2015, p. 77
[17] Science Magazine article by Andrew Lawler, 4/24/2018
[18] Music, A Pirate Looks at 40, Jimmy Buffet, 1974
[19] Music, REM, Losing My Religion, 1991, Michael Stipe/Peter Buck, I'm taking the song a little out of context
[20] Trading Freedom, Dael Norwood, bookTV, 2023

Chapter 5: Clever Instincts

[1] She said this on the James Corden show in 2022
[2] Mother's Finest is a Geogia band I've seen several times. The last time my wife and I heard them, and ZZ Top, everybody was standing while she was sitting, and she said "now I know what hell is like."
[3] The Sovereign Individual, Davidson and Rees-Mogg, 1997
[4] Music, Suddenly I See, K T Tunstall, 2005
[5] Blink, Malcomb Gladwell, 2005, p. 33
[6] University of New Mexico, Albuquerque, research by Miller, Tybur, and Jordan, 04/16/07
[7] University of Göttingen, Germany, research by Bernhard Fink and team
[8] Music, Those Were the Days, Lyrics by Gene Raskin, 1971, Music by Boris Fomin from early 20th century Russia
[9] The Edge of Evolution, Michael J. Behe, 2007, p. 41
[10] The Selfish Gene, Richard Dawkins, 1976, p. 215, Dawkins says that evolution itself is teleological
[11] Music, The Power of Love, Huey Lewis, 1985

Chapter 6: And the Story Begins

[1] Music, Have Yourself a Merry Little Christmas, Martin and Blane, 1943
[2] Churchill, Life & Legacy Part 3, 2022, Kevin Matthews, George Mason U. History department
[3] Churchill, taken from the Diaries of Lord Moran, the doctor who travelled with Churchill during WWII, 1966, p. 61
[4] Music, Time, David Gilmore and Richard Wright, 1973
[5] Music, Wish You Were Here, Rogers/Gilmour, 1975

[6] Berlin 1961, Frederick Kempe, 2011, p. 3
[7] Music, You Didn't Know Me When, Connick Jr/McLean, 1991
[8] Music, Rock Lobster, written by the B-52s, 1978
[9] Music, In the Mood, Glenn Miller's defining song, written by Joe Garland and an African American named Andy Razaf in 1938
[10] The Folly of Fools, Robert Trivers, 2011, p. 77 (Hamilton's Rule)
[11] Music, America, Paul Simon, 1968
[12] One Flew Over the Cuckoo's Nest, Ken Kesey, 1962
[13] en.wikipedia.org/wiki/PGM-19_Jupiter
[14] Russia Upside Down, Joseph Weisberg
[15] NewsNation Townhall w/Robert F. Kennedy Jr, 6/28/23
[16] JFK and Vietnam, John M. Newman, 1992, the book outlines JFK's withdrawal orders, step by step, also see The Kennedy Withdrawal by Marc Selverstone
[17] An Encounter with Evil, Jacob Hornberger, BookTV interview with Peter Slen, first aired 10/15/23
[18] PBS, Inside the Warren Commission, first aired 6/26/23
[19] Hotter than the Sun, Scott Horton, bookTV
[20] Wikipedia.org/wiki/Abolition_of_the_Caliphate
[21] Free Speech, Jacob Mchangama, 2022, p. 330
[22] Music, Year of the Cat, Al Stewart, 1976
[23] Music, Whipping Post, Gregg Allman, 1969

Chapter 7: Saving Jim's Privates

[1] fiddlersgreen.net
[2] The Lords of Finance, Liaquat Ahamed
[3] Music, Snoopy vs the Red Baron, Gernhard and Holler, 1966
[4] The Worldly Philosophers, Robert L. Heilbroner, 1972, p. 242
[5] George Nash, bookTV, Herbert Hoover, 5% of Americans farming
[6] Freedom's Furies, Timothy Sandefur, 2022, p. 17
[7] The Worldly Philosophers, Robert L. Heilbroner, 1972, p. 242
[8] Music, Wouldn't That Be Nice, Beach Boys, Wilson/Asher, 1966
[9] Wikipedia, Lynching of Raymond Gunn, revised 11/3/22
[10] How the Scots Invented the Modern World, Arthur Herman, 2001, p. 237
[11] Music, Strange Fruit, Abel Meeropol, 1939
[12] Ben Raines, The Last Slave Ship, bookTV
[13] Fetch the Devil, Clint Richmond, 2014, p. 7
[14] While You Were Out, Meg Kissinger, book TV, first aired 9/22/23

[15] Max Hastings, *Finest Years*, bookTV
[16] Enotes.com/homework-help/what-was-relationship
[17] Britannica.com/biography/Alois Hitler
[18] The Portable Jung, Joseph Campbell, 1971, p. xxiv of introduction
[19] Modern Man in Search of a Soul, 1933, translated by Dell and Baynes, Carl Jung, p. 188-189, 199-200
[20] Flowers for Algernon, Daniel Keyes, 1956, a genius mouse goes nuts
[21] Freedom's Furies, Sandefur, 2022, p. 285, 288
[22] Inferno, Max Hastings, 2011, p. 4
[23] Inferno, Max Hastings, 2011, p. 10
[24] Inferno, Max Hastings, 2011, p. 102
[25] Churchill, Life & Legacy Part I, 2022, Kevin Matthews, George Mason University History dept., bookTV
[26] Churchill, taken from the Diaries of Lord Moran, 1966, p. 63-64
[27] Inferno, Max Hastings, 2011, All Hell Let Loose, 2011
[28] Book by Dalton Trumbo, 1939
[29] Inferno, Max Hastings, 2011, p. 459
[30] Wikipedia, Theodor Weissenberger, revised 12/14/22

Chapter 8: Saturday Night at the Officer's Club

[1] A joke credited to Mae West in 1958, but this was 1944
[2] Music, Devil Baby, Mark Knopfler, 2002, he wrote "sawdust" not stardust; most songs call it stardust
[3] Music, The First Cut is the Deepest, Cat Stevens, 1967, legal name is now Sami Yusef
[4] How the Scots Invented the Modern World, Arthur Herman, 2001, p. 108
[5] John D. Keyser, research paper on Scottish History, Edith had this letter in her trunk
[6] How the Scots Invented the Modern World, 2001, p. 387
[7] All things liberty.com > 2013/03 > the-myth-of-the-rifleman-timothy murphy
[8] lithub.com > the-black-descendants-of-president-madison
[9] Thomas Jefferson: Author of America, 2005, p. 177
[10] Carole Bucy, Tennessee Through Time, bookTV, Erin Adams, Andrew Jackson's Hermitage, bookTV
[11] stlouisfed.org, A Foregone Conclusion
[12] History as It Happens, Martin Di Caro, bookTV

[13] en.wikipedia.org/wiki/History_of_central_banking_in_the_United_States, 1837-1862: Free Banking Era, see chart of increases in money supply
[14] Music, The Last Gunfighter Ballad, Guy Clark, 1977
[15] An Island Called Liberty, Joseph Specht, 2004, a reference to the book
[16] Choctaw Confederates, Fay Yarbrough, bookTV
[17] Tennessee Through Time, Carole Bucy, bookTV speech
[18] Tennessee Through Time, Carole Bucy, bookTV
[19] I heard and watched this story on PBS long ago and couldn't find it again to properly reference it
[20] Music, My Funny Valentine, Rogers and Hart, 1937

Chapter 9: Free Will, the Big Hail Mary

[1] Why Buddhism is True, Robert Wright, 2017, p. 130
[2] Candide, Voltaire, 2018, p. 16
[3] Music, Is That All There Is, Stoller and Leiber, 1969
[4] The Folly of Fools, Robert Trivers, 2011, p. 146
[5] Music, Dust in the Wind, Kerry Livgren, 1977
[6] Music, Fly Like an Eagle, Steve Miller, 1976
[7] The Moral Animal, Robert Wright, 1994, p. 11
[8] Existentialism is a Humanism, Jean-Paul Sartre, 2007, a translation, p. 10 of the introduction
[9] You Are the Placebo, Joe Dispenza, 2014, p. 57
[10] Memories, Dreams, Reflections, Carl Jung, translated by Aniela Jaffé, 1963, p. 107
[11] Until the End of Time, Brian Greene, 2020, p. 152
[12] Until the End of Time, Brian Greene, 2020, p. 153
[13] Until the End of Time, Brian Greene, 2020, p. 165, origin of speech is unknown, may be much older
[14] Until the End of Time, Brian Greene, 2020, p. 198
[15] The Theory of Money and Credit, Ludwig von Mises, 1981, p. 52
[16] The Sacred and Profane Love Machine, Iris Murdock, 1794
[17] Music, People Will Say We're in Love, Rodgers/Hammerstein, 1947
[18] A good book showing this is Time to Think Small, 2022, Todd Myers
[19] Nineteen Eighty-Four, George Orwell, 1949
[20] Music, Rocket Man, John/Taupin, 1972
[21] Music, A Many-Splendored Thing, Han Suyin, 1952

[22] The True Believer, Eric Hoffer, 1951, p. 23
[23] A funny line from Richard Gere in the movie Chicago
[24] A Troublesome Inheritance, Nicholas Wade, 2015, p. 25
[25] A Troublesome Inheritance, Nicholas Wade, 2015, p. 25

Chapter 10: Marriage is What We Came Here For

[1] Music, Hey Big Spender, Coleman/Fields, 1967
[2] Music, I Wonder What the King is Doing Tonight, Lerner and Loewe, 1960
[3] F.E.D. research
[4] The Moral Animal, Robert Wright, 1994, p. 108, studysmarter.us > History > Modern British Marriage
[5] Movie, Before Sunrise, 1995
[6] Music, Goodbye Horses, Q Lazarus, William Garvey, 1988
[7] Quote from Ruth Bader Ginsburg, confirmation hearings, 1993
[8] Music, Wish You Were Here, Waters/Gilmour, 1975
[9] George Mason's Gunston Hall, Scott Stroh, Stroh also said T. Jefferson never freed his slaves which is not true
[10] The Illimitable Freedom of the Human Mind, Andrew O'Shaughnessy, 2021, p. 238
[11] John Adams, David McCullough, 2001, p. 102
[12] Free Speech, Jacob Mchangama, 2022, p. 194
[13] Free Speech, Jacob Mchangama, 2022, p. 195-196
[14] Free Speech, Jacob Mchangama, 2022, p. 201
[15] Thomas Jefferson: Author of America, 2005, p. 15, 59
[16] Slaves in the Family, E. Ball, bookTV
[17] John Adams, David McCullough, 2001, p. 115
[18] First Among Men, Maurizio Valsania, C-SPAN2, book TV interview, first aired 9/23/23
[19] Thomas Jefferson: Author of America, Christopher Hitchens, 2005, p. 64, 104
[20] Y chromosome haplotype DNA study by Dr Eugen Foster, published in Nature, 11/98
[21] Music, Summertime, Gershwin/Heyward, 1934
[22] The Illimitable Freedom of the Human Mind, Andrew O'Shaughnessy, 2021, p. 194-195
[23] The Illimitable Freedom of the Human Mind, Andrew O'Shaughnessy, 2021, p. 204
[24] Music, The Pilgrim, Kris Christopherson, 1971

[25] John Adams, David McCullough, 2001, p. 116
[26] The Illimitable Freedom of the Human Mind, Andrew O'Shaughnessy, 2021, p. 44
[27] Britannica.com/Biography/Hamilton's Financial Program
[28] A Constitution, Beau Breslin
[29] The Illimitable Freedom of the Human Mind, Andrew O'Shaughnessy, 2021, p. 17
[30] James Madison, Jay Cost, 2021, p. 72
[31] Cowan, Sylia and Wright, Business History Review, Vol. 83, spring 2009, Fin. Crisis Management and the Lender of Last Resort, July 2006
[32] John Adams, David McCullough, 2001, p. 102, quote from James Harrington
[33] US law does not restrict censorship by the private sector but corporations are in the public sphere now, by many a definition.
[34] Founders Online, letter dated November 17, 1798, founders.archives.gov
[35] Thomas Jefferson: Author of America, 2005, p. 52
[36] John Adams, David McCullough, 2001, p. 131
[37] James Madison, Jay Cost, 2021, p. 49
[38] Thomas Jefferson: Author of America, 2005, p. 4
[39] Thomas Jefferson: Author of America, 2005, p. 149
[40] Music, This Land is Your Land, Woodie Guthrie, 1944
[41] Encyclopedia.com/history/news-wires-white-papers-and-books/1878-1899, page 1
[42] The Devil in the White City, Erik Larson, 2003, p. 49
[43] John Adams, David McCullough, 2001, p. 222
[44] James Madison, Jay Cost, 2021, p. 59
[45] John Adams, David McCullough, 2001, p. 36
[46] John Adams, David McCullough, 2001, p. 83
[47] Our Deist Founding Fathers, Rev. Andrew C. Kennedy
[48] James Madison, Jay Cost, 2021, p. 49
[49] James Hutson, James Madison and the Social Utility of Religion: Risks vs. Rewards
[50] The Faiths of the Founding Fathers, by David L. Holmes
[51] reddit.com, statements by many contributors, not scientific info
[52] JQA Speaks, The Last Word
[53] The Illimitable Freedom of the Human Mind, Andrew O'Shaughnessy, 2021, p. 166
[54] Free Speech, Jacob Mchangama, 2022, p. 238

[55] Thomas Jefferson: Author of America, Christopher Hitchens, 2005, p. 173-174

[56] The Illimitable Freedom of the Human Mind, Andrew O'Shaughnessy, 2021, p. 34

[57] Benjamin Franklin, 2 Part Series, CSPANN, first aired April, May, 2022

Chapter 11: Edith's Childhood

[1] Music, Five Foot Two Eyes of Blue, Henderson/Lewis/Young, 1925

Chapter 12: The Indefatigable Jim

[1] Music, Send in the Clowns, Stephen Sondheim, 1975

Chapter 13: US 1969—The Tipping Point

[1] Music, Back in the USSR, Lennon/McCarney, 1968

[2] Music, Everybody Knows, Leonard Cohen, 1988

[3] Movie and Play, Children of a Lesser God, 1986, Medoff/Anderson

[4] Music, Summer of 69, Brian Adams and Jim Vallance, 1984

[5] Music, High Hopes, James Van Heusen and Sammy Cahn, 1959

[6] Datalab.usaspending.gov > deficit > trends

[7] NPR article by Ron Elving, 11/19/21

[8] Inflation, Steve Forbes, 2022

[9] Music, 1999, Prince, 1982

[10] Music, Midnight at the Oasis, David Nichtern, 1973, and Do You Want to Know a Secret, Lennon/McCartney, 1962

[11] Quote from William Congreve's play The Morning Bride, 1967

[12] Music, All in Love is Fair, Stevie Wonder, 1973

[13] Music, The Glory of Love, Billy Hill, 1936

[14] Music, There'll Be Some Changes Made, Overstreet/Higgins, 1921, Atkins/Knopfler redo 1990

[15] Music, Mulligan Stew, 2002, Mark Knopfler

[16] Music, Vincent, Don McClean, 1970

[17] Music, Bad Moon Risin', John Fogerty, 1969

[18] Wikipedia.org/wiki/Bike_boom

[19] Churchill: The Power of Words, Martin Gilbert, 2012, p. 25

[20] Music, Jesse's Girl, Rick Springfield, 1981

[21] Music, Black Dog, John Paul Jones, 1971

[22] Lila, 1991, Robert Pirsig, p. 51

[23] Thomas Jefferson: Author of America, 2005, p. 178

Chapter 14: Einstein

[1] Einstein's War, Matthew Stanley
[2] The Biggest Ideas in the Universe, Sean Carrol on bookTV
[3] Einstein, 2007, Walter Isaacson, p. 16, 55
[4] Einstein, 2007, Walter Isaacson, p. 51, 56
[5] The Other Einstein, Marie Benedict, 2016, p. 219, Simultaneous events don't exist is my wording of time distortion
[6] The Other Einstein, Marie Benedict, 2016, p. 217
[7] The Other Einstein, Marie Benedict, 2016, p. 212-221
[8] The Other Einstein, Marie Benedict, 2016, 231-232
[9] $E=mc^2$, David Bodanis, 2000, p. 42-43
[10] $E=mc^2$, David Bodanis, 2000, p. 124-130
[11] $E=mc^2$, David Bodanis, 2000, p.141-142

Chapter 15: Only a Dream

[1] Music, On the Street Where You Live, Lerner and Loewe, 1956

Chapter 17: Our Dreams

[1] Homo Deus, Yuval Harari, 2017, p. 27
[2] Memories, Dreams, Reflections, Carl Jung, translated by Aniela Jaffé, 1963, p. 11-13
[3] Modern Man in Search of a Soul, 1933, translated by Dell and Baynes, Carl Jung, p. 59
[4] Memories, Dreams, Reflections, Carl Jung, translated by Aniela Jaffé, 1963, p. 118-133
[5] Music, Billy Ocean, Get Outa My Dreams, Get Into My Car, 1988
[6] The Folly of Fools, Robert Trivers, 2011, p. 27
[7] The Folly of Fools, Robert Trivers, 2011, p. 54
[8] The Emotional Brain, Joseph Ledoux, 1996, the whole book helped me with this paragraph
[9] You Are the Placebo, Joe Dispenza, 2014, p. 154
[10] The Moral Animal, Robert Wright, 1994, p. 11
[11] Modern Man in Search of a Soul, 1933, translated by Dell and Baynes, Carl Jung, p. 74
[12] Abual AF, Bunting SR, Klein S Carpenter, Thompson J. Javed, et al (2022)
[13] The Emotional Brain, Joseph Ledoux, 1996, p. 193
[14] Article by Henry Yin and Barbara Knowlton

[15] The Emotional Brain, Joseph Ledoux, 1996, p. 43
[16] Music, Undertow, Tony Banks, Genesis, 1978
[17] The Boy Crisis, Warren Farrell, 2018, p. 261
[18] The Emotional Brain, Joseph Ledoux, 1996, p. 142-143
[19] The Emotional Brain, Joseph Ledoux, 1996, p. 101
[20] In the dream I'm usually trapped in a tunnel or large pipe and as I keep working my way down, feet first, it keeps getting narrower. There are no words or sounds. It's worse than the worse feeling, like impending death. I have often relived the nightmare and traced it back to being born breach. This might have created a traumatic chemical reaction that turned into resentment toward Edith because I associated the pain to her.
[21] The Boy Crisis, Warren Farrell and John Gray, 2018, p. 259
[22] If I Ran the Circus, Dr Seuss, 1956
[23] Work, James Suzman, 2020, p. 114, plus research by Robin Dunbar 2006
[24] The Folly of Fools, Robert Trivers, 2011, p. 73, 69
[25] The Boy Crisis, Warren Farrell and John Gray, Gray 2018 is also the author of Men Are from Mars, Women Are from Venus, 1992
[26] Wikipedia.org/wiki/Gender_differences_in_suicide
[27] Suicide in the World, International Journal of Environmental Research and Public Health. 9 (3): 760-761 (Wikipedia)
[28] Music, Mamas Don't Let You're Babies Grow Up to Be Cowboys, Ed and Patsy Bruce, 1978
[29] Music, Desperado, Henley/Frey, 1973
[30] The Better Angels of our Nature, Stephen Pinker, 2011
[31] Music, Ode to Billy Joe, Bobbie Gentry, 1967
[32] Music, One Last Breath, Creed, Scott Stapp, 2002
[33] Music, Suicide is Painless, Mandel/Altman, 1970
[34] Music, Coldplay, Viva la Vida, 2008
[35] The Quiet Trailblazer, Mary Frances Early
[36] Music, Carpet Crawlers, Gabriel-Banks-Rutherford, 1975

Chapter 18: The House on Cielo Vista

[1] Music, Don McLean, Bye Bye Miss American Pie, 1971
[2] Music, Morning Girl, Tupper Saussy, 1969

Chapter 19: The House on Tomwood

[1] Music, Scotch and Soda, Dave Guard or unknown author, 1958

Chapter 20: The House at Marsh Glen Point

[1] Music, Ain't That a Kick in the Head, Van Huesen/Sammy Cahn, 1960
[2] Music, Depeche Mode, Precious, Martin Gore, 2005
[3] Music, Dreams of the Everyday Housewife, Chris Gantry, 1968
[4] Music, Desperados Waiting for a Train, Guy Clark, 1975
[5] Music, Hotel California, Felder/Henley/Frey, 1976
[6] Music, The Living Years, Mike Rutherford, 1988

Chapter 21: I Don't Always Use the Internet

[1] You Are the Placebo, Joe Dispenza, 2014, p. 188
[2] Music, A Quality Shoe, Mark Knopfler, 2002
[3] Music, As Time Goes By, Herman Hupfeld, 1931
[4] A term coined by Robert Trivers in the 1970s

Chapter 22: The Lying Gene

[1] The Folly of Fools, Robert Trivers, 2011, p. 7
[2] A Troublesome Inheritance, Nicholas Wade, 2015, p. 39
[3] Converus Inc., Dr John Kircher and Associates invented the Eye Detect
[4] A Troublesome Inheritance, Nicholas Wade, 2015, p. 86
[5] Memories, Dreams, Reflections, C. G. Jung, translated by Aniela Jaffé, 1963, p. 143
[6] Music, I Don't Know How to Love Him, Andrew Lloyd Webber, 1970
[7] Music, Nature Boy, eden ahbez (disputed by composer Harman Yablokoff), 1947

Chapter 23: Empathy Capitalism

[1] Research at Evron Quarry by Dr Filipe Natalio and associates from Wiezmann Institute
[2] Article in *New Scientist* magazine, 15 Nov. 2012
[3] Music, Someone to Watch Over Me, Ira and George Gershwin, 1926
[4] Your Brain is a Time Machine, Dean Buonomano, 2017
[5] Work, James Suzman, 2020, p. 183
[6] A Troublesome Inheritance, Nicholas Wade, 2015, p. 80
[7] A reference to the book The Forgotten Man, by Amity Schlaes
[8] The Righteous Mind, Johnathan Haidt, 2012, p. 226
[9] The Righteous Mind, Johnathan Haidt, 2012, p. 237
[10] M. C. Spock witnessed this in Costa Maya, Mexico, and posted a picture of it

Chapter 24: India, and West Meets East, Twice

[1] How the Scots Invented the Modern World, Arthur Herman, 2001, p. 370

[2] How the Scots Invented the Modern World, Arthur Herman, 2001, p. 374

[3] Genome Biology and Evolution, Vol. 6, Issue 3, 3/2014, pages 466-473

[4] Alaska, James A. Mitchener, 1988, p. 14-15

[5] Don't Know Much About History, 30th anniversary edition, Kenneth C. Davis, p. 4

[6] The Descent of Man, Charles Darwin, On the Races of Man, Chapter 7

[7] Don't Know Much About History, 30th anniversary edition, Kenneth C. Davis, 2011, p. 14

[8] Colin. C Gillespie, Annals of Applied Statistics, 2017, Vol. 11, No. 4

[9] Free Speech, Jacob Mchangama, 2012, p. 244-246

[10] Thomas Jefferson: Author of America, Christopher Hitchens, 2005, p. 187

[11] Mark Moyar, Hillsdale College, first aired on C-SPAN2, 5/20/23

[12] Arguably, Christopher Hitchens, 2011, p. 485

[13] Arguably, Christopher Hitchens, 2011, p. 482

[14] Until the End of Time, Brian Greene, 2020, p. 207

[15] Until the End of Time, Brian Greene, 2020, p. 207

[16] Arguably, Christopher Hitchens, 2011

[17] The Jungle Books, edited by Lisa Makman, 2004, p. xxix, of the Introduction

[18] NONZERO, Robert Wright, 2000, p. 120

[19] Joke from the Indian-American comedian, Russell Peters

[20] Wikipedia, Black Hole of Calcutta, last revised 1/13/23

[21] Thomas Jefferson: Author of America, Christopher Hitchens, 2005, p. 11

[22] www.britannica.com/story/5-fast-facts-about-the-east-india-company

[23] battlefields.org > learn >articles > royal-navy

[24] How the Scots Invented the Modern World, Arthur Herman, 2001, p. 354, 358

[25] Max Hastings Speech, Book TV

[26] Churchill, taken from the Diaries of Lord Moran, the doctor who travelled with Churchill during WWII, 1966, p. 29-33

[27] Inferno, Max Hastings, 2011, p. 223

[28] Inferno, Max Hastings, 2011, p. 544

[29] Lew also jokes about how my wife walks and says she makes a spiral staircase look straight
[30] Free Speech, Jacob, Mchangama, 2022, p. 329
[31] Comprehensive comparative family study by Roger Penn of Queen's University in Belfast
[32] Music, Love is a Battlefield, written by Holly Knight and Mike Chapman, 1983
[33] A Hidden Reality for Adolescent Girls, a paper by Plan International

Chapter 25: Well, I'll Be a Monkey's Uncle

[1] The Edge of Evolution, Michael J. Behe, 2007, p. 70
[2] The Moral Animal, Robert Wright, 1994, p. 49
[3] The Third Chimpanzee, Jared Diamond, 1992, p. 15, 20
[4] Almost Human: Rise of the Apes, 8/3/22, Discovery Channel
[5] Oxford article, Pfefferle, et al, 2011
[6] Oxford Handbook of the Anthropology of Hunter-Gatherers, 2014
[7] Music, Bohemian Rhapsody, Queen, 1975
[8] The Third Chimpanzee, Jared Diamond, 1992, p. 42
[9] Big Brain, Gary Lynch and Richard Granger, 2008, p. 186
[10] The Kids in the Hall, Improv Comedy Team
[11] HOX gene, discovered by Lewis, Nüsslein-Volhard, and Wieschaus; Dr Mario Capecchi of University of Utah won the Nobel Prize for shutting off some of these genes in mice

Chapter 26: Lamarck, Scerri, and Quammen

[1] This age-old wisdom may no longer hold water. We can physically change using our brain. You Are the Placebo, Joe Dispenza, 2014, p. 86
[2] The Summer Knows, Music, 1971, written by Berman and Legrand
[3] PLoS One, 2008; 3(7): e2700, published online 7/16, 2008, Rice University research confirms
[4] Genome, Matt Ridley, 1999, Gist of Chapter 1
[5] The Rise and Fall of Nations, Ruchir Sharma, 2016
[6] The Better Half, Dr Sharon Moalem, p. 11, 29
[7] Shay, J.W., Wright, W.E. Nat Rev Genet 20, 299-309 (2019)

Chapter 27: I Got 50¢ more than I'm Gonna Keep

[1] Music, White America, Eminem, 2002
[2] Music, Celebration, Ronald Bell, 1980

[3] The Second Founding, Eric Foner, 1999, last page of preface
[4] Music, Taint Nobody's Business If I Do, Porter Grainger and Jimmy Witherspoon, 1922
[5] Music, I Only Wanna Be with the Ones Who Burn Burn Burn, Ronnie Elliot, 2001
[6] Winton Marsalis, Bloomberg interview, David Blumenthal
[7] Music, Help Me Rhonda, Brian Wilson and Mike Love, 1965

Chapter 28: The Best Kept Secret in the World

[1] The Bodies of Others, Naomi Wolf, 2022, p. 136, 137
[2] Why Minsky Matters, L. Randall Wray, 2016, p. 92-94
[3] Article by Richard H. Timberlake, Money in the 1920s and 1930s, fee.org, end of paragraph 9, page 2. Timberlake says that Rothbard's 62% number incorrectly includes M2 and M3 (money that's slow to get into the economy) however, it did get into circulation. In fact, it gained interest and allowed more purchasing of fiat paper, and pressured more spending, until the fiat market crashed 8 years later. The reason the FED stopped reporting M3 money in 2005 is because their ultra-wealthy "non-spenders" had gotten so rich it was getting embarrassing to tell us.
[4] Free Speech, Jacob Mchangama, 2022, p. 64
[5] federalreserve.gov > careers-for-students
[6] The Bodies of Others, Naomi Wolf, 2022, p. 207, 201
[7] The Theory of Money and Credit, Ludwig von Mises, 1981
[8] Music, Camelot, Lerner and Loewe, 1960
[9] Material Girl, Madonna, 1985, also a song by George Harrison
[10] Music, Gangsta's Paradise, Coolio LV/Doug Rasheed, 1995
[11] Music, First We Take Manhattan, Leonard Cohen, 1983, I probably take this song out of context
[12] Work, James Suzman, 2020, p. 350
[13] Work, James Suzman, 2020, p. 352
[14] Mises Wire article, Daniel Fernandez Mendez, 2/22/22, he says benefits upped wages to par
[15] Springer Nature Journal, Globalization and Health
[16] Permanent Record, Edward Snowden, 2019, p. 208 (exiled by Senator John Kerry)
[17] Founders Online, letter dated November 17, 1798, founders.archives.gov
[18] Free Speech, Jacob Mchangama, 2022, p. 354

[19] Free Speech, Jacob Mchangama, 2022, p. 365

[20] Wall Street Journal, How to Make a Killing on B.K., by Michael Corkery, 9/1/2010

[21] The Week, The Week Magazine Staff, 1/10/15

[22] James Madison, Jay Cost, 2021, p. 60

[23] Lords of Finance, Liaquat Ahamed, one of Ben Bernanke's favorite books

[24] The Worldly Philosophers, Robert L. Heilbroner, 1972, p. 208

[25] Behind Copper Prices: 1850-1950, Marc Badia-Miró, Anna Carreras-Marín, Christián Ducoing

[26] It Usually Begins with Ayn Rand, 1971, Jerome Tuccille

[27] Ayn Rand and the World She Made, 2009, Anne C. Heller, p. 242

[28] Friedrich Hayek, The Road to Serfdom, 1944

[29] Wikipedia.org/wiki/Gold_standard

[30] The Evolution of Everything, Matt Ridley, 2016, p. 93

[31] The Communist Manifesto, 1848, Marx and Engels

[32] Mises Wire, Marx and Central Banks, Thorsten Polleit, 2/8/19

[33] Mary Poppins, 1969, quote from Banker/Father

[34] Electric City, Thomas Hager, bookTV

[35] Music, My Way, lyric Paul Anka, originally a French song by Revaux, Thibaut, and Francois